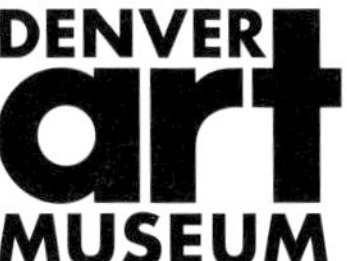

MUSEUM BARBERINI

POTSDAM

The Honest Eye

Camille Pissarro's Impressionism

Exhibition:
Claire Durand-Ruel Snollaerts
Clarisse Fava-Piz
Nerina Santorius

Catalog:
Clarisse Fava-Piz
Nerina Santorius

Edited by
Angelica Daneo
Clarisse Fava-Piz
Christoph Heinrich
Michael Philipp
Nerina Santorius
Ortrud Westheider

With contributions by
Claire Durand-Ruel Snollaerts
Clarisse Fava-Piz
Nerina Santorius
Emily Willkom
Daniel Zamani

PRESTEL Munich · London · New York

The Honest Eye: Camille Pissarro's Impressionism
is co-organized by
the Museum Barberini, Potsdam, and
the Denver Art Museum.

MUSEUM BARBERINI
POTSDAM

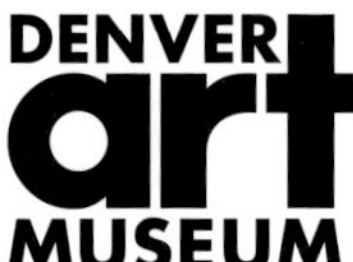

The exhibition in Denver is presented by Barbara Bridges, Bridget and John Grier, and the Kristin and Charles Lohmiller Exhibitions Fund, and is supported by the Tom Taplin Jr. and Ted Taplin Endowment, Adolph Coors Exhibition Endowment Fund, Birnbaum Social Discourse Project, Lori and Grady Durham, Kathie and Keith Finger, Sally Cooper Murray, Ellen and Morris Susman, Lisë Gander and Andy Main, Mary Pat and Richard McCormick, Kent Thiry and Denise O'Leary, Christie's, the donors to the Annual Fund Leadership Campaign, and the residents who support the Scientific and Cultural Facilities District (SCFD). This exhibition is supported by an indemnity from the Federal Council on the Arts and the Humanities.

Contents

Lenders

Van Gogh Museum, Amsterdam
The Baltimore Museum of Art
Szépművészeti Múzeum / Museum of Fine Arts, Budapest
The Art Institute of Chicago
The Cleveland Museum of Art
Wallraf-Richartz Museum & Fondation Corboud, Cologne
Ordrupgaard, Copenhagen
National Gallery of Ireland, Dublin
Indianapolis Museum of Art at Newfields
The Nelson-Atkins Museum of Art, Kansas City, Missouri
Staatliche Kunsthalle Karlsruhe
Musée d'art moderne André Malraux, Le Havre
The Courtauld, London
The National Gallery, London
Tate, London
The J. Paul Getty Museum, Los Angeles
Musée des Beaux-Arts de Lyon
Kunsthalle Mannheim
Yale University Art Gallery, New Haven
The Metropolitan Museum of Art, New York
Joslyn Art Museum, Omaha, Nebraska
National Gallery of Canada, Ottawa
The Ashmolean Museum, University of Oxford
Musée d'Orsay, Paris
Musée Marmottan Monet, Paris
Norton Simon Art Foundation, Pasadena, California
Philadelphia Museum of Art
Carnegie Museum of Art, Pittsburgh
Hasso Plattner Collection, Museum Barberini, Potsdam
National Gallery Prague
Musée des Beaux-Arts de la Ville de Reims
Virginia Museum of Fine Arts, Richmond
Saint Louis Art Museum
Fine Arts Museums of San Francisco
Staatsgalerie Stuttgart
Toledo Museum of Art
Art Gallery of Ontario, Toronto
Amgueddfa Cymru—Museum Wales
National Gallery of Art, Washington, DC
Clark Art Institute, Williamstown, Massachusetts
Kunst Museum Winterthur

Isabelle and Scott Black Collection
Collection of Prof. Mark Kaufman, Monaco
Drs. Tobia and Morton Mower
Colección Pérez Simón
Colección Patricia Phelps de Cisneros
Pissarro Family Archives
Pissarro & Associates Fine Art

Private collection, Colorado
Private collection, Switzerland
Private collection, UK

as well as several private collectors who wish to remain anonymous

Introduction

> I just read the book by Kropotkin. One must admit that if it is utopian, in every way it is a beautiful dream. As we often have had examples of beautiful dreams become realities, nothing prevents us from believing that it will be possible one day, unless man fails and returns to complete barbarism.[1]

As the oldest of the artists who later became known as Impressionists, Camille Pissarro (1830–1903) inspired many colleagues in Paris who had embraced plein-air painting. Born and raised on the island of Saint Thomas in the Caribbean, then a Danish colony, and under the influence of the Romantic painting of Scandinavia, Pissarro already made plein-air studies in Venezuela. He brought to his Parisian circle a worldview that was free of academic rules. Together with his artist friends in France, Pissarro organized eight Impressionist exhibitions. He painted with Claude Monet in the region around Paris, introduced Paul Cézanne to the group, and advocated for the work of Mary Cassatt. He was open to the concerns of the Neo-Impressionists and, unlike Monet and Pierre-Auguste Renoir, even showed with these younger artists.

In recent years, exhibitions of the artist's work have focused on the personality behind this important oeuvre. Richard R. Brettell's *Pissarro's People,* presented in Williamstown and San Francisco in 2011–12, was far more than a portrait exhibition. For the first time, it examined Pissarro's network, his intellectual milieu, and his reception of writings on social philosophy and political ethics. It also investigated Pissarro's network of friends and family in the context of his Jewish origins; as his correspondence shows, relatives who lived abroad were also important to him. In 2017 the Musée Marmottan Monet in Paris gave him a retrospective; the same year, the museum Ordrupgaard, Copenhagen, explored Pissarro's collaboration with Danish painter Fritz Melbye on Saint Thomas and exposed connections between early nineteenth-century Danish painting and French Impressionism. In 2021 the Kunstmuseum Basel devoted an exhibition to Pissarro's cooperation with artists such as Cassatt, Cézanne, Edgar Degas, Paul Gauguin, and Monet, complemented at the Ashmolean Museum in Oxford by drawings and letters by Pissarro and his sons, who were also artists, from the Pissarro family archives.

The retrospective in Potsdam and Denver builds on these milestones of Pissarro research. The title *The Honest Eye: Camille Pissarro's Impressionism* points to Pissarro's understanding of perception as a vital impulse of his artistic practice. On May 13, 1891, Pissarro wrote to his son Lucien, "The Impressionists are right, [Impressionism] is a healthy art based on sensations, and it is honest."[2] Trusting his "sensations" while seeking "honesty" in the presence of nature drove Pissarro, who not only became a central figure in the development of Impressionism but was unwavering in his artistic independence to constantly reinvent himself.

Everyday motifs from the industrial suburbs and provincial France bear witness to the painter's sensitivity to the upheavals of the modern age. Pissarro worked on a new image of the landscape. In every painting, he strove for compositional balance and harmony; he searched for equilibrium and wove forms and colors together in an effort to unify the picture plane. His works pay homage to the present moment in all of its unassuming qualities. Whether fieldworkers or domestic servants, Pissarro's figures are monuments to human activity. Timothy J. Clark has characterized the sense of time conveyed by these images as a "unique, unnoticeable, difficult, unrepeatable persistence."[3] For Pissarro, being an artist was a way to develop without constraints, and with a pedagogical ethos, he encouraged his children to embrace the artistic calling as well. As a reader of the social-utopian writings of Pyotr Kropotkin as well as the political and economic literature of his time, Pissarro developed a reserved humanism that was never boastful. With an honest eye, he inscribed this idealism into his art.

The exhibition is organized cooperatively by the Museum Barberini and the Denver Art Museum. Clarisse Fava-Piz, Associate Curator of European and American Art Before 1900 at the Denver Art Museum; Nerina Santorius, Curator and Head of Impressionism at the Museum Barberini; and Claire Durand-Ruel Snollaerts, coeditor of the Pissarro catalogue raisonné, curated the exhibition. We are grateful to them for opening up new perspectives on Pissarro's artistic activity. Together with Angelica Daneo, Chief of Curatorial Affairs, Collections, and Exhibitions/Curator of European Art Before 1900 in Denver, and Daniel Zamani, a longtime curator at the Museum Barberini and now Artistic Director at the Museum Frieder Burda in Baden-Baden, they succeeded in gaining the confidence of major museums, who generously entrusted their valuable works to us. We would also like to thank the many private collectors whose holdings were indispensable for our project, in particular the collections of Isabelle and Scott Black, Mark Kaufman, Tobia and Morton Mower, Juan Antonio Pérez Simón, Patricia Phelps de Cisneros, and Pissarro & Associates Fine Art, as well as those who wish to remain anonymous.

The essays in this catalog were developed in the context of a symposium that took place in Potsdam on May 22, 2024. We are grateful to the authors and museum teams in Denver and Potsdam, especially Curatorial Assistants Valentina Plotnikova and Emily Willkom, for their contributions and careful editing. We would also like to thank Olga Osadtschy, independent curator, who supervised the catalog.

The Pissarro exhibition is the second cooperative project between the Denver Art Museum and the Museum Barberini. In 2019–20 the two institutions organized the highly acclaimed *Monet: The Truth of Nature* in Denver and *Monet: Places* in Potsdam. Just as the wealth of works by Monet in both collections formed the basis for the earlier collaboration, so now the exhibition builds on our Pissarro holdings. There are seven paintings by the artist in the Hasso Plattner Collection, and we are grateful to the museum founder as well as the Hasso Plattner Foundation for permitting them to travel to Denver.

Seven works by Pissarro from the Denver Art Museum's collection will be on view in Potsdam, including two paintings bequeathed to the museum with the Impressionist collection of Frederic C. Hamilton in 2014, a gift that will continue to have an impact well into the future. In Denver, the exhibition is presented by Barbara Bridges, Bridget and John Grier, and the Kristin and Charles Lohmiller Exhibitions Fund, and is supported by the Tom Taplin Jr. and Ted Taplin Endowment, Adolph Coors Exhibition Endowment Fund, Birnbaum Social Discourse Project, Lori and Grady Durham, Kathie and Keith Finger, Sally Cooper Murray, Ellen and Morris Susman, Lisë Gander and Andy Main, Mary Pat and Richard McCormick, Kent Thiry and Denise O'Leary, Christie's, the donors to the Annual Fund Leadership Campaign, and the residents who support the Scientific and Cultural Facilities District (SCFD). This exhibition is supported by an indemnity from the Federal Council on the Arts and the Humanities.

Ortrud Westheider
Director
Museum Barberini, Potsdam

Christoph Heinrich
Frederick and Jan Mayer Director
Denver Art Museum

Acknowledgments

Bringing together well over a hundred works, including some iconic paintings from both sides of the Atlantic, our exhibition traces five decades of Pissarro's career, honoring the evolution of the artist's practice from his early years in the Caribbean and South America to his time in France as a central figure of the Impressionist movement. Due to his Jewish and Danish Caribbean roots, his pictorial interests that eschewed his peers' choice of upper-class subject matter to depict scenes of the mundane and his anarchist sympathies, Pissarro brought an important external perspective to the Impressionist group. Arranged thematically, the exhibition explores subjects that occupied a central role in the artist's oeuvre, including landscapes, portraits of his family, the domestic life in Éragny-sur-Epte, the artist's studio practice, scenes of the rural world and the local markets, Neo-Impressionist experiments, as well as urban motifs, such as the harbors of Normandy and the bustling streets of Paris.

We are deeply grateful to all our lenders, and we kindly acknowledge the following individuals and their colleagues: Emilie Gordenker and Lisa Smit-Vermeer, Van Gogh Museum, Amsterdam; Asma Naeem, Katy Rothkopf, and Lara Yeager-Crasselt, The Baltimore Museum of Art; László Baán, Szépművészeti Múzeum / Museum of Fine Arts, Budapest; James Rondeau and Gloria Groom, The Art Institute of Chicago; William M. Griswold and Heather Lemonedes Brown, The Cleveland Museum of Art; Marcus Dekiert and Barbara Schaefer, Wallraf-Richartz Museum & Fondation Corboud, Cologne; Gertrud Oelsner and Dorthe Vangsgaard Nielsen, Ordrupgaard, Copenhagen; Caroline Campbell and Janet McLean, National Gallery of Ireland, Dublin; Belinda Tate and Robin Cooper, Indianapolis Museum of Art at Newfields; Julián Zugazagoitia and Aimee Marcereau DeGalan, The Nelson-Atkins Museum of Art, Kansas City, Missouri; Frédéric Bußmann and Leonie Beiersdorf, Staatliche Kunsthalle Karlsruhe; Géraldine Lefebvre, Musée d'art moderne André Malraux, Le Havre; Ernst Vegelin van Claerbergen and Karen Serres, The Courtauld, London; Gabriele Finaldi and Christopher Riopelle, The National Gallery, London; Maria Balshaw, Tate, London; Timothy Potts, Davide Gasparotto, and Scott Allan, The J. Paul Getty Museum, Los Angeles; Sylvie Ramond and Stéphane Paccoud, Musée des Beaux-Arts de Lyon; Johan Holten and Inge Herold, Kunsthalle Mannheim; Stephanie Wiles and Laurence Kanter, Yale University Art Gallery, New Haven; Max Hollein, Susan Alyson Stein, and Alison Hokanson, The Metropolitan Museum of Art, New York; Jack Becker and Taylor J. Acosta, Joslyn Art Museum, Omaha, Nebraska; Jean-François Bélisle and Anabelle Kienle Ponka, National Gallery of Canada, Ottawa; Alexander Sturgis and Colin Harrison, The Ashmolean Museum, University of Oxford; Sylvain Amic, Paul Perrin, Isolde Pludermacher, and Anne Robbins, Musée d'Orsay, Paris; Érik Desmazières and Aurélie Gavoille, Musée Marmottan Monet, Paris; Walter W. Timoshuk and Emily M. Talbot, Norton Simon Art Foundation, Pasadena, California; Sasha Suda, Jennifer Thompson, and Laurel Garber, Philadelphia Museum of Art; Eric Crosby and Marie-Stéphanie Delamaire, Carnegie Museum of Art, Pittsburgh; Alicja

Knast, National Gallery Prague; Georges Magnier, Musée des Beaux-Arts de la Ville de Reims; Alex Nyerges, Michael R. Taylor, and Sylvain Cordier, Virginia Museum of Fine Arts, Richmond; Min Jung Kim and Simon Kelly, Saint Louis Art Museum; Thomas P. Campbell and Emily Beeny, Fine Arts Museums of San Francisco; Christiane Lange, Staatsgalerie Stuttgart; Adam M. Levine, Robert Schindler, and Lori Mott, Toledo Museum of Art; Stephan Jost and Caroline Shields, Art Gallery of Ontario, Toronto; Kath Davies, Amgueddfa Cymru—Museum Wales; Kaywin Feldman, Mary Morton, and Kimberly A. Jones, National Gallery of Art, Washington, DC; Olivier Meslay, Esther Bell, and Anne Leonard, Clark Art Institute, Williamstown, Massachusetts; Konrad Bitterli, Kunst Museum Winterthur. Our gratitude is also due to the private lenders of this exhibition.

We would also like to thank those who helped carry out this project: Marcela Caruso, Julien Domercq, Archives Durand-Ruel, Alma Egger, Amelia Harris, Ileen Kohn, Olga Osadtschy, Joachim Pissarro, Lionel and Sandrine Pissarro, Stern Pissarro Gallery, Vincent Pruchnicki, Graciela Téllez Trevilla, and especially Daniel Zamani, Artistic Director at the Museum Frieder Burda in Baden-Baden, who has co-conceptualized the exhibition. We also extend our thanks to the research staff at the Documentation Center of the Musée d'Orsay in Paris, The Metropolitan Museum of Art in New York, and the National Gallery of Art in Washington, DC.

At the Museum Barberini, we are deeply grateful to the entire team behind this ambitious project. Special thanks are due to Ortrud Westheider, Director; Janine Meyer, Managing Director; Michael Philipp, Chief Curator; Linda Hacka, Provenance Research Associate; Valentina Plotnikova, Curatorial Assistant; Anne Barz, Annelies Legein, and Anna Seidel, Registrars; Achim Klapp, Marte Kräher, Valerie Maul, and Carolin Stranz, Communications and Marketing; Dorothee Entrup, Isabel Acosta, and Andrea Schmidt, Education and Inspiration; Stefan Scholze, Digitization and Information Security; and Leonie Schmidt, Student Assistant.

At the Denver Art Museum, we were fortunate to receive unstinting support from our Frederick and Jan Mayer Director, Christoph Heinrich, and our Chief of Curatorial Affairs, Collections, and Exhibitions, Angelica Daneo. A project of this scale would have never come to fruition without the contribution of our stellar team: Emily Willkom, Senior Curatorial Assistant; Lauren Thompson, Senior Interpretative Specialist; Renée Albiston, Associate Provenance Researcher; Sarah Cucinella-McDaniel, Director of Registration, Collections, and Exhibitions; Caitlin R. Rumery, Associate Registrar; Eric Berkemeyer, Project Manager; Valerie Hellstein, Managing Editor of Publications; Christina Jackson, Manager of Photographic Services; Renée B. Miller, Manager of Rights and Reproductions; Pam Skiles, Senior Paintings Conservator; Felicia Martinez, Assistant Project Manager; Jeff Keene, Senior Preparator for Exhibitions; Ruby Dorchester, Assistant Preparator for Exhibitions; Erwin Erkfitz, Associate Preparator for Registration; David Griesheimer, Associate Director of Exhibition Production; Haley Hartmann, Manager of Exhibition Lighting; and interns Chloe Ponzio and Valentine Karrer. Credit for the stunning exhibition design goes to Stephen Saitas and to Evan Cotgageorge for exhibition graphic design.

Claire Durand-Ruel Snollaerts
Guest curator
Pissarro expert

Clarisse Fava-Piz
Associate Curator of
European and American
Art Before 1900
Denver Art Museum

Nerina Santorius
Curator and
Head of Impressionism
Museum Barberini,
Potsdam

"Absolutely Free"
Camille Pissarro's Dedication as an Artist

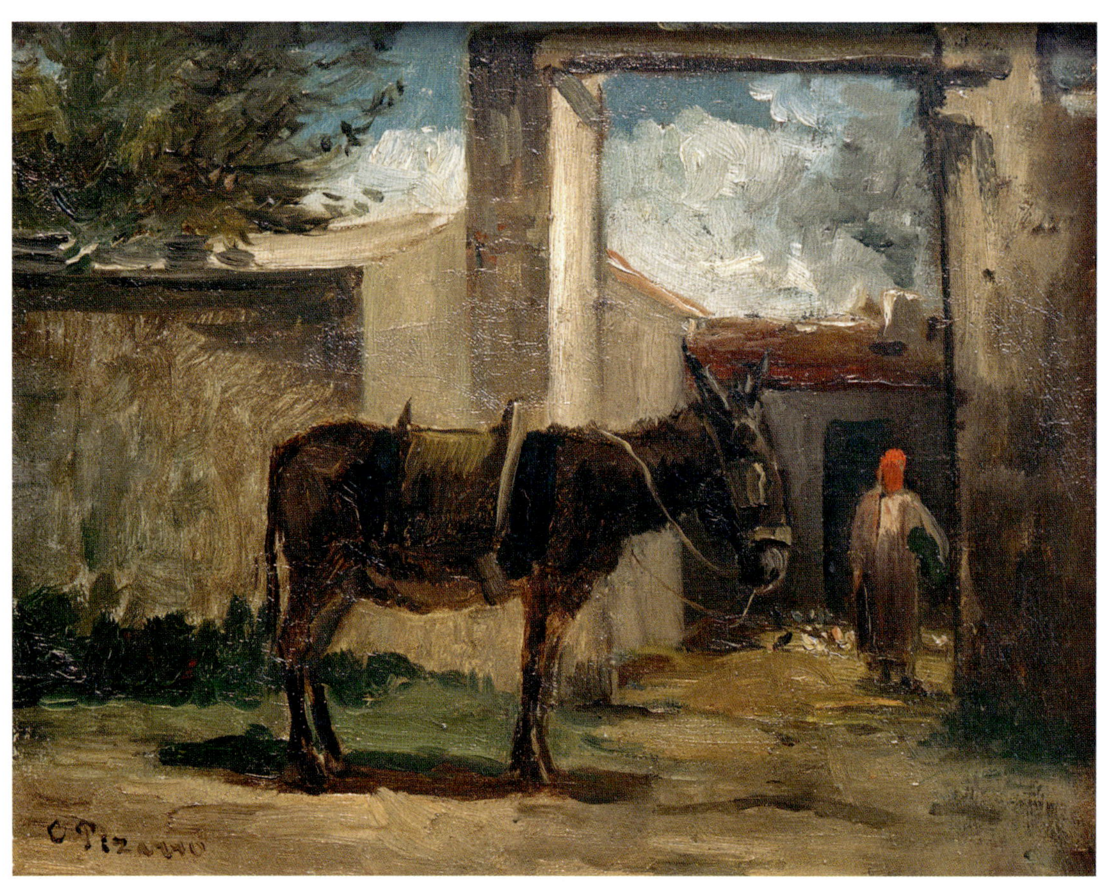

1
Landscape at Montmorency, ca. 1859, Musée d'Orsay, Paris

> It's almost impossible to keep a young man from going where his passions lead him. [...] When I think that, as a young man, left to my own devices like anyone else, I found myself in a foreign land, free, absolutely free, and lucky enough to never encounter misfortune, I wonder what advice I could possibly give. [...] The author of this letter had a powerful distraction: art!!![1]

Passion, freedom, art: Camille Pissarro articulated these three key terms at the age of sixty-eight in a letter to his son Lucien. Yet nothing in Pissarro's background—neither his place of birth nor his family origins—predisposed him to become a painter. The following essay explores Pissarro's dedication to developing free opportunities for creating art outside the Salon and academies, tracing his role in the group of Impressionists and his advocacy for the artists of the next generation.

"Where He Learned to Draw Without a Master": Early Years on Saint Thomas and in Venezuela

Camille Pissarro was born on July 10, 1830, in Charlotte Amalie—a port town on the island of Saint Thomas in the Danish Antilles, now the US Virgin Islands—to a French merchant family of Jewish faith. Later in life, he rarely spoke about his youth or his artistic beginnings on Saint Thomas. The young Pissarro grew up in a diverse, cosmopolitan environment, interacting with Europeans—the community of French, Danish, Spanish, and English merchants who, like his father, conducted business on the island—as well as with the enslaved people from various colonized African countries who lived there.[2] As a child, he attended a Moravian elementary school that provided instruction to children from all these communities.[3] In 1842, at the age of twelve, he was sent to boarding school near Paris.[4] Its director is said to have advised him, "When you return to your country, be sure to draw the coconut trees!"[5] It is not documented whether Pissarro was already interested in drawing at this time or if he visited the museums of Paris during his boarding school period, which ended when he returned to Charlotte Amalie in 1847. When he went back to France in 1855, at the age of twenty-five, Pissarro was already an accomplished artist, with a substantial portfolio of works on paper and paintings.[6] Paul Cézanne later remarked, "He had the good luck of being born in the Antilles, where he learned to draw without a master."[7] Though not entirely accurate—Pissarro did have some instruction—Cézanne's observation reflects how Pissarro started his early training far from the rigid methods of the French academic workshops.

When he returned to Charlotte Amalie in 1847, Pissarro reluctantly joined the family business, a haberdashery and hardware firm. At every opportunity, he would slip away with his sketchbook to capture the lively scenes at the harbor. With a sure hand, he also made portraits and drew women returning from market with their wares balanced on their heads, animals, landscapes dotted with coconut palms, and huts nestled at the foot of lush hills.

One day, while overseeing the arrival of merchandise, Pissarro met Danish painter Fritz Melbye (1826–1869), an encounter that would profoundly alter the course of his life. Melbye, a marine painter, traveled the world producing work for European collectors. Together, they left Saint Thomas—Pissarro departing without his family's permission—for Venezuela, where they lived as bohemian artist-adventurers from 1852 to 1854. Melbye became the first of many artistic companions in Pissarro's life. Years later, Pissarro recalled this bold leap into the unknown:

> In '52, working as a well-paid clerk on Saint Thomas, I couldn't stand it any longer—without further reflection, I left everything behind and fled to Caracas to break the tie that bound me to bourgeois life. I suffered terribly, of course, but I lived.[8]

The two painters traveled across Venezuela, discovering new cultures and ways of life. Most importantly, they created numerous works inspired by the surrounding natural world. Two paintings—*A Plaza in Caracas* (cat. 6), from Venezuela, and *Two Women Chatting by the Sea, Saint Thomas* (cat. 8), painted on Saint Thomas but later redated to 1856—demonstrate the artistic mastery that Pissarro had developed under the guidance of his Danish mentor. His cosmopolitan childhood in the Antilles and his time in Venezuela, enriching and sometimes painful, profoundly shaped Pissarro's adult character. From these experiences, he developed a strong work ethic, determination, a love of art, a deep yearning for freedom and independence, generosity, a spirit of sharing, and a remarkable open-mindedness.

In 1855 his father accepted his vocation as a painter and allowed him to continue his training in France. Yet when he arrived in Paris, the young Pissarro was already an experienced artist. His time in Venezuela had exposed him to a wide range of subjects and motifs. He had also experimented with drawing, watercolor, and oil painting. His preferred themes on Saint Thomas and in Venezuela anticipated those of the Impressionist movement: he depicted daily life and local customs without artifice. His subjects were market scenes, animals, tree-lined roads, the seashore, and people working, conversing, or resting. This interest in using brush and pencil to express the reality of a simple, authentic life would remain central to his work. Later, in Louveciennes, Pontoise, and Éragny-sur-Epte—towns near Paris, but still largely untouched by industrialization—Pissarro captured, with delicacy and sensitivity, the peaceful countryside through the changing seasons, peopled by dignified peasant figures. Yet while his choice of subjects remained largely consistent, Pissarro's artistic style evolved significantly over the decades, influenced by his close ties to other artists.

"Not the Least Delectation for the Eye": The Critics at the Paris Salon

At the time of Pissarro's return to France, the only way to gain recognition from dealers and collectors was to have works accepted at the official Salon de Peinture et de Sculpture, or Salon de Paris. Four years after his arrival in the French capital, in 1859, Pissarro tried his luck and was thrilled when his work was accepted—a small painting titled *Landscape at*

Montmorency, depicting a woman with a donkey by a farmyard (fig. 1). In the catalog, he was listed as a "student of Anton Melbye," the brother of Fritz Melbye.[9] The Salon accepted his work six more times, through 1870, when he sent his last submission. *The Banks of the Marne in Winter* (cat. 13), an austere, melancholy painting exhibited at the Salon in 1866, attracted the attention of two critics and can be considered one of the first works to establish his reputation.

The reviewer of *L'Univers illustré* astutely noted Pissarro's gift for deeming even the most banal or ugly motifs worthy of painting:

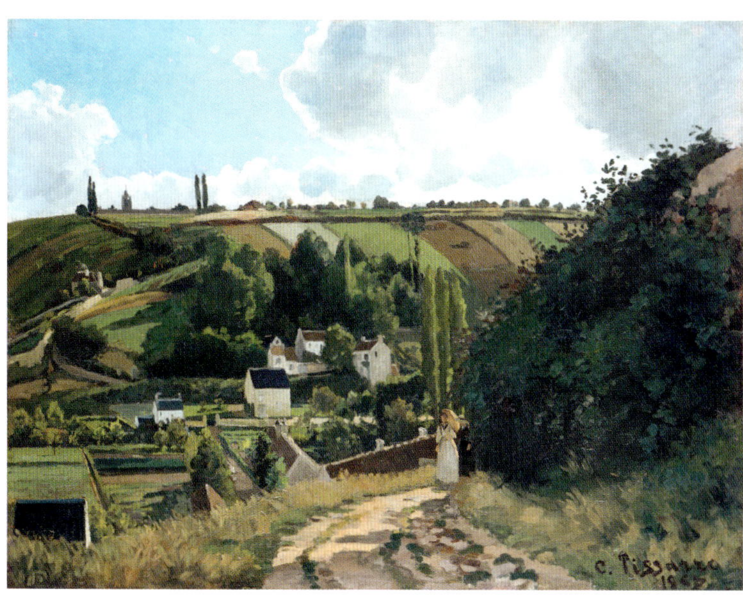

2
Jalais Hill, Pontoise, 1867,
The Metropolitan Museum of Art,
New York

> Surely there is nothing more vulgar than this view and nevertheless I challenge you to pass by without noticing it. It becomes original by the abrupt energy of execution, which underlines these uglinesses, instead of seeking to conceal them. One sees that M. Pissarro is not banal through an inability to be picturesque.[10]

The second review came from Émile Zola, writing in *L'Événement* after discovering the artist's work:

> M. Pissarro is an unknown and probably no one will talk about him. I consider it my duty to give him a vigorous handshake before leaving. Thank you, Monsieur, your winter landscape refreshed me for a good half hour, during my trip through the great desert of the Salon. I know that you were admitted only with great difficulty and I congratulate you on that. Besides which, you ought to know that you please nobody and that your painting is thought to be too bare, too black. So why the devil do you have the arrant awkwardness to paint solidly and study nature so honestly! Look, you choose wintertime, you have there a little bit of a road, then a hillside in the background, and open fields to the horizon. Not the least delectation for the eye. A grave and austere kind of painting, an extreme care for truth and rightness, an iron will.[11]

In *The Banks of the Marne in Winter,* Pissarro had painted a landscape devoid of any significant event—a scene that, as both critics observed, was not even beautiful. Throughout his career, Pissarro made a point of rendering reality as he saw it, without embellishment or picturesque details. The "pretty," he often warned his son, was a greater danger than the "ugly." His commitment to this philosophy sometimes put him at odds with his dealers and collectors.[12]

The year 1866 also marked Pissarro's move to Pontoise, a town some twenty miles northwest of Paris. He and his family lived there for two years, before returning to make it their home once again from 1872 to 1882.[13] The paintings *Pontoise* (cat. 15) and *Jalais Hill, Pontoise* (fig. 2) belong to the group of works from his first stay. Using quite large formats, Pissarro set about depicting the panoramas of L'Hermitage, an area on the outskirts of town. The first shows vegetable gardens set against a hillside of terraced housing. The second work depicts a view of a bend in a road from which two elegantly dressed women emerge, illuminated by the light. They pass an embankment that blocks the view of the path they have taken and casts a shadow over the foreground. When the painting was shown at the Salon of 1868, Zola once again praised Pissarro:

> This is the modern countryside. [...] And this little valley, this hill, have a heroic simplicity and forthrightness. Nothing would be more banal if it were not so grand. From ordinary reality the painter's temperament has drawn a rare poem of life and strength.[14]

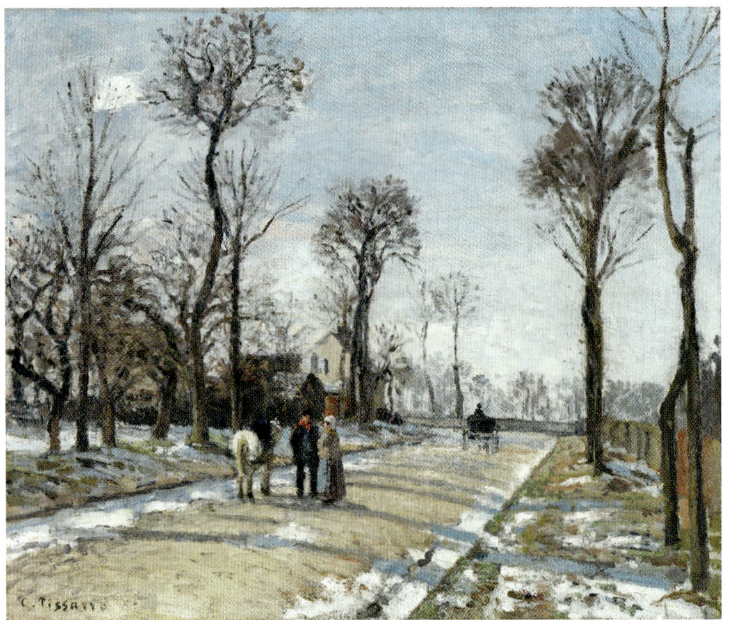

3
Route de Versailles, Louveciennes, Winter Sun and Snow, ca. 1870, Museo Nacional Thyssen-Bornemisza, Madrid

Zola's emphasis on simplicity and forthrightness perfectly described the artist's character as well.

From 1869 to 1872, the Pissarro family moved closer to Paris, renting a house in the town of Louveciennes at the foot of the Marly aqueduct. Pissarro often painted outdoors alongside Claude Monet, Alfred Sisley, and Pierre-Auguste Renoir, who had also settled in the area. During this period, Pissarro's work underwent its first stylistic changes: his palette became brighter, his brushstrokes lighter, and above all, he used smaller formats that were easier to transport. A topographical study of the sites Pissarro depicted in Louveciennes reveals his distinctive working method: he rarely ventured far from his home on the Route de Versailles, creating twenty-two works from this road alone, most of them just yards from his doorstep. The outdoors served as his studio, and his immediate surroundings provided him with an abundance of subjects. From this fixed location, Pissarro demonstrated remarkable versatility, often revisiting the same motifs from slightly different angles and in varying weather conditions to achieve a sense of constant renewal. In *Route de Versailles, Rain Effect* (cat. 21) his house appears on the left, with the blacksmith's house opposite. *Route de Versailles, Louveciennes, Winter Sun and Snow* (fig. 3) presents the reverse view, with his house hidden behind him and the posthouse visible across the street. The twenty-two paintings of the Route de Versailles do not constitute a formal series due to their varying viewpoints. Standing in front of his house, Pissarro turned in different directions and depicted buildings from close up or from a distance. However, the exhaustive exploration of a single location anticipates both Monet's later serial works and Pissarro's own series of urban panoramas, created from the 1890s onward. *The Thaw* or *The House of Monsieur Musy, Louveciennes* (cat. 22) depicts a nearby house that appears in six distinct paintings, each with such different perspectives and framing that the subject is not immediately recognizable as the same building.[15] This ability to generate multiple motifs from a single subject was characteristic for Pissarro's approach. In Éragny-sur-Epte he would take up this approach again.

The Conversation, Louveciennes (fig. 4), dated 1870, is notable for its exceptional size: 39 ½ by 31 ⅞ inches. In this highly structured composition, Pissarro shows a conversation between his wife, Julie, seen from behind with their daughter Jeanne-Rachel ("Minette") at her side, and a neighbor. The fence marking the boundary of the family home guides the viewer's gaze toward these three figures; the eye pauses on the neighbor's face before being drawn further toward the Route de Versailles, bathed in brilliant light. The tree's foliage, rendered in small brushstrokes, separates the shaded private space on the left from the sunlit public space on the right. Despite its large format, the canvas was certainly painted *en plein air.* Pissarro and his friends adopted a technique of small brushstrokes and hatchings that allowed them to more accurately capture the texture of foliage and flowers, as well as the shimmering interplay of light and shade on objects. Though relatively subdued in color, this painting represents a significant step in Pissarro's progression toward Impressionism.

"Our Exhibition Is Going Well": Pissarro's Role in the Impressionist Group

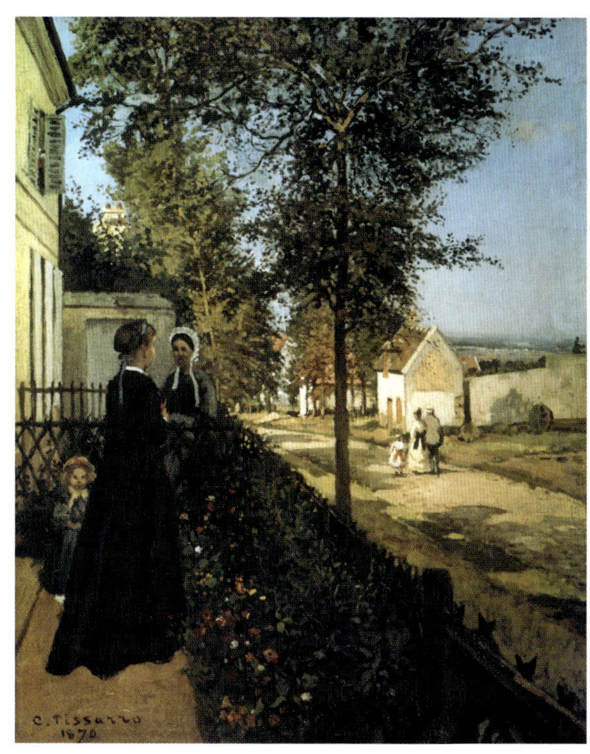

4
The Conversation, Louveciennes, 1870, Emil Bührle Collection, Zurich

After spending a year in London starting in late 1870 to escape the Prussian troops who had occupied their house in Louveciennes, Pissarro and his family returned to Pontoise in 1872 and remained there for ten years. This second period in Pontoise marked a significant chapter in the painter's artistic development and his growing influence within the Impressionist movement. In particular, it coincided with the first of seven independent Impressionist exhibitions. Pissarro was the only artist to exhibit in all eight (the final one in 1886, when he was living in Éragny-sur-Epte). While Renoir and Monet, discouraged by the poor reception of their work, occasionally preferred to try their luck at the official Salon, and others such as Gustave Caillebotte, Mary Cassatt, Cézanne, Edgar Degas, and Sisley eventually abstained entirely, Pissarro never wavered in his decision to participate in these independent exhibitions, despite facing humiliation with each one. The rigid, academic style of the Salon was too stark a contrast to the artist's commitment to independence and freedom.

In 1874 Pissarro, along with Monet, Renoir, and Degas, actively participated in the group's founding and in the selection of artists for its first independent exhibition. At this inaugural showing, he exhibited five landscapes of Pontoise, including *Hoarfrost* (cat. 33), which startled many viewers with its enigmatic grid-like arrangement of shadows. Louis Leroy, one of the harshest opponents of this new style of painting, recounted a dialogue in front of the picture:

> "Those furrows? That frost? But they are palette-scrapings placed uniformly on a dirty canvas. It has neither head nor tail, top nor bottom, front nor back."—"Perhaps . . . but the impression is there."—"Well, it's a funny impression!"[16]

Despite the disparaging remarks, Pissarro remained confident. He reported to his friend Théodore Duret, "Our exhibition is going well, it's a success. The critics are tearing us apart and accusing us of not studying—I'm going back to my studies, it's better than reading the reviews; there's nothing to be learned from them."[17] Criticism continued to be fierce throughout the eight exhibitions, often focusing on the use of colors deemed too garish and the seemingly unfinished quality of the works.

Among the thirty exhibitors in 1874 was Paul Cézanne, who gained admission thanks to Pissarro. During the decade from 1872 to 1882, Cézanne often stayed in the Pontoise region to paint alongside his mentor. "He was like a father to me," he later said. "You could always ask him questions; he was something like the good God."[18] From their artistic dialogue emerged works of strong similarity.[19] *View of the Maison des Mathurins, Pontoise* (fig. 5) by Pissarro and *Road at Pontoise* (fig. 6) by Cézanne were painted side by side in 1875. Their shared use of the palette knife, limited color range, and reduction of composition to essential elements reflect the intensity of their artistic exchange. Pissarro later recalled of this period, "Cézanne was under my influence in Pontoise and I was under his. Of course—we were always together!"[20]

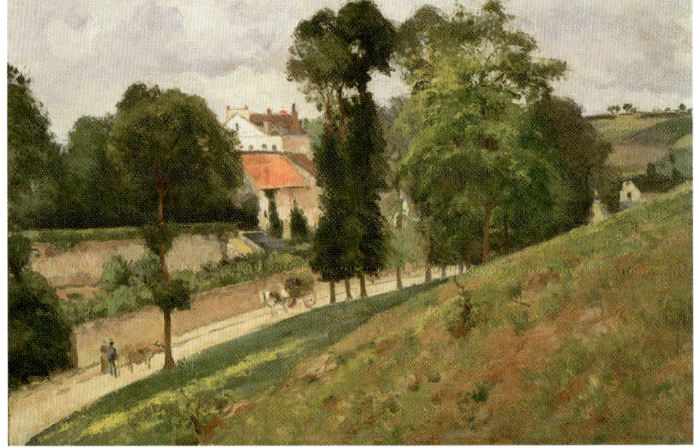

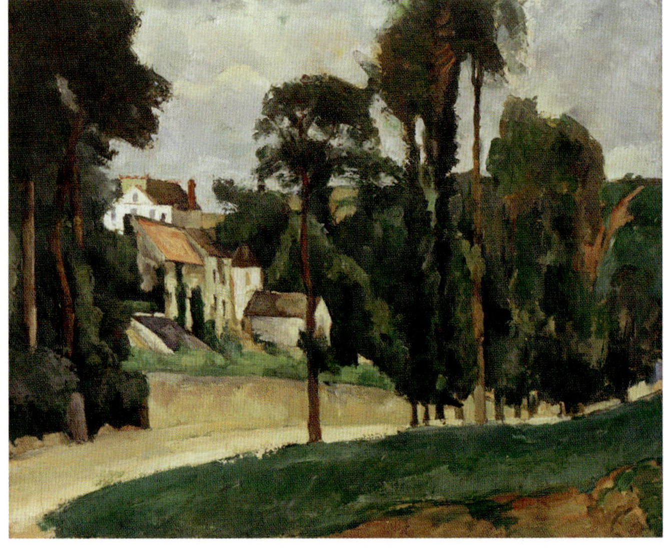

5
View of the Maison des Mathurins, Pontoise, 1875, private collection

6
Paul Cézanne, *Road at Pontoise,* 1875, State Pushkin Museum of Fine Arts, Moscow

Pissarro was a mentor not only to Cézanne but also to Paul Gauguin, who, until 1885, drew heavily on his example: "He was one of my masters, and I would never deny it."[21] Gauguin, eighteen years Pissarro's junior, visited Pontoise frequently between 1879 and 1883 to paint in his mentor's style, copying his subjects and absorbing lessons about broken brushwork. Patient, attentive, and nonauthoritarian, Pissarro was a dedicated teacher throughout his life, guiding and encouraging both his artist friends and his five sons in their artistic growth.

"I Accept the Fight": The Neo-Impressionist Adventure

While Pissarro had fought to have Cézanne admitted in 1874, in 1886, the year of the final exhibition of the Impressionist group, he insisted on including Georges Seurat and Paul Signac, two unknown young artists who were the pioneers of the Divisionist technique, also known as Neo-Impressionism. This new approach to painting, rooted in modern scientific principles, was rejected by the rest of the group. The organization of this final exhibition was thus more chaotic than ever; never before had such diverse styles been displayed in one show. Caillebotte, Monet, Renoir, and Sisley desisted. Pissarro's success in imposing painters whose technique was so far removed from Impressionism highlights his dedication to innovation:

> I explained [...] that Seurat was bringing something new that, despite their talent, these gentlemen could not appreciate, and that I personally am convinced of the progress in this art which will, at some point, produce extraordinary results. Besides, I couldn't care less about the opinion of any artists whatsoever, and I don't accept the casual judgments of the romantics [i.e., the Impressionists], who have a vested interested in fighting new trends. I accept the fight, that's all.[22]

In a separate room, Pissarro proudly exhibited his Divisionist works—including *View from My Window in Cloudy Weather* (cat. 78) and *Apple Picking* (fig. 7)—alongside Seurat's *A Sunday on La Grande Jatte* (fig. 8).[23] While criticism persisted, many welcomed this new way of painting. Jean Ajalbert was dazzled upon entering the room blazing with Pissarros, Signacs, and Seurats:

> These artists are seeking something new only in their technique. They arrive at intense coloration through observations that are as accurate as they are simple. They color shadows with the complementary color of light areas; they avoid muddy mixtures by painting with small touches, dots, or by juxtaposing colors: the mixing happens in the eye, not on the palette. They paint by softening, by endlessly modifying an object's local color by the reflections from stronger neighboring colors.[24]

Of Pissarro, Ajalbert perceptively wrote, "He is an old-time wrestler, a master always making progress, and courageously shaping himself according to new theories."[25]

The Divisionist adventure brought Pissarro closer to Neo-Impressionists such as Henri-Edmond Cross, Albert Dubois-Pillet, Léo Gausson, Maximilien Luce, and Belgian painter Théo Van Rysselberghe. Alongside them, he produced a series of works using tiny dots that achieved exceptional luminosity. However, after four years of intense dedication to the technique, he abandoned it, finding the long and painstaking process stifling. He lamented "the impossibility of following my fleeting sensations, and thus of giving life and movement; the impossibility of capturing the many varied efforts of nature, the impossibility or difficulty of giving character to my drawing, of avoiding repetition [. . .]. I had to give it up, it was more than time!"[26] He noted that creating a painting using the dotted technique took him twice as long as his previous methods. The slow, almost mechanical gesture felt ill-suited to the spontaneity of his sensations. A tally of his output between 1885 (the year before he began Divisionism) and 1890 (the year he abandoned it) shows the decline in his production during his Divisionist period. In 1885 he completed thirty-five paintings; in 1886, twenty-two; in 1887, sixteen; in 1888, eight; in 1889, twelve; and in 1890 he returned to twenty-eight.

This interlude, which sparked disagreements with his Impressionist friends and led to the cessation of purchases by his dealer Paul Durand-Ruel, further underscores Pissarro's independence and his openness to exploring new techniques, even at an advanced age.

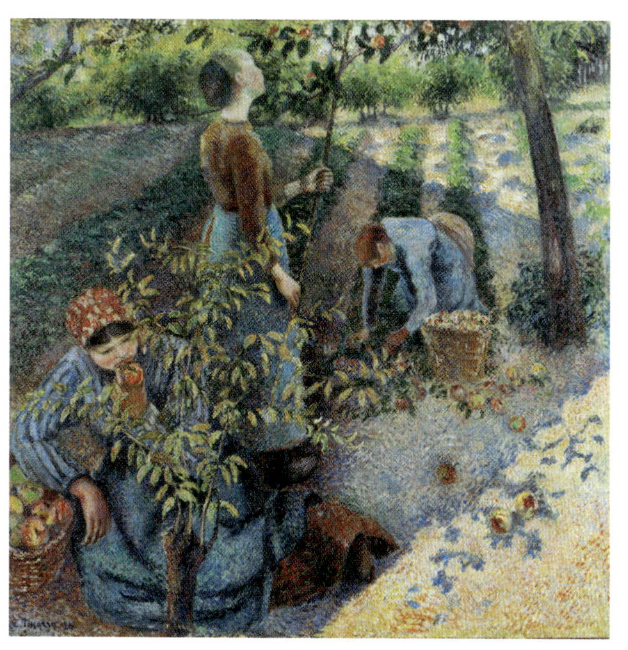

7
Apple Picking, 1886,
Ohara Museum of Art, Kurashiki

The eight Impressionist exhibitions—spread across twelve years—served as a springboard for Pissarro's career. Not only did he play a key role in organizing them, but each exhibition also introduced the public to new facets of his evolving work. Alongside oils, he exhibited gouaches, fans, and engravings, demonstrating both his technical versatility as well as his curiosity and openness to new approaches. In 1881 and 1882, at the sixth and seventh exhibitions, Pissarro distinguished himself with a number of plein-air figure studies (cats. 40–42). While some praised these works, others compared his figures to those of Jean-François Millet, much to his annoyance: "They throw Millet in my face, but Millet was biblical! For a Hebrew, I seem to be far less so—curious, isn't it?"[27] Unlike Millet, who often portrayed peasants as struggling under hardship (fig. 9), Pissarro depicted them as content and harmoniously absorbed in their environment (fig. 10). The portrait-figures, painted either individually or in groups, often fill the entire canvas space, standing out against natural backgrounds that do not represent any specific landscape. Sensitively rendered, Pissarro's peasant figures were, above all, a tribute to his friend Degas.

"View from My Window": Éragny-sur-Epte, Le Havre, Paris

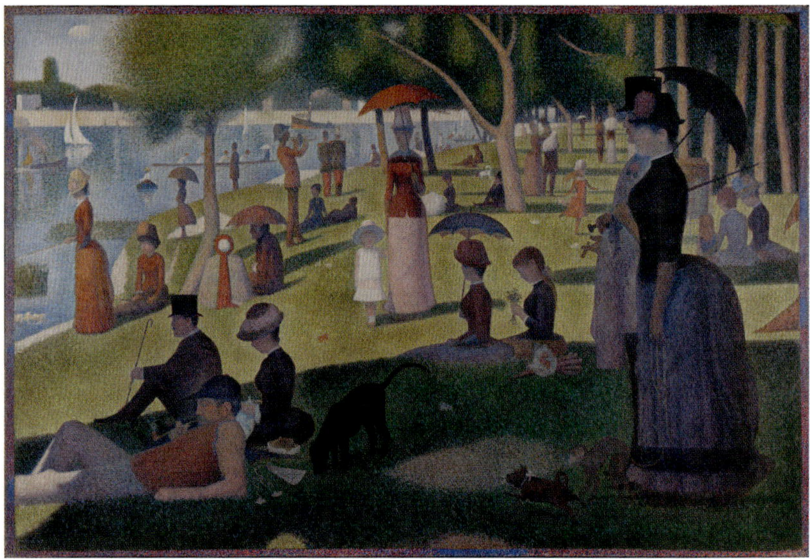

8
Georges Seurat,
A Sunday on La Grande Jatte, 1884–86,
The Art Institute of Chicago

From 1884 until Julie Pissarro's death in 1926, the Pissarro family lived in Éragny-sur-Epte, a small rural village of around five hundred inhabitants—both then and today—located in the French Vexin region. Their home, situated along a country road, had a large kitchen garden that extended into wide meadows. Despite the limited range of subjects, Pissarro created as many works here as in Pontoise (about 350 oil paintings), though over a period twice as long: twenty years. *View from My Window in Cloudy Weather* (cat. 78), executed in small dots, encompasses all the Éragny motifs—subjects he captured at all hours, in all seasons, and from various angles. Like his earlier views of Louveciennes, the paintings of this motif group demonstrate his practice of returning repeatedly to the same landscape, each time introducing subtle variations in framing and light (cats. 59–61, 69–72).

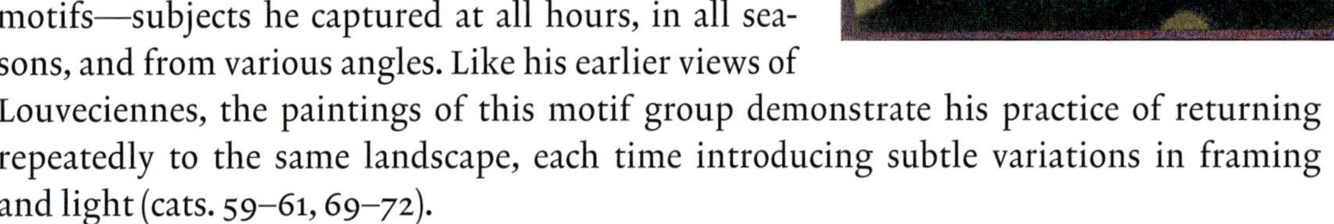

By the early 1890s, Pissarro undertook numerous painting campaigns away from Éragny-sur-Epte, returning home only to rest with his family. He began to tackle large cityscapes when he was over sixty, despite his fragile health. From 1893 until his death in 1903, he produced nearly three hundred urban views, always from a window, alternating each year between the three Normandy ports of Rouen, Dieppe, and Le Havre (cats. 87–96) and Paris, where he depicted the city's busy neighborhoods (cats. 97–109).

Pissarro left behind an impressive body of work: more than 1,500 paintings, thousands of pastels, gouaches, aquarelles, fans, and drawings, as well as prints—a demanding medium that he mastered with technical excellence. Among his Impressionist friends, he was almost unique in his exploration of such a wide range of techniques. His extensive correspondence reflects his artistic ideas.[28] Pissarro died on November 13, 1903, in Paris, surrounded by his family and friends, shortly after completing a series of paintings in Le Havre. Cézanne later reflected:

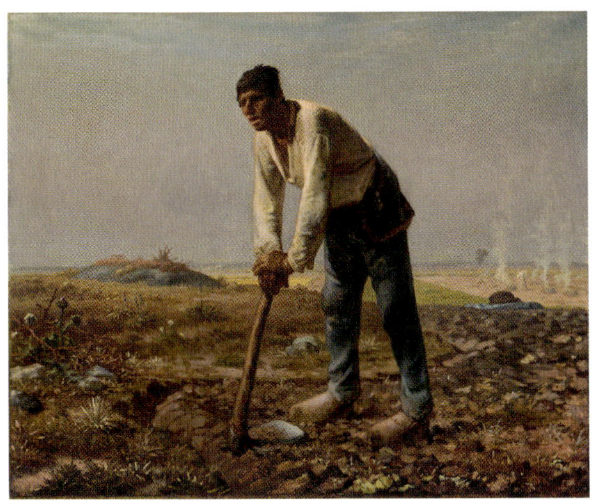

> And so perhaps all of us come out of Pissarro. [. . .] Never paint with anything but the three primary colors and their immediate derivatives, he told me. Yes, he really was the first Impressionist.[29]

Indeed, Pissarro was the first Impressionist: as the group's senior and in his complete dedication to the movement. But he also deserves this title because his voice carried great weight in the group's crucial decisions. Pissarro was known as a patient listener, a generous mentor, and an enthusiastic explorer of new ideas. Throughout his career, he maintained an uncompromising standard, painting according to his deepest convictions, while always experimenting and renewing his approach. In every sense, Pissarro earned his title as "father" of the Impressionists.

Translated from French by Helge R. Dascher

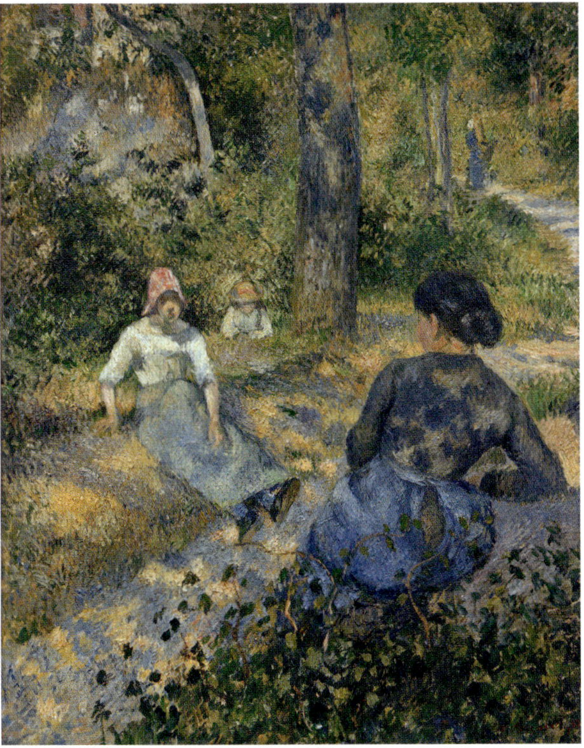

9
Jean-François Millet,
Man with a Hoe, 1860–62,
The J. Paul Getty Museum, Los Angeles

10
Peasants Resting, 1881,
Toledo Museum of Art

In Pissarro's Studio
A Window into Impressionist Experimentation

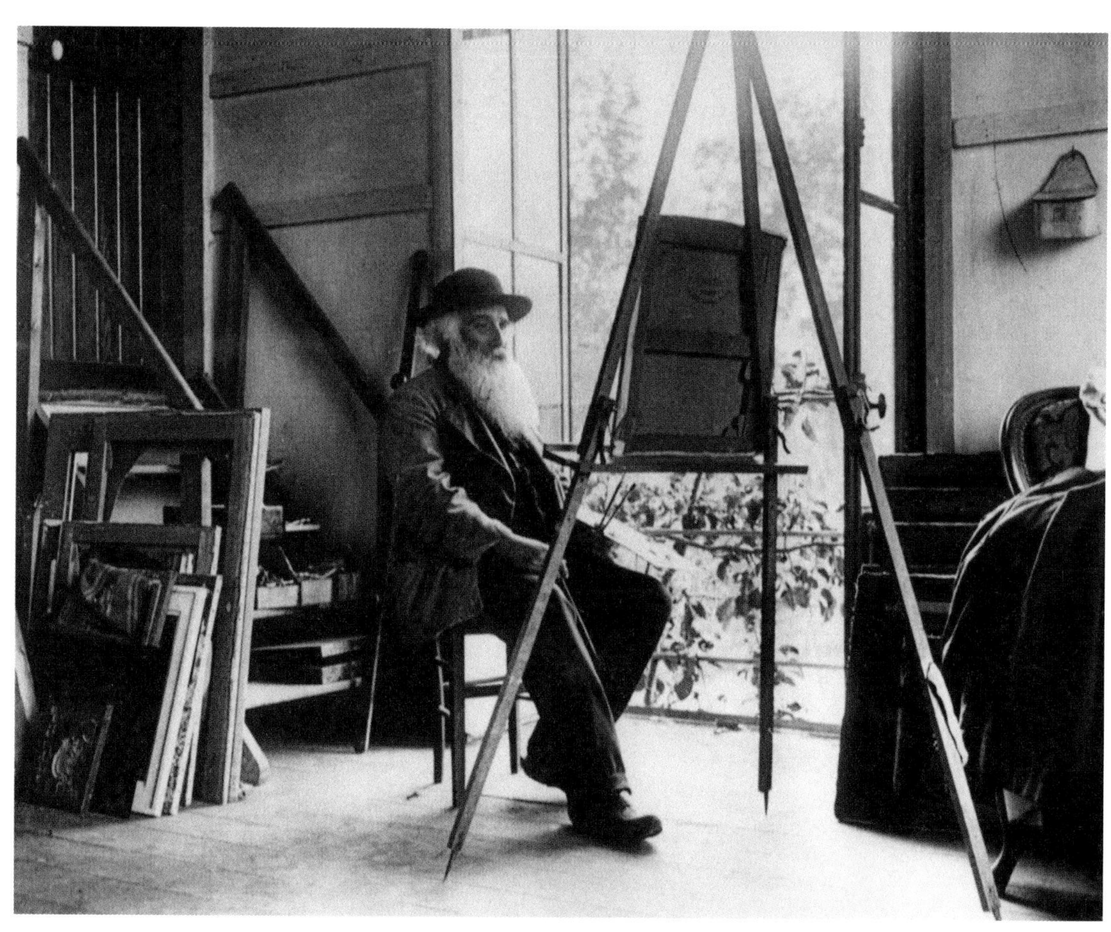

1
Camille Pissarro at a window in his studio in Éragny-sur-Epte, undated (unknown photographer), Musée d'Art et d'Histoire Pissarro—Pontoise

In 1893, at the age of sixty-three, Camille Pissarro transformed the barn on his property in Éragny-sur-Epte into an atelier, and the studio windows framed the artist's view of the surroundings that he would then repeatedly paint (fig. 1). However, Pissarro worried about the implications of this workspace on his artistic practice. In a letter to his sons Lucien, Georges, and Félix, Pissarro shared his apprehension regarding the new arrangement:

> It's a first-rate atelier, but I keep saying to myself, what's the point of having a studio? In the old days, I did my painting anywhere; in every season, in sweltering heat, under rain, in horrid cold spells, I found it in me to work enthusiastically [. . .]. Am I going to be able to work in this new environment??? My painting's bound to be affected; my painting will put on gloves, gosh almighty, I'll be official!!![1]

Pissarro's anxiety reflects his association of a studio with official art. He feared that by confining himself to working indoors, the nature of his paintings would change and turn into much-loathed academic art. Plein-air painting is still considered a major principle of Impressionism, in opposition to the stuffy aesthetic rules of the nineteenth-century academy. But the image of the Impressionist artist standing in front of the easel outdoors, directly transcribing immediate sensations onto the canvas, is a reductive understanding of Pissarro's complex practice.

Not content to just paint outdoors, Pissarro, a prolific draftsman, exercised his eye and hand on a near-daily basis and used his drawings to build a wide repertoire of figures and motifs that he incorporated into his paintings. Moreover, the artist often annotated in pencil the colors that he intended for his painted compositions. Pissarro also carefully prepared his paintings before working at the easel. He did not necessarily design the drawing in such a way that it could be transferred directly to the canvas, but rather he gathered enough visual data to develop and refine his final composition.[2] Pissarro's rigorous artistic process destabilizes the common understanding of Impressionist painting as the direct and immediate transcription of atmospheric effects directly experienced by the artist.

Plein-air practice dominated Pissarro's early Impressionist years, but even before the creation of a dedicated studio space at Éragny-sur-Epte, Pissarro sometimes worked indoors. Weather conditions could affect the artist's progress on his paintings initiated outdoors, forcing him to pursue his work inside.[3] Moreover, Pissarro's dacryocystitis, which he had been suffering from for some time, worsened around 1889. The chronic eye infection made it difficult for him to paint outside. Even at the time, critics noted that Pissarro's work was constructed and rigorous, and while initiated *sur le motif,* his paintings were completed in the studio. In 1892 art critic and novelist Georges Lecomte was one of the first to comment on Pissarro's artistic process:

> For a long time now, Mr. Pissarro had ceased to work exclusively in front of nature, to render its momentary and incidental details. After having fixed in watercolor or pastel the physiognomy of a site, the appearance of a farmer or an animal, he devotes himself, far from the motif, to a work of composition during which the relative and the superfluous are pruned: only the essential aspects contributing to the meaning and the decorative whole of the work remain.[4]

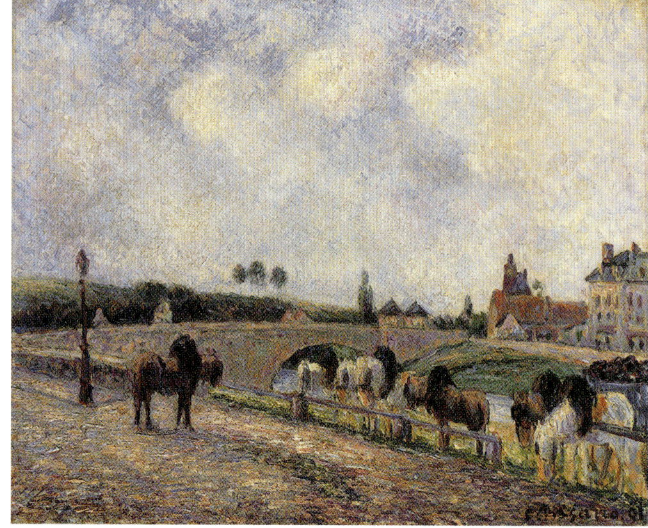

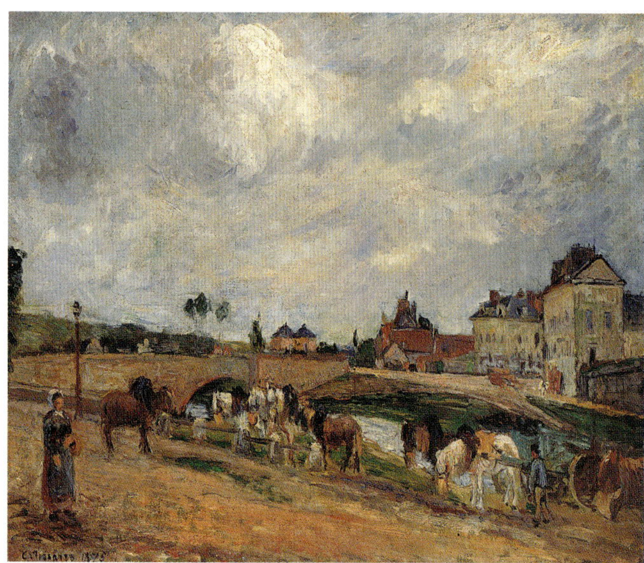

2
The Pontoise Bridge, 1891,
private collection, Luxembourg

3
The Pontoise Bridge, 1875,
private collection

Lecomte understood the studio as a necessary stage in Pissarro's artistic process, where the artist was able to distance himself from the motif in order to capture the essence of his subject and achieve the unity of his composition. Moreover, Lecomte portrays Pissarro as an artist who navigated fluidly between watercolor, pastel, and oil on canvas without any aesthetic hierarchy in the artist's mind. Other contemporary critics concurred, including Charles Kunstler, who noted:

> One thing generally unknown to the public is that Pissarro is not just a plein-air painter, a painter of impressions. He executed *in his studio* not only numerous pastels and gouaches, but also large paintings of tedders and harvests, looking for new layouts, but nevertheless using direct studies, after nature, some very advanced.[5]

Although often compared to contemporary landscape painters Claude Monet and Alfred Sisley, Pissarro had more in common with Edgar Degas in his insatiable search for new technical and pictorial problems. This essay aims to provide a more nuanced understanding of the artist's process and oeuvre beyond the wide-spread recognition of Pissarro as a well-known Impressionist plein-air painter. It will also examine how seriality is implicated in Pissarro's studio aesthetic and unveil the artist's studio practice through the study of the proliferation of motifs and experiments across disparate media. It posits a definition of the studio not only as the physical space where the artist pursued his creative endeavors but also as a laboratory of experimentation with forms, media, and motifs.

Seriality

Throughout his career, Pissarro used seriality and multiples to create his compositions and advance his artistic experimentations. This essay states that a serial production is the reworking of one image into another and is different from multiplicity, which consists of creating multiple views of the same scene, perhaps from different angles. Importantly, serialization is more inherently a studio practice, both in the physical sense of where the work was created and in the conceptual sense of how the work was conceived and assessed.[6] In some cases, the whole composition is serialized; in others, just a motif. Sometimes, images and motifs are reworked across media—paintings, prints, and decorative arts. While seriality and multiplicity are two different processes, artists can use one or the other, or some combination of the two, and sometimes it is not completely clear if the repetition is a multiple or a series, especially in the case of the paintings inspired by what Pissarro saw from his studio window.[7]

Looking at *The Pontoise Bridge,* painted in 1891, one might think that Pissarro had set up his easel alongside the river on the Quai Bucherelle in Pontoise, where the artist frequently painted, next to the group of horses grazing in the foreground (fig. 2). The bridge running across the composition leads to a group of customs houses on the Saint-Ouen-l'Aumône bank of the river. However, far from being done *sur le motif,* this painting is a reappropriation of an earlier composition painted in 1875, when Pissarro still lived in Pontoise (fig. 3).[8] Locals would have noticed that by 1891 the stone bridge had been replaced by an iron bridge.[9] In the new version of *The Pontoise Bridge* executed in his studio, Pissarro abandoned the figures, flattened the perspective, cropped the composition, and recentered it around the horses and the streetlight to the left. Less naturalistic than the older version, this painting gives more prominence to the vivid colors applied in small touches across the surface, an approach that is characteristic of the Impressionist technique.

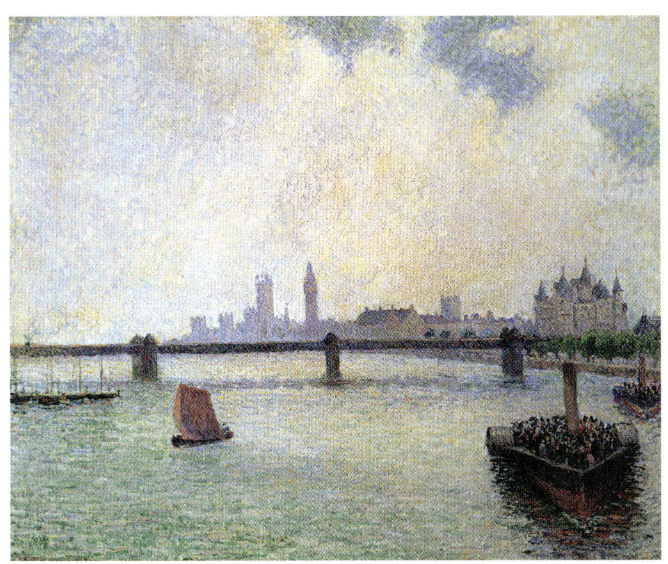

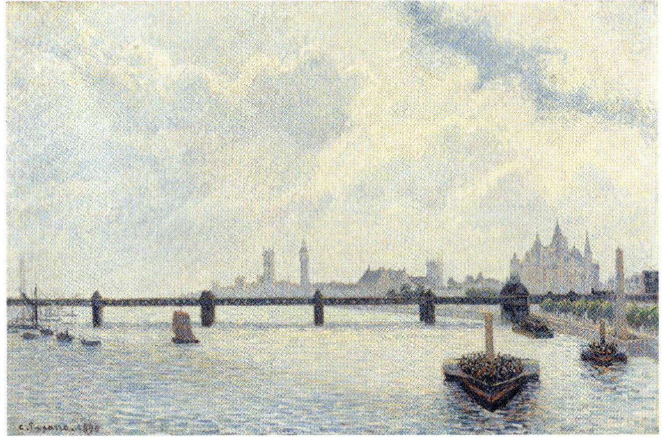

4
Charing Cross Bridge, London, 1891, private collection, Switzerland

5
Charing Cross Bridge, London, 1890, National Gallery of Art, Washington

This case is not an isolated example in Pissarro's oeuvre since that same year the artist created *Snow Effect with Cows in Montfoucault* (1891, private collection), the third of a series of paintings on the same motif dated 1874 and 1882, respectively.[10] Here again, Pissarro used a more naturalistic composition from the early 1870s to experiment with a new style. In the 1882 version, he dramatically cropped the composition. A decade later, he used his first version of the painting as a point of reference to experiment with a more varied chromatic palette and vibrant touches of colors.

This practice of seriality and reworking not only included motifs close to home, such as Pontoise and Montfoucault, but also views reconstructed after trips across the English Channel. For instance, *Charing Cross Bridge, London* from 1891 (fig. 4) constitutes a small-scale version of another painting of the same subject, itself painted in the artist's studio after Pissarro's trip to London in 1890 (fig. 5).[11] One recognizes Charing Cross Bridge viewed from Waterloo Bridge, the high towers of the Houses of Parliament with Westminster Hall and Westminster Abbey in the center background, and Whitehall Court to the right. In his letters to his niece Esther Isaacson, based in London, Pissarro asked her about the exact topography of the site, which he was trying to recollect to execute his painting back home.[12] The smaller 1891 version exemplifies the artist's attempt at using a new style. Instead of constantly looking for new motifs, Pissarro revisited earlier compositions in his studio over time to experiment with new techniques and styles, such as Neo-Impressionism.

As art historian Joachim Pissarro has demonstrated, many examples of "this vast program of 'repeats' of earlier themes" abound, and in the 1890s, another type of artistic revision appears in which Pissarro reworked many of his Neo-Impressionist paintings.[13] While this practice of repetitions and variations in Pissarro's oeuvre has been little studied, it sheds new light on the serial paintings of his late career. Furthermore, it recasts Pissarro's studio at the center stage of his artistic production.

In 1884, after many years marked by constant moves, Pissarro settled in the village of Éragny-sur-Epte, a commune located about fifty-six miles northwest of Paris, in the Département de l'Oise.[14] Thanks to a loan from Monet and a contribution from Paul Durand-Ruel, Camille and Julie Pissarro bought the property they were renting in 1892. It was composed of a house, an orchard, and a barn—which the painter would shortly convert into his studio. Even before transforming the barn into a studio space, Pissarro painted indoors from the second-floor window of the house. The artist multiplied the views of his surroundings from this elevated viewpoint, capturing the atmospheric changes of the alluvial plain of the Epte River at different times of the day. The four views of nearby Bazincourt, ranging from 1884 to 1892, are part of one of the earliest and largest series of pictorial variations completed by the artist (cats. 69–72).

In 1893 Pissarro hired Parisian architect Alfred Besnard to plan and oversee the conversion of his barn into a studio. The correspondence between Pissarro and Besnard not only lists the contractors, masons, carpenters, and locksmiths who worked on the project but also highlights Pissarro's involvement in the various phases of the studio transformation. The artist provided feedback on the successive architectural plans that Besnard submitted, weighing in on every aspect of the new studio.[15]

A side-by-side comparison of *View from My Window, Éragny* (cat. 78) and *Plum Trees in Blossom, Éragny* (cat. 59) highlights the transformations of Pissarro's property. In 1893 the thick wall running alongside the artist's garden was torn down, creating an opening leading to the meadow. In *Plum Trees in Blossom, Éragny,* painted in 1894, a figure carrying a bucket stands at the juncture where the wall would have previously stood, signaling a newly opened path. The old barn depicted on the left side of *View from My Window*, begun in 1886, was transformed into the artist's studio as seen in *Plum Trees in Blossom, Éragny*: the henhouse was removed, and a set of stairs was added to the building. Access to the studio was possible via a covered exterior staircase (fig. 6). Pissarro commented on the completion of his studio to his son Lucien in August 1893, accompanying his letter with a sketch of the stairs of the newly built studio (fig. 7):

> My studio is coming along, they're putting in the ceiling, it [the studio] measures seven by eight and a half yards and has a very high ceiling, there will be a sizable window to the west, which I would have liked to have square, but I thought of it too late, the door will be right by the entrance to the barn, [with] the stairway in the yard, there will be a roof of old tiles. [. . .] I forgot the main thing, an arched picture window three yards wide to the north, which will give a good light.[16]

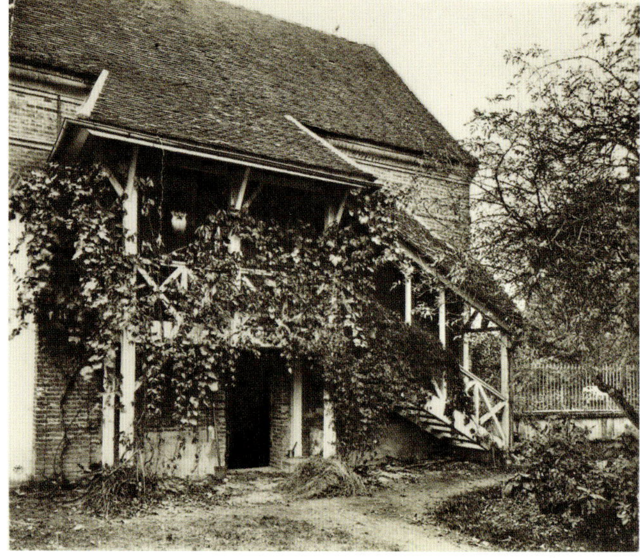

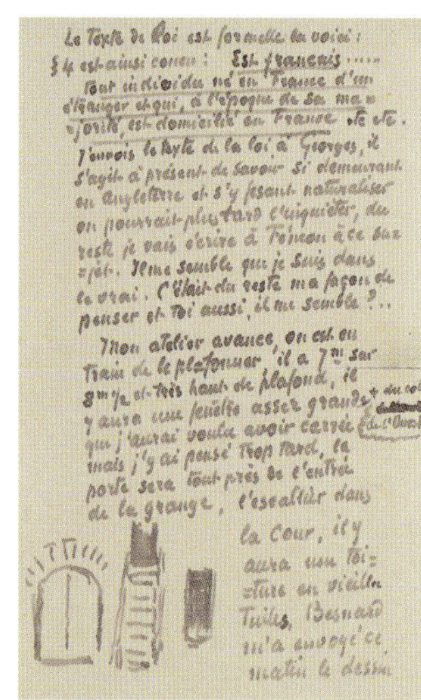

Le Texte de loi est formelle la voici :
§ 4 est ainsi conçu : Est français .....
Tout individu né en France d'un
étranger et qui, à l'époque de sa ma-
-jorité, est domicilié en France etc etc.
J'envoie le texte de la loi à Georges, il
s'agit à présent de savoir si demeurant
en Angleterre et s'y faisant naturaliser
on pourrait plus tard l'inquiéter, du
reste je vais écrire à Tenon à ce su-
-jet. Il me semble que je suis dans
le vrai. C'était du reste ma façon de
penser et toi aussi, il me semble ?..
Mon atelier avance, on est en
train de le plafonner il a 7m sur
8m ½ et très haut de plafond, il
y aura une fenêtre assez grande + au côté de l'Ouest
que j'aurai voulu avoir carrée
mais j'y ai pensé trop tard, la
porte sera tout près de l'entrée
de la grange, l'escalier dans
la cour, il y
aura une toi-
-ture en vieilles
tuiles. Besnard
m'a envoyé ce
matin le dessin

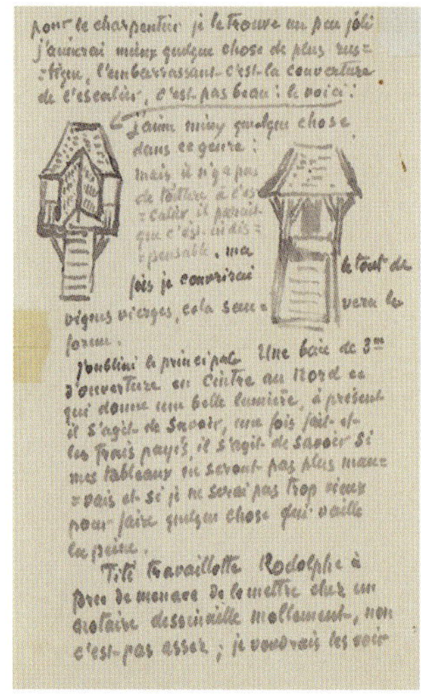

Pour le charpentier je le trouve un peu joli
j'aimerai mieux quelque chose de plus rus-
-tique, l'embarrassant c'est la couverture
de l'escalier, c'est pas beau : le voici :
j'aime mieux quelque chose
dans ce genre :
mais il n'y a pas
de toiture à l'es-
-calier, il paraît
que c'est indis-
-pensable. ma
fois je couvrirai le tout de
vignes vierges, cela sera vers la
forme.
J'oubliai le principal. Une baie de 3m
d'ouverture en cintre au Nord et
qui donne une belle lumière, à présent
il s'agit de savoir, une fois fait et
les frais payés, il s'agit de savoir si
mes tableaux ne seront pas plus mau-
-vais et si je ne serai pas trop vieux
pour faire quelque chose qui vaille
la peine.
Titi travaille, Rodolphe à
force de menace de le mettre chez un
notaire dessine mollement, non
c'est pas assez ; je voudrais les voir

6
Camille Pissarro on the stairs to his studio in Éragny-sur-Epte, undated (unknown photographer), Pissarro Family Archives

7
Sketch of studio stairs, in a letter from Camille Pissarro to his son Lucien, Éragny-sur-Epte, August 27, 1893, The Ashmolean Museum, University of Oxford

In October 1893, the studio space was greatly enhanced by a large north-facing window, and Pissarro was eager to start working.[17] From this window, he completed a series of paintings including *The Steeple at Éragny Viewed from the Studio* (1894, private collection) and *The Deaf Woman's House and the Steeple at Éragny* (ca. 1894, private collection), which are variations of the same subject. The vertical formats highlight the church's steeple, with the so-called deaf woman's house to the left. In the foreground, the enclosed space corresponds to Pissarro's back garden. The second version constitutes a more intimate painting in which the space is compressed, and the vertical format is emphasized by the placement of a figure walking toward the viewer. The distinction between serial and multiple is blurred here because Pissarro was painting in his studio in both cases. Did he create the same scene with a slightly different perspective by looking out of the studio window again, or did he rework a previous composition?

Printmaking Experiments

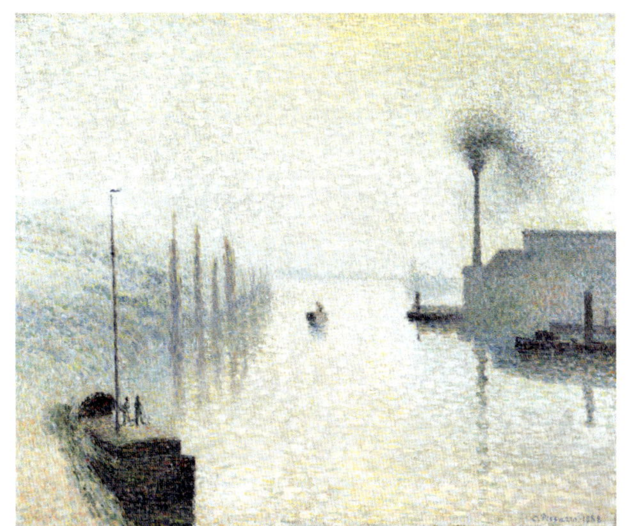

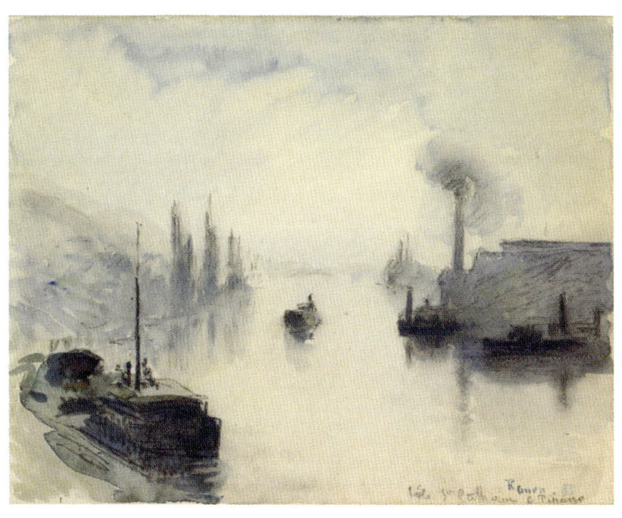

8
L'Île Lacroix, Rouen (The Effect of Fog), 1888, Philadelphia Museum of Art

9
L'Île Lacroix, Motif, 1883, Musée des Beaux-Arts de Rouen

The painting *L'Île Lacroix, Rouen (The Effect of Fog)* is not only a magnificent example of Pissarro's brief Neo-Impressionist period, but it also illustrates how Pissarro's printmaking experiments advanced his pictorial efforts (fig. 8). Indeed, this painting is part of a long series of works in various media, which started with a series of works on paper, including a watercolor completed on the motif five years prior in 1883 (fig. 9) and a cycle of prints.[18] The painting closed the cycle of Pissarro's experimentation with the motif of the Seine in Rouen, at a time when he was not traveling there anymore. According to Christophe Duvivier, former director of the Musée d'Art et d'Histoire Pissarro—Pontoise, Pissarro's Neo-Impressionist works originate from the artist's technical experiments with prints and works on paper.[19] Duvivier's assessment of Pissarro's oeuvre complicates the common understanding of the emergence of Neo-Impressionism as the direct evolution of the Impressionist touch.

Furthermore, Pissarro's interest in series and multiples, best highlighted in his late cityscapes, can also be attributed to his printmaking experiments. While printmaking has traditionally been considered a reproductive medium, some Impressionists such as Mary Cassatt, Edgar Degas, and Pissarro appreciated it for its emphasis on the artistic process. They executed each step of the process themselves, from creating the image and producing a matrix to printing the image on paper, believing that it allowed them to develop singular techniques that served their artistic innovations.[20] Pissarro first used Degas's press and his expertise to print his etchings. Later, in 1894, he installed a printing press in his newly renovated studio in Éragny-sur-Epte and shared his excitement with his son Lucien: "The press that I bought from Delatre is installed in the large studio, I am waiting for ink to print. We tried it with oil color, it will be amazing. This will give me a taste."[21] Pissarro's fascination with printmaking is discernible here in his impatience to experiment with new materials in his studio.

Throughout his career, Pissarro completed about 230 prints, including 131 etchings, 67 lithographs, and approximately 30 monotypes.[22] For a brief period following the close of the fourth Impressionist exhibition in 1879, Cassatt, Degas, and Pissarro worked together on the publication of the journal *Le Jour et la nuit* (Day and Night), which ultimately failed to materialize.[23] However, this collective enterprise had an important influence on Pissarro's printmaking, which he integrated fully into his artistic practice.[24] During the fifth Impressionist exhibition in 1880, he exhibited multiple states of the same printing plate in a single frame, considering each state of the print a finished work.[25] The multiplicity of states made it possible to preserve variations of the same composition, a principle that Pissarro applied to his large urban and port series of Paris, Rouen, Dieppe, and Le Havre, in which he worked on multiple canvases simultaneously at different hours of the day, capturing the changing atmosphere (cats. 95–98, 102–06). Like the states of an etching, the painter developed multiple interpretations of the same pictorial motif unfolding before his eyes. One can argue that Pissarro's experiments in etching instigated and sometimes advanced his research in other techniques. Throughout the 1890s, Pissarro used a variety of print media to treat his favorite subjects, such as fieldworkers and cityscapes.[26] His affinity for these themes and motifs is manifest across media beyond painting.

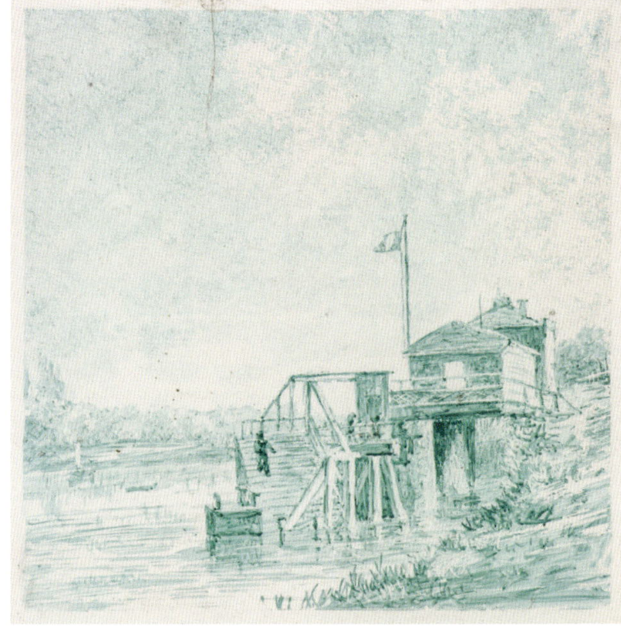

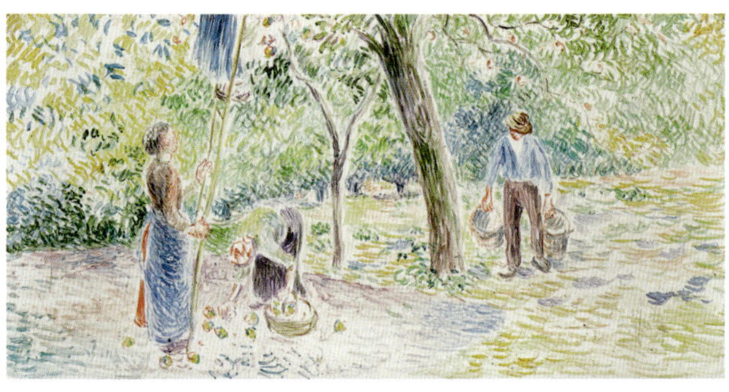

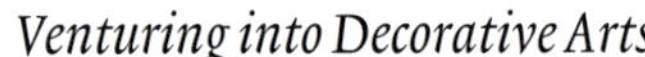

Venturing into Decorative Arts

In 1876, while in Montfoucault at the invitation of his friend artist Ludovic Piette, Pissarro first toyed with the idea of painting on ceramics.[27] According to his biographers, to save costs, he painted ceramics without using a professional workshop, as he hoped to make up for the financial shortfall of his lackluster painting sales by selling painted tiles. *Landscape* (1880, Musée d'Art et d'Histoire Pissarro—Pontoise) and *The Jetty* (fig. 10) are two examples of these delicate objects, painted in green monochrome on white porcelain, which were probably fired in the local ceramic factory in Osny.[28] Pissarro constructed detailed landscapes in the small format tiles. He also used the rectangular format of a ceramic planter to create paintings on earthenware tiles, as in *Apple Picking* (fig. 11) and *Saint-Martin Fair at Pontoise* (ca. 1883, private collection). Taking advantage of the light background of the earthenware to create a luminous effect, Pissarro skillfully transposed the principles of Impressionism to a utilitarian object.

10
The Jetty, ca. 1880,
Musée d'Orsay, Paris

11
Apple Picking, ca. 1883,
private collection

In *Interior of the Studio,* Pissarro's son Lucien depicted such a ceramic planter, decorated with his father's recognizable apple-picking scene, standing on a side table to the left (fig. 12). Here, art pervades the Pissarro household through its everyday objects, and the apple-picking scene takes on a new meaning as it functions as the base for a floral ensemble that expands beyond its support. Pissarro had considered the functionality of the support in creating the tile's design: the cropping of the tree trunk and the legs of a figure climbing on the ladder suggest that the scene ought to be completed by the actual plant in the planter. Indeed, the figure on the ladder is absent from the paintings based on the same composition (fig. 13). There, the main protagonist, a standing young woman, is not holding a ladder but a long stick—a motif of which a drawing also exists (ca. 1885, Musée d'Orsay, Paris). While motifs circulate through several compositions across media, such as the standing figure in this apple-picking scene, the artist introduces variations. The stick held by the figure in the drawing and in the painted versions becomes the ladder in the ceramic in order to emphasize the functionality of the planter. *Apple Picking* exemplifies Pissarro's serialization and can be linked clearly to the experimental nature of his printmaking practice, as discussed earlier.

Saint-Martin Fair, Pontoise constitutes another instance in which the artist circulated a motif from one medium to another, on a painting on canvas (1883, private collection) and on the earthenware tile mentioned above. In both instances, the scene is organized into horizontal bands with people mingling in the foreground and the rooftops of the village in the back. However, while a horse takes center stage in the work on canvas, a central road opens onto a vista on the tile. These variations demonstrate how Pissarro adapted his compositions to the constraints of various media. In his fan-shaped gouache of the same topic (cat. 56), exhibited at the sixth Impressionist exhibition in 1881, a post with a hanging lamp to the center left structures a unified and crowded composition where villagers socialize among small pavilions. Again, the artist explored the same topic in a series of etchings. By transferring his rich repertoire of rural motifs and themes such as apple-picking and market scenes into a variety of formats and media, Pissarro masterfully transformed it.

Pissarro's Fans

Pissarro exhibited fans for the first time in 1879 at the fourth Impressionist exhibition: twelve fans accompanied twenty-five other works.[29] They were shown alongside fans by Jean-Louis Forain and Edgar Degas, the latter of whom had envisioned a room devoted entirely to fans but was unable to fulfill the plan.[30] Exhibiting his work in various media would not be an exception for Pissarro, both at the Impressionist exhibitions and at Galerie Durand-Ruel in Paris.[31] While fans were not an Impressionist invention, the artists considered them particularly conducive to formulating the transience of phenomena. This "epidemic of fans," as contemporary critics defined it, grew out of the exhibition of Japanese objects at the 1867 and 1878 Expositions Universelles in Paris, when a Japanese pavilion was built on the Rue des Nations on the Champs de Mars.[32] The Impressionists seemed particularly attracted by the way Japanese artists applied the same principles of composition on various supports and in different techniques.

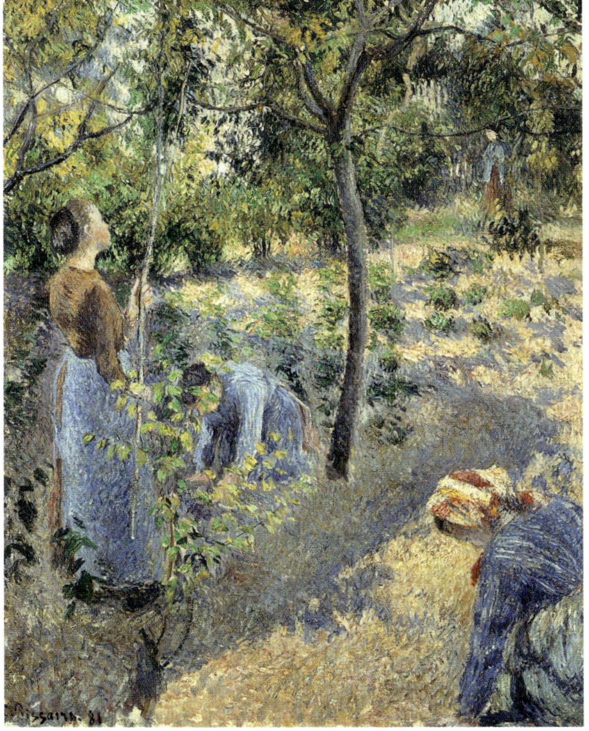

12
Lucien Pissarro, *Interior of the Studio,* 1887, Indianapolis Museum of Art at Newfields

13
Apple Picking, 1881, private collection

Fans offered an experimental ground for Pissarro, who multiplied the techniques of ink, gouache, oil, and watercolor on surfaces such as Japanese paper, cotton, vellum, and silk (cats. 50–53, 56, 58). In a letter to his son Lucien in 1890, Pissarro described his excitement regarding two new fans whose surfaces allowed for unexpected artistic effects:

> Since your departure, I have made, in addition to canvases, five fans with which I am happy. I have two *Fogs* [. . .]; there is one on Japanese paper, it's magical, and the other one on the back of a skin, onion skin paper, this one unexpected. It is a red setting sun, like an aurora borealis, with a strip of pearl-gray fog with cows blurred in the mist and a tall, young girl in the foreground. I bet Durand won't want it![33]

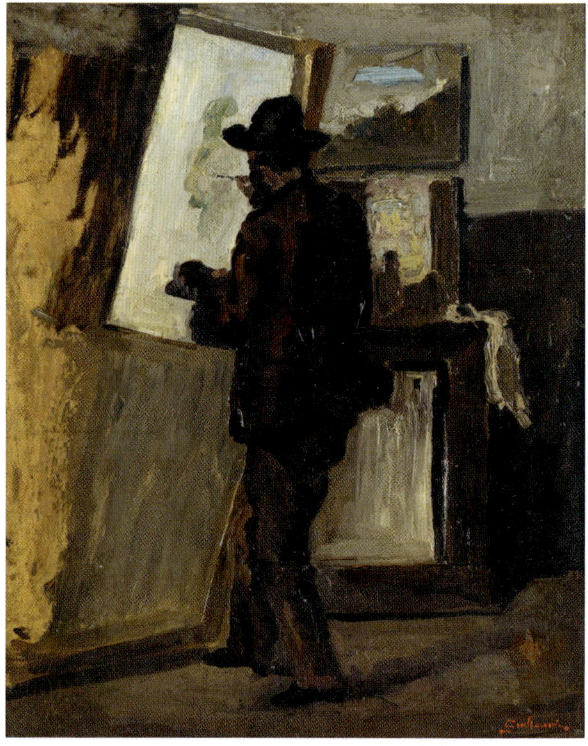

14
Armand Guillaumin,
Portrait of Pissarro, ca. 1868,
Musée d'Orsay, Paris

More often decorative than functional, Impressionist fans were framed and hung on picture rails and could seduce a new clientele at lower prices than oil paintings. Artists valued the research that the fan allowed on the specific form and material of the fan, rather than the purpose of the work.[34] More than just a fertile ground for experimentation, Pissarro's fans can be analyzed as an additional medium through which the artist challenged artistic expectations in his search for compositional unity.

Pissarro mastered the arc-shaped format with its emphasis on its two ends and made the curvature of the fan a compositional element, in contrast to other artists, such as Paul Gauguin, who adapted the cutout of the fan window to the preexisting work. Indeed, the constrained format of the semicircle allowed the artist to play with decentering, ellipsis, and the scattering of patterns and planes. In most cases, Pissarro reused the compositions of earlier paintings or drawings. However, there are instances when it is difficult to know whether the fan was created first. This is the case with *The Pea Stakers,* where female figures labor in rhythm, and which was executed both as a fan (1890, The Ashmolean Museum, University of Oxford) and as a painting (fig. p. 40).

Pissarro's Window

With his back to the viewer, a painter is caught in action, holding a brush in his right hand (fig. 14). Several paintings and frames are stacked against the wall to the right in a confined space that is hard to identify. While one might expect to witness the banal scene of an artist in the act of painting on canvas, it is in fact a window shade that the artist paints. Pissarro is portrayed here by his friend, fellow artist Armand Guillaumin, with whom he produced shades in the 1860s.[35] Far from the typical portrait of the Impressionist painter, who at the end of his life depicted himself gazing out toward the viewer, his palette at hand, in an interior framed with a window to the left (fig. 15), Guillaumin's depiction of his friend highlights a lesser-known aspect of Pissarro's artistic identity. The artist who would become primarily known as a plein-air painter and leader of the Impressionist group appears here as an everyday painter and a humble artisan on the one hand, and as a multifaceted artist resistant to fixed ideas and settled formulas on the other hand.

The motif of the window became characteristic of Pissarro's late artistic production; in addition, the window was always a site that allowed Pissarro to shift from outdoor to indoor, to go back and forth between plein-air painting and studio practice.[36] He did not choose just any window, but the ones that would allow him to paint specific motifs, painting from the studio but directing his gaze outward. Pissarro also experimented with various materials and supports, repurposing motifs in different compositions over time, working in and outside the studio. The serial reworking of an image through brushstroke and color, like his serial reworking of the etching plate, is less about capturing a fleeting sensory impression than it is about manipulating the pictorial elements of the medium on the canvas or on paper. Pissarro sought aesthetic sensation in the material and support of his work rather than in nature. Pissarro came back to the term *sensation* repeatedly in his letters. In 1890 he gave some words of advice to his son Georges, which encapsulate his artistic approach:

> The only thing to do is to let the young man follow his sensations as much as possible; if he has the stuff of a man of talent within him, like the bee, he will know how to find the nectar of the flowers that will sustain him. [. . .] Create your project according to your sensations, as long as it is new and harmonious.[37]

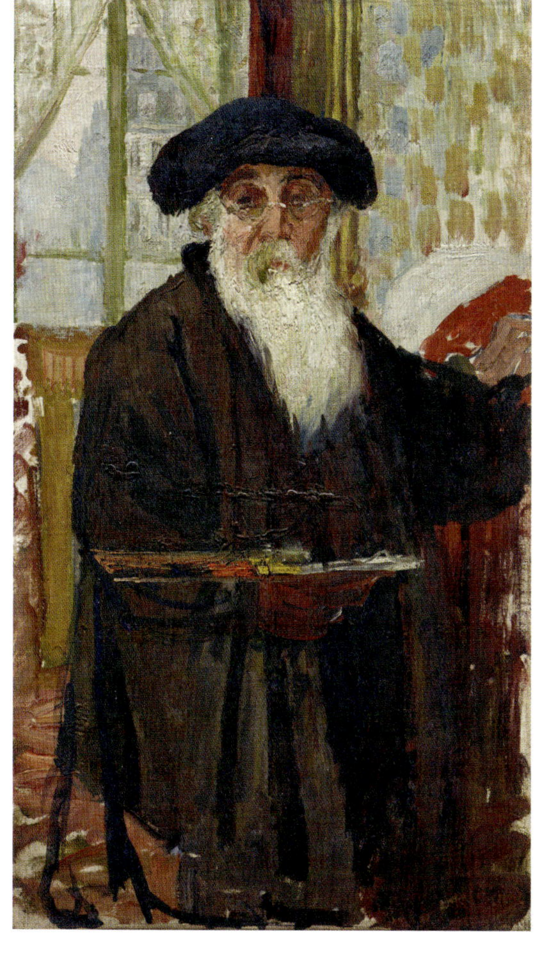

15
Self-Portrait, ca. 1896,
Dallas Museum of Art

Realism or Utopia?
Pissarro's Depictions of Rural Labor

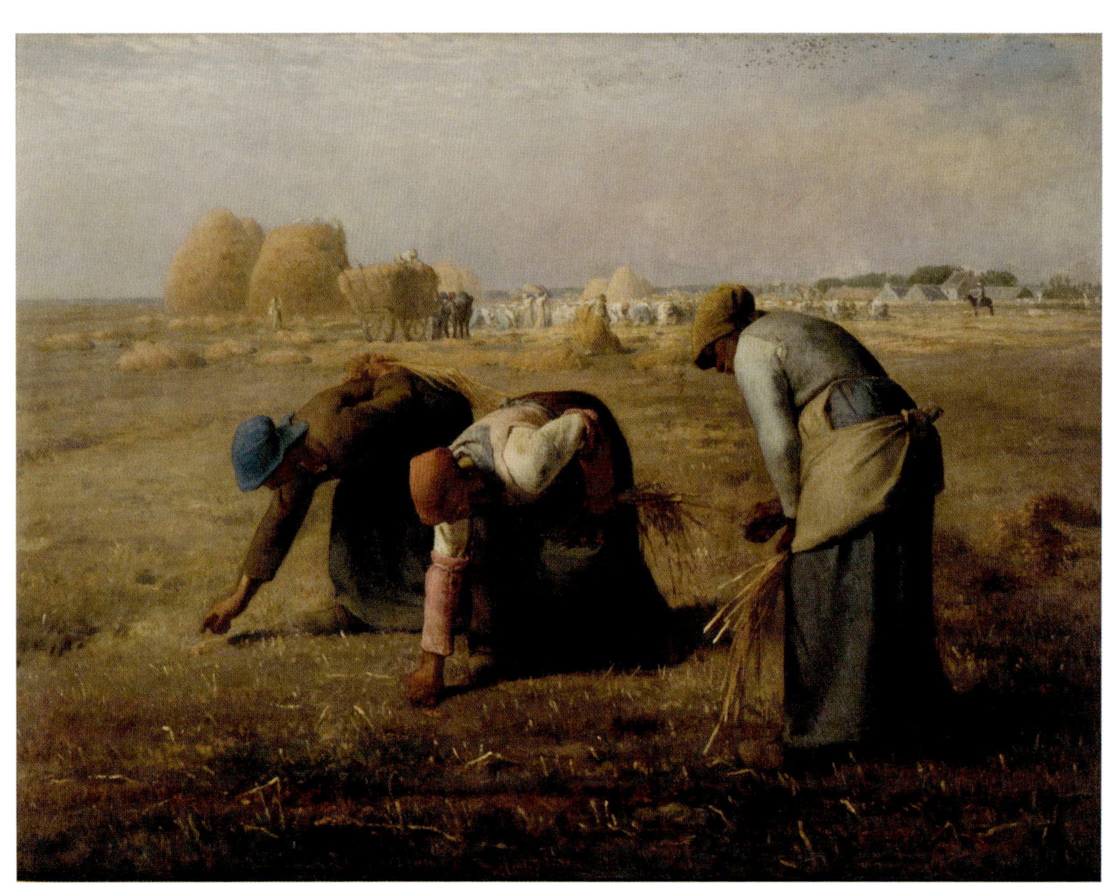

1
Jean-François Millet, *The Gleaners*, 1857, Musée d'Orsay, Paris

Of all the artists associated with the Impressionist movement, Camille Pissarro was the only painter who accorded the figure of the peasant a significant role in his oeuvre.[1] Especially after his move to Éragny-sur-Epte—a small village around fifty-six miles northwest of Paris, to which he relocated in 1884—a considerable part of his output pertained to scenes of rural labor, often in ambitious multifigure compositions that were minutely prepared through a wide range of preliminary studies. For these paintings, Pissarro drew inspiration from the work of Jean-François Millet, that stalwart of French Realist painting, whose work was most closely associated with peasant imagery and the depiction of the poorer rural population.[2] Pissarro much admired Millet and on occasion appropriated distinct compositional formulas of the slightly older artist into his own pictorial arrangements. Yet as this essay demonstrates, the peasants we encounter in Pissarro's works are far removed from the haggard and downtrodden figures inhabiting Millet's compositions such as *The Gleaners* (fig. 1) or *Man with a Hoe* (fig. p. 21). Instead of men and women who embody hardship, misery, and toil, Pissarro presents his cast of working figures—sowers and plowmen, shepherds, farmers, and gardeners—as healthy and joyful beings who thrive on life in the country. A surprising number of paintings show them not at work but instead engaged in leisure and respite, communally resting in the shade (fig. p. 21) or lost in moments of solitary reverie and introspection. Yet, even in scenes that foreground the actual process of labor, the figures seem to perform their tasks with unimpeded contentment—conveying the sense that the landscape surrounding them is timeless and fertile, removed from any impingement by modern progress. This essay discusses Pissarro's representations of rural labor within the wider context of French nineteenth-century peasant imagery, arguing that his unfailingly joyful rendering of the motif mirrored his political stance as a fervent advocate of anarchism and its ideological focus on the aspired harmony between man and nature.

"Superb Work of the Earth"

As a figure of ideological contestation, the peasant, or more generally the rural worker, was a key trope in nineteenth-century art and literature well before the dawn of the Impressionist movement—and one that had already staunchly come to the fore in George Sand's novella *La Mare au diable* (The Devil's Pool), published in 1846. The first of Sand's celebrated *romans champêtres,* the account takes place in the rural province of Berry, among peasant characters, described in Sand's preface as "the story of a laborer."[3] Its hero is Germain, a peasant who is described throughout as strong, kind, intelligent, and gentle. Breaking with convention, he falls in love with and eventually marries Marie, a poor young girl from his village, finding happiness with her. At the outset of the book, Sand explains that her interest in conceiving the story was prompted by a print by Hans Holbein the Younger—a sixteenth-century woodcut depicting death and a plowman, part of a series of allegorical images related to "The Dance of Death."[4] The artistic vision of a poor husbandman, who at the end of his life is worn out by work and toil, is reinforced by an old French verse that Sand recalls for the attention of her readers:

À la sueur de ton visaige,
Tu gagnerais ta pauvre vie:
Après long travail et usaige,
Voicy la mort qui te convie.

In toil and sorrow thou shalt eat
The bitter bread of property.
After the burden and the heat,
Lo! It is Death who calls for thee.[5]

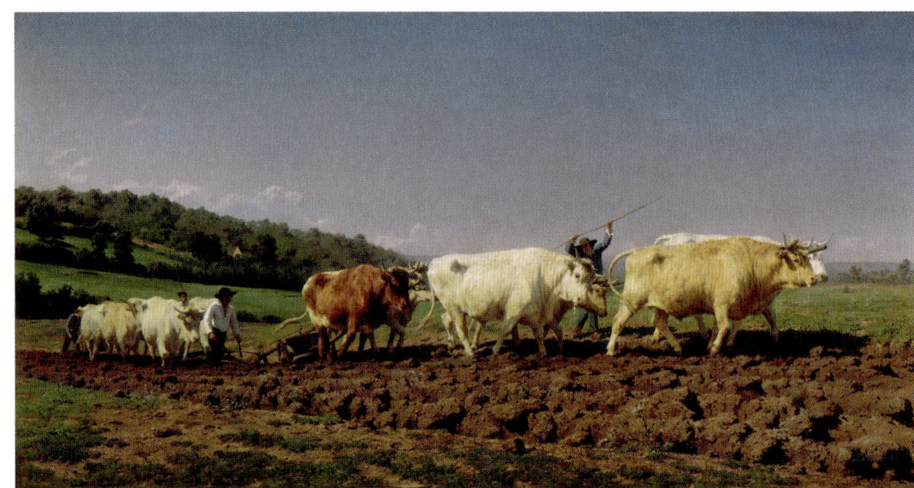

2
Rosa Bonheur,
Plowing in the Nivernais, 1849,
Musée d'Orsay, Paris

According to Sand, the print and its allegorical explanation challenged her to produce a different, positive vision of life among the peasantry. Describing the social circumstances of French rural workers of her time as "abject," "wretched," and "fearful,"[6] she voices her hope in reform and renewal, outlining her optimistic faith that "the dream of a serene, free, poetic, laborious, and simple life for the tiller of the soil is not so impossible that we should banish it as a chimera."[7] If Holbein's vision of the peasant as a cipher of poverty and toil still held true for many rural laborers who were active in France during the first half of the nineteenth century, Sand's novel proposed to sketch an alternative view—one in which the farmers are depicted as happy and healthy characters whose lives are in harmony with the natural cycle of the year. A key scene is dedicated to Germain tilling the ground with the help of four pairs of cattle, accompanied by his young son, who, as Sand highlights, looks "lovely as an angel, [. . .] like a little Saint John the Baptist out of a Renaissance picture."[8] In a marked counterpoint to the worn-out plowman in Holbein's print, Germain is both vigorous and handsome, joyously singing a peasant's chant, a "noble song," which Sand muses to have probably been "sacred in its origin."[9] Calling the scene "a truly noble subject for a painter,"[10] Sand exults in its picturesque quality: "The whole scene was beautiful in its grace and strength; the landscape, the man, the child, the oxen under the yoke; and in spite of the mighty struggle by which the earth was subdued, a deep feeling of peace and sweetness reigned over all."[11]

Sand's idyllic pastoral romance is widely considered to have been the catalyst for one of the nineteenth century's most celebrated depictions of rural labor—Rosa Bonheur's monumental *Plowing in the Nivernais* of 1849 (fig. 2), which was commissioned by the French government and awarded a First Medal when shown at the Salon de Paris the very same year it was executed. Bonheur, who had gained considerable reputation as a painter of animals, here shows four laborers who plow the ground with the help of twelve strong Charolais oxen, tilling the field in two groups of six. The plowmen and the animals seem to perform their task in perfect unison, their rhythmic actions set against a majestic landscape panorama that exudes a sense of freshness and vitality. The sun-filled composition was conceived one year after the uprisings of 1848, glorifying the supposedly timeless beauty of French peasant life in the countryside at a time when Paris had only recently been the site of bloodshed and revolutionary fervor.[12] The lasting appeal of such panegyrics to rustic life, far removed from the hustle and bustle of modern urban experience, was reflected by the fact that the work was later not only chosen for display at the Musée du Luxembourg but also included at the 1889 Exposition Universelle in Paris, in which agricultural imagery was strategically given a prominent role.

In the 1880s and 1890s, when most of Pissarro's depictions of peasant labor were produced, paintings focused on rural labor also marked an immensely popular genre at the annual Salon in Paris—an important yet often neglected context when considering agricultural motifs depicted in Impressionist painting. The contemporary reception of Claude Monet's *Grainstack* series, which he executed in 1890–91, also stands in this context.[13] In these compositions, Monet offered variations on one basic compositional formula: showing a view of one or two grainstacks in the fore- or middle ground, set against a silhouette of distant hills or the sky. The differences in color and light result from observation of the motif in different seasons and at varying times of the day, expressing Monet's wish that each part of the series should constitute the impression of one particular effect. As the outcome of the annual harvest from the fields, the grainstacks represent the livelihood of local farming families, essentially nodding to Giverny's identity as an agrarian community. However, viewed as a series, the motif also reflects the seasonal cycle of the year—a subtext that some commentators understood as a pictorial reference to the inevitable passage of time and, by extension, human aging and the cosmic duality of life and death. For critic Gustave Geffroy, the paintings certainly had a strong emotional appeal, as he referred to Monet as "a great pantheistic poet" and further described the *Grainstacks* as "changing portraits, the faces of the landscape, the manifestations of joy and despair, of mystery and fate."[14]

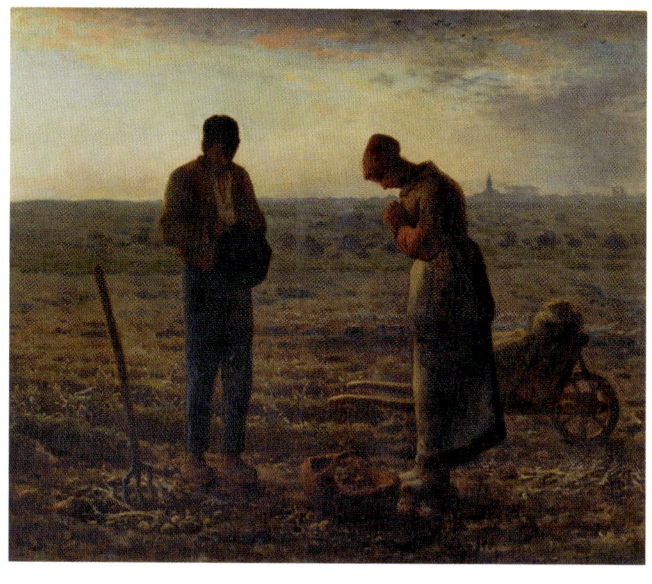

3
Jean-François Millet,
The Angelus, 1857–59,
Musée d'Orsay, Paris

Writing in 1891, critic Roger Marx read Monet's images in terms that suggested a dialogue with traditional celebrations of peasant humility, taking them to "symbolize and sum up the labor, the sowing, and the harvesting, all of the harsh fight with the elements to fertilize the land, all the arduous and superb work of the earth."[15] In hindsight, such assessments seem baffling, given that Monet resolutely eclipsed any direct references to menial work in open nature. As a motif, the grainstacks encapsulated Giverny's identity as an agricultural community—representing the very essence of the considerable wealth of Normandy's farming villages. Yet the local laborers are nowhere represented in Monet's usually uninhibited landscapes showcasing Giverny and its surrounding countryside—notable exceptions being views of nature that include figures from the artist's own family circle. The rural scenes that Pissarro concurrently executed in the village of Éragny-sur-Epte are strikingly different in outlook, as the local farmers and rural workers here ranked among his preferred protagonists.

Due to Pissarro's serial representations of peasants within idyllic landscape settings, his Éragny figure paintings can be read as Impressionist heirs to Realist country images including Millet's *The Angelus* (fig. 3), whose status as an icon of French art history would become firmly cemented during the late 1880s and early 1890s. Now considered one of the most important paintings of the nineteenth century, the meaning of the work remains ambiguous, capturing the poor French peasantry in a sympathetic way but damping any message of outright social critique by its apparent emphasis on piety—framing the meek couple in the foreground as both humble and staunchly devout. Millet's slightly earlier painting *The Gleaners* (fig. 1), executed in 1857 and exhibited at the Salon of the same year, can be considered more straightforwardly as a piece of political commentary. Measuring an impressive 32 ⅞ by 43 ¼ inches, this ambitious composition was an unflinching take on the harsh conditions of rural life, showing three female paupers gleaning a field of stray stalks of wheat left after a day of harvest—a backbreaking activity that was associated with the lowest members of country society and strictly limited in terms of access and duration. Millet's compositional choice was audacious in his placement of the three women in direct proximity to the perceived standpoint of the viewer, countering their miserable work and bent backs with a view of the rich harvest in the background—and thus also foregrounding the stark economic divide between wealthy landowners and paupers, who were essentially reduced to scavenge for leftover scraps on fields that were not part of their own property.

The Dignity of Labor

Millet's *Gleaners* flopped at the Salon of 1857, with one critic noting that "his three *Gleaners* have gigantic pretensions, they pose as the Three Fates of poverty. They are scarecrows in tatters [. . .]. His ugliness lacks emphasis, his grossness is unrelieved."[16] Yet the same work was evidently held in high regard not long after Millet's death in 1875, as reflected by its purchase at auction in 1889 by Jeanne-Alexandrine Pommery, the widow of a wealthy champagne maker, for the staggering sum of 300,000 francs and its subsequent donation to the collection of the Musée du Louvre. A change in attitude toward Millet and his representations of rural poverty was reflected around the same time by the public outcry about the fate of his painting *The Angelus,* after the Louvre's attempt to secure it at auction on July 1, 1889, failed and it was instead secured for the collection of the American Art Organization in New York.[17]

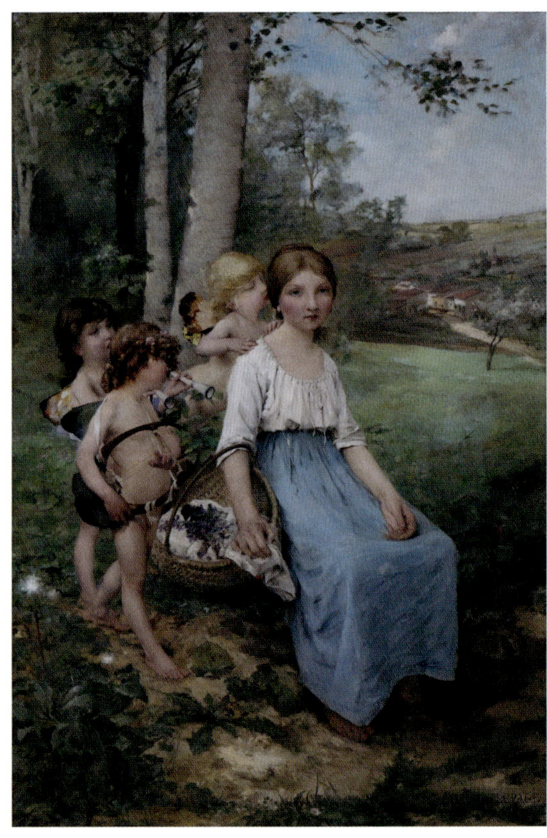

4
Jules Bastien-Lepage,
Song of Spring, 1874,
Musée de la Princerie, Verdun

After being defeated in the Franco-Prussian War of 1870–71, France had done much to fuel its economic growth as an industrial nation, resolutely committed to progress and modernization. Yet this forward notion was accompanied by a growing, and in many ways regressive, nostalgia for the country's irretrievable past as an agrarian nation. In Sand's *La Mare au diable,* modern city life had already been foiled by the supposedly healthy and timeless ways of the country—inhabited not by an uneducated and vulgar class but by steadfast upholders of traditional virtues such as modesty alongside honest labor. Such a notion of rustic wholesomeness would increasingly come to the fore in the visual arts toward the end of the nineteenth century. Indeed, the gradual canonization of Millet's paintings was part of an increasing hype around the literary and visual representation of peasants. Although they were already in the process of becoming a "vanishing breed," they were soon enough accommodated as a staple subject in more popular consumer media, including children's books and, from the early 1900s, illustrated postcards.[18]

The burgeoning fascination with the representation of peasants also facilitated the success of academic painters such as Jules Breton and Jules Bastien-Lepage, who both became darlings of the official Salon with imagery that was decidedly nostalgic in outlook and at times tinged with a sense of the erotic. This was certainly the case with Bastien-Lepage's figure painting *Song of Spring* (fig. 4), in which he cast a beautiful, barefoot peasant girl as an allegorical representation of spring, accompanied by three naked or half-naked children with wings—fairies or wood nymphs—who give the composition a distinctly mythical touch and who, reminiscent of cupid figures, also reinforce the sexual undertones of the scene. The classicizing painting earned the young artist a medal at the Salon of 1874, held the same year in which Pissarro participated in the first Impressionist exhibition in Paris, and was soon after acquired by the French government. Bastien-Lepage's older colleague Jules Breton had been inspired to take up rural subject matter following the example of Millet and Gustave Courbet, and some of his first public successes had been elaborately crafted renderings of rural labor, among them *Calling in the Gleaners* of 1859 (fig. 5). Breton here focused on the moment of the women's imminent return from work. The approach of night is marked by the shimmering sickle moon in the upper-left-hand corner, while the soft glow of the setting sun cloaks the distant horizon in soft golden hues. Realistic details such as the gleaners' bare feet and ragged outfits notwithstanding, their healthy bodies, fair complexions, and upright, proud postures all serve to transmit a sense of nobility and grandeur—an impression heightened by the artfully arranged grouping of the figures, which recalls a frieze from antiquity. Much admired at the Salon of 1859, the work soon entered the collection of the Musée du Luxembourg as a much-telling gift of Emperor Napoleon III. Another peasant painting, which Breton successfully showed at the Salon, was his *Song of the Lark* of 1884—a depiction of a young girl returning from work, set against the red glowing orb of the sinking sun, apparently transfigured by listening to the melodious song of a bird in the distance (fig. 6).

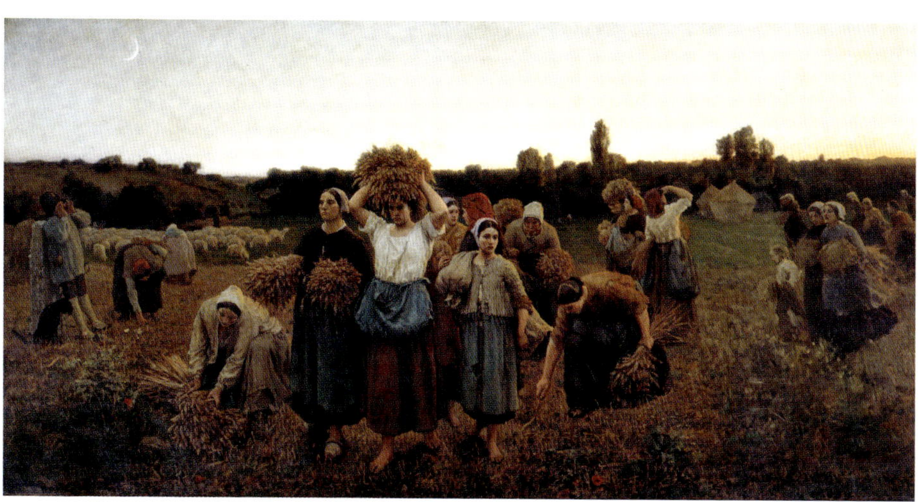

5
Jules Breton,
Calling in the Gleaners, 1859,
Musée d'Orsay, Paris

In works such as *Song of Spring* or *Song of the Lark*, Bastien-Lepage and Breton both turned to classicizing devices in ennobling peasant imagery, while conspicuously casting their female sitters as beautiful, sensuous, and alluring. In Pissarro's rural scenes, the representation of working women (both solitary and communal) far outweighs that of men. Many of these also exude an oneiric atmosphere, especially when single sitters are portrayed in moments of introspection and reverie, as is the case in images including *Peasant Girl with a Straw Hat* (cat. 41) or *The Shepherdess* (cat. 42). Yet Pissarro's figures are never characterized by a sense of erotic appeal. Rather, they appear as self-sufficient and autonomous, a quality that also comes to the fore in Pissarro's numerous dignified depictions of country maids and female domestic workers—carefully rendered portraits of substantial scale, which find no real equivalent in the paintings of his Impressionist peers, who often preferred to focus on the leisure and luxury of French high society. Conversely, glimpses into the elusive world of Parisian high-end entertainment, so cherished by Impressionist artists including Mary Cassatt, Edgar Degas, and Pierre-Auguste Renoir, are conspicuously absent from Pissarro's otherwise vast and varied repertoire of subjects.

While Pissarro admired the work of Millet and would have certainly been familiar with the images of academic painters such as Breton and Bastien-Lepage, his own take on peasant imagery cut a markedly different line. With regard to Millet, the most obvious change was a shift in perspective, which transformed the peasant from a figure triggering the viewer's pity into one of positive identification, inviting associations with health, vitality, and pride in honest labor, as well as the joy of communal work in nature. It has been pointed out that this distinction would have been partially due to the many current changes in the circumstance of French peasantry, which resulted from widespread rural reforms in the last quarter of the nineteenth century. While the worn-out women in Millet's painting belong to the lowest ranks of French rural society, Pissarro's works show landowning laborers who could tend to their own property and who, even in a small way, actively contributed to the growing economy of local country markets, which the painter also frequently depicted.[19] Yet Pissarro's rendering of the harvest in painstakingly worked-up compositions, in which warm, vibrant light caresses both the earth and the hardy workers, also speaks to his wish to present country life and the conditions of farming as quintessentially healthy and in tune with the primal forces of nature.

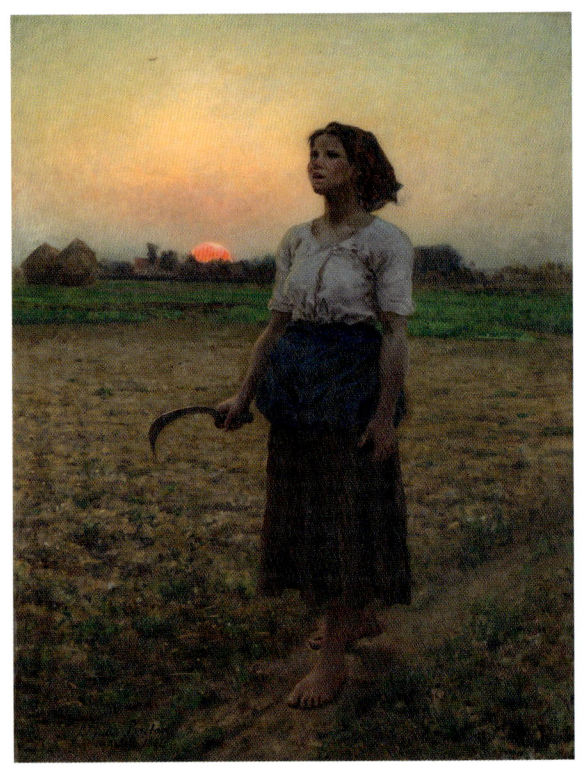

6
Jules Breton,
Song of the Lark, 1884,
The Art Institute of Chicago

Indeed, there is a strikingly theatrical quality to Pissarro's harvesting scenes and a repetition of formula that betrays that these are by no means images copied from real life, caught on canvas like snapshots—the kind of spontaneously executed plein-air production so often associated with Impressionist painting. Many of Pissarro's most ambitious multifigure compositions were created between the late 1880s and 1901—time-consuming images that were often only executed after completing numerous preparatory studies on paper, both in pen and ink or in gouache or pastel. A case in point is Pissarro's *Apple Harvest* of 1888 (fig. 7), a canvas that he worked on for more than a year and prepared through countless sketches. The painting shows four figures shaking apples from a solitary tree on a sun-filled autumn day. The entire scene is cloaked by a shimmering haze, vibrant hues of yellow, orange, and green coalescing into an almost golden sheen across the jewel-like surface structure. The vertical thrust of the tree finds a soothing counterweight in the curved furrows of the field behind. Similarly, the branch formation and the tree's lush foliage are counterbalanced by the shadow on the ground, in which the harvesters seem to find a refreshing shelter from the sun. In the far-right background and barely visible on first sight, a single horse-drawn wagon animates the peaceful scenery.

In 1889 Pissarro submitted his *Apple Harvest* to the annual art exhibition of the Belgian avant-garde society Les Vingt, which had been founded in 1883. One of the group's members, artist, architect, and designer Henry van de Velde, gave a lecture titled "On the Peasant in Painting" in 1891. In it, he discussed different aspects of modern labor and cited Pissarro's agricultural images of the late 1880s and early 1890s as role models, whose "honesty" and lack of artifice he positively contrasted to the supposedly more contrived and "sentimental" peasant images by artists including Millet, Breton, and Bastien-Lepage—a distinction that is hard to verify on the visual basis of Pissarro's paintings themselves.[20] *The Gleaners* of 1889 (fig. 8), for instance, reflects the same compositional rigor as *Apple Harvest,* and in many ways it epitomizes the theatrical mise-en-scène so typical of Pissarro's multifigure scenes of agricultural labor. Even at a brief glance, it becomes obvious that the women here represent a generic type rather than individual characters—a carefully choreographed grouping that is no less artificial in nature than the classicizing arrangement we encounter in Breton's aforementioned *Calling in the Gleaners* of 1859 (fig. 5). Pissarro's success in fusing the figures harmoniously with their surrounding was not lost on critic Albert Aurier, who reviewed the artist's 1890 solo show at Boussod, Valadon & Cie. Writing that the work was "marvelously composed," he further noted that "the lines of those raised or bent bodies, those folded spines or extended rumps are very cleverly linked and harmonized with the soft, languid sinuosity of the horizon line."[21] In another skillfully balanced composition, *Haymaking at Éragny* (cat. 43), Pissarro's arrangement of the women and their rhythmic movements evoke the performance of a joyful round dance in much the same way as his 1891 painting *Peasant Women Planting Poles* (fig. 9), in which the peasants seem cast as modern-day nymphs denoting fertility and abundance. Pissarro may have shied away from directly allegorizing cues such as the overtly kitschy fairy children in Lepage's *Song of Spring,* but his own peasant images also harked back to the sentimentality of the pastoral and were in many ways distinctly "mythic" in outlook.[22]

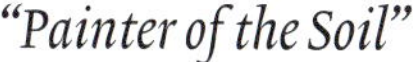

"Painter of the Soil"

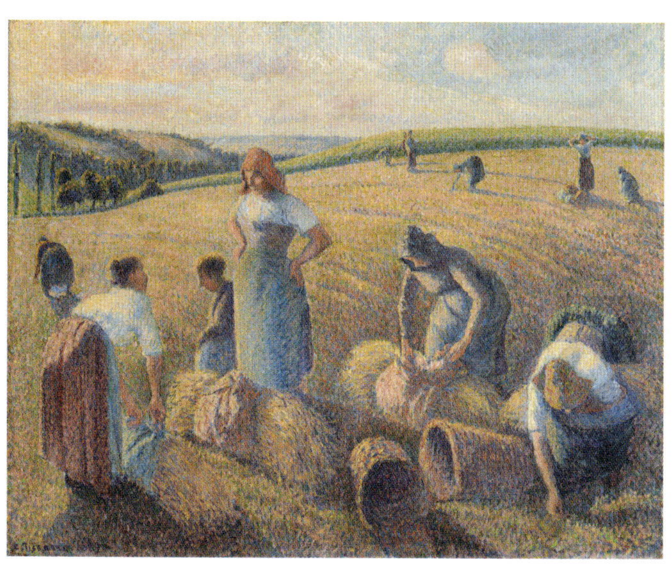

Pissarro's political convictions as a committed anarchist were likely key to his sustained interest in dignified depictions of peasant life. They also must have been one of the reasons that facilitated his early entry into the coterie of Neo-Impressionist painters around Georges Seurat, which had gathered momentum in the mid-1880s and could, from the very beginning, rely on Pissarro's support as a mentor.[23] Fascinated by Seurat's new technique of Divisionism, in which objects are rendered as a mosaic of dots of pure color that only blend optically at some distance in the eye of the viewer, Pissarro experimented with the method for a significant number of years and exhibited with the group of the younger "Néos" as early as the eighth and last of the Impressionist exhibitions in Paris in 1886—a show in which Seurat's groundbreaking *A Sunday on La Grande Jatte* (fig. p. 20) was set in a visual dialogue with Pissarro's magisterial *Apple Picking* of 1886 (fig. p. 19). Like many other painters associated with Neo-Impressionism, among them Henri-Edmond Cross and Paul Signac, Pissarro supported the anarchist movement in a variety of ways. These ranged from direct donations to illustrations he contributed to publications championing the anarchist cause—essentially aspiring to a revolutionary new social order characterized by liberty, freedom from social, institutional, and state tutelage, and the individual's unhindered striving for happiness and self-realization.

7
Apple Harvest, 1888,
Dallas Museum of Art

8
The Gleaners, 1889,
Kunstmuseum Basel

One of Pissarro's more overtly propagandist images was reproduced on the title page of a special issue of the French literature and art journal *La Plume,* published on May 1, 1893, dedicated to the theme of anarchism and featuring an opening essay titled "La Philosophie de l'anarchie" (fig. p. 220). Pissarro's drawing shows the toilsome labor of dockworkers.[24] At least three more images were published in the more radical journal *Les Temps nouveaux,* edited since its beginning in 1895 by militant anarchist Jean Grave, who was on friendly terms with Pissarro and whose publishing venture was also supported by both Cross and Signac. One of these was a color lithograph titled *The Plow* (cat. 48), which was executed in 1901 and served as frontispiece for a literary supplement of *Les Temps nouveaux* in June of the following year.[25] Pissarro's choice of motif can here be seen as an "ideal pictorial symbol for his anarchist beliefs," as it shows a solitary male laborer who tills the earth with a rustic wooden wheel plow rather than a modern tilling machine.[26] Like Pissarro's contemporaneous paintings from Éragny-sur-Epte, the work exudes an atmosphere of peaceful quiet, depicting the husbandman as a stout laborer whose task on a sun-drenched field could be related to ideas of fertility, regeneration, and the bounty of nature.

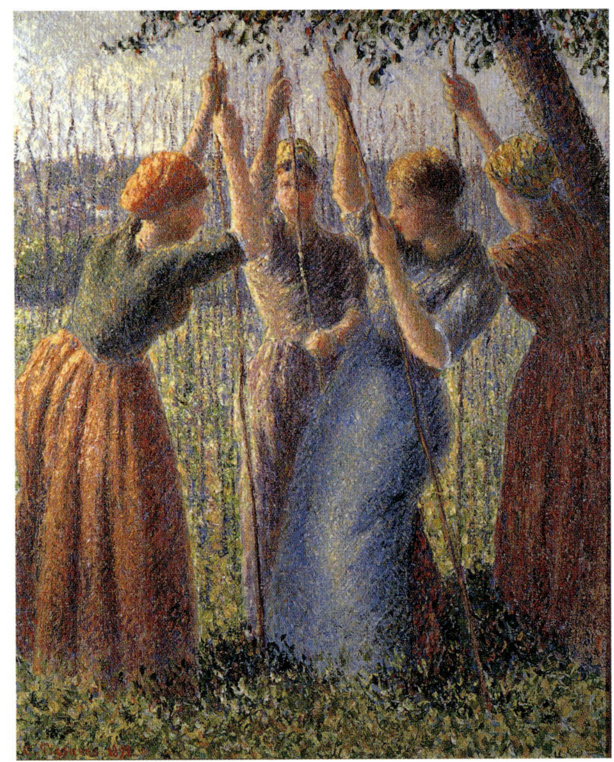

9
Peasant Women Planting Poles, 1891, private collection, on loan to the Sheffield Galleries and Museum Trust

Pissarro was an avid writer of letters and discussed his interest in anarchism with a number of his correspondents, including his son and fellow artist Lucien, to whom he confided in 1891 that "our ideas, impregnated with anarchist philosophies, spread through our work."[27] One source for Pissarro's immersion in anarchist belief systems were the writings of Pyotr Kropotkin, whose publications were hotly debated in French avant-garde circles of the 1890s. Among his staunchest supporters was Grave, who published one of Kropotkin's lectures with a cover featuring the figure of a sower, which had been drawn by Pissarro in a rather obvious homage to Millet. Born into an aristocratic family in Russia in 1842, Kropotkin was imprisoned for his left-wing political activism in 1874 and, after his successful escape into exile, became one of Europe's most prominent spokesmen for the anarchist movement. A geographer by training, Kropotkin propagated his belief in the possibility of a future utopia in several groundbreaking theoretical treatises, including his 1892 book *La Conquête du pain* (The Conquest of Bread), which was first published in serialized form in the anarchist journal *Le Révolté* and soon after as a monograph, which contained a preface by his colleague Élisée Reclus.[28] The middle of the book sketched out Kropotkin's vision of a future anarchist society, while its last chapter was essentially a eulogy to the history and practice of agriculture and its role as a source of communal happiness. On April 21, 1892, Pissarro wrote about his admiration for the book in a letter he sent to Octave Mirbeau—a successful novelist and vociferous champion of anarchism, who was a friend of Pissarro's and whose house and garden at Les Damps the artist depicted that same year in four sun-drenched compositions (cat. 79). In a passage worth quoting at length, Pissarro specifically highlighted Kropotkin's interest in the life of rural workers, writing:

> I have just read Kropotkin's book. It must be admitted that if it's utopian, in any case it's a beautiful dream. And because we have often had examples of utopias become realities, nothing prevents us from believing that it will be possible one day, unless man sombers and returns to complete barbarity. [. . .] Kropotkin thinks that one has to live like peasants in order to understand them well; it seems to me that one has to be enthusiastic for one's subject to render it well, but is it necessary to be a peasant? Let's be artists first, and we'll have the faculty of appreciating everything, even a landscape, without being a peasant.[29]

Pissarro's interest in the work of Kropotkin was shared by Cross, whose mature works provide an interesting parallel to many of Pissarro's pictorial preoccupations of the 1880s and 1890s. In 1891 Cross moved to the South of France, whose mesmerizing light and ebullient vegetation entranced him. With his friend and fellow artist Signac he discussed their mutual fascination for anarchist thought, and in 1893 they challenged each other to produce a depiction that would best encapsulate their shared enthusiasm for the South of France as a terrestrial paradise. "Why, since both of us love this land of sun, don't we try to erect a joint monument to it [. . .] supporting each other with mutual advice," Signac asked in a letter sent in April 1893.[30] The resulting images would become two of the artists' most arresting compositions, Cross's *Evening Air* (ca. 1893, Musée d'Orsay, Paris) and Signac's *In the Time of Harmony* (1895, Hôtel de Ville de Montreuil), both complex multifigure paintings, in which the idyllic decor of the Mediterranean serves as an Edenic setting. Yet such a vision of the rural South as the mirror image of an anarchist utopia, more generally colors a great number of Cross's and Signac's southern landscapes and genre scenes. In the early 1890s, for instance, Cross produced a small but significant group of works that cast rural labor in the Var in idyllic terms: in addition to a magisterially executed harvesting scene called *Grape Harvest (Var)* (1891–92, private collection), a pair of images titled *The Farm (Morning)* (1893, Musée des Beaux-Arts de Nancy) and *The Farm (Evening)* (fig. 10). The latter shows a single female figure who carries a wooden basket on her right shoulder, set against a farm building and a group of majestic pine trees. The light of the sinking sun makes the scene radiate with shimmering hues, giving the depiction of labor a decidedly oneiric outlook.

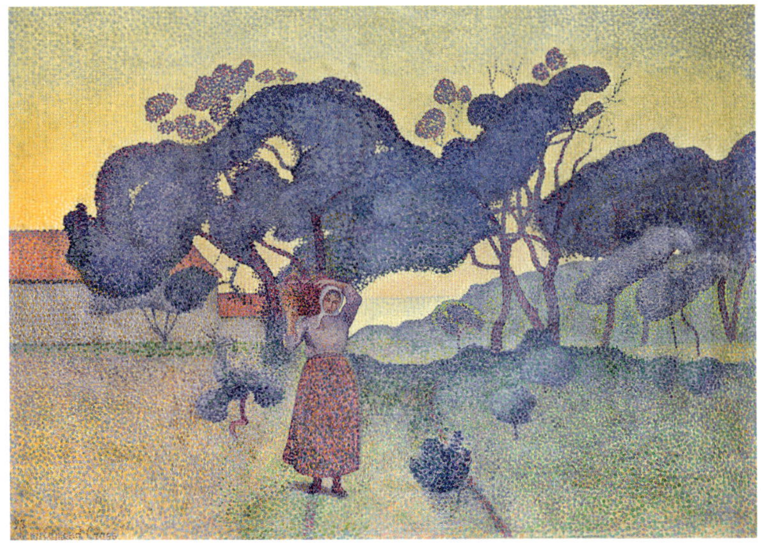

10
Henri-Edmond Cross, *The Farm (Evening)*, 1893, private collection

Pissarro's images from Éragny-sur-Epte transmit a sense of village life in similarly joyful terms, often tinged with a touch of downright Romanticism. His numerous paintings of peasants, who seem to flourish during hours of hardy work on the fields, must be contextualized within the vast array of compositions that depict Éragny itself as a quintessentially idyllic terrain—ranging from images of Pissarro's own house and its attendant kitchen garden to sun-filled views of orchards or farms, in which a sense of blissful quiet reigns supreme (cats. 59–66).[31] The aspect of pastoral charm in these oil paintings also characterizes the representations on the many silk fans that Pissarro covered in gouache and pastel and in which he again frequently turned to themes of agricultural labor (cats. 50–53). Painted at a time when peasant imagery of the Realist school became firmly canonized as part of the French artistic *patrimoine* (national heritage) and when France's identity as a primarily agrarian nation had long ceased to be a reality, such images successfully catered to a widely shared sense of yearning. At the same time, Pissarro's wish to cast menial work in nature (and particularly work concerned with the fertile power of the earth such as sowing, harvesting, or tending to orchards or gardens) also chimed with his sympathies for the ethics of the anarchist movement and its search for a peaceful harmony between man and nature.[32] Certainly, this was a reading espoused by Mirbeau in a perceptive analysis of 1904, published in the catalog that accompanied the Pissarro retrospective staged at the gallery of Paul Durand-Ruel several months after the artist's death on November 13, 1903:

> It's the life of the land that Camille Pissarro expresses, without resorting to sentimentality or extraordinary effects. More than any other, he will have been truly the painter of the soil. [. . .] When he paints figures in scenes of agrarian life, man always takes his proper place within a vast earthly harmony.[33]

Mirbeau's choice of the word *harmony* was significant here, since it was frequently deployed by anarchist writers such as Kropotkin and Reclus much in the same way as Signac's famous verdict "Justice in sociology, harmony in art: the same thing."[34]

Pissarro's glorification of country life and the time-honored, seasonal work in the fields also spilled over into a project, which he first conceived in 1886 in collaboration with his son Lucien, who was a talented printmaker. Titled *Les Travaux des champs,* it was to become an illustrated book on the art of agriculture, with prints made by Lucien after drawings provided by his father. In this cycle, which was probably again inspired by the model of Millet, the artists wanted to feature scenes of country life reminiscent of medieval depictions of the labors of the months, placing their focus on the ethics of communal work. Although the project was never completed to the full scale they had originally envisioned, a first portfolio was published in 1895, containing six images that were respectively titled *Plowing, Woman Guarding Cows, Studies, Woman with Chickens, Women Gathering Herbs* (fig. 11), and *Weeders* (fig. 12). The images reflect the artists' shared fascination with the colorful and distinctly flat rendering of forms in

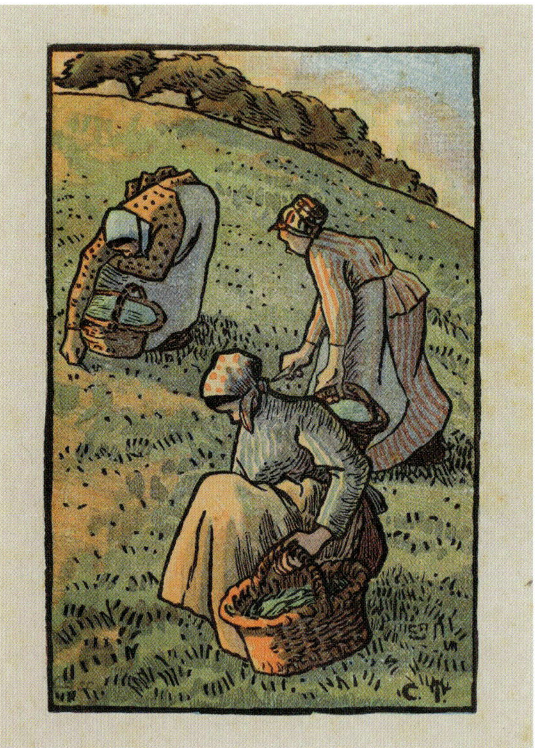

11
Women Gathering Herbs, 1893, Toledo Museum of Art

Japanese woodcut prints, which they both greatly admired. But they also show their decision to cast rural work as a wholesome and joyous exercise and to allocate significant space to the role of women as active and autonomous agents.[35] Woodcut prints such as *Women Gathering Herbs,* which shows three figures wearing colorful headscarves in addition to pretty dresses and neat aprons, more straightforwardly embody the tendency to romanticize contemporary country life, which also comes to the fore in Pissarro's numerous paintings of Éragny-sur-Epte and its agricultural workers—compositions, in which men and women were unfailingly cast as the rightful and blessed participants in "a vast earthly harmony." In pictorial terms, Pissarro's peasant paintings made palpable that "dream of a serene, free, poetic, laborious, and simple life for the tiller of the soil," such as it had already been conjured in Sand's pastoral romances of the 1840s and 1850s.

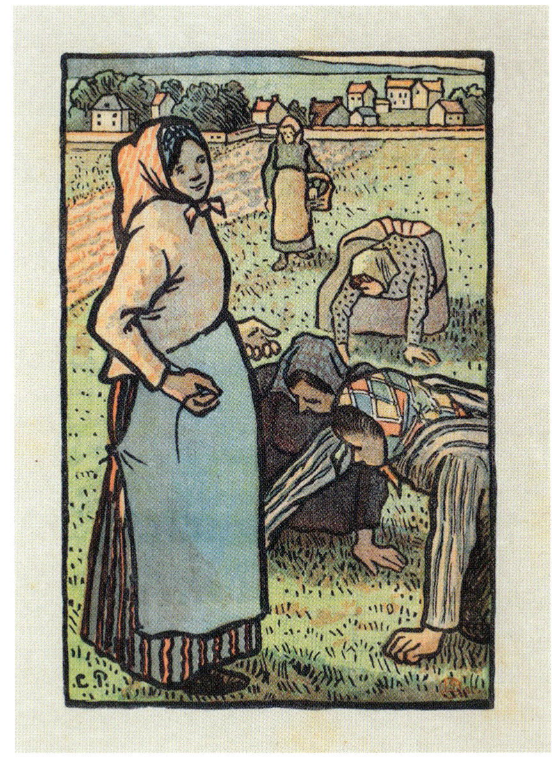

12
Weeders, 1893,
Toledo Museum of Art

Clarisse Fava-Piz

Under Palm Trees and at the Port

Artistic Beginnings in the Caribbean

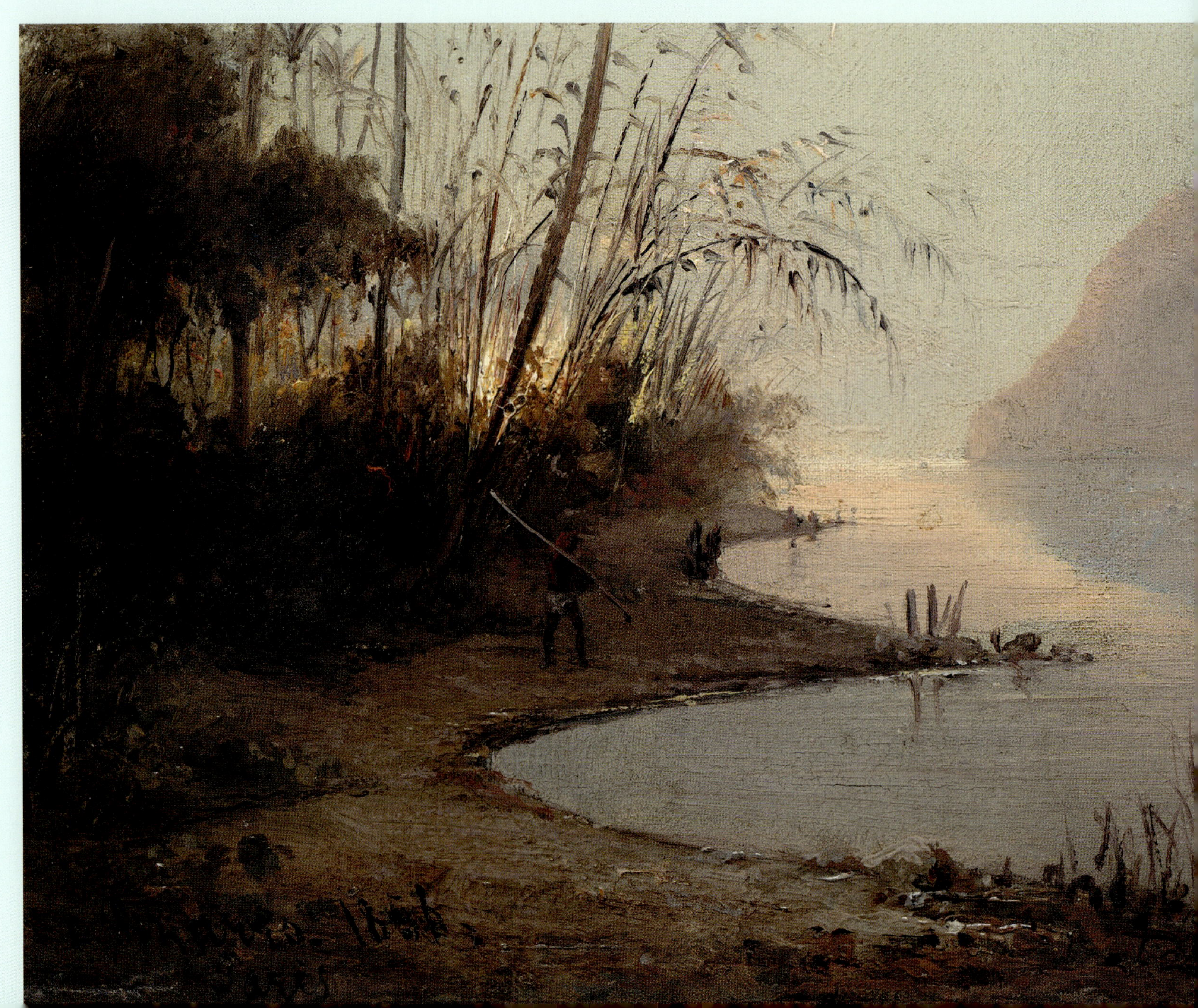

Shore landscapes with palms and simple huts in a tropical setting—such motifs shape the earliest works of Camille Pissarro. His artistic origins lie on the island of Saint Thomas in the Caribbean, where he was born, and in Venezuela, where he lived from 1852 to 1854. Pissarro's interest in plein-air painting and atmospheric landscapes as well as the life of ordinary people is already evident in his first paintings and drawings. The son of a Jewish merchant family, he grew up in a culturally diverse environment and experienced the abolition of slavery as a young man. In France, Pissarro introduced an international perspective to the Impressionist group.

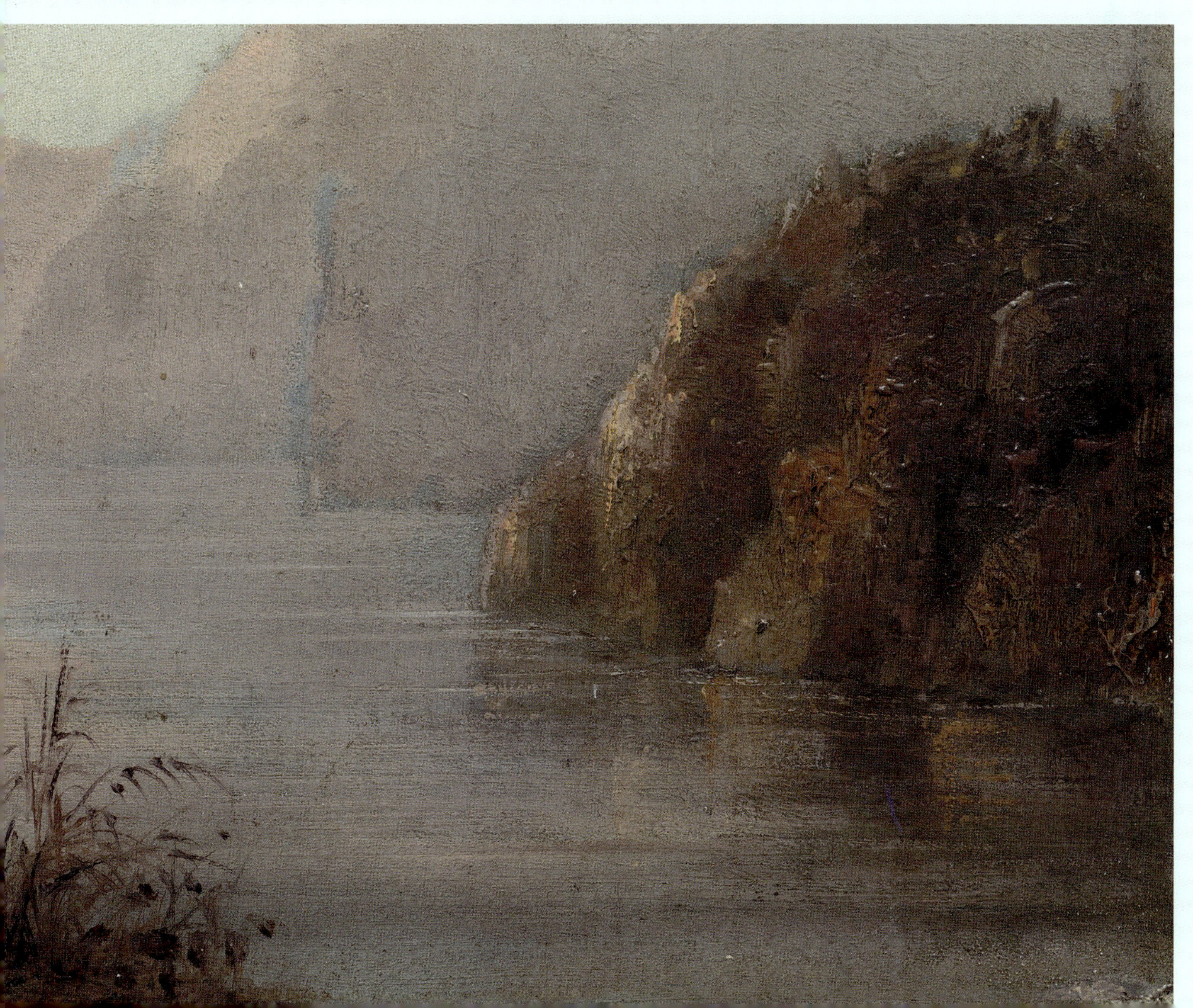

A native of Charlotte Amalie, the capital of the Saint Thomas archipelago, in the Danish West Indies (now part of the US Virgin Islands), Camille Pissarro was the son of Frédéric Abraham Gabriel Pissarro and Rachel Manzana-Pomié, who were merchants of Jewish faith with French ties.[1] They represented the upper-bourgeois merchant class of Charlotte Amalie, a thriving free port city during the first half of the nineteenth century. Saint Thomas was a central commercial hub for the Caribbean and North and South America because of its open ports and international trade that attracted French, Portuguese, Dutch, and Spanish people, among others.[2]

The majority population of the island was Afro-Caribbean, and Pissarro was educated with Afro-Caribbean children at a Moravian school until he was sent to boarding school in Passy, a suburb of Paris, at the age of twelve.[3] Everything predestined him to take the reins of the prosperous family business. However, in Passy, where he first learned drawing, his teacher noticed that he had a natural disposition for art and encouraged him to practice drawing and copy the flora and fauna of his island. Upon his return to Saint Thomas in 1847, Pissarro showed little interest in his parents' mercantile business, preferring a life of art instead.

In 1850 Pissarro met the slightly older Danish painter Fritz Melbye (1826–1869), who came from a family of marine artists. Pissarro and Melbye became professional partners, sketching and painting together throughout the Virgin Islands.[4] In 1852 they embarked on a trip to Venezuela, arriving in the port city of La Guaira on November 12. The two artists then made their way to the capital of Caracas, where they established a studio until the summer of 1854. They traveled the country and produced drawings, watercolors, and some oil paintings—fruits of a collaboration that makes attributions from this period difficult.[5]

Melbye and Pissarro traveled to Venezuela at a time of political instability and extreme poverty, and their works demonstrate their interest in the daily life of local people. The appeal of Venezuela may have been its relative proximity to Saint Thomas, as well as the political liberalism that the country represented. The two artists completed a considerable number of small-scale sketches and drawings, probably intended for sale to private collectors.[6] In search of virginal landscapes and exoticism, many artists had traveled to South America before them. But unlike earlier European traveler-artists, who were commissioned by royalty or government, Melbye and Pissarro's journey was not part of an exploratory expedition.

A popular subject during the nineteenth century, La Guaira was sketched by Pissarro in 1852 (cat. 1), most likely soon after his arrival. Here, Pissarro depicts in pencil and ink on paper a genre scene of locals, who are carrying jugs on their heads, beneath a lush, tropical tree. The diagonal hatching in this work—particularly in the tree stump on the left—is one of the most important characteristics of Pissarro's early years as a graphic artist. *Landscape with Donkeys, Venezuela* (cat. 2) also highlights his use of diagonal hatching during his formative years. In Maiquetía, a suburb of La Guaira, Pissarro drew its river (cat. 3) in December 1852, conveying the sensation of the waterfall instead of exactly rendering the landscape details.[7] The insertion of a group of explorers at the foot of the waterfall, in the lower left, transforms the work from a mere landscape into a narrative scene.

In April 1853, Pissarro completed the watercolor *Pariata* (cat. 4), depicting a place near Maiquetía. A modest dwelling appears amid the flora in hues of grays, greens, blues, and earth tones, which capture the bright tropical light. Several unfinished figures in pencil populate the scene. Pissarro's mastery of the medium of watercolor—where he first introduced color to his compositions—is again highlighted in his splendid *Bridge at Caracas* (cat. 5). The artist's interest in capturing the effects of the light of coastal Venezuela anticipates his Impressionist work later in his career.

In 1855 Pissarro settled in France and arrived in Paris just in time to visit the first Exposition Universelle. At first, he continued to paint Caribbean and South American subjects and even used the Spanish spelling of his name—Pizarro—to sign his paintings, perhaps an attempt to establish his identity as a foreigner in the Parisian artistic milieu. It is likely that Pissarro hoped that his exotic scenes would appeal to a European market.

In *Two Women Chatting by the Sea, Saint Thomas* (cat. 8), Pissarro depicts the encounter of two Afro-Caribbean women on a seaside path outside Charlotte Amalie: one carries a bundle of freshly laundered clothes and sheets on her head, the other a wicker basket in the crook of her arm. The theme of conversation will reappear as a leitmotif in Pissarro's later figure paintings (fig. p. 17). In the middle distance, a group of women wash their laundry in the bay. While this humble scene could have been sketched on site, the artist transposed it in a sort of private reverie, probably combining fact and fiction. The carefully structured composition is imbued by a light made of soft blues and silvers, a contrast to the vivid, intense tropical light. The landscape is also completely generalized, with no identifiable details of particular vegetation or architectural structures that would allow us to locate the scene.

A Creek in Saint Thomas (Virgin Islands) (cat. 7), *Cove with Sailboat* (cat. 9), and *Landscape, Saint Thomas* (cat. 10) are also idyllic scenes of Pissarro's native island, probably painted from memory. The paths in these paintings function as an invitation for viewers to immerse themselves in this local terrain with tropical vegetation. A pair of iconic palm trees structures each of these compositions, and the rest of the rich tropical flora lacks botanical details. Rather, Pissarro emphasizes the tropical sunlight that encompasses the scenes, as in *Cove with Sailboat,* which features two figures walking along a peaceful beach with a sailboat floating in the calm waters of the bay.

In *A Plaza in Caracas* (cat. 6), Pissarro likely reused sketches made during his Venezuelan trip. One recognizes the Altagracia church in the background and the marketplace of Caracas in the foreground. More so than in any other paintings from this period, there is a greater emphasis on human activity, and it is worth noting that the motif of the market is one that Pissarro would take up again in later works in Pontoise and Éragny-sur-Epte (cats. 54–58). In *A Plaza in Caracas,* the composition is centered around a female figure whose back is turned toward the viewer, strolling along the market square with a jug balancing on her head. To her right, a group of figures lounges in the shade of an open tent. These compositional elements recall Orientalist tropes depicting non-Europeans trapped in a supposed uncivilized past, a pictorial tradition well established in France at the time of Pissarro's arrival in the mid-1850s.

With his Caribbean origins, Pissarro stands as an outsider among his fellow Impressionists, and while his career and life would remain associated with France after his move there in 1855, he retained his Danish nationality. Pissarro's beginnings as a plein-air painter can thus be linked to the international environment in which he evolved on Saint Thomas and in Venezuela and not simply to the French pictorial tradition of the Barbizon School, which he would only discover after his arrival in France.[8] There, Pissarro would revisit the subjects that he saw and drew during his years on Saint Thomas and in Venezuela: the rural landscapes, market scenes, ports, and representations of local life became a leitmotif that Pissarro would pursue throughout his career.

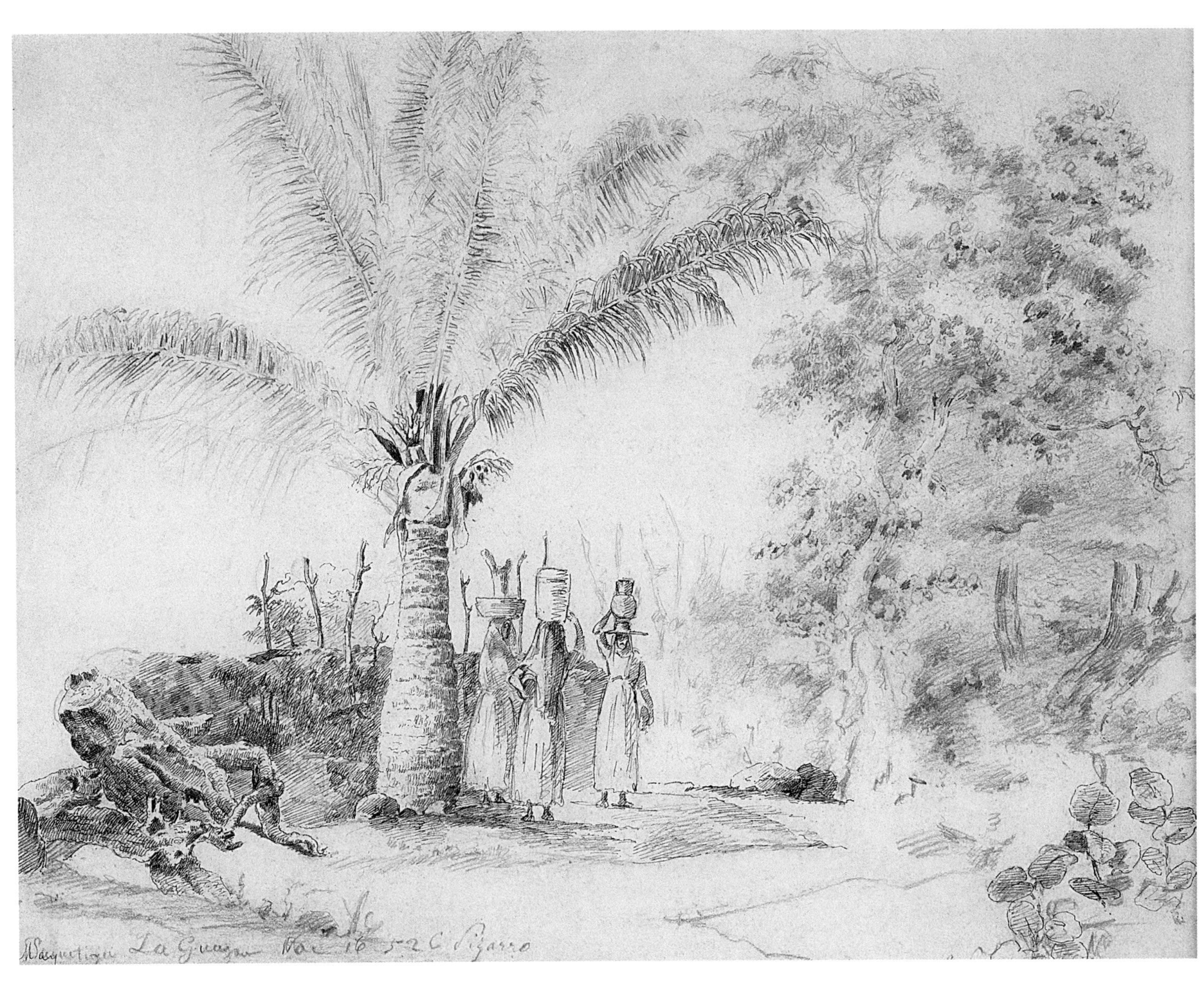

1
La Guaira, 1852
Colección Patricia Phelps de Cisneros

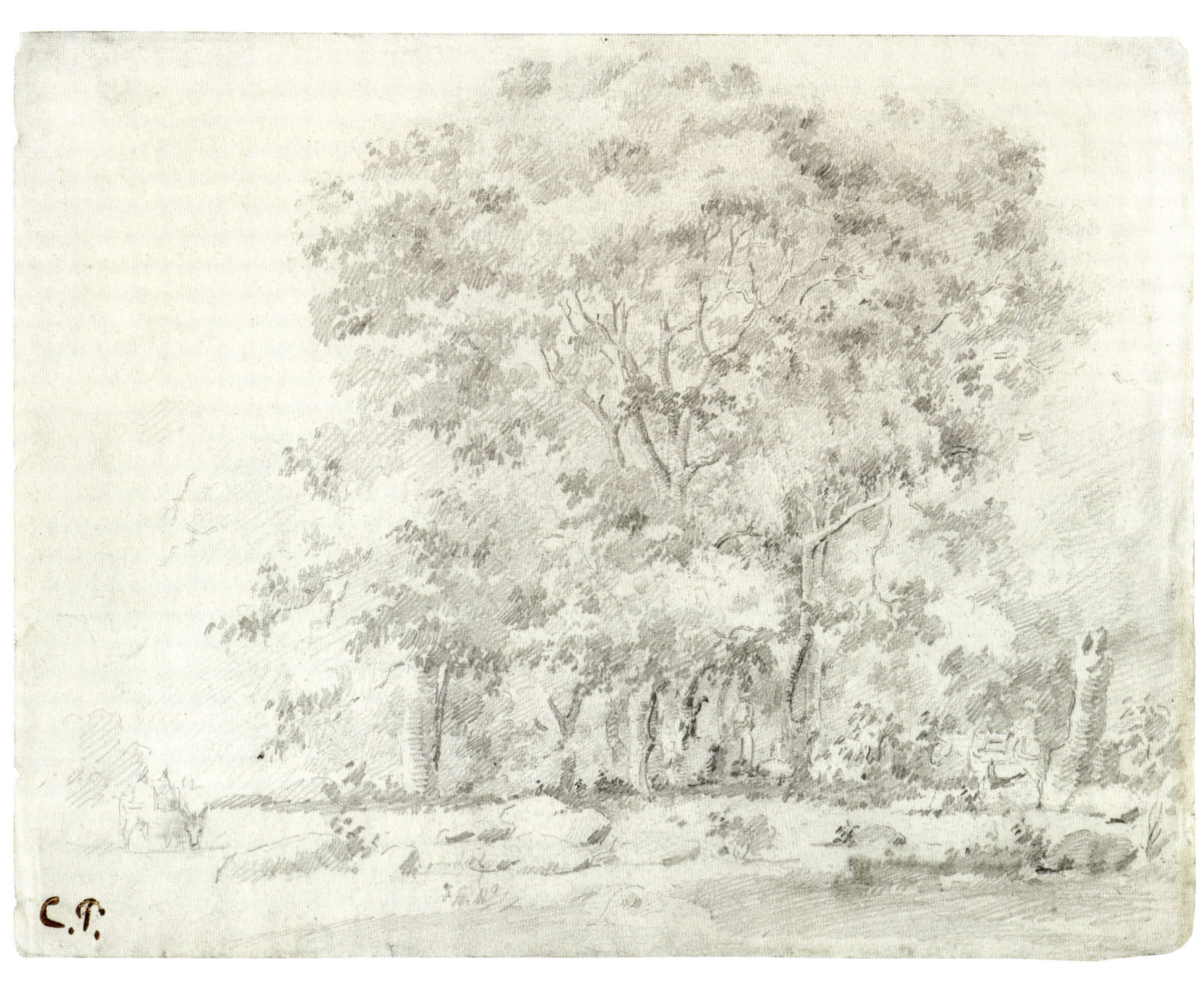

2
Landscape with Donkeys, Venezuela, ca. 1854
Clark Art Institute, Williamstown, Massachusetts, Gift of Gayllis R. Ward in memory of Chester D. Ward, Jr.

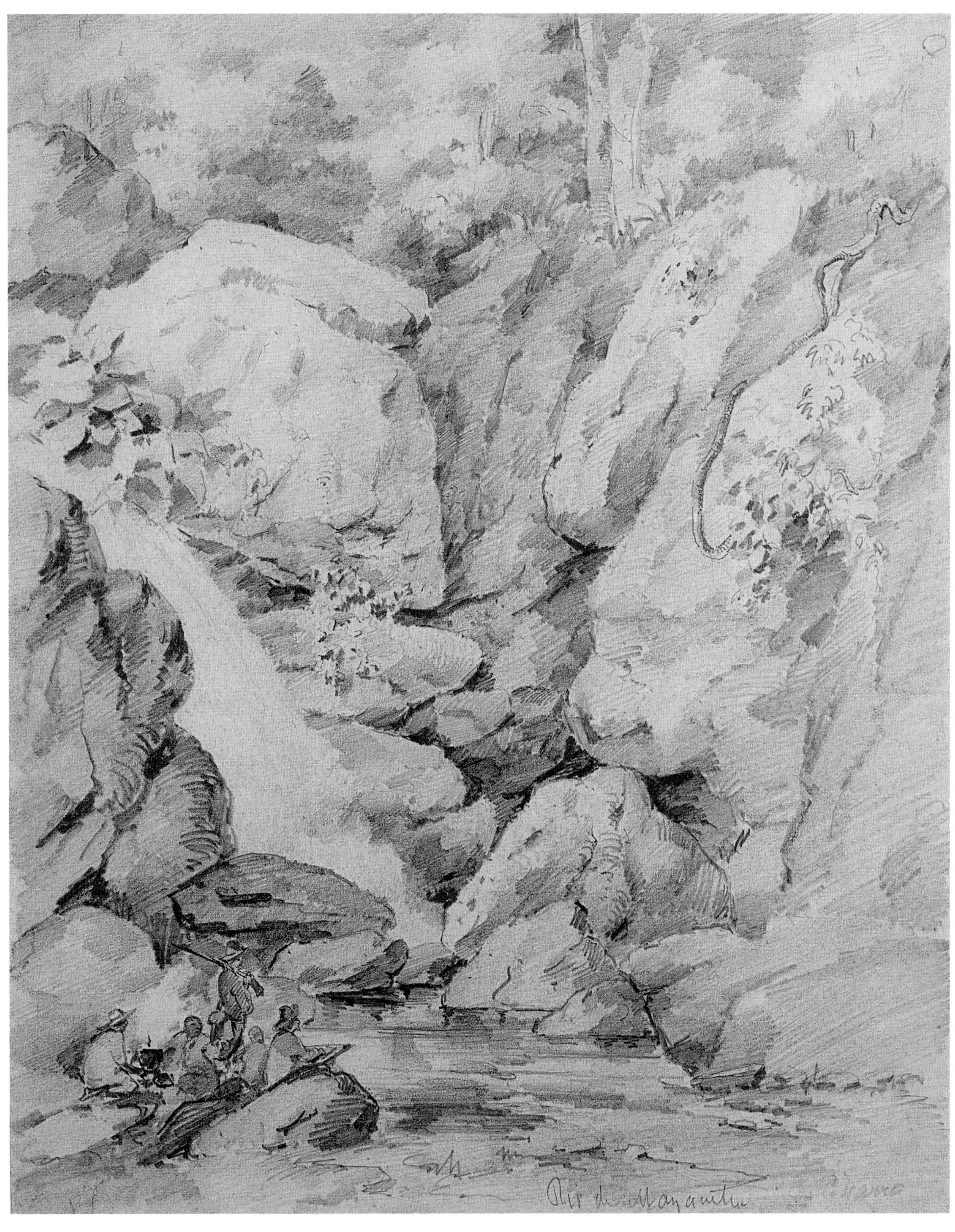

3
Rio de Maiquetía, 1852
Colección Patricia Phelps de Cisneros

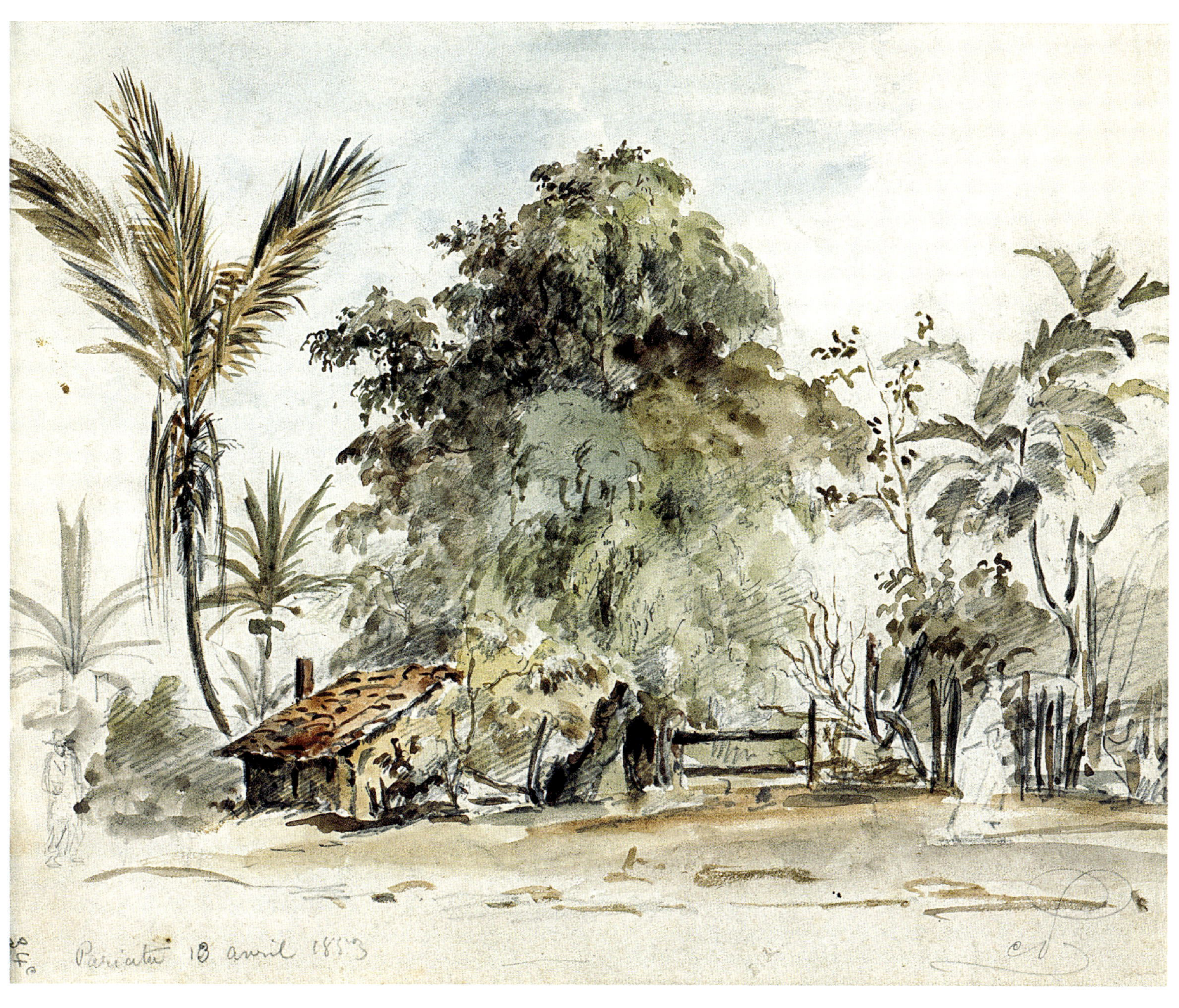

4
Pariata, 1853
Colección Patricia Phelps de Cisneros

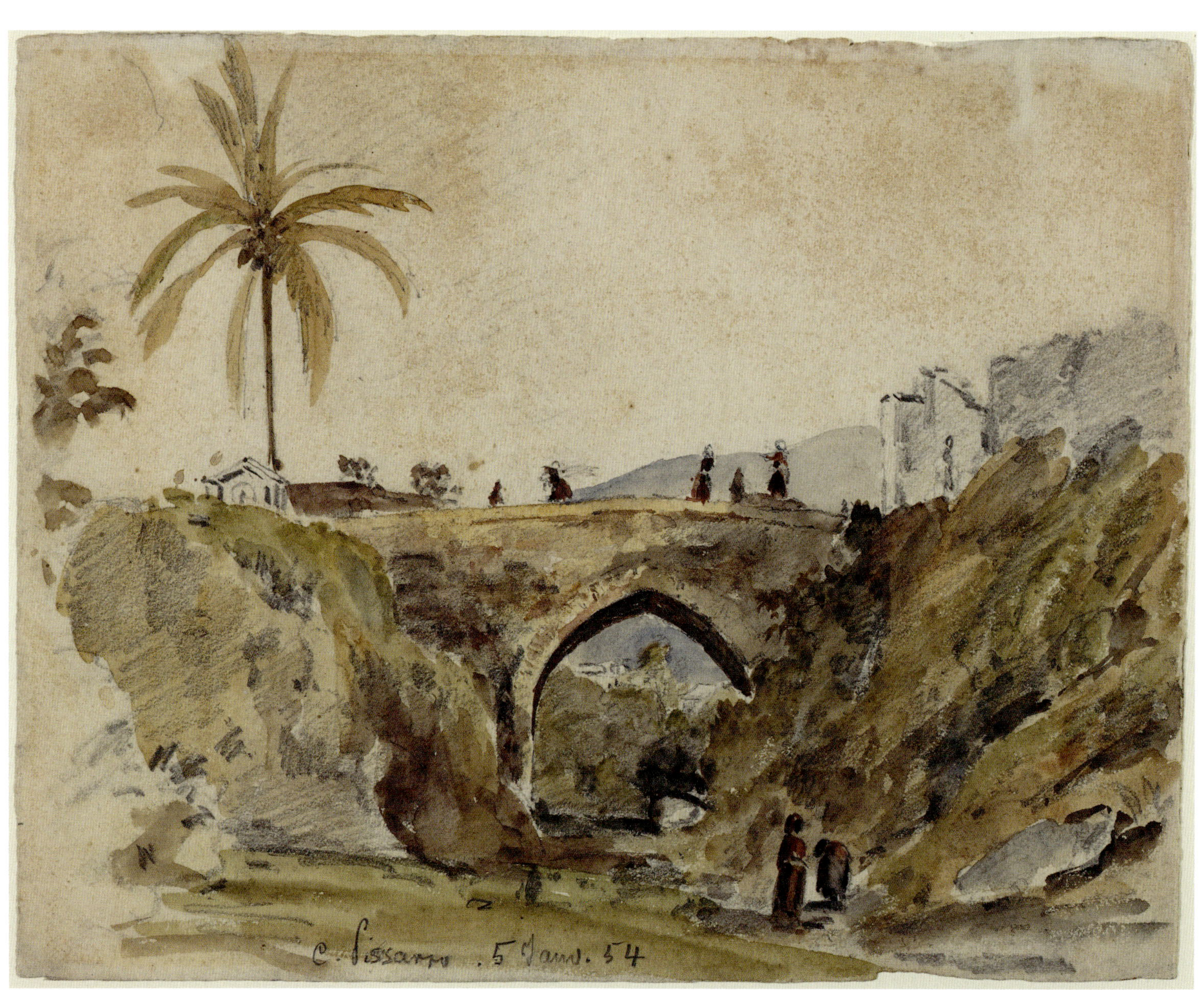

5
Bridge at Caracas, 1854
National Gallery of Art, Washington, Collection of Mr. and Mrs. Paul Mellon, 1985

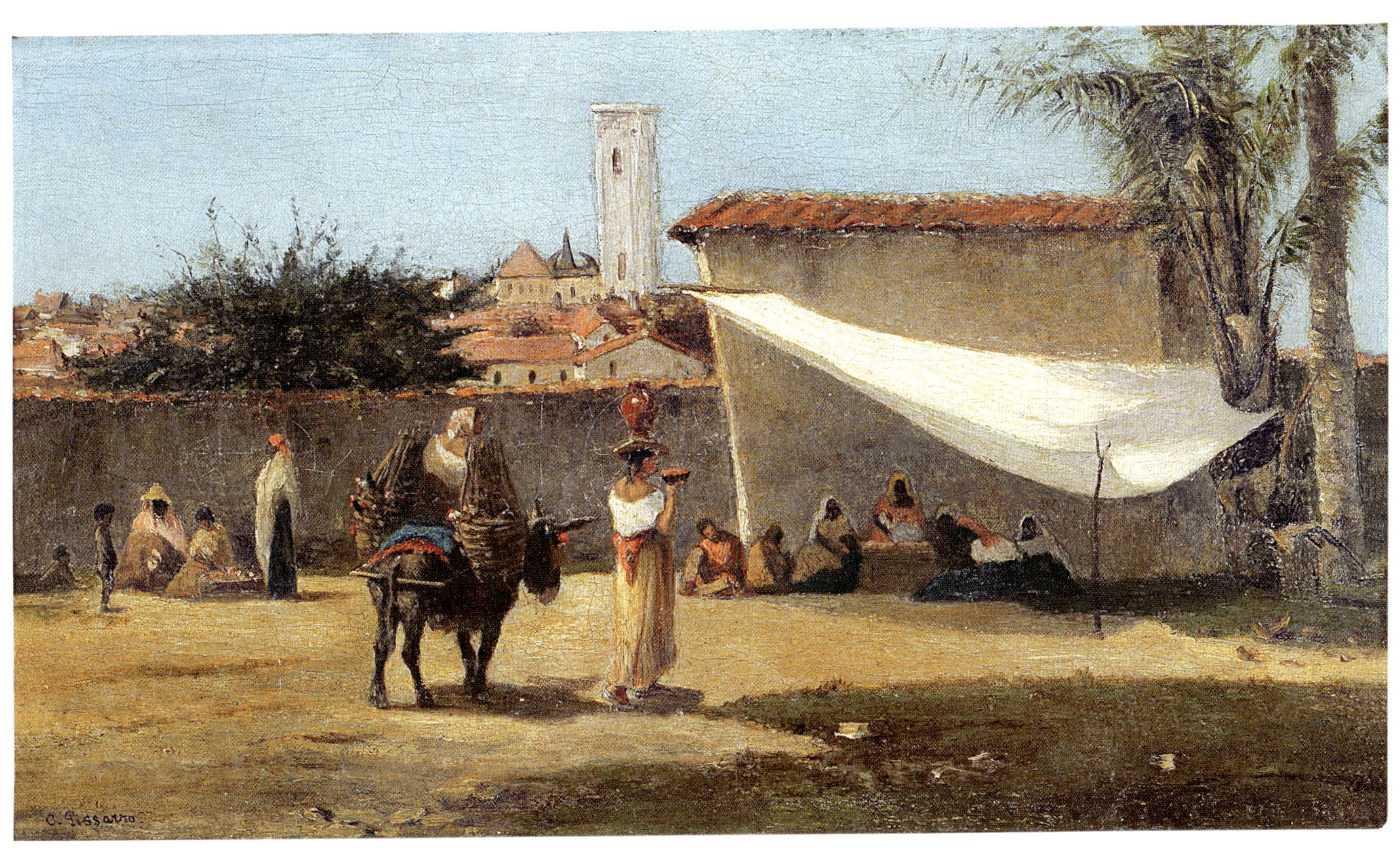

6

A Plaza in Caracas, ca. 1854

Colección Patricia Phelps de Cisneros

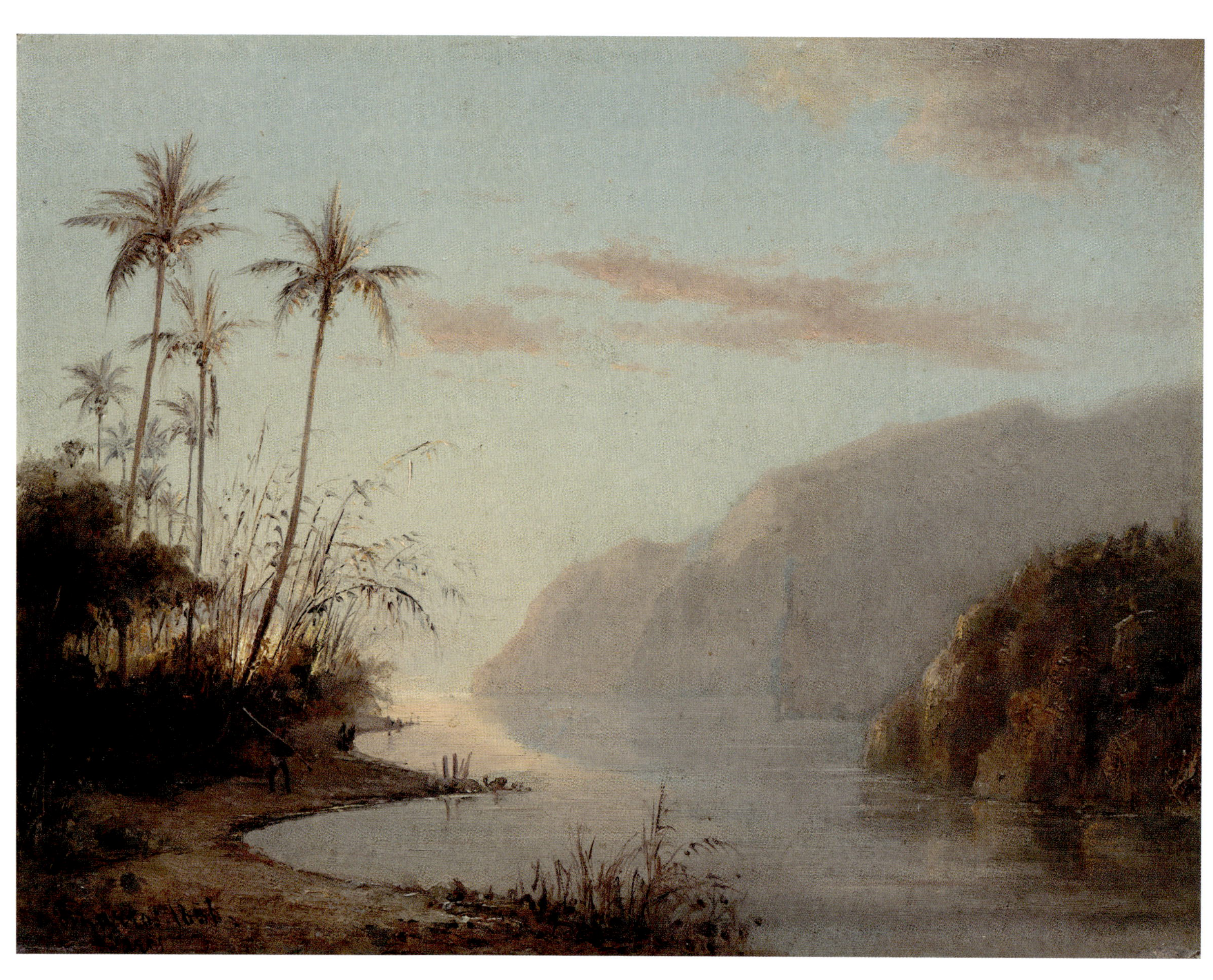

7
A Creek in Saint Thomas (Virgin Islands), 1856
National Gallery of Art, Washington, Collection of Mr. and Mrs. Paul Mellon

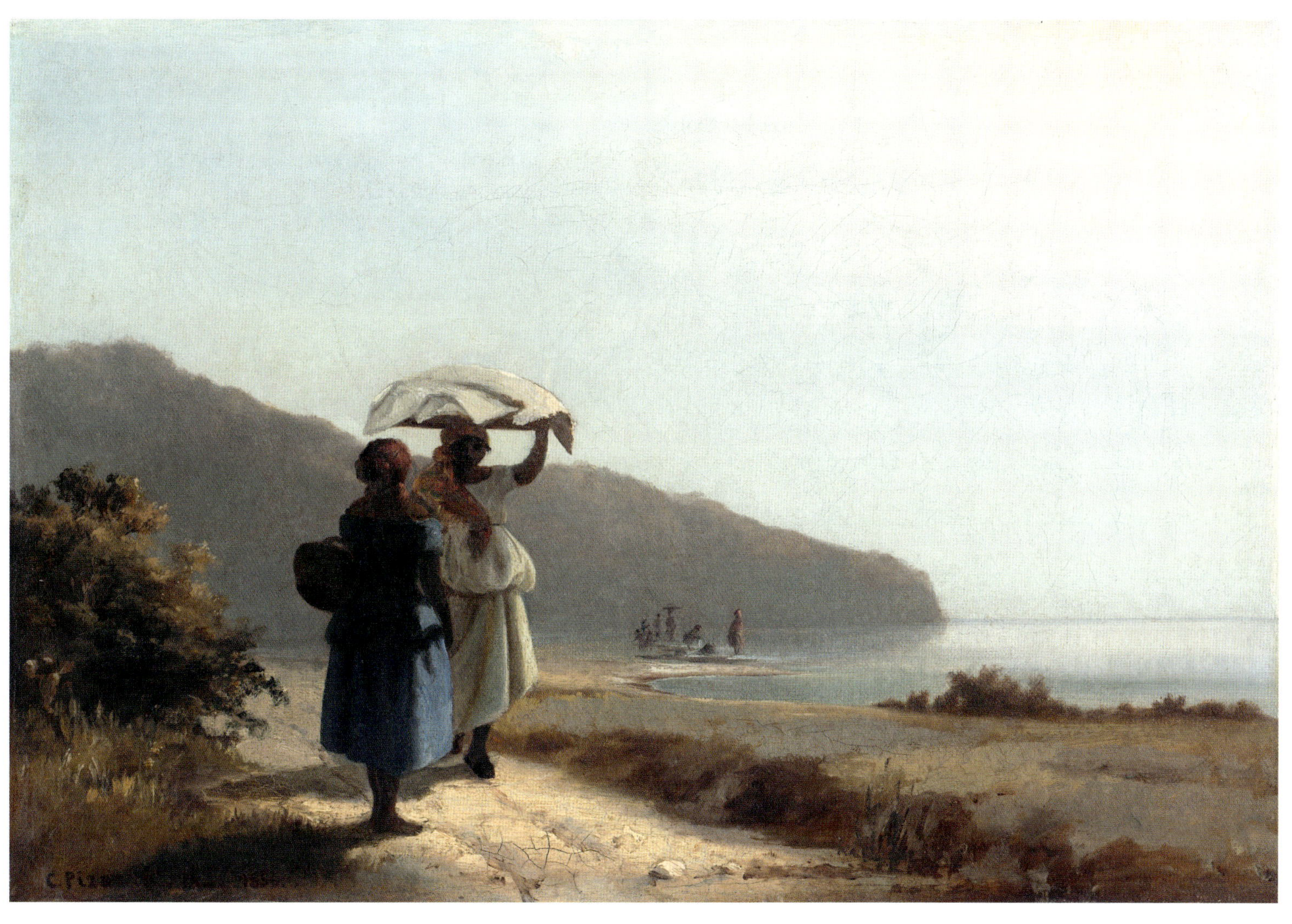

8
Two Women Chatting by the Sea, Saint Thomas, 1856
National Gallery of Art, Washington, Collection of Mr. and Mrs. Paul Mellon

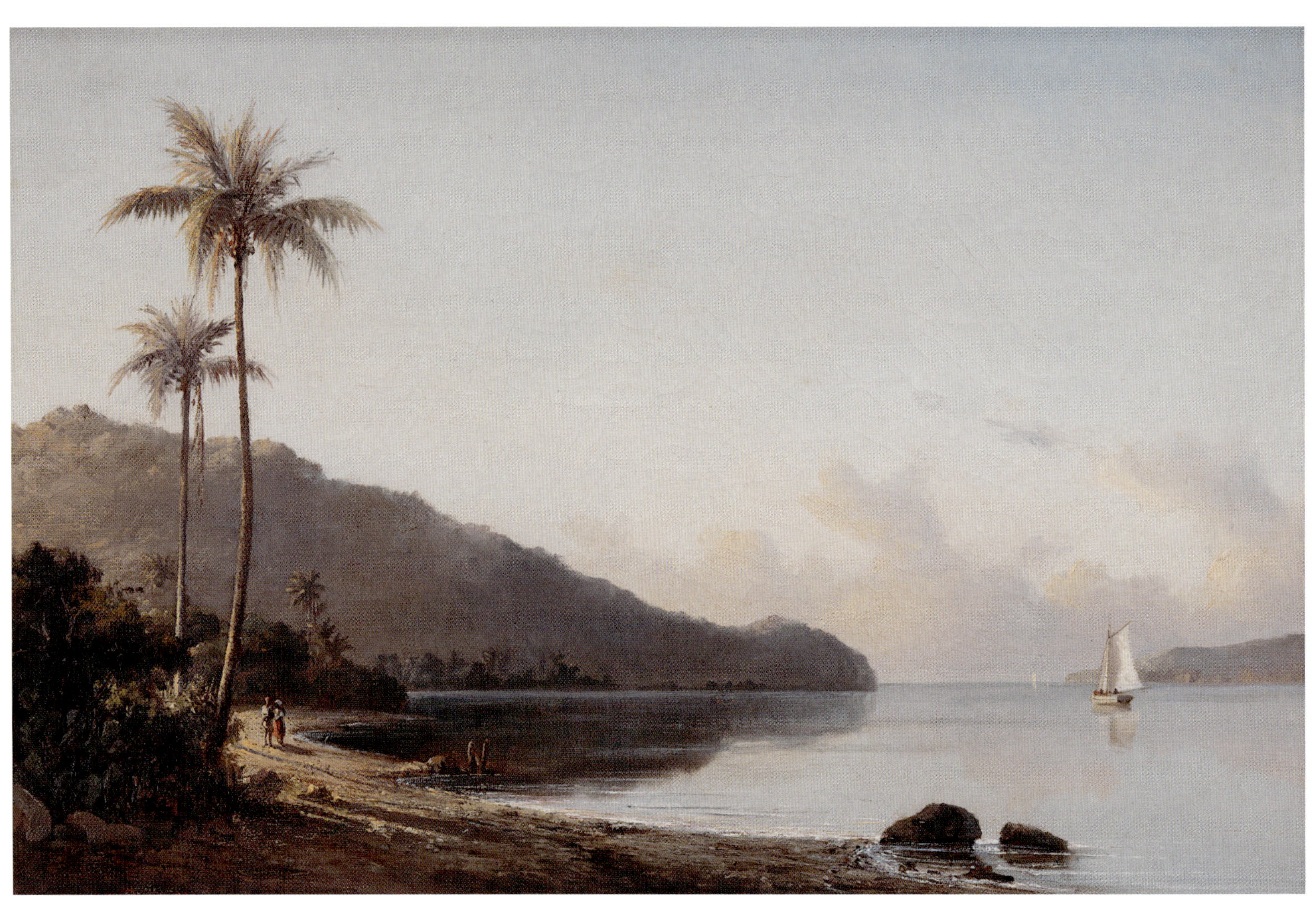

9
Cove with Sailboat, 1856
Colección Patricia Phelps de Cisneros

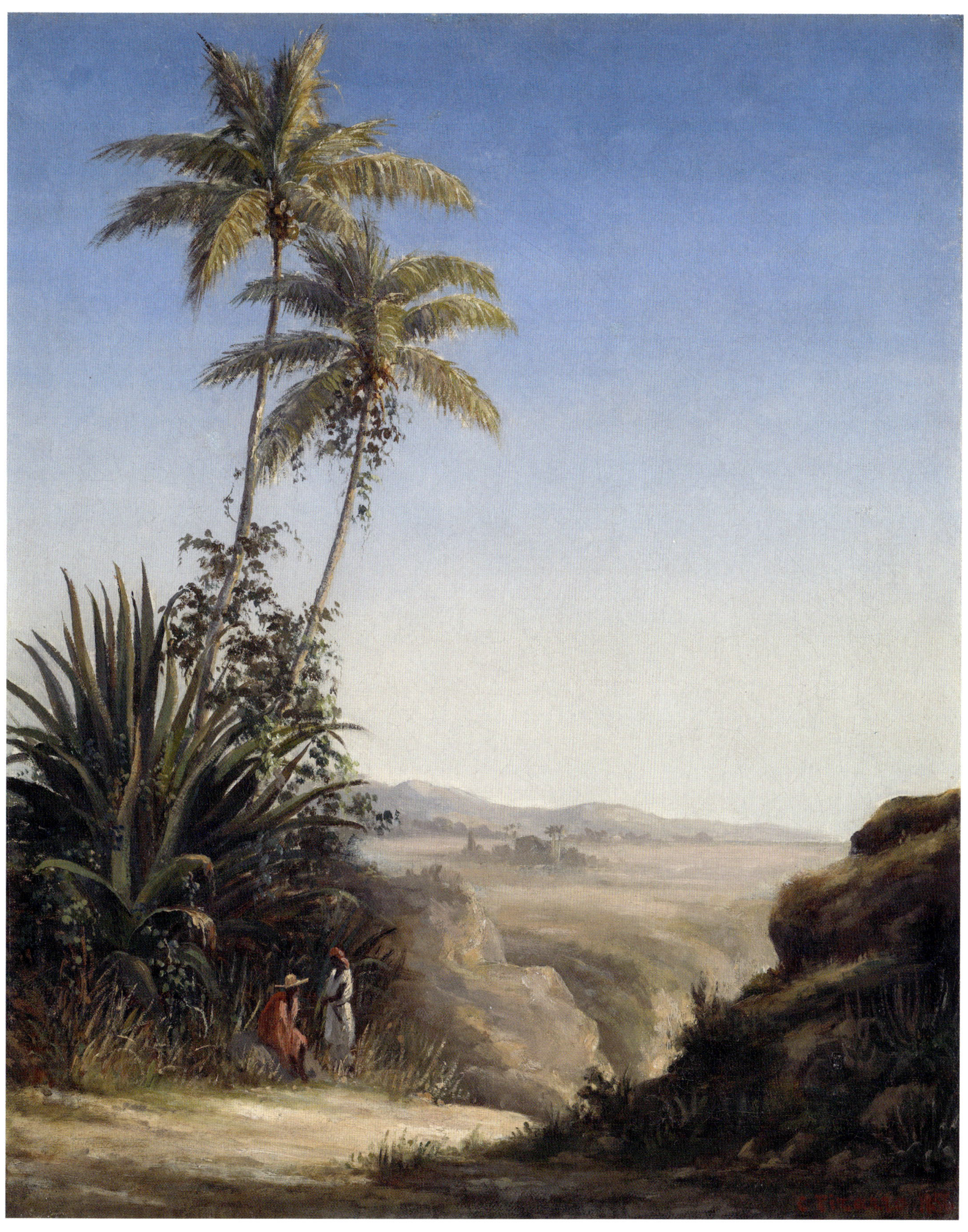

10
Landscape, Saint Thomas, 1856
Virginia Museum of Fine Arts, Richmond, Collection of Mr. and Mrs. Paul Mellon

Clarisse Fava-Piz

The Path to Impressionism
Modern Landscapes

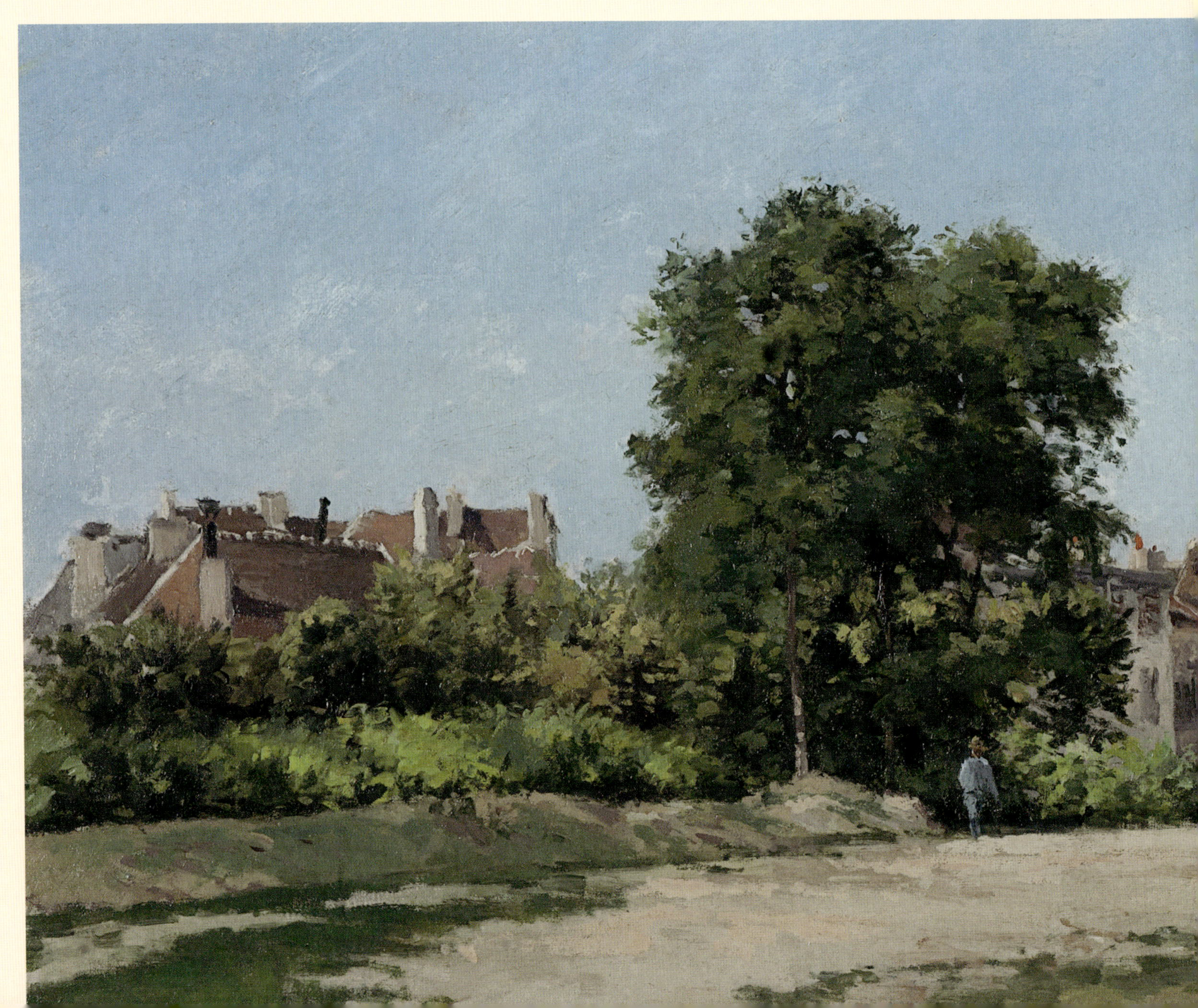

Camille Pissarro moved to France in 1855. The realistic style of his early landscape paintings was influenced by artists of the Barbizon School such as Camille Corot and Gustave Courbet. Pissarro often painted the vegetable gardens, fields, and roads in the towns of Pontoise and Louveciennes, where he lived. Many viewers criticized these motifs as banal, while others celebrated them as genuine and honest. Pissarro was one of the first Impressionists to embrace the industrialized suburbs of Paris as a worthy subject for modern landscape painting. He began to explore the transformation of motifs at different times of day and year. During the Franco-Prussian War of 1870–71, he fled to London, where he met art dealer Paul Durand-Ruel.

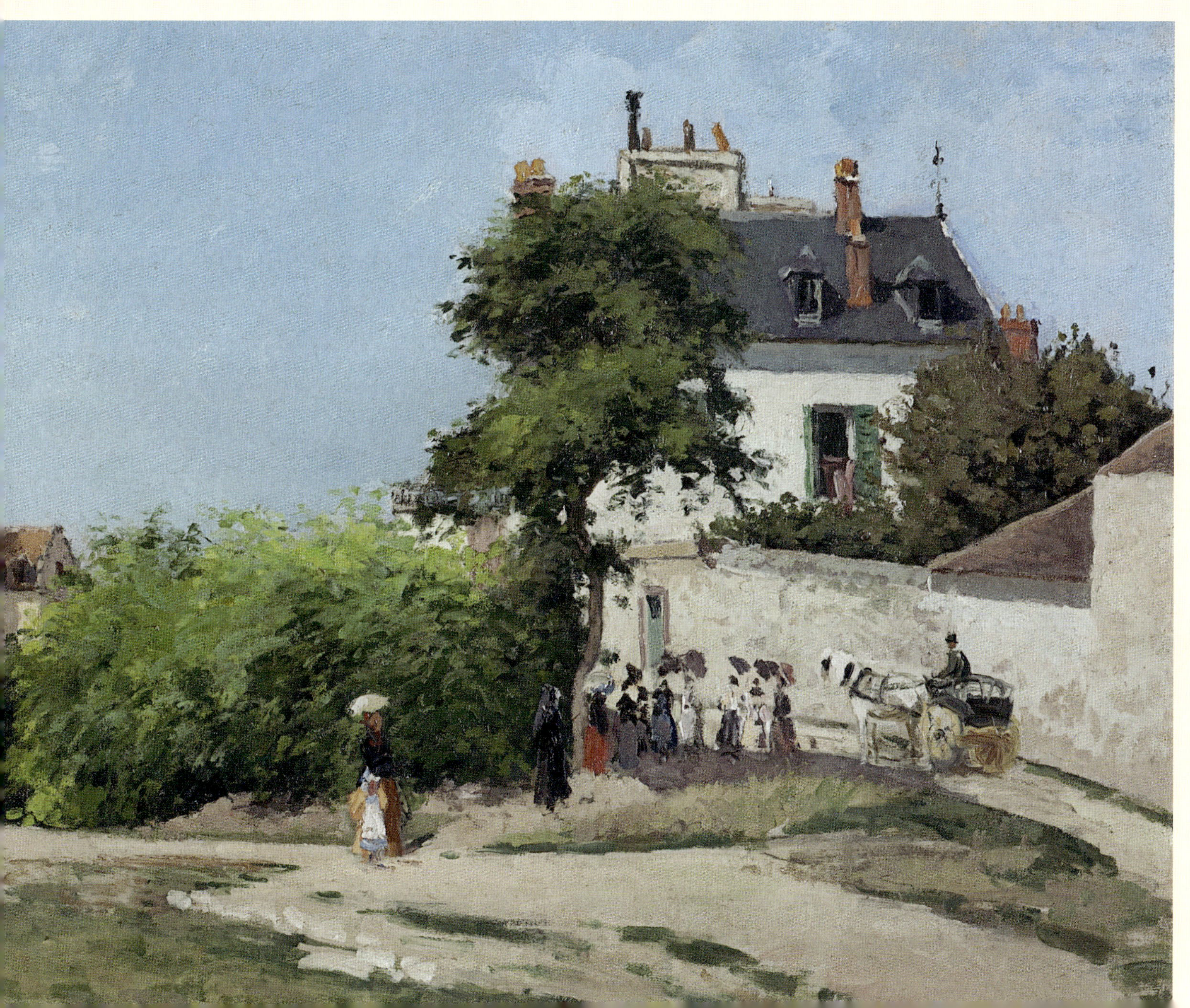

In 1855 Camille Pissarro moved to France to devote himself entirely to his career as an artist. His early years in Saint Thomas and Venezuela provided him with a solid foundation to develop his art. He arrived in Paris in time to visit the Exposition Universelle, where he discovered the works of Camille Corot, Gustave Courbet, and Eugène Delacroix. By 1858 he shifted from painting scenes of the Caribbean to the French countryside, and he chose a painting of Montmorency, north of Paris, where he spent his summers painting outdoors, to submit at the Paris Salon of 1859. *Landscape at Montmorency* (fig. p. 12) was his first work accepted at the Salon, the prestigious French institution that made artists' careers, where Pissarro would regularly submit his work until 1870. Pissarro's paintings from the late 1850s and 1860s explore motifs painted by members of the Barbizon School, as evidence of his training with Corot, and his knowledge of Courbet and Charles-François Daubigny. For a short time, Pissarro enrolled in private classes taught by official teachers at the École des Beaux-Arts, but it was at the Académie Suisse, a free drawing school, that he met a group of artists, including Paul Cézanne, Armand Guillaumin, and Claude Monet, moving in a new direction that privileged painting local life *en plein air.*

Although Pissarro rented a studio in Paris with other artists for a while, he chose to paint and live in the small towns outside the French capital, and his landscapes represented the countryside near Montmorency, La Roche-Guyon, La Varenne-Saint-Hilaire, Louveciennes, and Pontoise. His submissions to the Salon attracted the interest of some critics, including Émile Zola, who praised his ambitious painting *The Banks of the Marne in Winter* (cat. 13) in the 1866 Salon for its simplicity and realism. While some critics characterized this desolate winter landscape alongside the Marne River as "ugly" and "banal," Zola described it enthusiastically as an honest, simple, and straightforward depiction of nature's unassuming beauty.[1] Bareness and utter bleakness define this large-scale winter scene, where two figures trudge along a path lined with young trees bare of leaves. The foreground of this tightly constructed composition is left open to an empty field of green grass. The upper third of the painting is dominated by a gray sky filled with heavy, rain-laden clouds. Zola would become one of Pissarro's most ardent defenders and was one of the first to recognize Pissarro's embrace of rural life and his understanding of the country landscapes that he depicted.

In 1866 Pissarro moved to Pontoise, a small provincial town located twenty miles northwest of Paris, where he lived intermittently until 1882. This period was one of the most productive and pictorially diverse of his career. Several years before Monet and Alfred Sisley, Pissarro explored industrial motifs in a sequence of pictures of the banks of the Oise River in which small factories on the bank play a prominent role. In *Banks of the Oise at Pontoise* (cat. 16), *Quai du Pothuis, Pontoise* (cat. 17), *The Seine at Bougival* (cat. 18), and *The Seine near Port Marly* (cat. 19), Pissarro embraced, rather than ignored, the industrial character of the landscape. In contrast with Daubigny, who depicted the countryside around Paris untouched by technical progress, Pissarro included modern architectural elements, such as riverside factories and new railroad bridges, in his early rural landscapes—and he was one of the first Impressionists to do so.[2] In *Banks of the Oise at Pontoise,* a man with a walking stick stares at a smokestack across the river, drawing the viewer's attention to it. The smoking chimney of a local factory towers over the steeple of the Romanesque cathedral of Saint-Maclou to the left, while an iron railway bridge, built in 1863 to connect Pontoise and Paris, spans the Oise to the far right. X-radiographs of the work reveal that the smokestack was a later addition to the painting, emphasizing the artist's purposeful inclusion of this modern element in a landscape in transformation.

The Lock at Pontoise (cat. 20), painted in 1872, features the site where the Oise rushes over a low dam and splits to flow around the island of Saint-Martin. Canal barges are moored to the far bank, signaling the importance of the commercially navigable river for the town's industrial development. Indeed, the much-increased barge traffic along the Oise played a major role in the proliferation of factories in and near Pontoise. The river in Pissarro's paintings does not appear as a natural space but rather as a site of human intervention.[3]

Pissarro does not conform to the widespread notion of the Impressionist as a direct transcriber of sensations onto the canvas. Rather, the artist often altered and edited the landscapes that he saw before working on the canvas, in accordance with his social agenda.[4] Even though Pissarro is primarily known as a painter of rural life, he devoted considerable attention to industrial forms. His preoccupation with labor contrasts with Impressionist painters such as Monet and Pierre-Auguste Renoir, who at that time depicted the leisurely world of bourgeois figures moving along the banks of the Seine in Paris.

The Pissarro family moved to the village of Louveciennes in 1869, where almost all the future Impressionists— Cézanne, Edgar Degas, Berthe Morisot, Renoir, and Sisley—resided or sojourned. Pissarro's paintings from this period demonstrate a shift away from the muted colors of the Barbizon School toward a brighter, more varied palette and the broken brushwork that became hallmarks of Impressionism. The motif of the road or the path, whether paved or unpaved, is particularly prominent in these early Impressionist paintings.[5] *Route de Versailles, Louveciennes, Rain Effect* (cat. 21) is one of numerous small-scale paintings exploring that motif under different atmospheric conditions and at different times of the day. These paintings reflect the artist's new interest in observing seasonal effects on the same view. It also demonstrates Pissarro's affinity with Monet, who painted this same road twice in 1870. In some cases, Pissarro depicted major thoroughfares, such as the Route de Versailles, a wide, paved artery linking Louveciennes with Marly-le-Roi and Versailles. In other instances, he focused on smaller paths such as the unpaved Rue des Creux (now Rue du Maréchal Joffre), in *Landscape at Louveciennes (Autumn)* (cat. 14). In this large landscape painting, the village path is fronted by modest homes and vegetable gardens populated with a few locals. Instead of depicting the imposing country residences of the rich, Pissarro celebrated rural France.

The Franco-Prussian War broke out in 1870, and the Pissarros—at that time the artist and Julie Vellay had two children—went into exile in London. Across the English Channel, Pissarro studied the works of Joseph Mallord William Turner and John Constable and was introduced to French gallerist Paul Durand-Ruel, who would become his main art dealer. *Lordship Lane Station, Dulwich* (cat. 23) dates from that brief but decisive time in London. It is one of the first appearances of a train in Impressionist painting, well before Monet's well-known evocations of trains and bustling stations. Here, the locomotive heads directly toward the viewer, cutting this South London landscape in two. As in the suburbs of Paris, a network of railways was created around London in the mid-1850s. This painting features the now-demolished station at Lordship Lane in Upper Norwood on the old Crystal Palace and South London Junction Railway that was motivated by the construction of the Crystal Palace at Sydenham in 1852–54.[6] It is arguably the most emblematic image of industrial progress Pissarro painted in England.

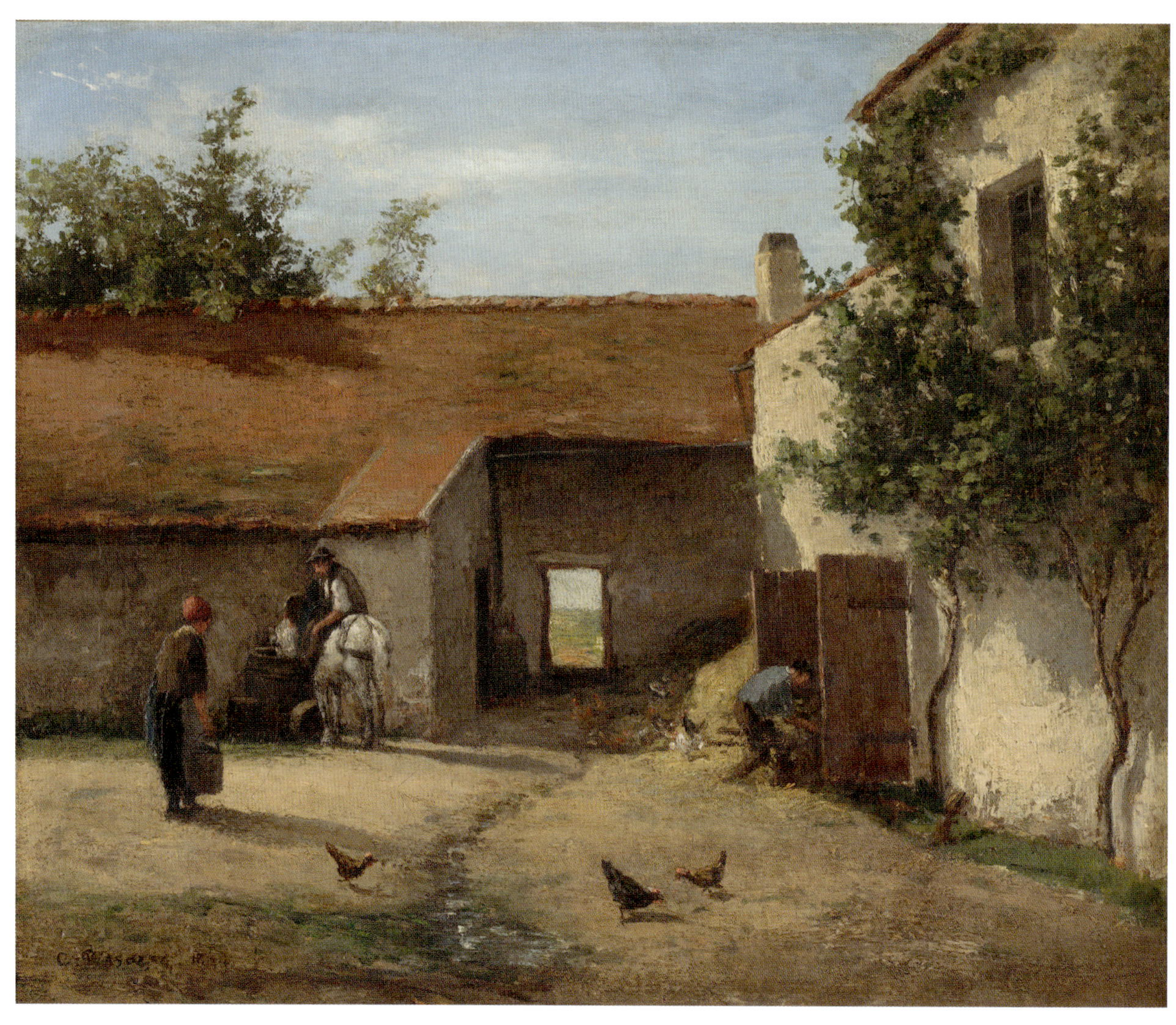

11
Farmyard, ca. 1863
Private collection, Colorado

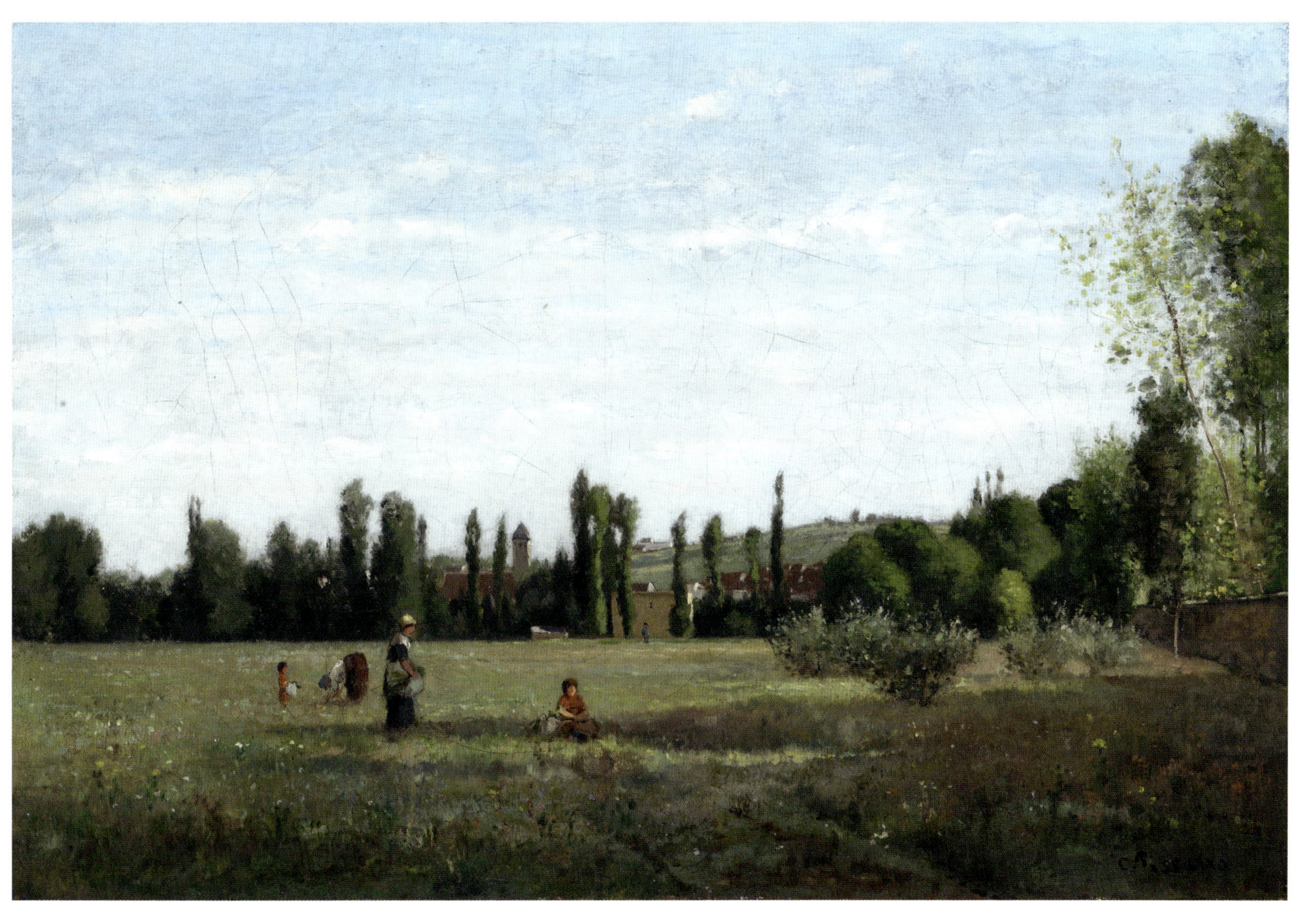

12
La Varenne-Saint-Hilaire, ca. 1863
Szépművészeti Múzeum / Museum of Fine Arts, Budapest

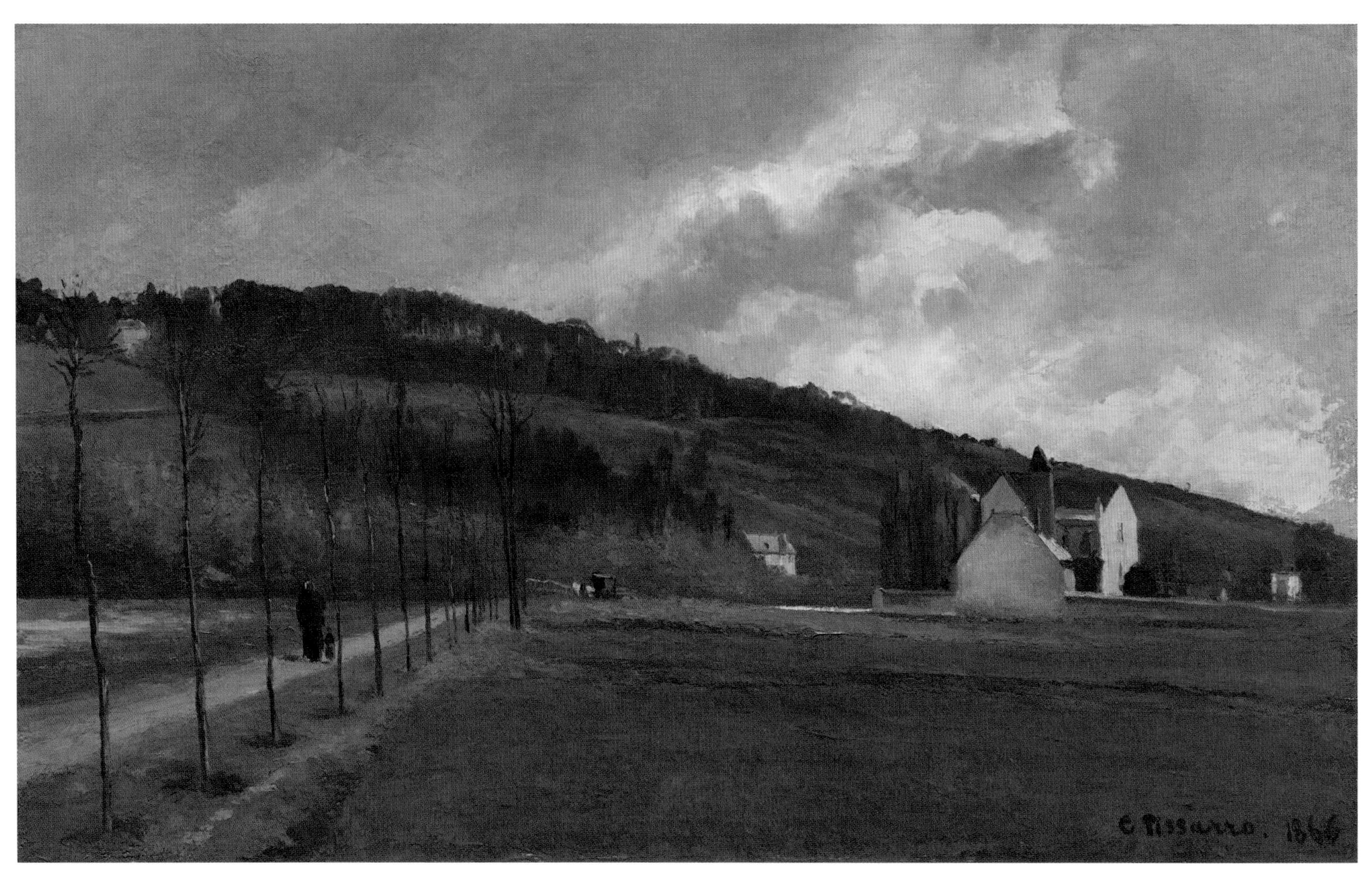

13
The Banks of the Marne in Winter, 1866
The Art Institute of Chicago, Mr. and Mrs. Lewis Larned Coburn Memorial Collection

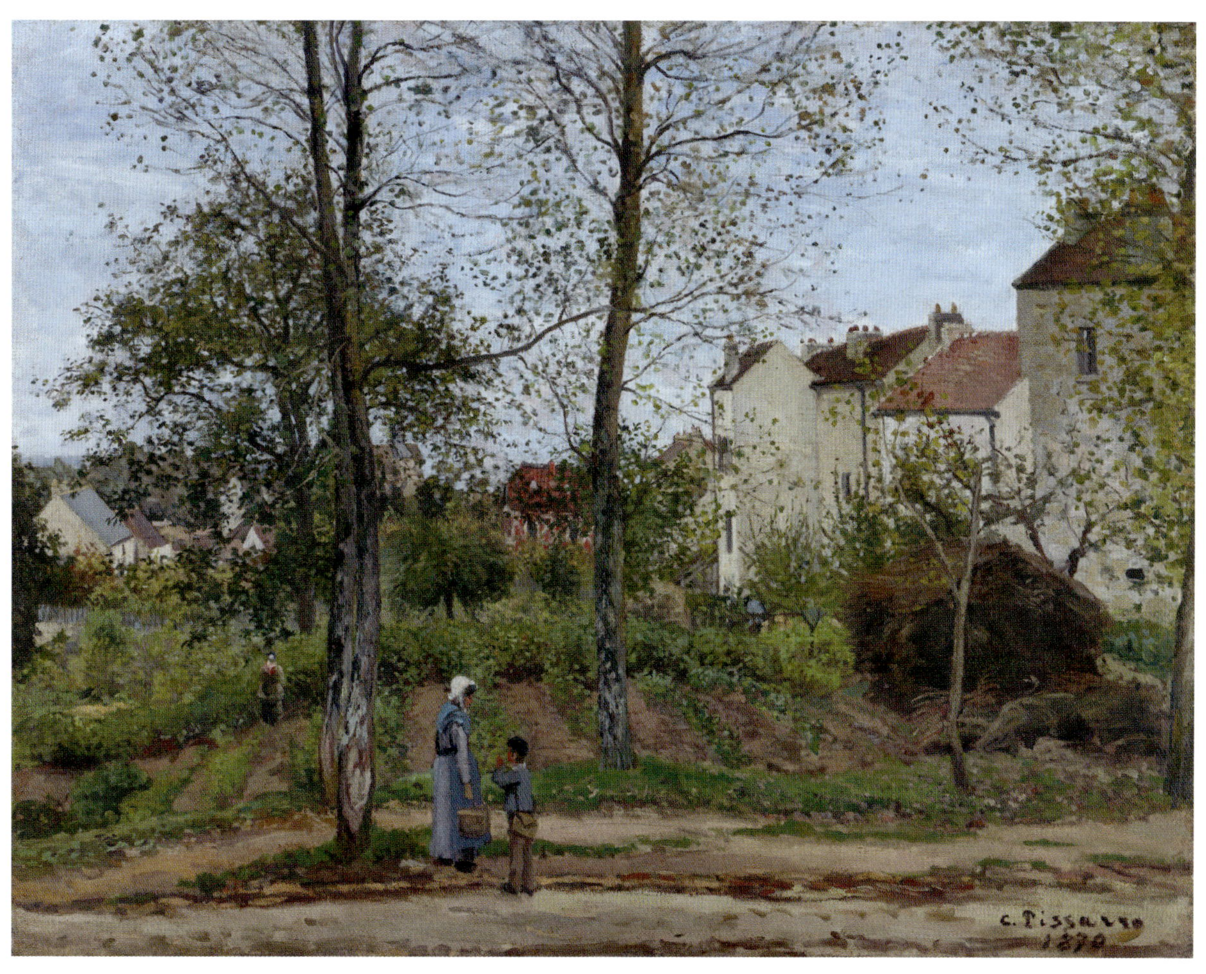

14
Landscape at Louveciennes (Autumn), 1870
The J. Paul Getty Museum, Los Angeles

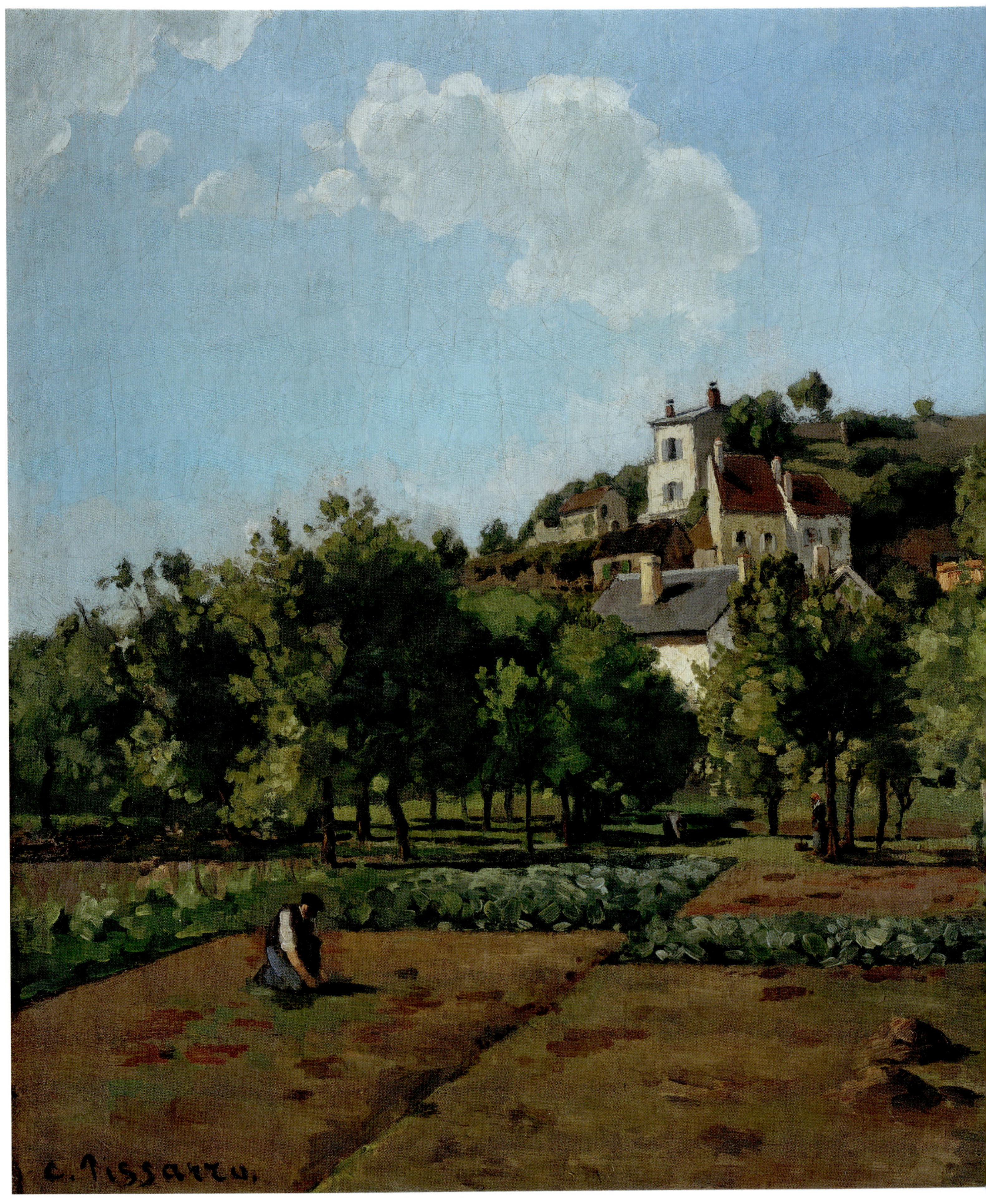
C. Pissarro.

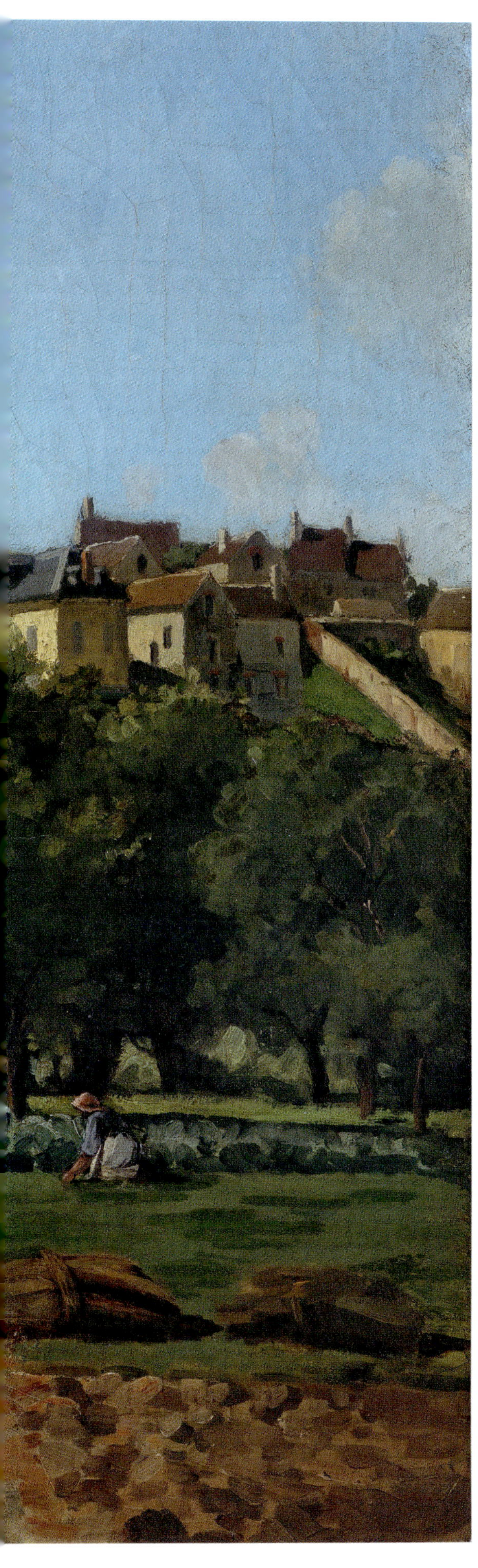

15
Pontoise, ca. 1867
National Gallery Prague

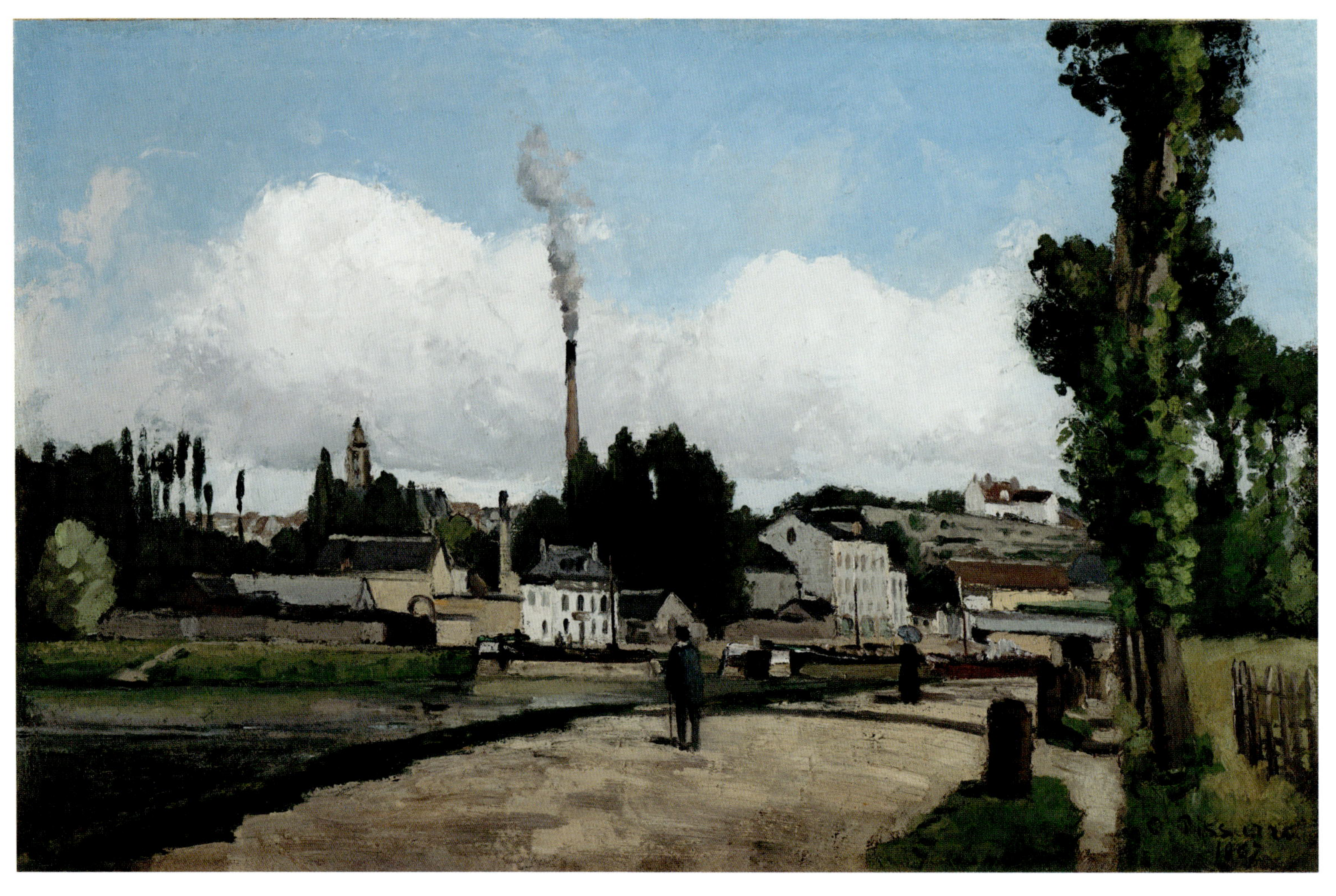

16
Banks of the Oise at Pontoise or *Banks of the Oise at Saint-Ouen-l'Aumône,* 1867
Denver Art Museum, Gift of the Barnett and Annalee Newman Foundation in honor of Annalee G. Newman

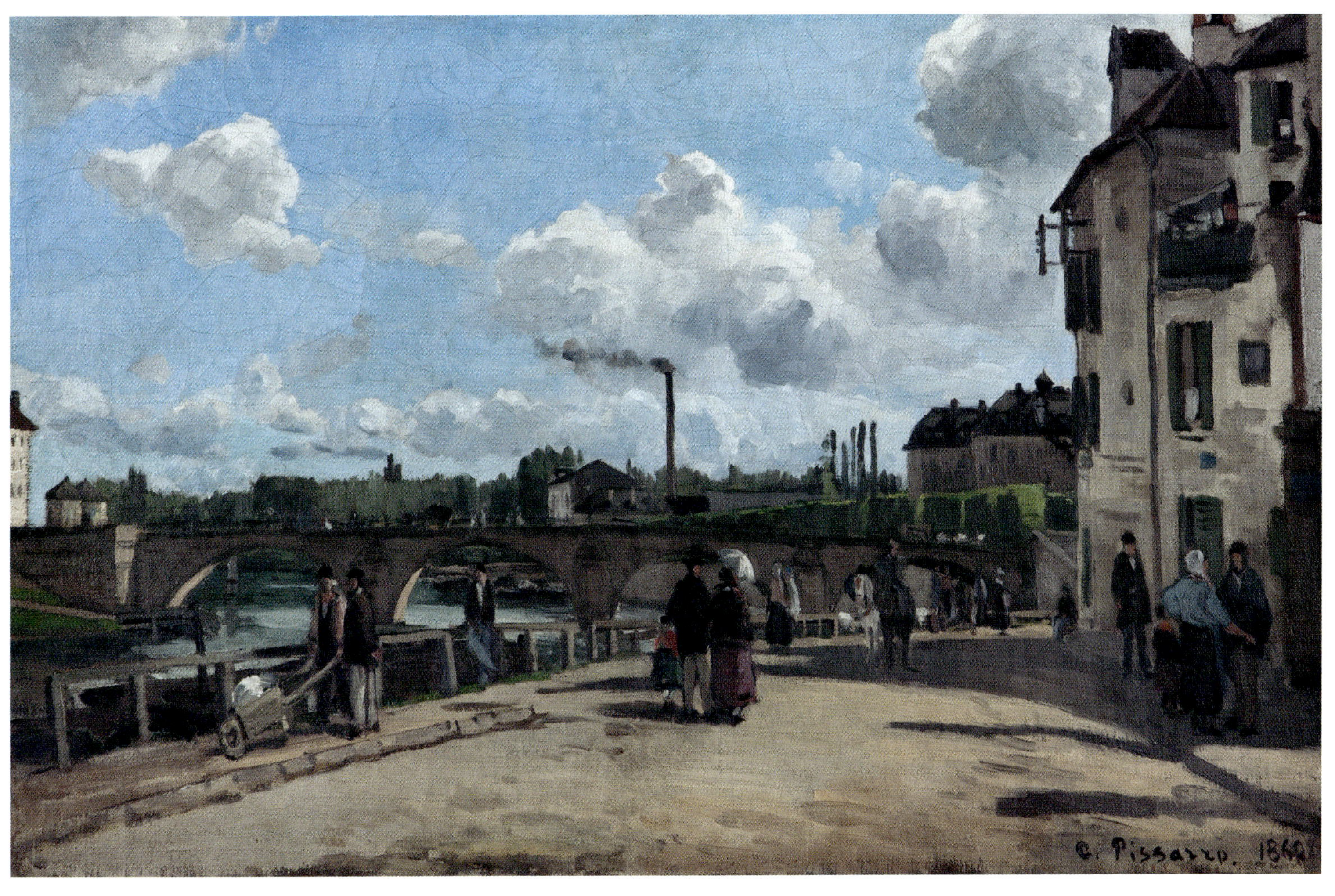

17
Quai du Pothuis, Pontoise, 1868
Kunsthalle Mannheim

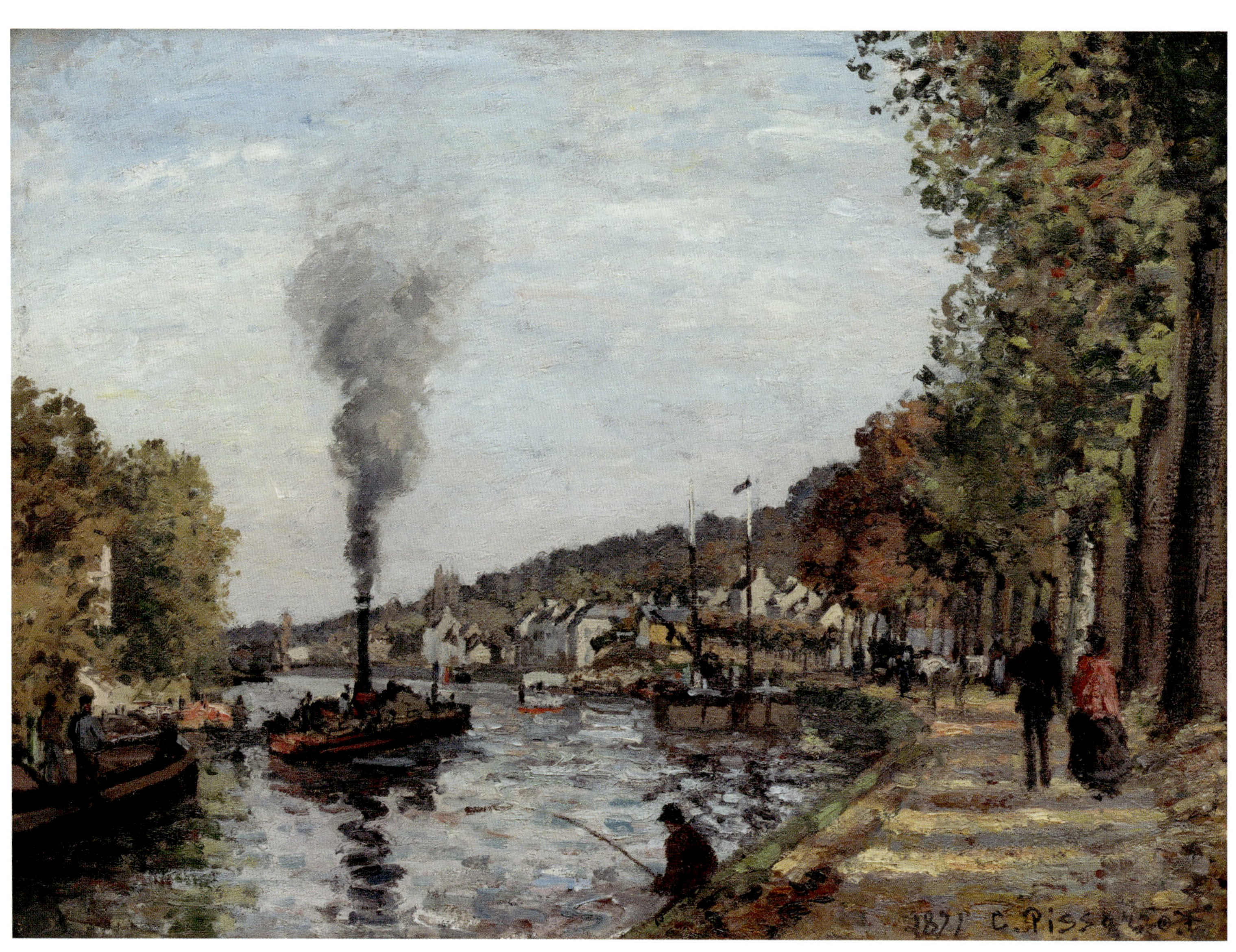

18
The Seine at Bougival, 1871
Private collection

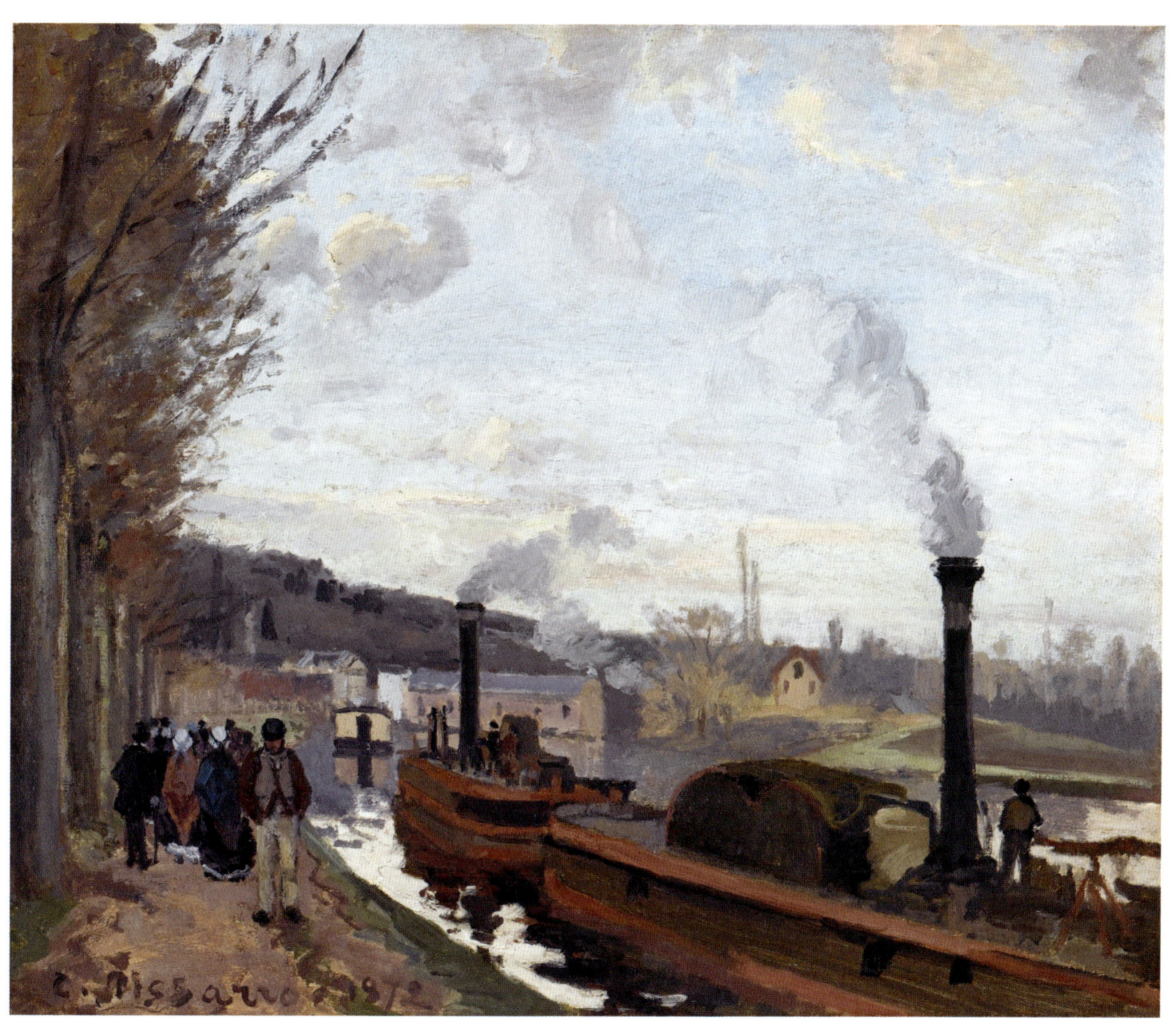

19
The Seine near Port Marly, 1872
Staatsgalerie Stuttgart, Purchased with lottery funds in 1965

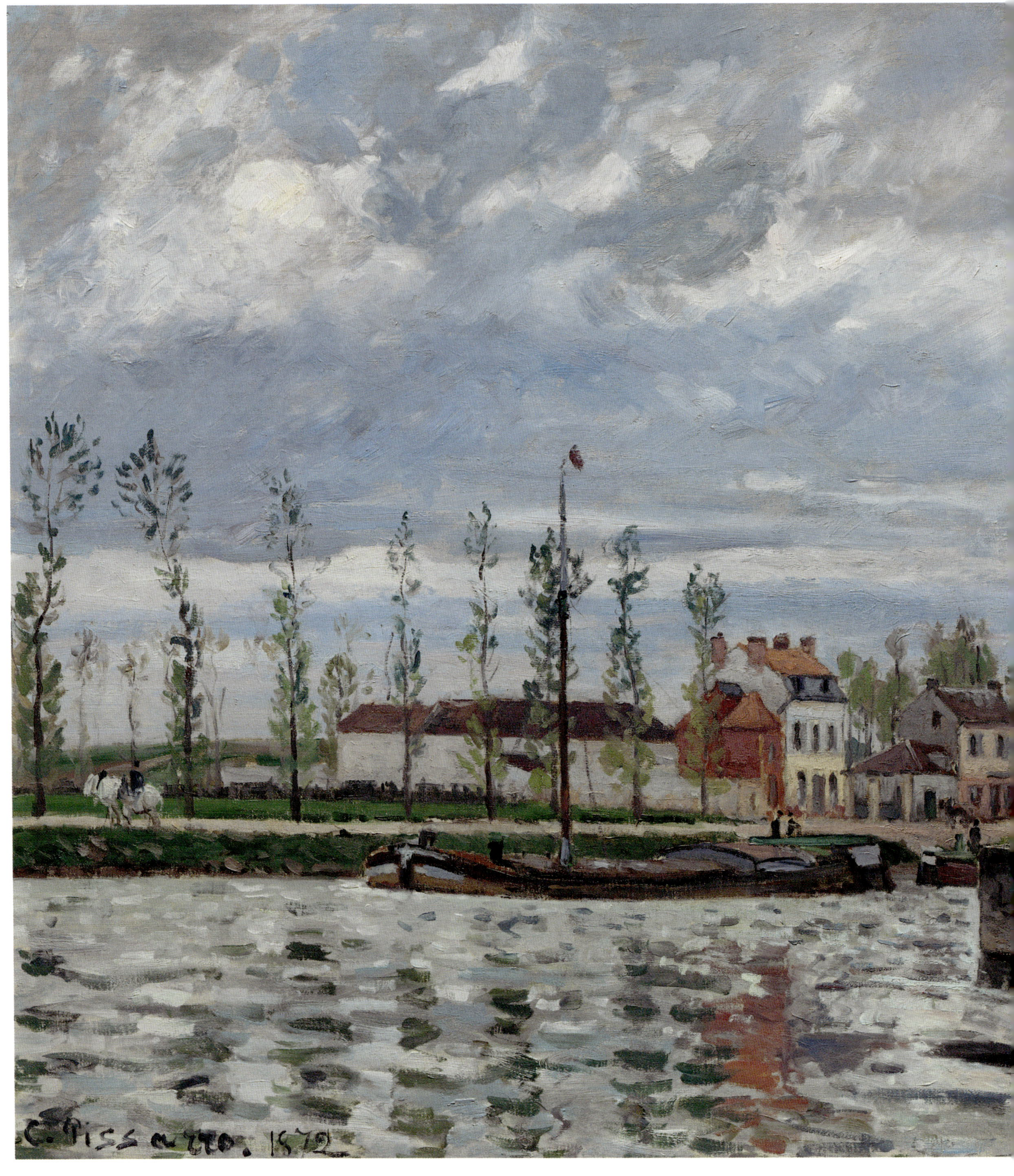
C. Pissarro. 1872

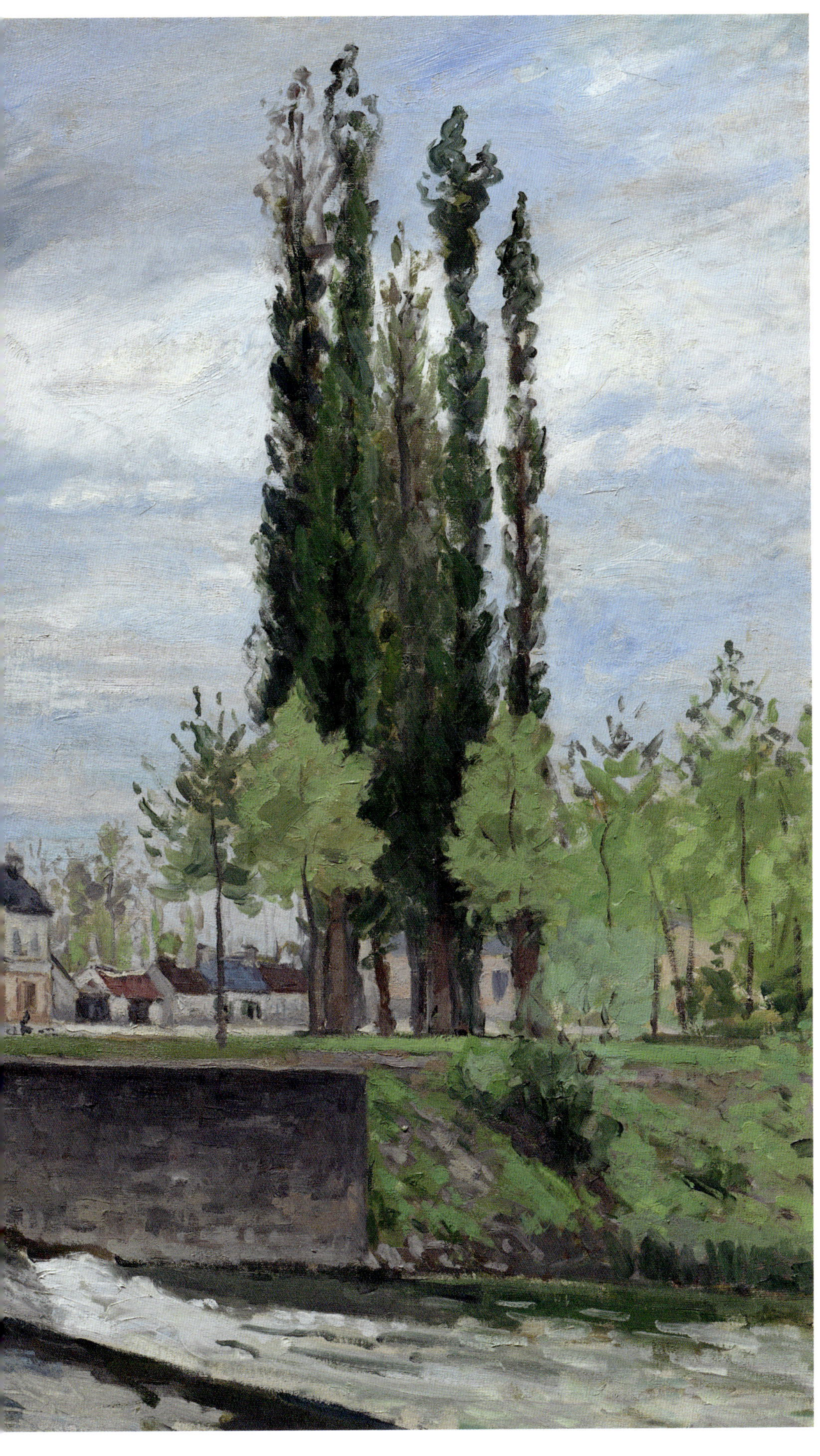

20
The Lock at Pontoise, 1872
The Cleveland Museum of Art,
Leonard C. Hanna Jr. Fund

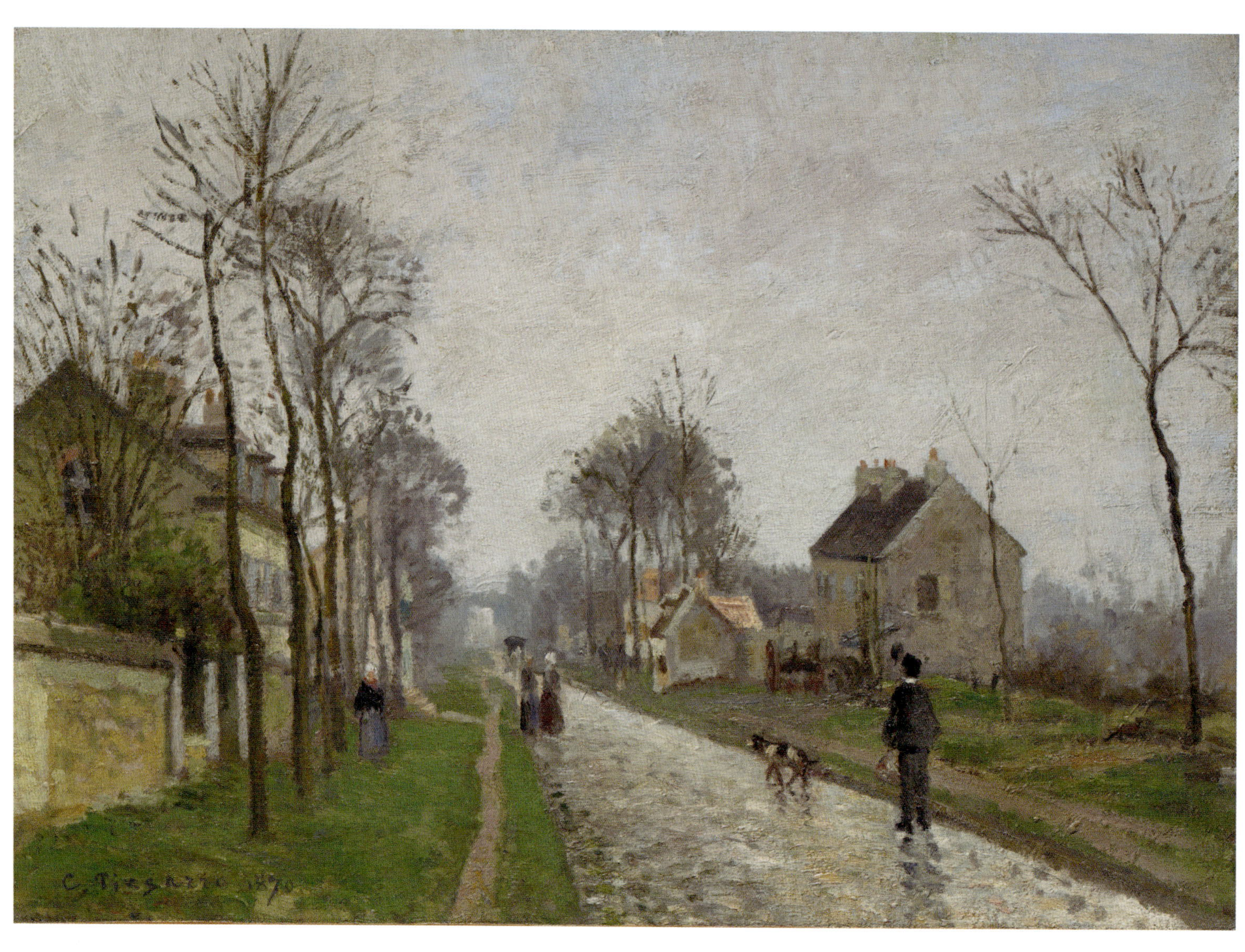

21
Route de Versailles, Louveciennes, Rain Effect, 1870
Clark Art Institute, Williamstown, Massachusetts

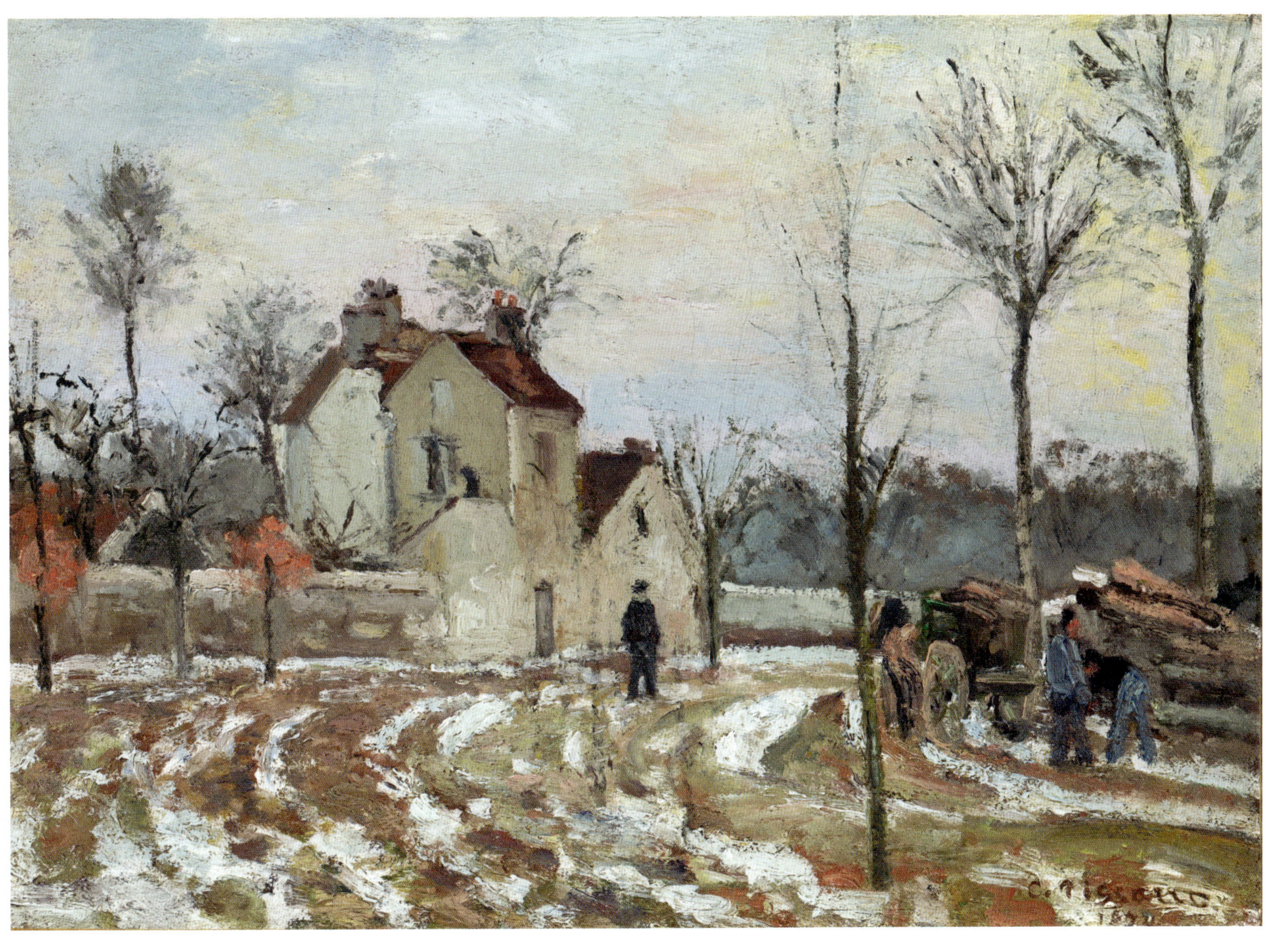

22
The Thaw or *The House of Monsieur Musy, Louveciennes,* 1872
Denver Art Museum, Frederic C. Hamilton Collection

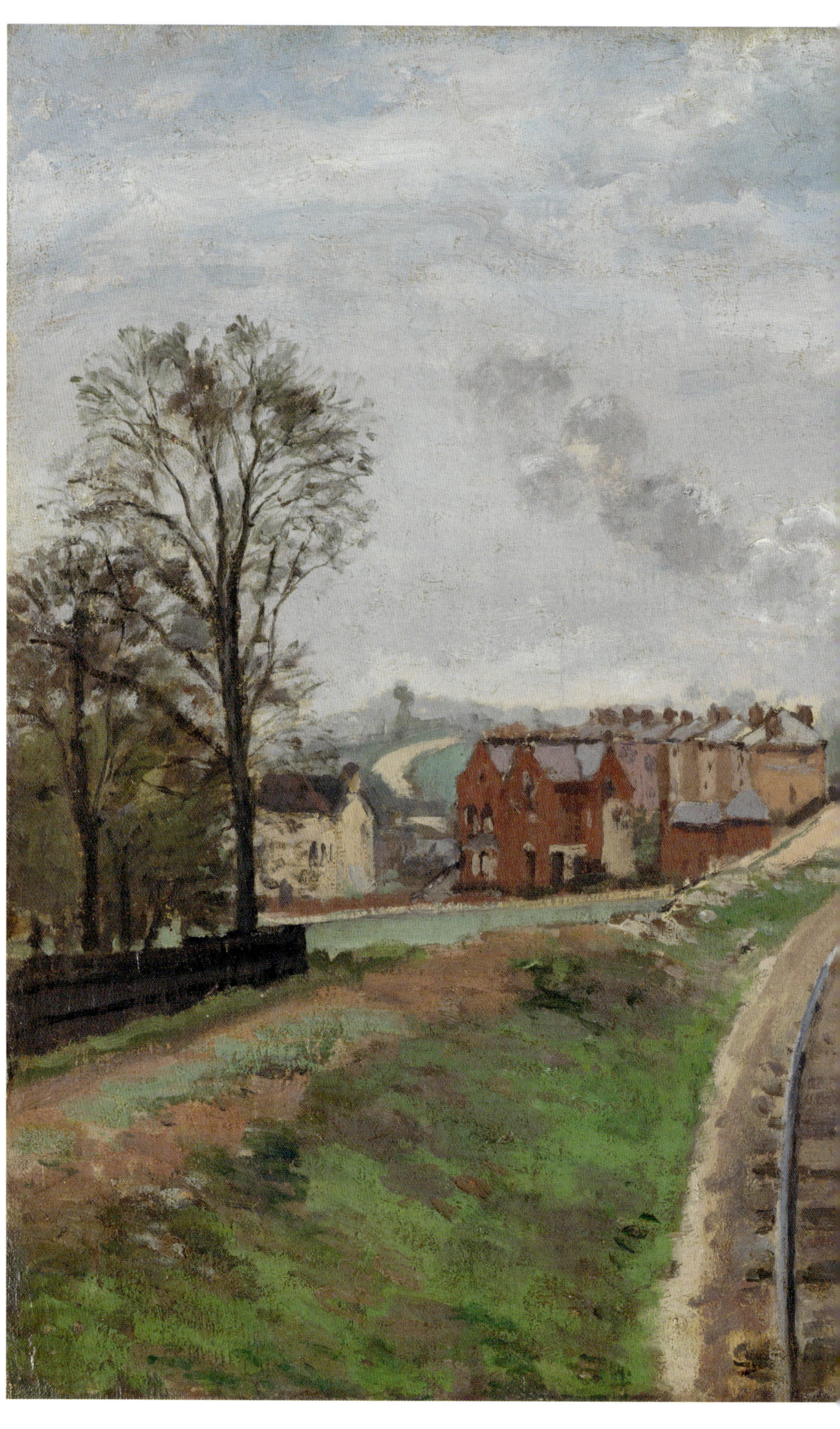

23
Lordship Lane Station, Dulwich, 1871
Courtauld, London (Samuel Courtauld Trust)

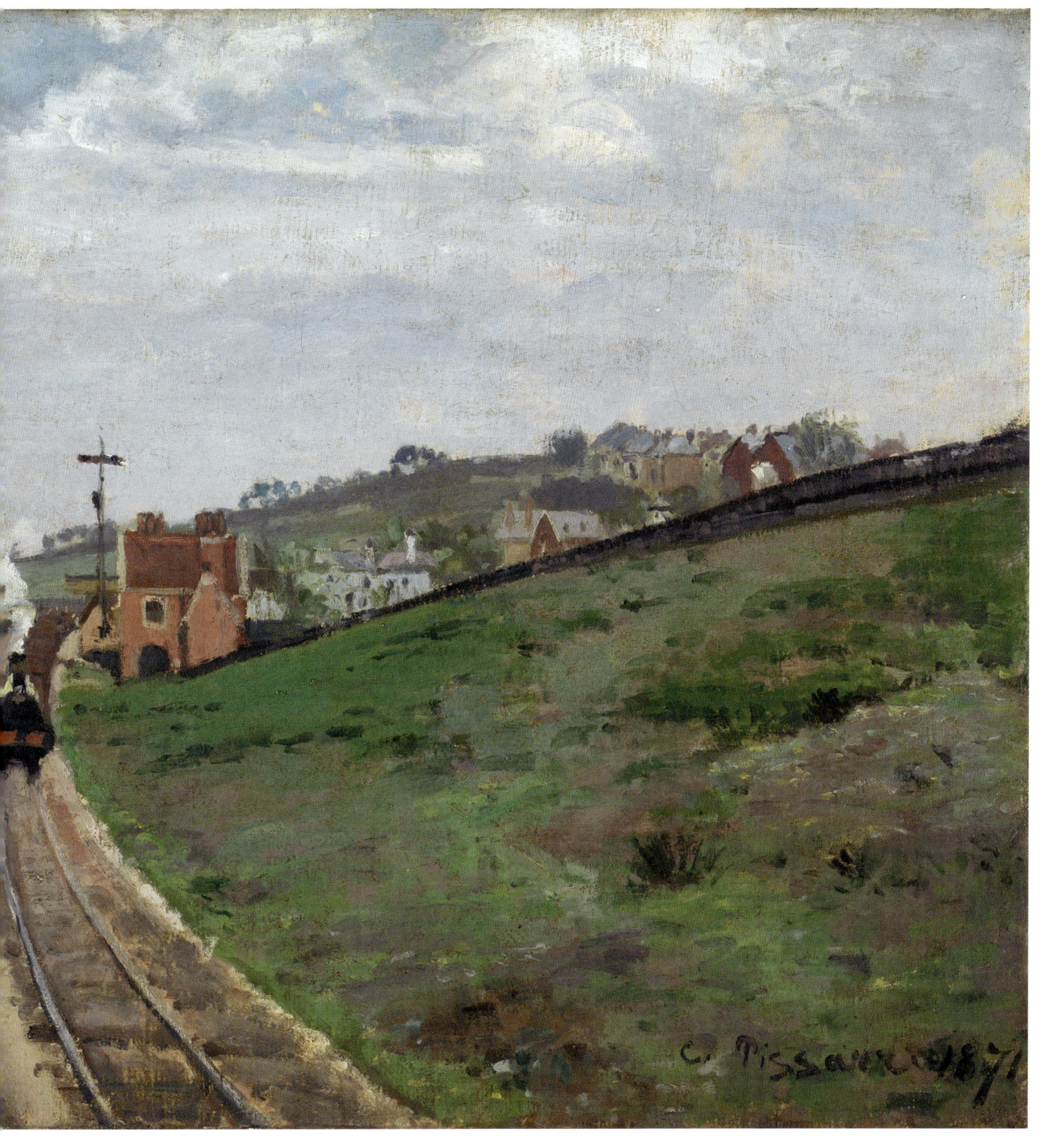
C. Pissarro 1871

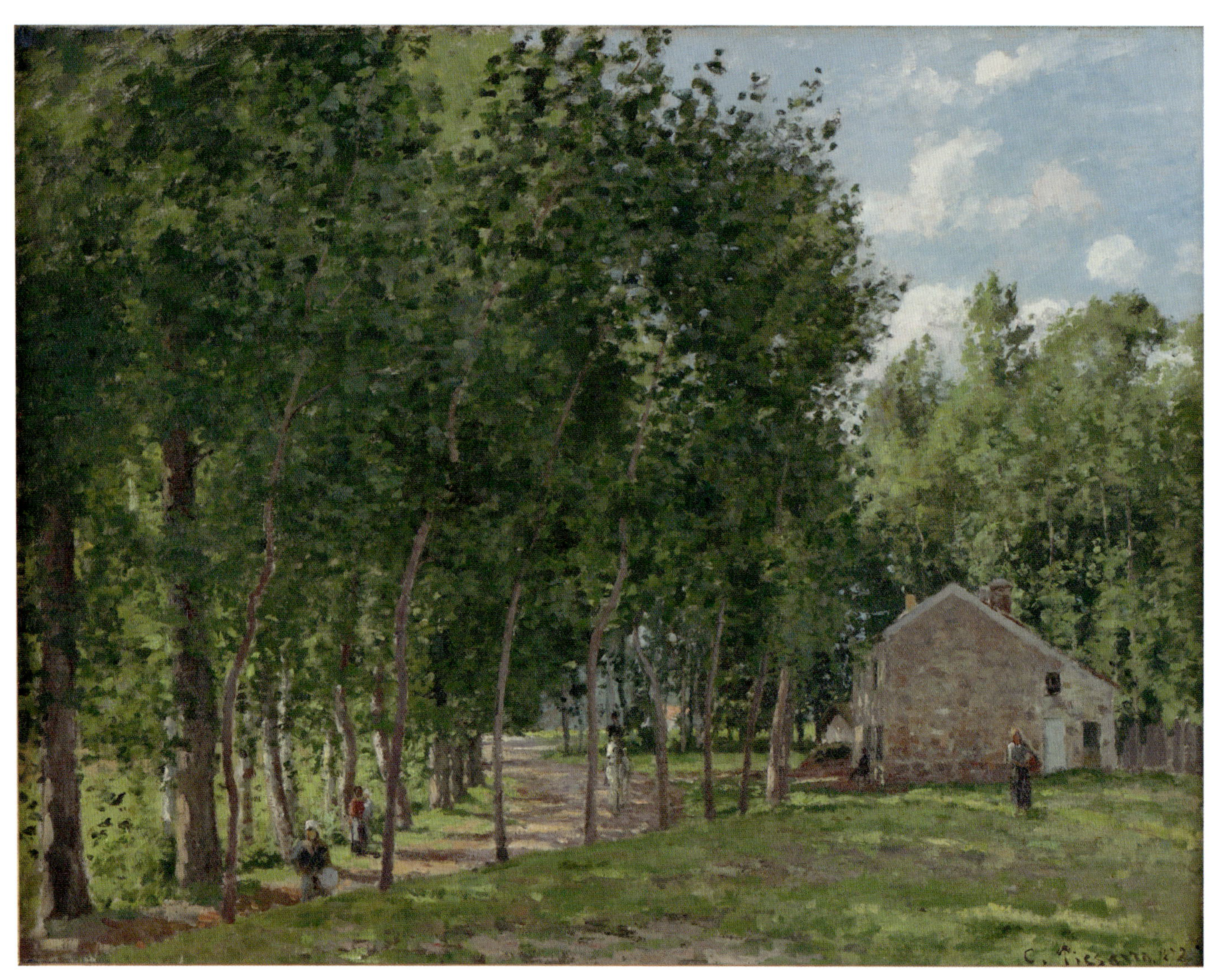

24
The House in the Woods, 1872
Drs. Tobia and Morton Mower

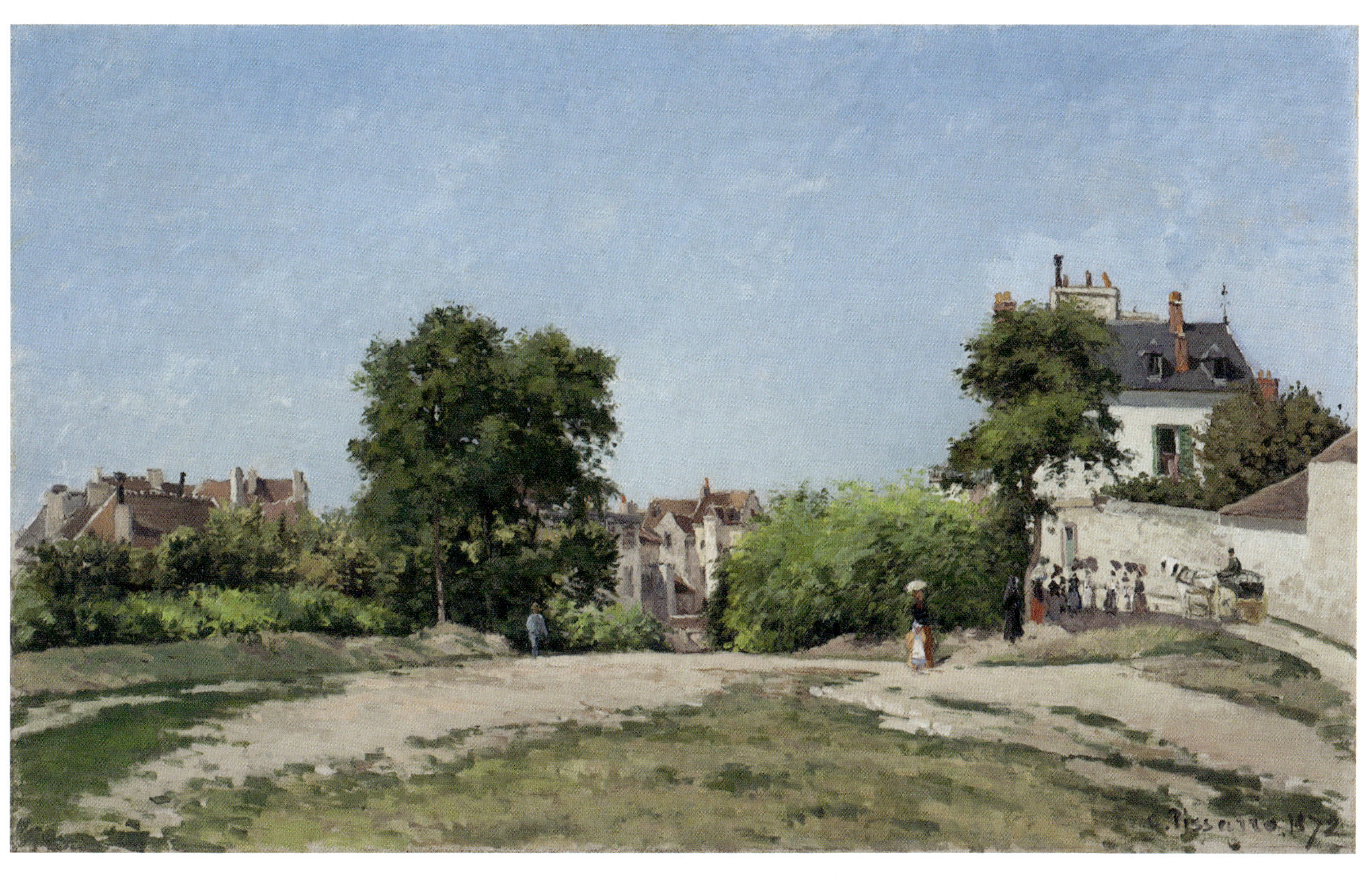

25
The Crossroads, Pontoise or *Square at the Old Cemetery, Pontoise*, 1872
Carnegie Museum of Art, Pittsburgh, Acquired through the generosity of the Sarah Mellon Scaife Family

Family Pictures
Portraits and Still Lifes

Clarisse Fava-Piz

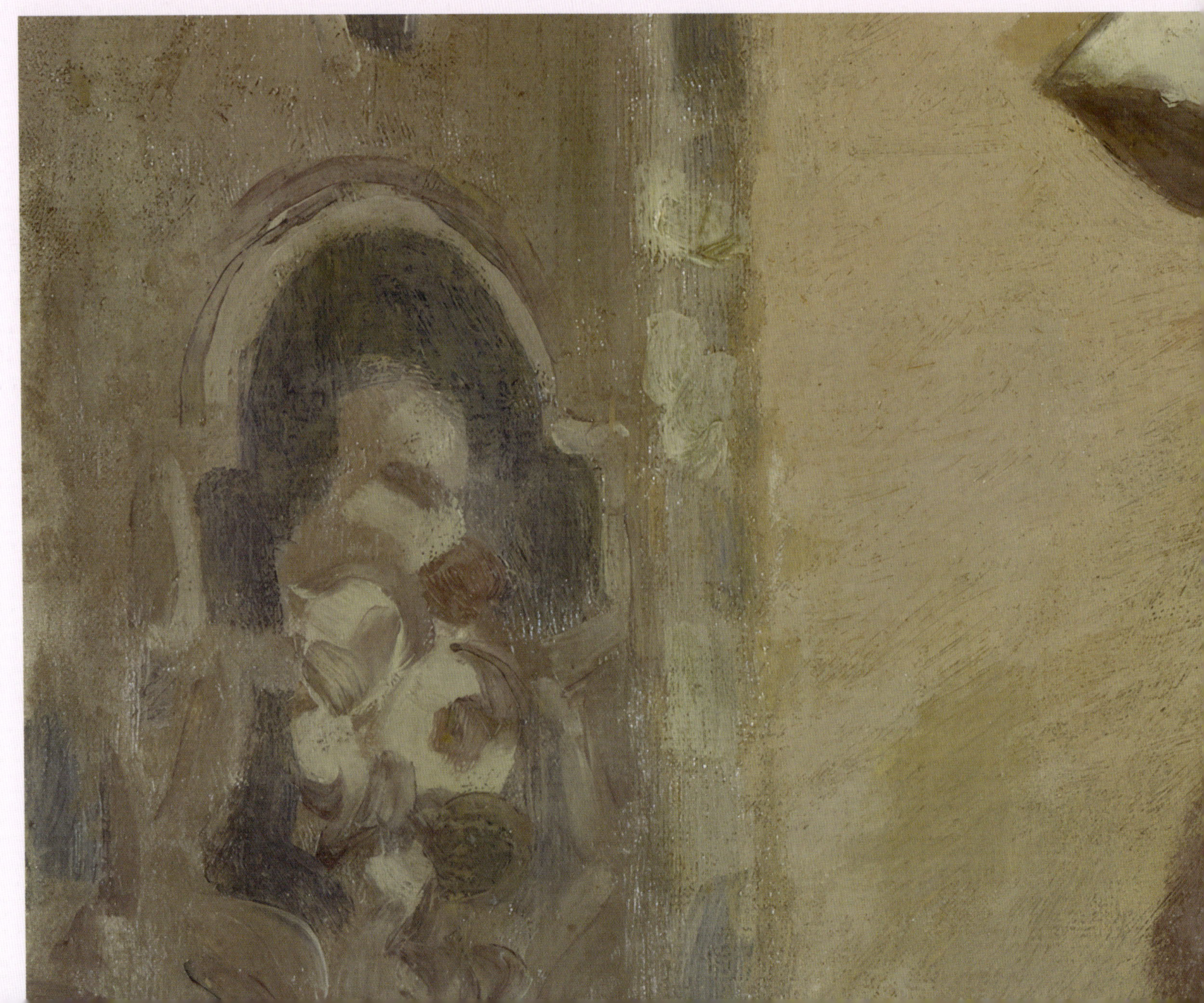

Camille Pissarro's large family played an important role in his life. Against his parents' will, he married Julie Vellay, a French Catholic winegrower's daughter who had been employed as a maid in his family home. The couple had eight children, three of whom died: one son as a young adult and two daughters during childhood.

Pissarro's portraits of his family members tend to be private in character. He used powerful, impasto brushstrokes to express his wife's strength and life experience and evoked the frail constitution of his young daughter Jeanne-Rachel with muted tones and a more transparent application of paint. Pissarro also encouraged his children to acquire artistic training, and five of them followed in his professional footsteps.

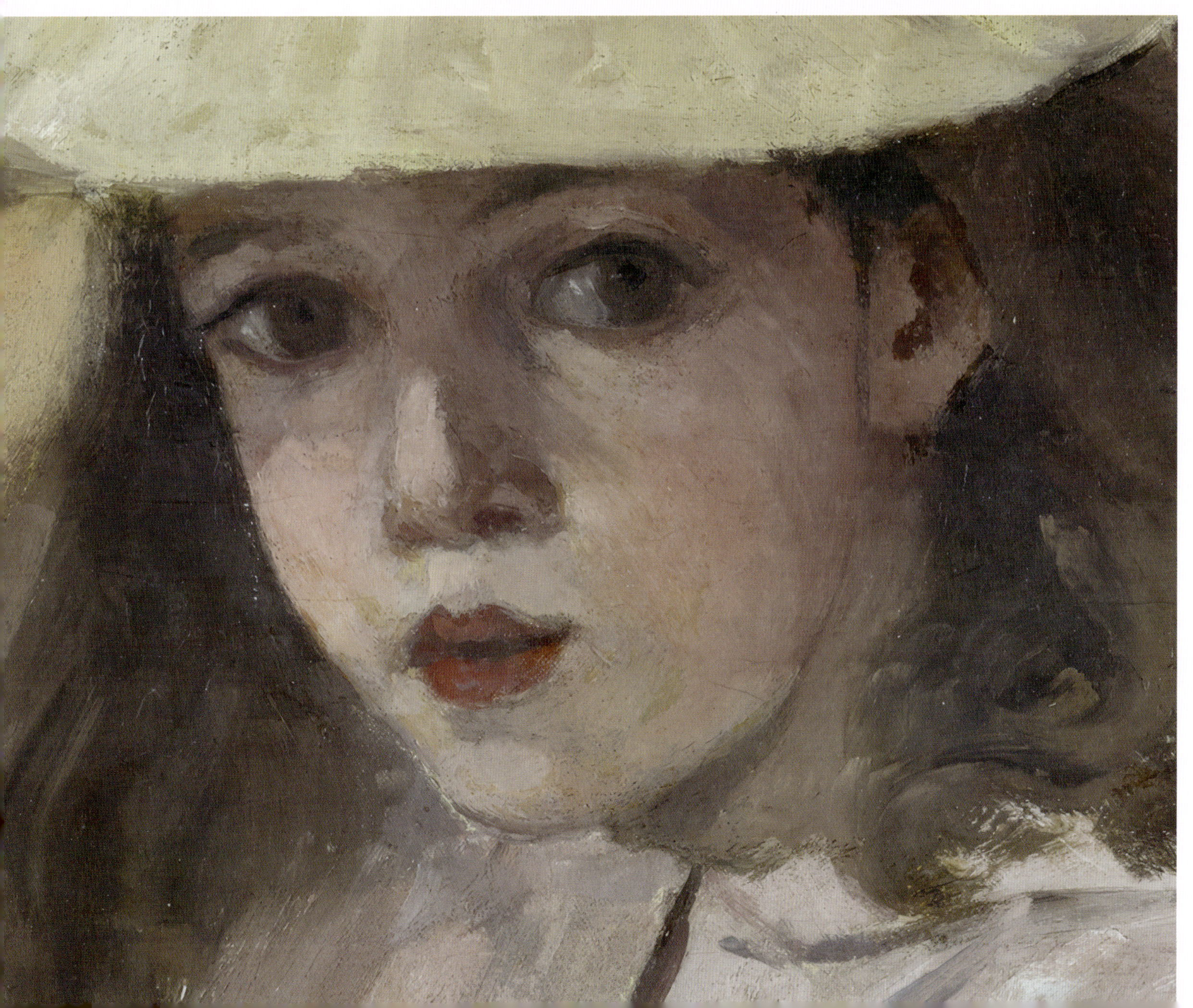

Set in a domestic interior, Camille Pissarro's self-portrait from 1873 (cat. 26) depicts him as a man calm and clear-eyed at age forty-three. Pissarro only painted four self-portraits during his life, and the three others came in his final decade. However, these works reveal little about the artist and his life. In contrast with many fellow Impressionists, Pissarro was "a quintessential family man."[1] He and his wife, Julie Pissarro (née Vellay), had eight children, making them an exceptionally large family for an artist in nineteenth-century France. Even more, Pissarro was determined to transmit his artistic ideals to his children, and his letters to them are filled with advice on how to draw, what to read, and encouragement to think more ambitiously and develop intellectually.[2] He believed that being an artist was the most beautiful *métier* (occupation) in the world. Even if Julie Pissarro constantly worried about the monetary hardships that a life devoted to art would bring them, all five of the Pissarros' sons became artists in their own right.

Julie Vellay met Camille Pissarro in 1860, when she was working as a maid at his mother's home. The daughter of Catholic wine workers from Burgundy, she lacked upper-level education, and her ability to read and write was limited. She was never accepted by Pissarro's parents, who disapproved of their relationship. After already having two children, they married in a quiet civil ceremony in London in 1871 while in exile during the Franco-Prussian War. Despite these hurdles, the two would become lifelong partners.

Julie Pissarro was the backbone of the family as her husband struggled to sell his art until well into his sixties. Thanks to her industriousness, the family lived reasonably comfortably yet frugally. Julie Pissarro took care of their children, maintained their successive family households, kept a kitchen garden as well as chickens, ducks—and sometimes a cow—to reduce costs, and regularly negotiated for credit in the shops.[3] She also took the initiative to buy their house in Éragny-sur-Epte and secured a loan from Claude Monet to help with the purchase in June 1892.[4] Although not directly involved in her husband's artistic business, she visited his exhibitions, expressed her opinions about them, and was friendly with his many artist friends, even becoming the godmother of Monet's first son, Jean. Among those friends, some perceived her as the dominant figure of the couple, including art dealer Theo van Gogh, who wrote about Pissarro to his artist brother in 1889, "I don't think he has much say in the household, where his wife wears the pants."[5]

Given her central role in the artist's life and though she is often present as an industrious figure in his landscape paintings, Julie Pissarro only rarely appears as a portrait model. *Julie Pissarro Sewing Beside a Window*, painted around 1877 (cat. 27), is arguably the most accomplished of the six portraits that Pissarro dedicated to his wife. She is shown fully immersed in her sewing, as if unaware of being portrayed. With her hair tied up in a bun, she sits in profile in front of a wrought-iron balcony. The dense texture of the painting emphasizes the sitter's presence, and the lively handling of the skin tones reflects her outdoor work.[6] Her flushed cheeks perhaps signify the difference in temperature between the cold winter air outside and the warmth of the domestic space. Modest in formal terms, this charming portrait of Julie is a testament to her dedication to her household and its chores, which she rarely paused, even to sit for a portrait by her husband. The way that the bare canvas is exposed in the area of the cloth she is holding additionally draws a subtle parallel between her sewing and Pissarro's canvas. This is also ultimately achieved through their simultaneous pursuit of a productive activity.

The portraits of Pissarro's children are intimate, both in size and subject matter. Surprisingly, Pissarro rarely painted his firstborn son, Lucien, to whom he wrote extensive letters. Jeanne-Rachel, nicknamed "Minette," however, was a favorite model for Pissarro, who painted her often during her short nine years. The portraits tragically document her long illness and deteriorating health. In a portrait painted in 1872 (cat. 28), Minette sits in a conventional three-quarter pose and gazes directly at the viewer while holding a bouquet of freshly cut flowers. A straw hat trimmed with pale blue ribbons embellishes her long ash-blond hair framing her delicate face. In the full-length painting *Jeanne Pissarro (Minette) Holding a Fan,* from around 1874 (cat. 29), Minette's hair has been cut short and darkened to a reddish brown. The sickly child appears seated in a simple white dress with a blue apron and holds a large white Asian fan in an interior—perhaps her bedroom—looking at the viewer with large, tired eyes and slumped shoulders. The dry painting style, which reveals traces of the canvas in the contours, and the darkness of the surrounding interior, reduced to flat planes with little detail, contribute to the impression of fragility and melancholy.[7] Minette's health began to deteriorate by October 1873, and she died on April 6, 1874. At the time, Julie and Camille had lost two of their four children and both of their daughters. Pissarro would paint his last three children—Ludovic-Rodolphe ("Rodo," born 1878), Jeanne-Marguerite ("Cocotte," born 1881), and Paul-Émile (born 1884, cat. 30)—more often than their elder siblings. Despite the centrality of his children in his artistic life, Pissarro exhibited only one portrait of them among the hundreds of works he sent to the Impressionist exhibitions: the gouache *The Children* (1880, National Gallery of Art, Washington, DC) showing most probably his sons Félix and Ludovic-Rodolphe drawing at a table, which emphasizes the role of art in Pissarro's pedagogical approach.[8]

Landscapes filled with sunlight and atmospheric effects dominate the popular understanding of Impressionism. However, Pissarro also inventively engaged with the still life genre and, like many of his peers, defied artistic conventions.[9] During the 1870s, Pissarro created still lifes of floral compositions in domestic spaces. The featured bouquets were often arranged by Julie Pissarro and included flowers from her garden. Early in their relationship, Julie worked as a florist, and she later took pride in growing pink peonies, which Pissarro depicted in several of his still lifes, including *Vase of Peonies and Mock Orange* (cat. 32). These paintings provide us with a lens into their domestic interior as we get to see it on several occasions. For instance, *Chrysanthemums in a Chinese Vase* (cat. 31) shows the same patterned wallpaper as Pissarro's self-portrait from 1873 and two other still lifes from the early 1870s.[10] The delicately executed flowers on the wallpaper repeat the colors and shapes of the bouquet of white, yellow, and red chrysanthemums. They also resonate with the exotically patterned vase in which the chrysanthemums are displayed. Like the family portraits, these still lifes celebrate the Pissarros' domestic life in the country while rendering artistic homage to this modest way of living.

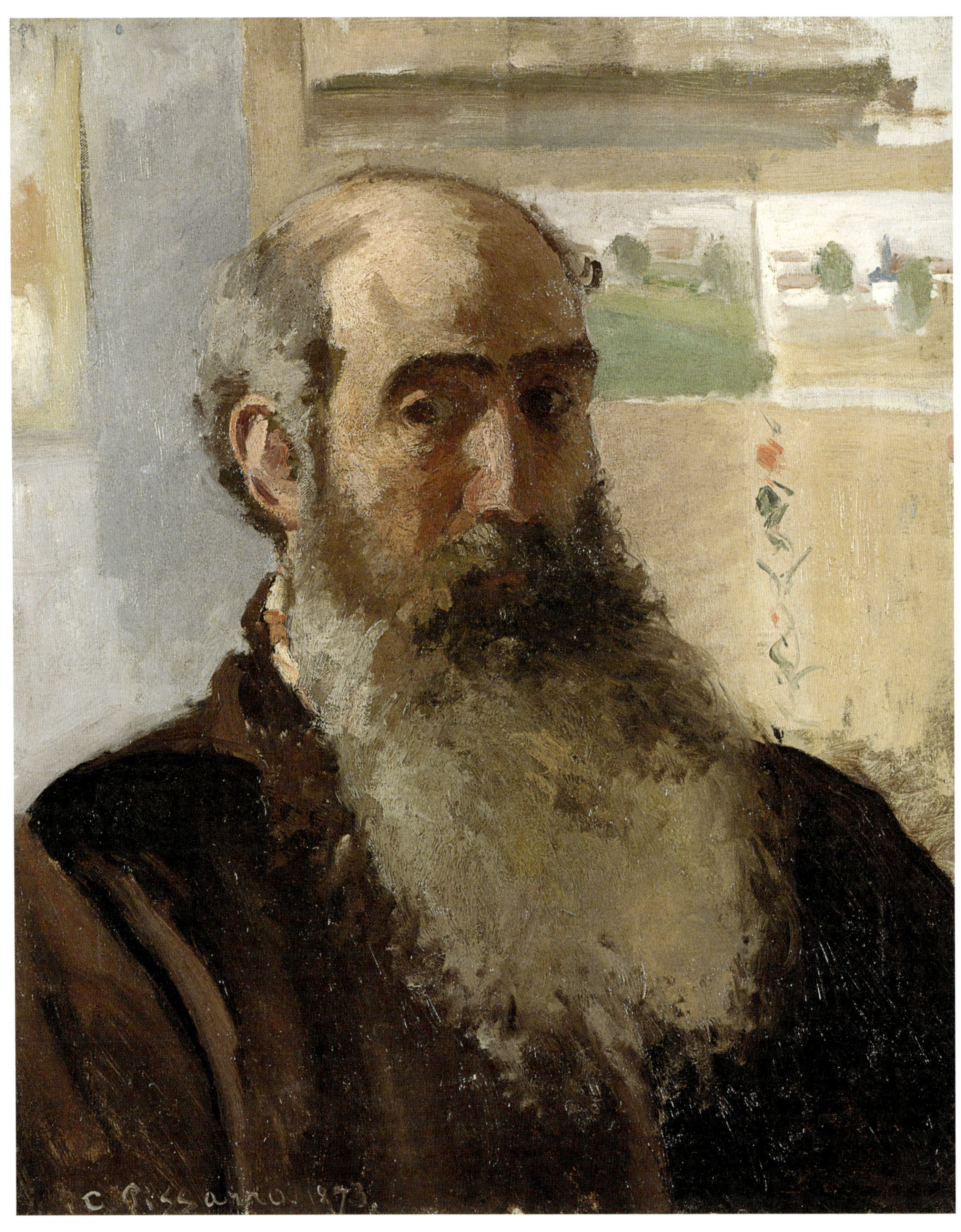

26
Portrait of the Artist, 1873
Musée d'Orsay, Paris, Paul-Émile Pissarro Donation, 1930

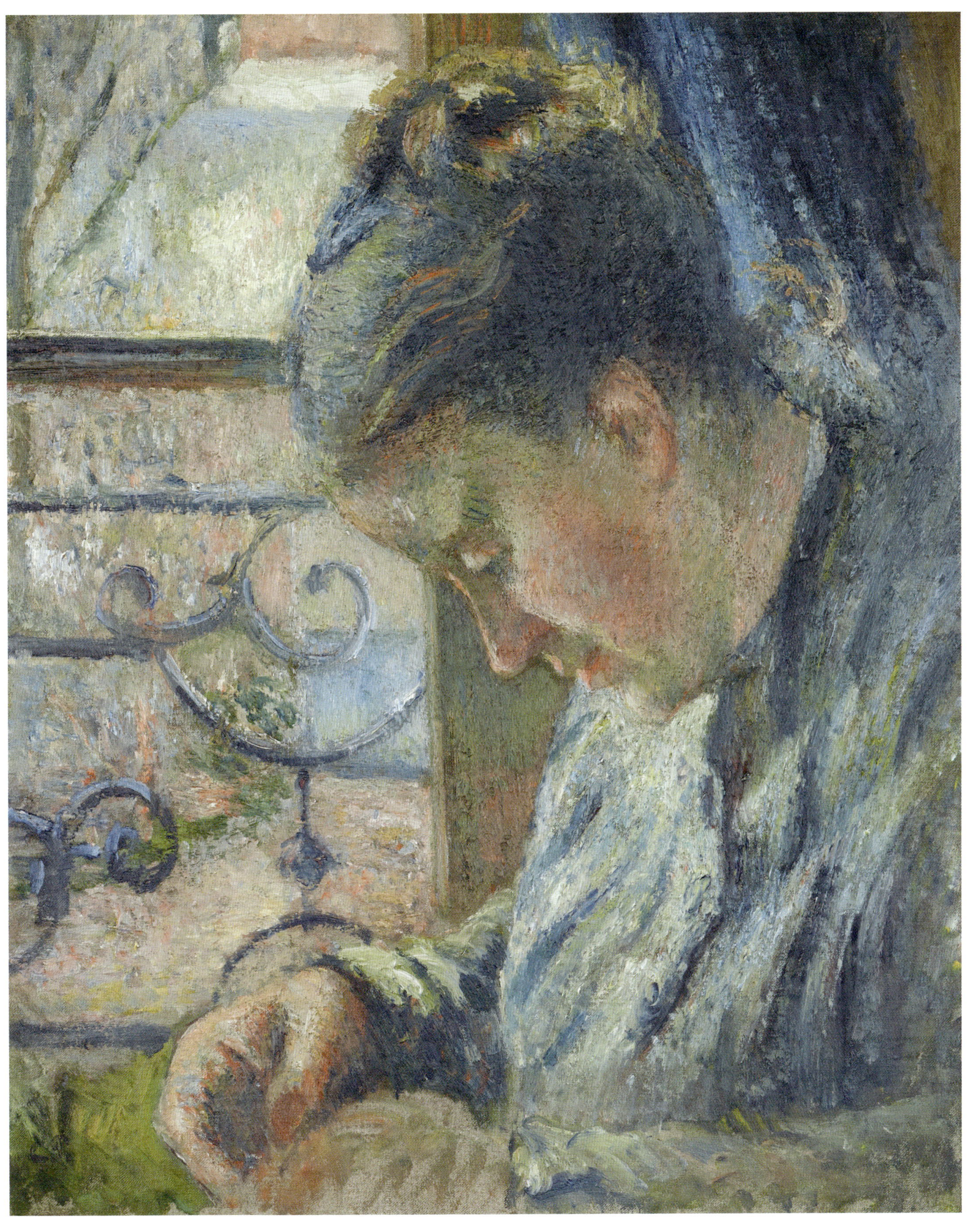

27
Julie Pissarro Sewing Beside a Window, ca. 1877
The Ashmolean Museum, University of Oxford, Presented by Esther Pissarro, 1951

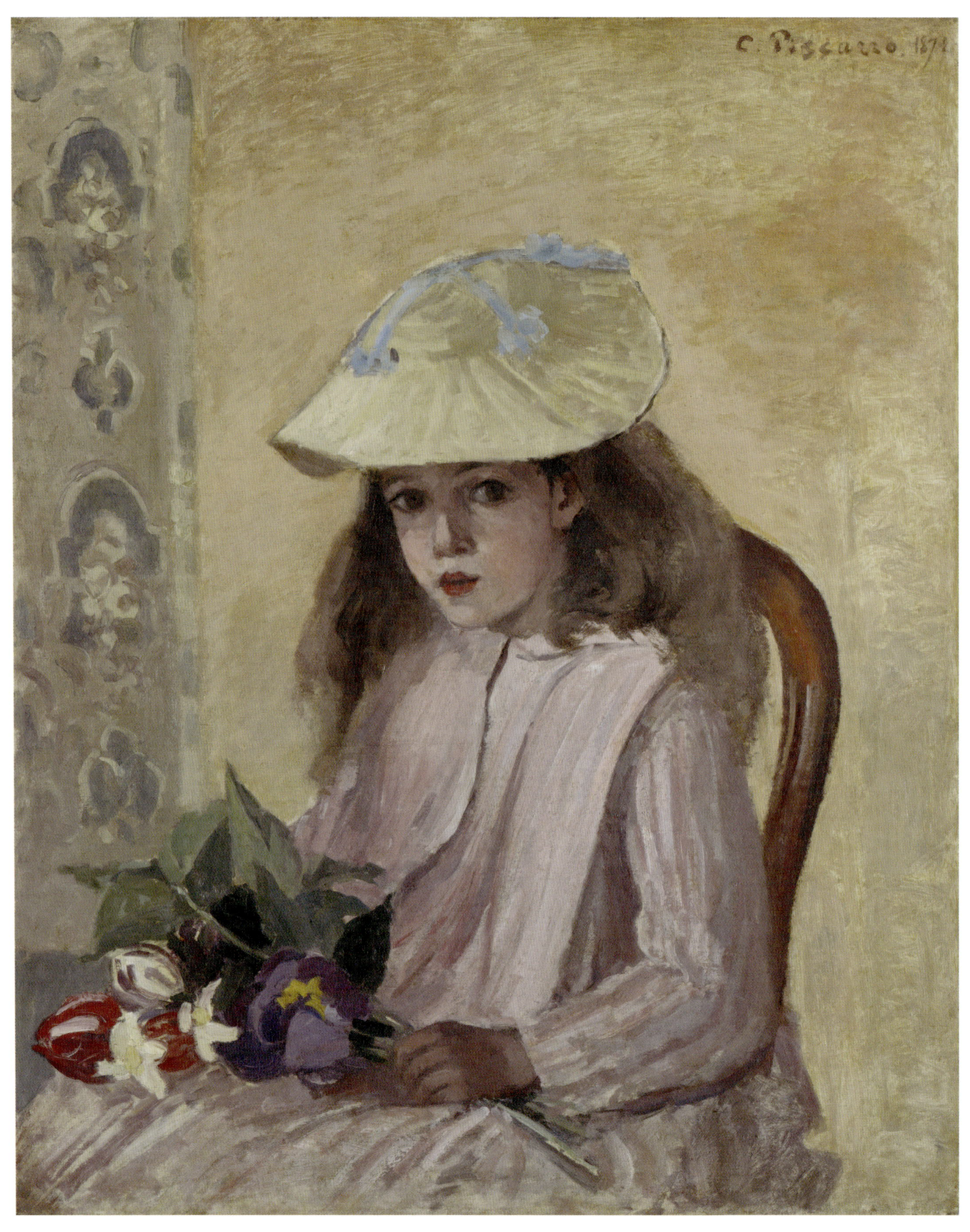

28
Portrait of Jeanne Pissarro, 1872
Yale University Art Gallery, New Haven, John Hay Whitney, B.A. 1926, M.A. (Hon.) 1956, Collection

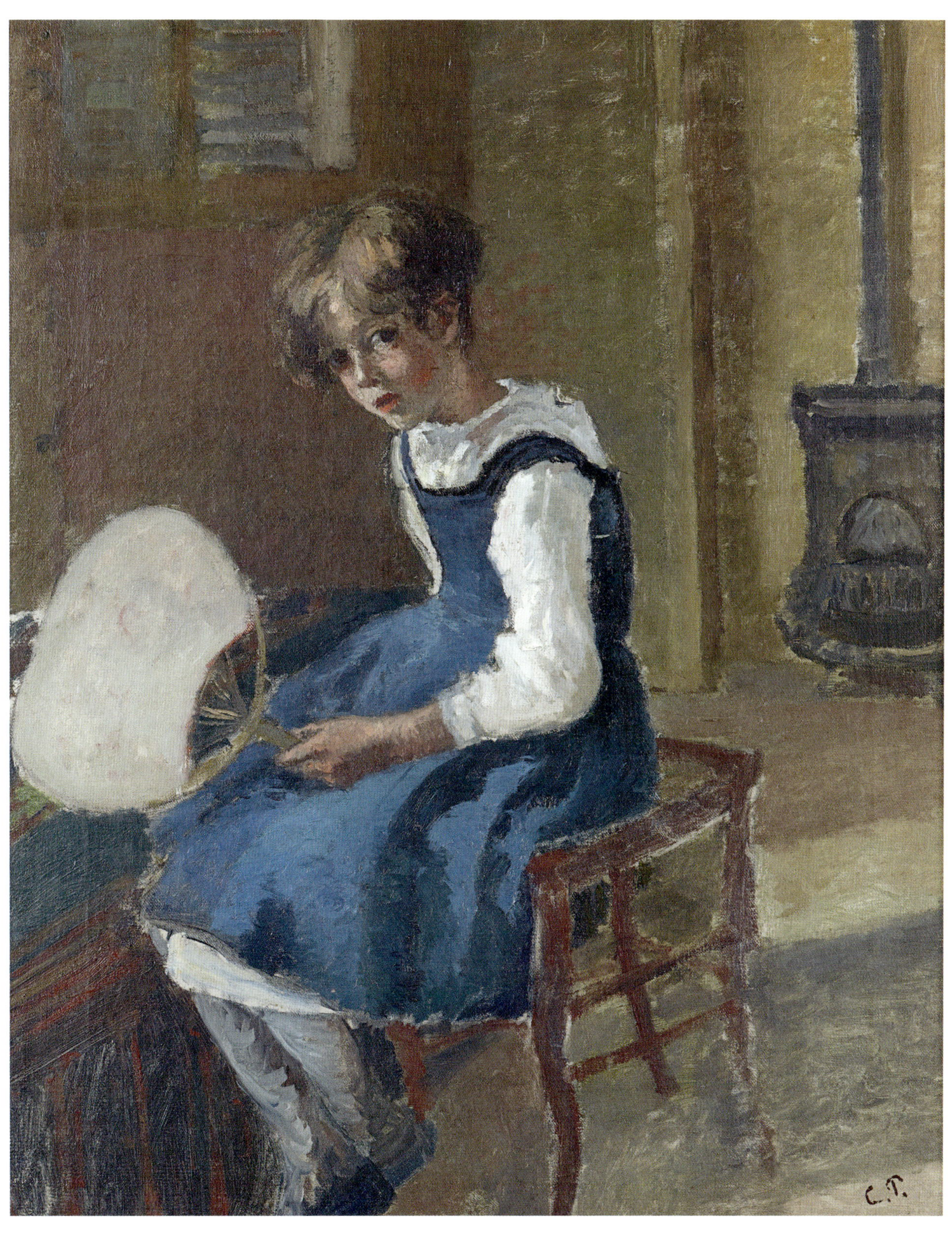

29
Jeanne Pissarro (Minette) Holding a Fan, ca. 1874
The Ashmolean Museum, University of Oxford, Bequeathed by Esther Pissarro, 1952

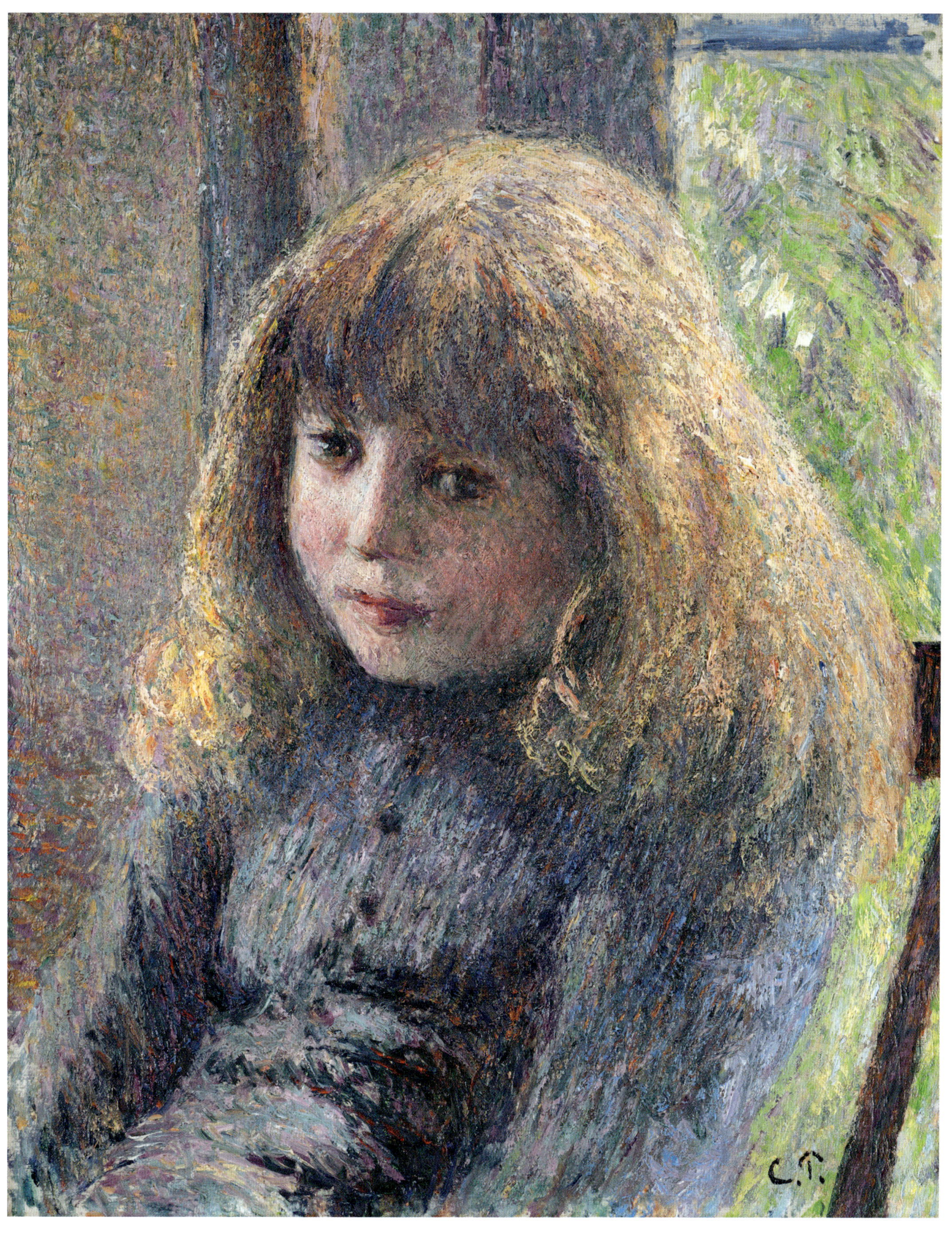

30
Portrait of Paul-Émile Pissarro, ca. 1890
Private collection

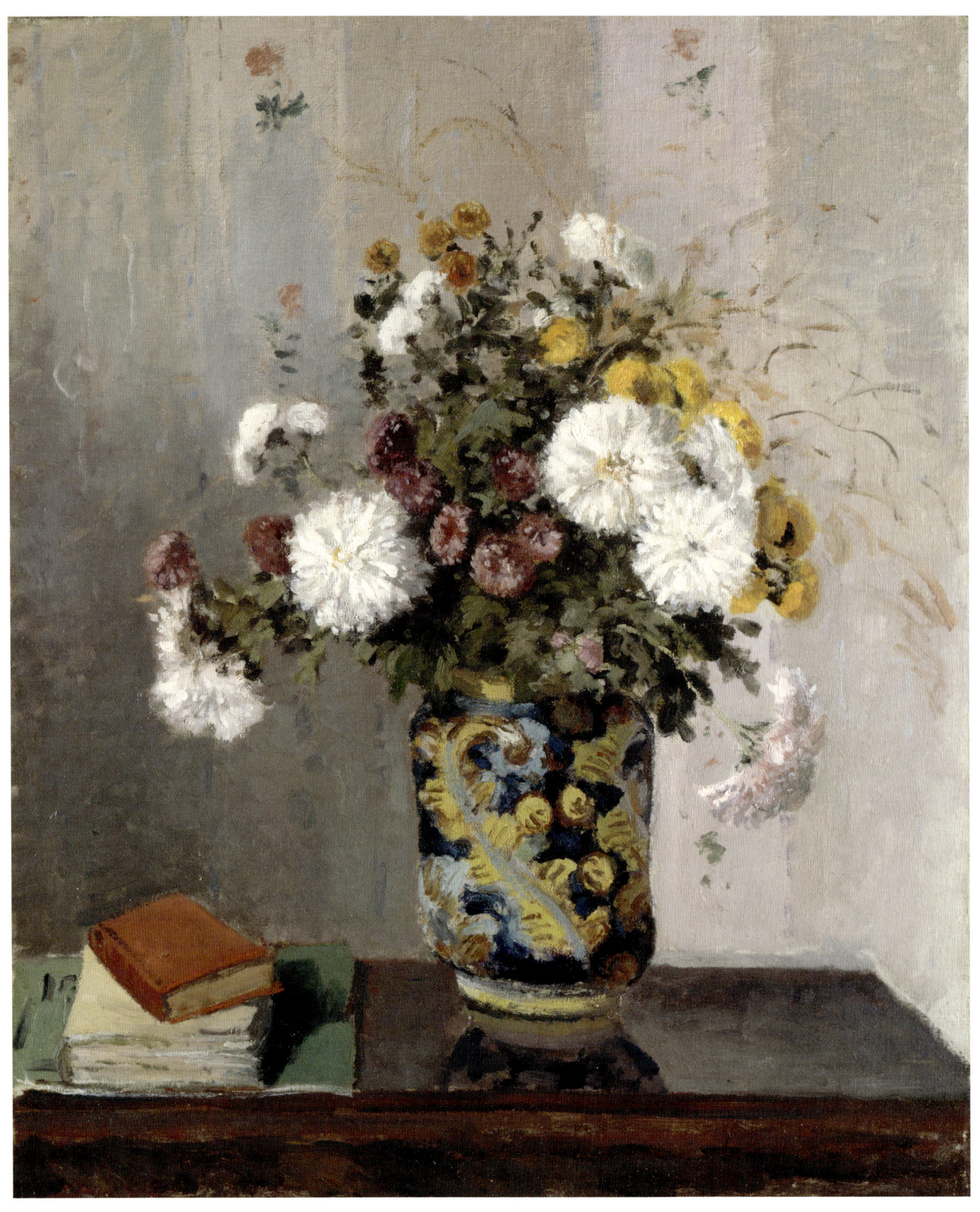

31
Chrysanthemums in a Chinese Vase, 1873
National Gallery of Ireland, Dublin, Purchased, 1983 (Shaw Fund)

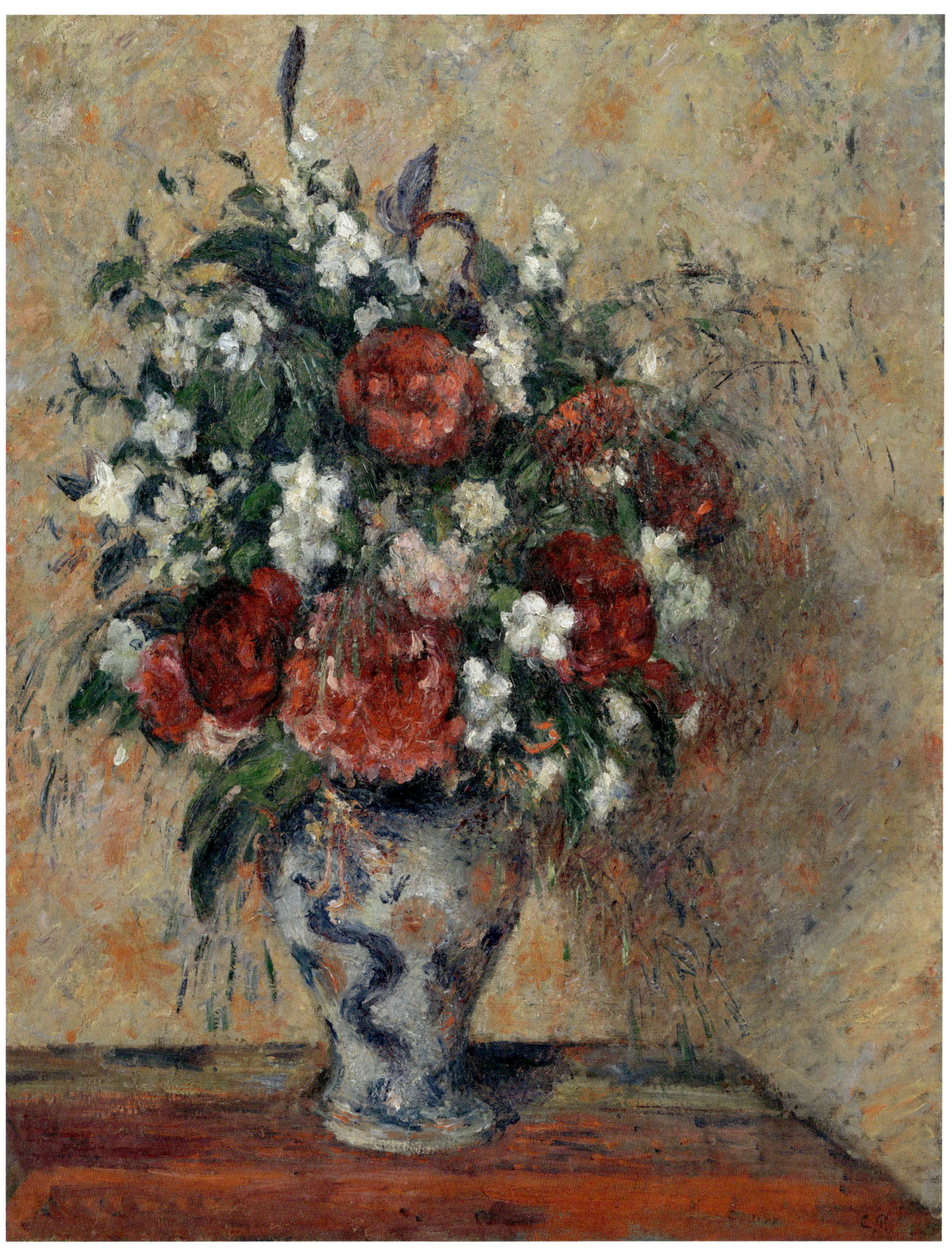

32
Vase of Peonies and Mock Orange, 1872–77
Van Gogh Museum, Amsterdam (gift from Sara Lee Corporation)

Clarisse Fava-Piz

Painting Outdoors
Pissarro's Impressionism

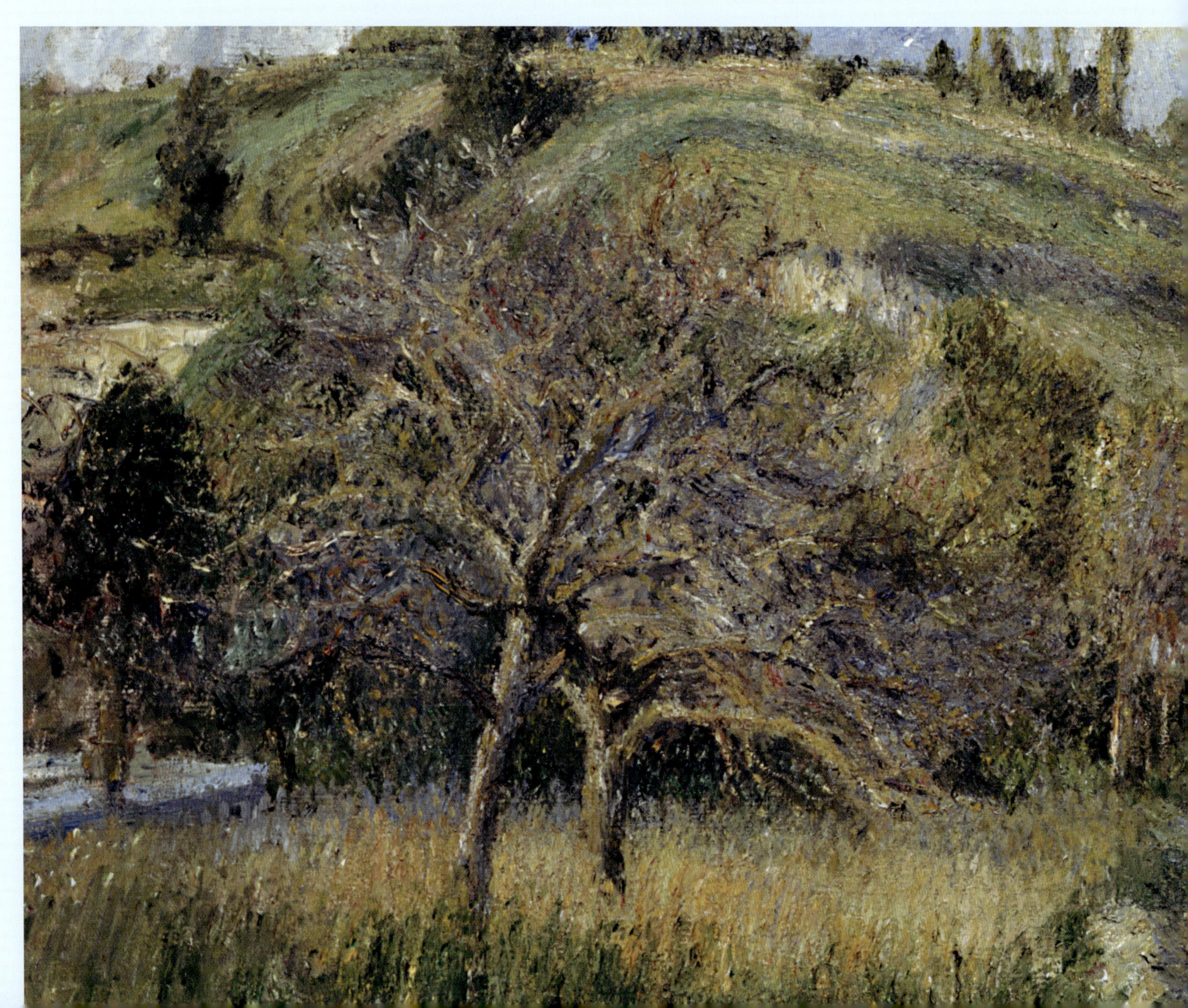

Camille Pissarro's unconventional, sketch-like plein-air painting was repeatedly rejected by the jury of the Paris Salon. To gain independence from these state-sponsored exhibitions, he helped found the Société Anonyme des Artistes Peintres, Sculpteurs, Graveurs, etc. in 1873 with fellow painters, including Claude Monet and Edgar Degas. Pissarro was the only artist to participate in all eight of the exhibitions organized by the group between 1874 and 1886. In the early years, he concentrated on landscapes painted at different times of day and year. From 1880 on, his interest shifted to figural peasant scenes, portraying contemporary rural life as a positive, fulfilling experience, without nostalgia or social criticism.

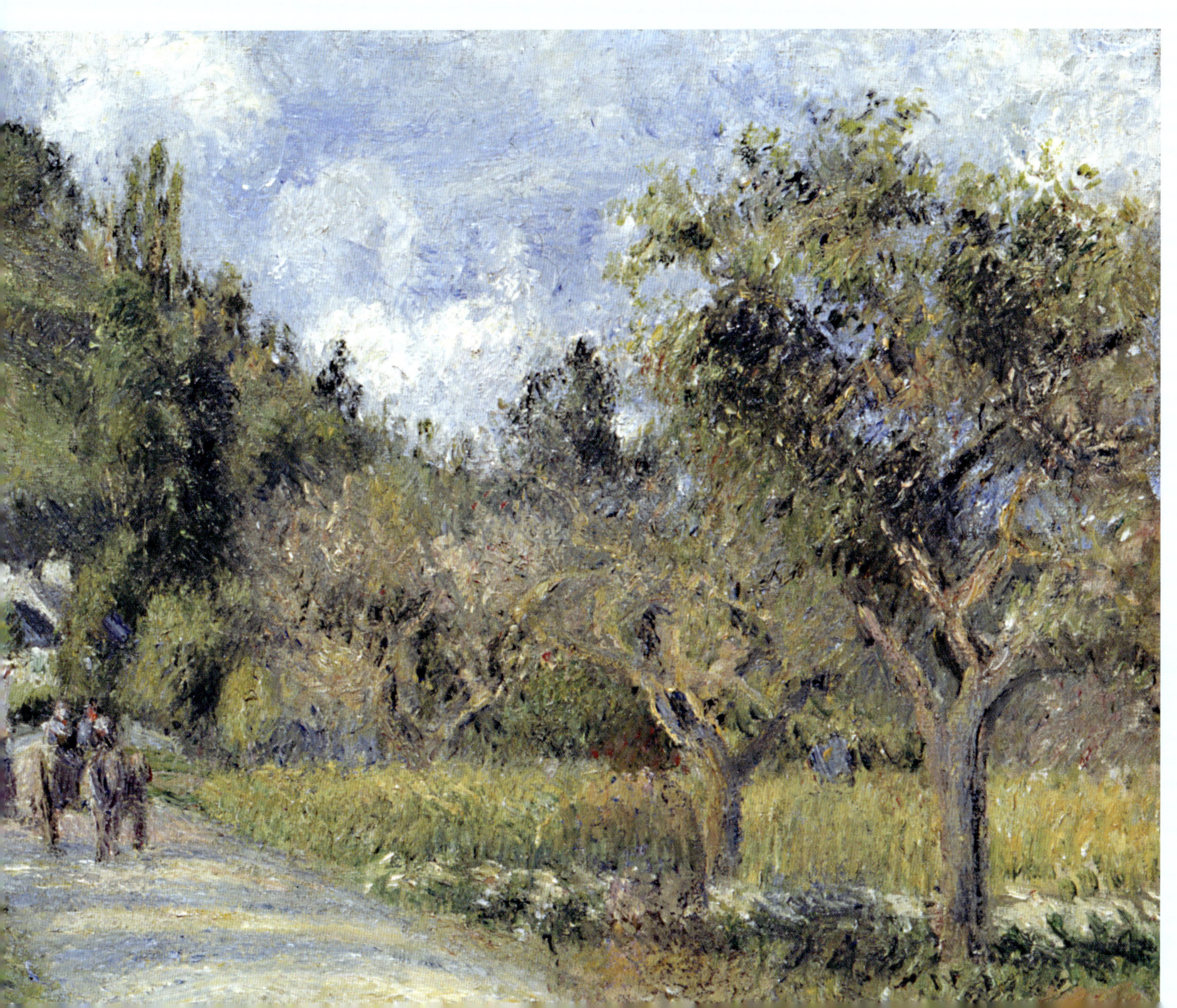

Despite its widespread popularity today, the art of the Impressionists was originally viewed as radical and unconventional. From the beginning, critics raged against this group of artists, using the term *impressionist* to denigrate the quick and summary nature of their works. In 1873 Pissarro was part of the group, alongside Claude Monet and Edgar Degas and others, who founded the Société Anonyme des Artistes Peintres, Sculpteurs, Graveurs, etc. (Anonymous Society of Painters, Sculptors, Engravers, etc.). They sought to break away from academic conventions and promote a new way of painting. Taking inspiration from contemporary life and everyday landscapes, they often worked outdoors and not solely in their studios like the academicians. The following year, they organized their first exhibition in the studio of the photographer Nadar at 35, Boulevard des Capucines in Paris, which displeased critics.

An indisputable figure in the Impressionist adventure, Pissarro was the only artist to renounce the Salon from that point on and participate in all eight Impressionist exhibitions.[1] Called the "father" or "pioneer" of the Impressionists, and even "first among the Impressionists," Pissarro has long been revered for his catalyzing role.[2] The eldest in the group—he was forty-four in 1874—he played a leading role in organizing the successive exhibitions and was not only friends with but also a mentor for many younger artists. Notably, he invited several artists working in the Neo-Impressionist vein—a style he himself was experimenting with—to participate in the last Impressionist exhibition in 1886. That same year he reported to Paul Durand-Ruel, his art dealer, "As for the rest of my history as a painter, it is linked to the Impressionist group."[3]

Hoarfrost (cat. 33) is one of the five paintings that Pissarro exhibited at the first Impressionist exhibition in 1874. This winter scene depicts the old road that led to the village of Ennery, located over the hillside northeast of Pontoise. The hill forms a horizontal strip that takes up two thirds of the composition. It is crisscrossed by the plowed furrows in the earth and the tall shadows of leafless trees, which to the dismay of critics were not visible in the painting. A man with a cane, carrying a large burden of sticks on his back, seems dwarfed by the heaviness of this winter landscape. The hoarfrost glitters in the frigid air, in a harmony of yellow, blue, and green. To convey the sensation of light, Pissarro let the brushstrokes remain visible, a loose painting style that many saw as revolutionary at the time.

Exhibited at the third Impressionist exhibition in April 1877, *The Garden of Les Mathurins at Pontoise* (cat. 39) is exceptional in Pissarro's oeuvre. Not only is it an unusually large painting for Pissarro, its subject matter is an anomaly within the artist's depictions of the rural world and everyday labor painted up to that point. Indeed, the pleasure garden of the Château des Mathurins, located in the neighborhood of L'Hermitage, a short distance from Pissarro's home in Pontoise, reveals the prosperous life of the wealthy—a subject more typically seen in Monet's paintings of bourgeois life in the 1860s and 1870s.[4] However, there is certainly more to this painting than the artificial veneer of its richly textured surface, well-ordered composition, saturated brushstrokes, and vivid colors. In the middle ground, the small figure of a woman in a long white dress, facing a gazing globe while reading a letter or a pamphlet, might be feminist Maria Deraismes (1828–1894), who lived on this prosperous estate. Far from the type of bourgeois women of leisure celebrated by Monet and Pierre-Auguste Renoir, she was an activist, with whom Pissarro shared political views. During and after the Paris Commune, she wrote political pamphlets and contributed to one of the earliest feminist newspapers in France, *Le Droit des femmes.* Despite its manicured luxuriousness, the garden signals a politically charged space—the stage for feminist gatherings.[5]

Starting in 1880, figures took on greater importance in Pissarro's paintings until, for an extended period of time, they became the main subject. While Pissarro had previously carefully integrated them into their environments, they now dominated the compositions, and the landscape became secondary. Pissarro sent several figure paintings to the sixth and seventh Impressionist exhibitions of 1881 and 1882. *Washerwoman, Study* (cat. 40), *Peasant Girl with a Straw Hat* (cat. 41), and *The Sheperdess* (cat. 42) were among the fourteen figure paintings he displayed at the 1882 exhibition, which also included six figure paintings by Gustave Caillebotte, five by Paul Gauguin, four by Berthe Morisot, and ten by Renoir.[6] These three paintings, remarkable for their aesthetic quality and monumentality, are steadfastly "rural portraits" and continue Pissarro's interest in workers and daily life.[7] In the late 1800s, it was uncommon to dedicate portraits to ordinary people. Pissarro's portraits of female workers seated, leaning, or lying on the grass (fig. p. 21) were radical in their celebration of the French rural life.

In *The Sheperdess,* a young peasant girl rests on the grass, carried away in her own thoughts. The full-length figure and the shallow space around her give the painting a sense of theatricality. *Peasant Girl with a Straw Hat* also shows a young girl seated on a grassy hillside but in a classic three-quarter portrait pose. With her hands clasped in her lap and looking away from the viewer, she possesses restraint and dignity. While the identity of the young girl is unknown, *Washerwoman, Study* represents fifty-six-year-old Marie Adeline Larchevêque, Pissarro's neighbor in Pontoise, also called "Mother Larchevêque." She sits quietly in a contained and meditative pose, showing the wisdom of her age. Perhaps to comply with the expectations on the subject matter for an audience who expected portraits of well-to-do sitters—not workers—Pissarro displayed the painting under the generic title *Washerwoman, Study,* turning it into the depiction of a type instead of identifying the sitter of the portrait.[8]

Pissarro's portraits of rural women presented at the Impressionist exhibitions did seduce some prominent contemporary critics, including Joris-Karl Huysmans, who commented in 1882, "Mr. Pissarro has completely freed himself from Millet's memories; he paints his country people, without false grandeur, simply, as he sees them. His delightful little girls in red stockings, his old woman resting, his shepherdesses and washerwomen, his peasant women eating lunch or working the grass are real little masterpieces."[9] Indeed, Pissarro's rural figures were often compared to those painted by Jean-François Millet, but the artist did not embrace the comparison.[10] Instead, as Huysmans astutely analyzed, Pissarro invented new ways to depict rural life, based on his intimate observation of it and not on nostalgic tropes popular in earlier nineteenth-century interpretations of the subject. Pissarro's Impressionism was tied to the artist's representation of the contemporary rural world in which he lived, driven by his anarchist sympathies and care for his neighbors.

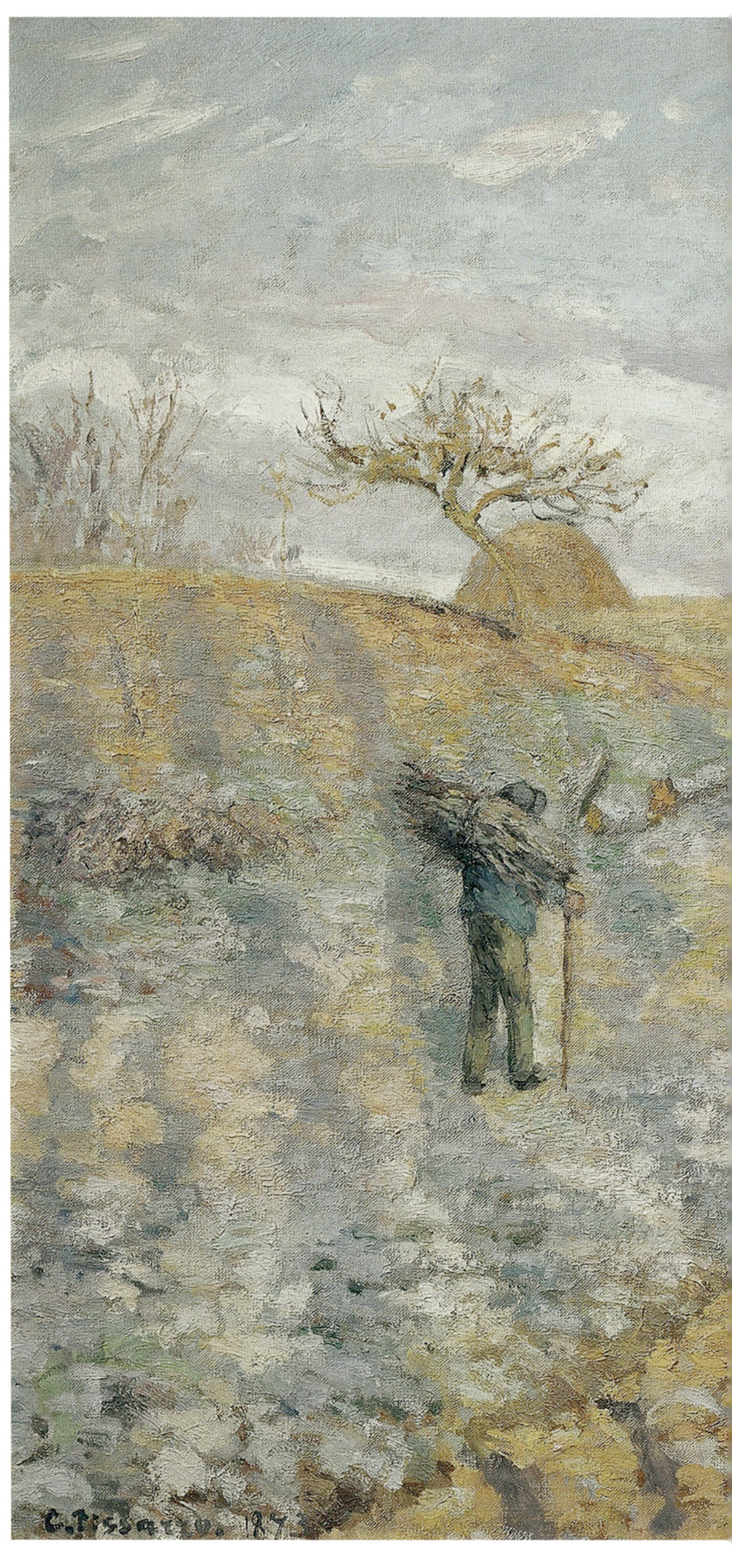

33
Hoarfrost, 1873
Musée d'Orsay, Paris, Bequest of Enriqueta Alsop
in the name of Dr. Eduardo Mollard, 1972

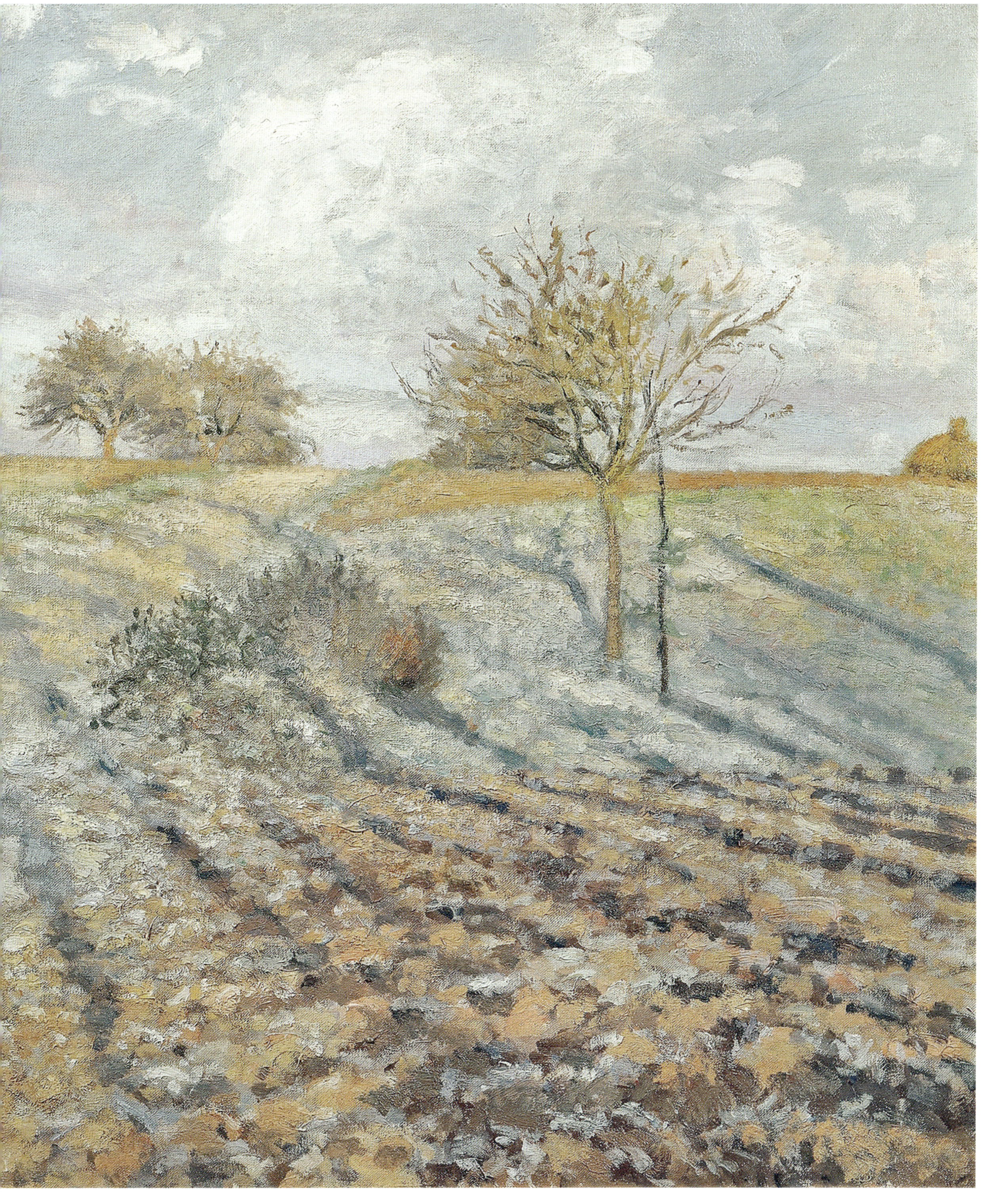

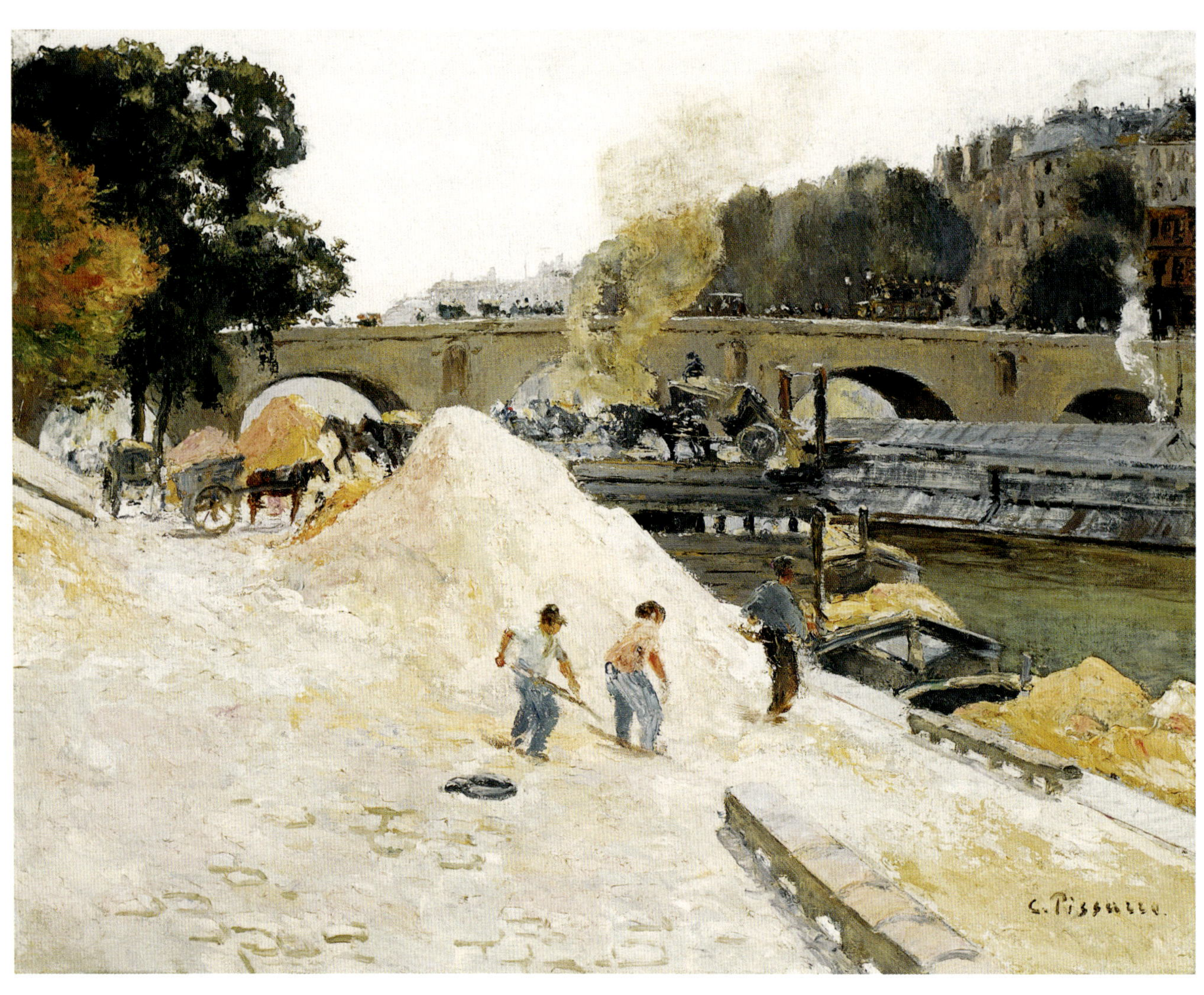

34
The Pont-Marie Viewed from the Quai d'Anjou, Paris, ca. 1875
Colección Pérez Simón

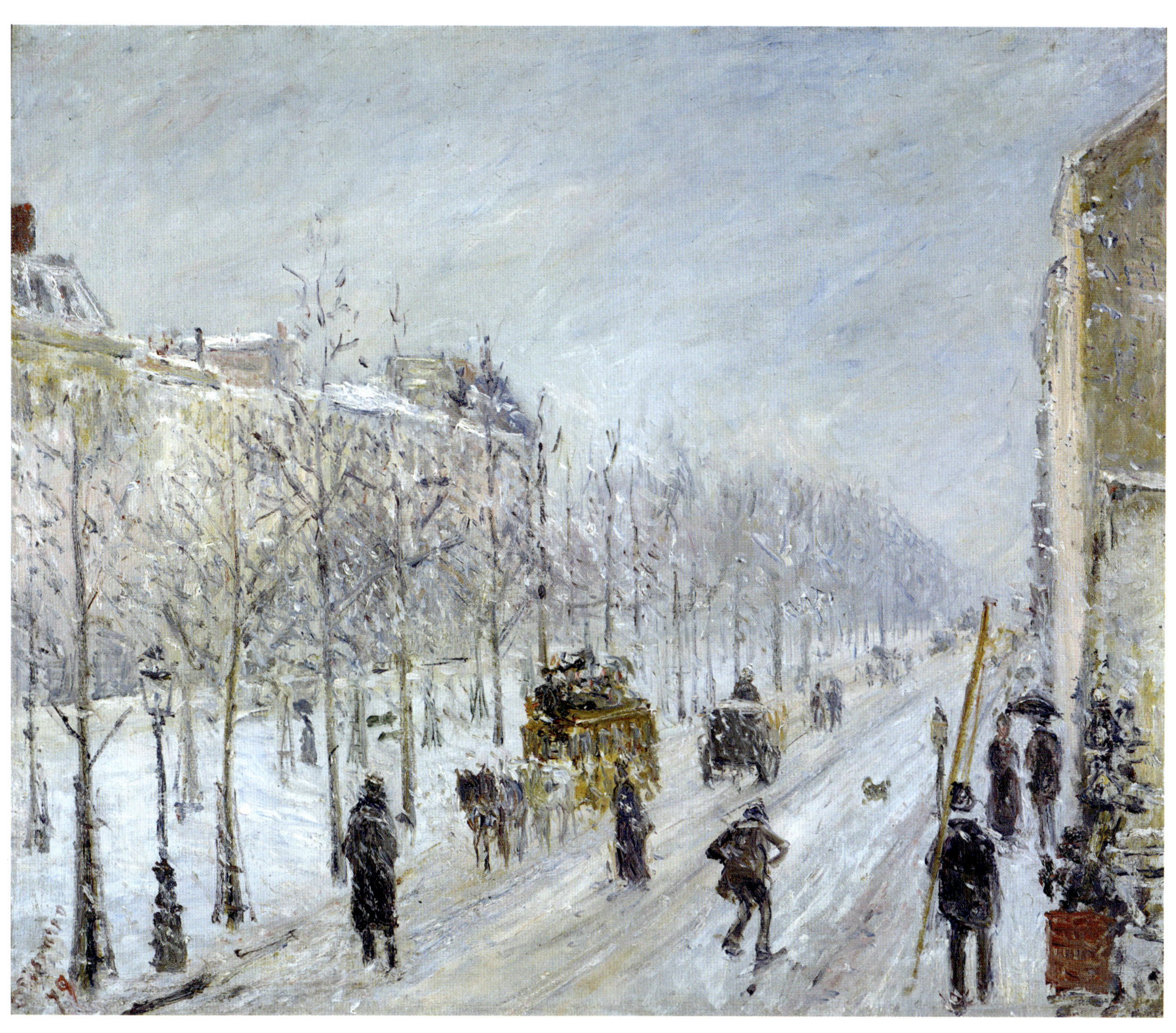

35
The Boulevards Extérieurs, Effect of Snow, 1879
Musée Marmottan Monet, Paris, Gift of Eugène and Victorine Donop de Monchy, 1940

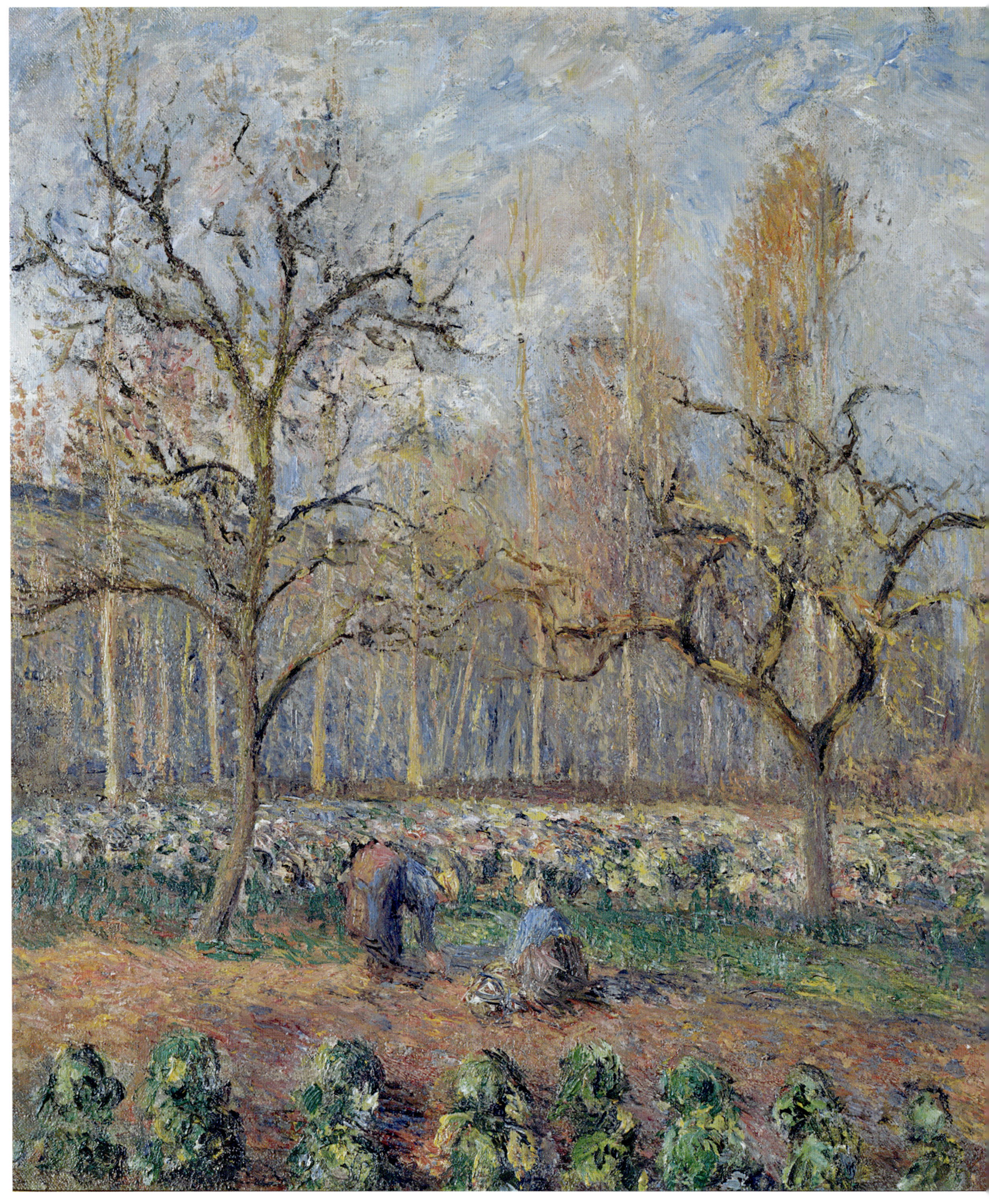

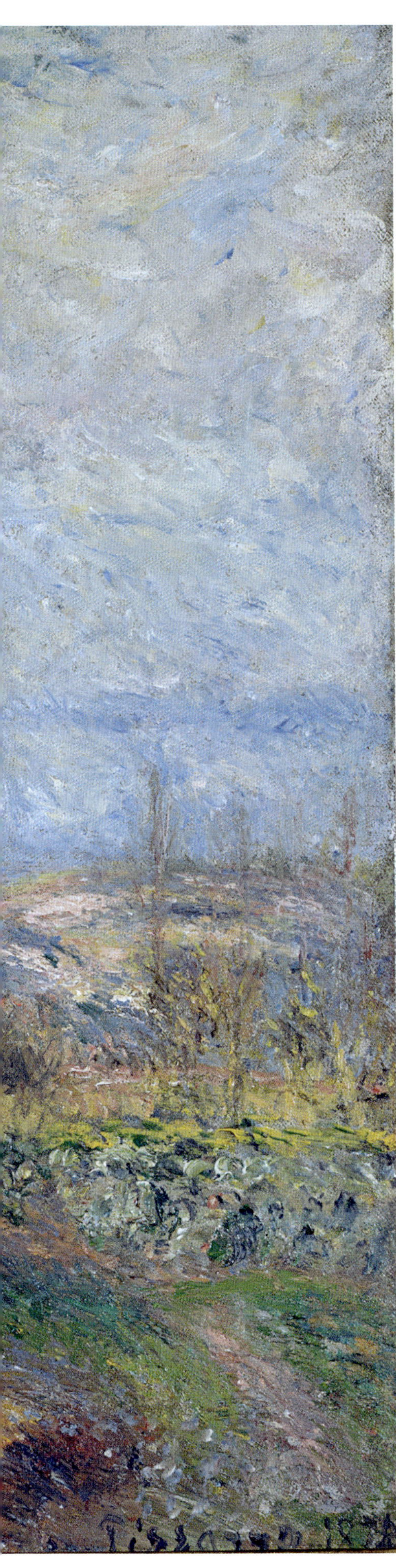

36
Orchard at Pontoise, Sunset, 1878
Wallraf-Richartz-Museum & Fondation Corboud, Cologne

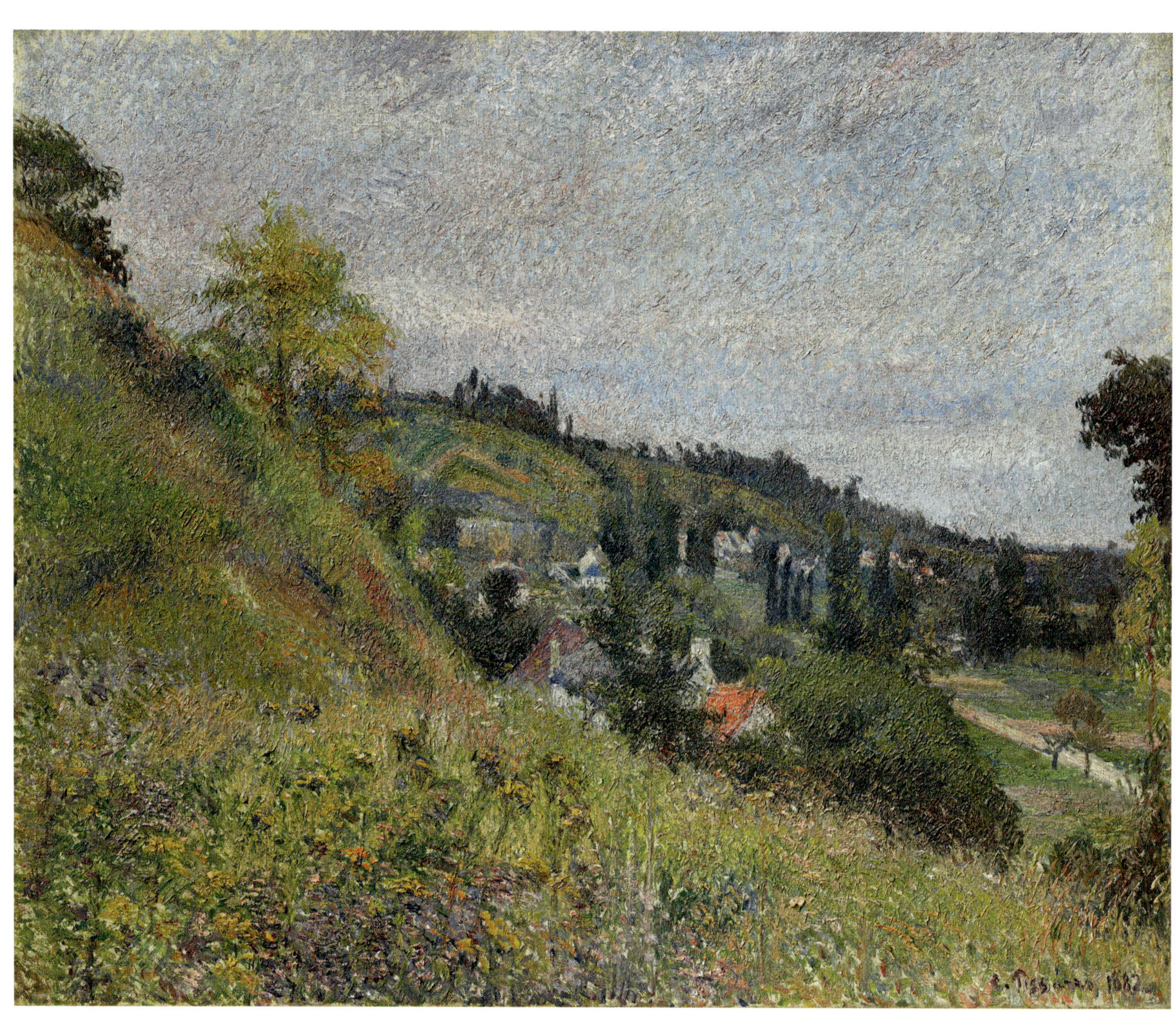

37
The Hills at Le Chou, Pontoise, 1882
Hasso Plattner Collection, Museum Barberini, Potsdam

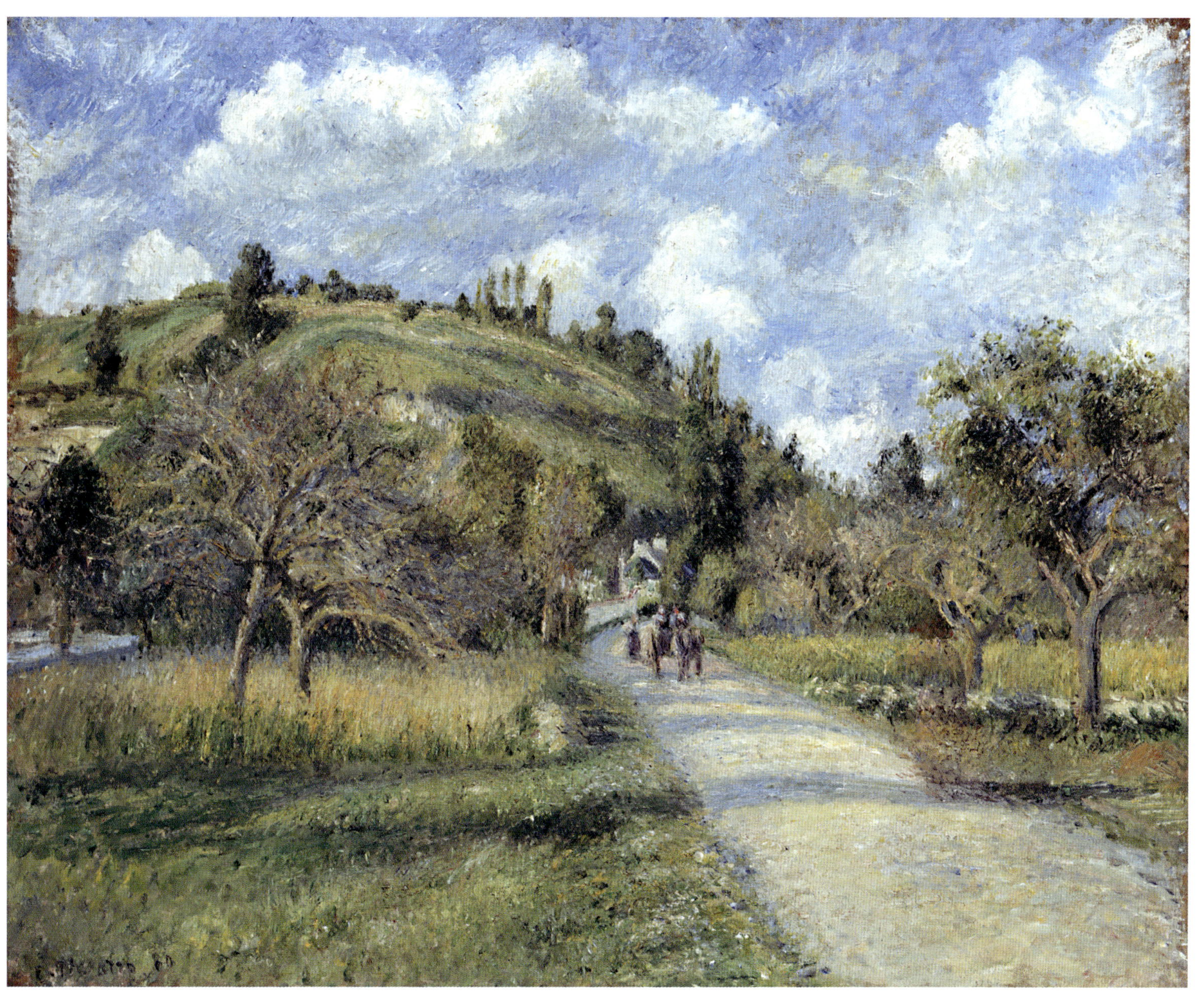

38
The Highway (La Côte du Valhermeil, Auvers-sur-Oise), 1880
The Baltimore Museum of Art, The Cone Collection, formed by Dr. Claribel Cone and Miss Etta Cone of Baltimore, Maryland

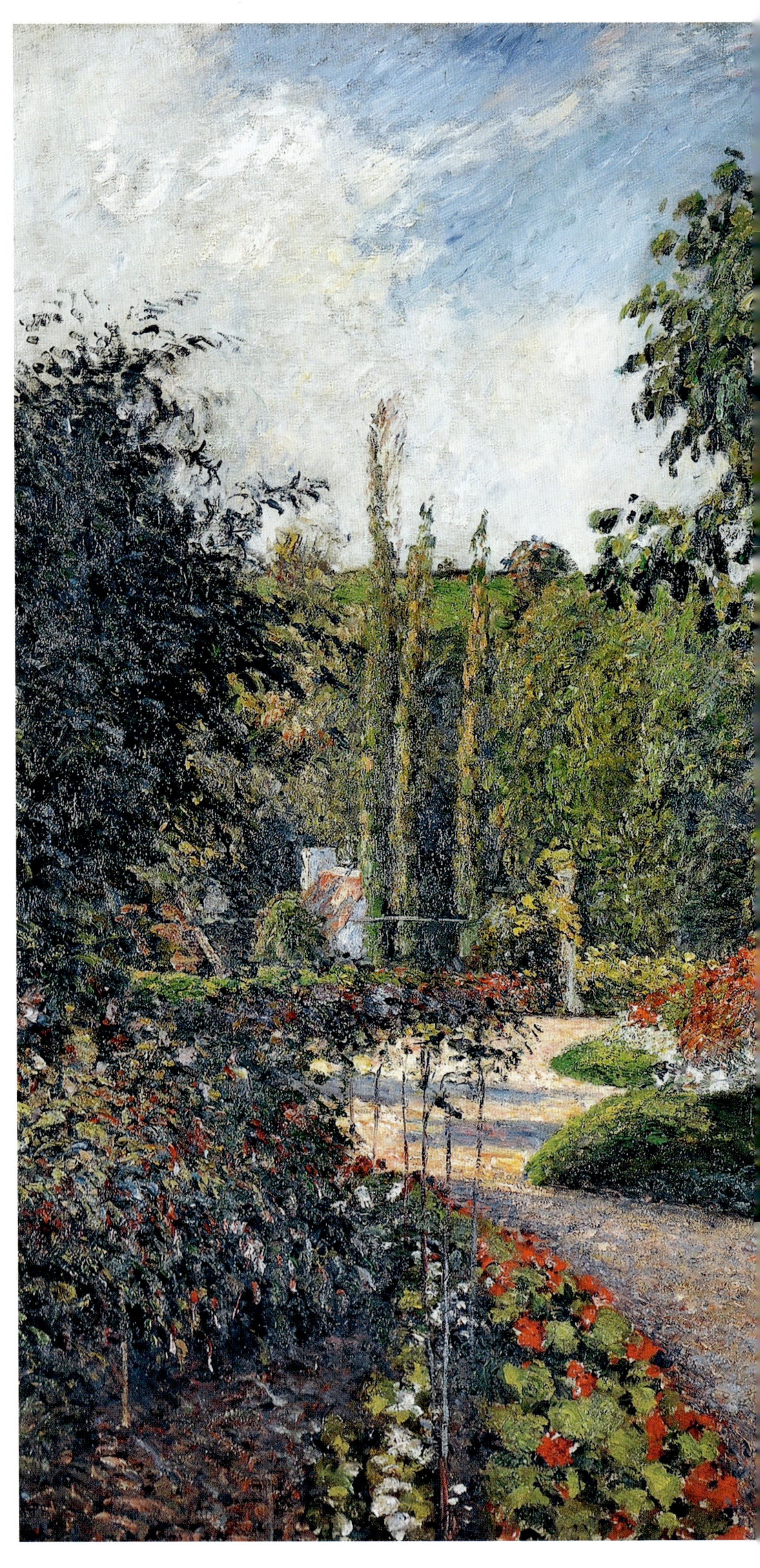

39
The Garden of Les Mathurins at Pontoise, 1876
The Nelson-Atkins Museum of Art, Kansas City, Missouri,
Purchase: William Rockhill Nelson Trust

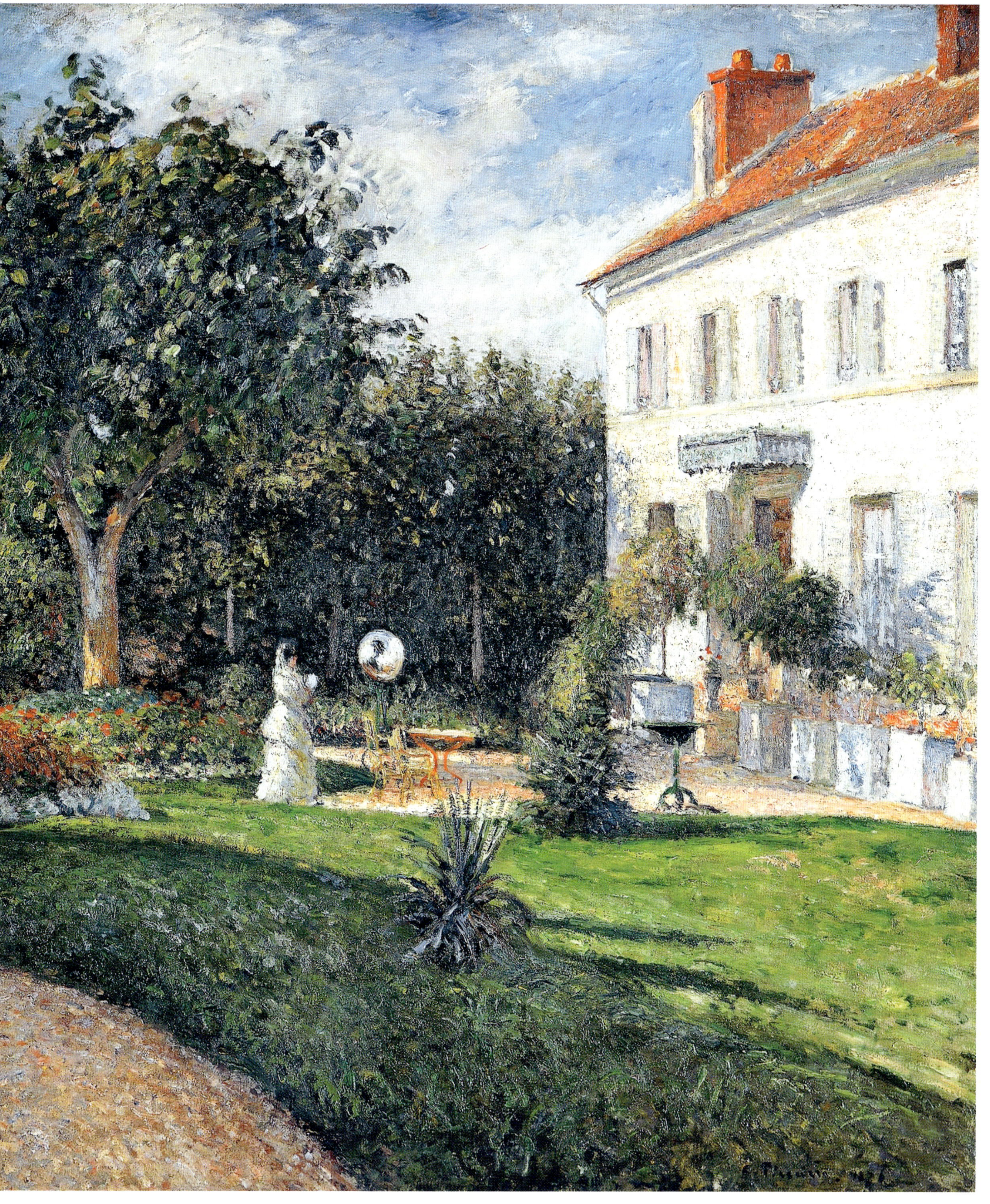

Rural Community
Harvest and Market Scenes

Clarisse Fava-Piz

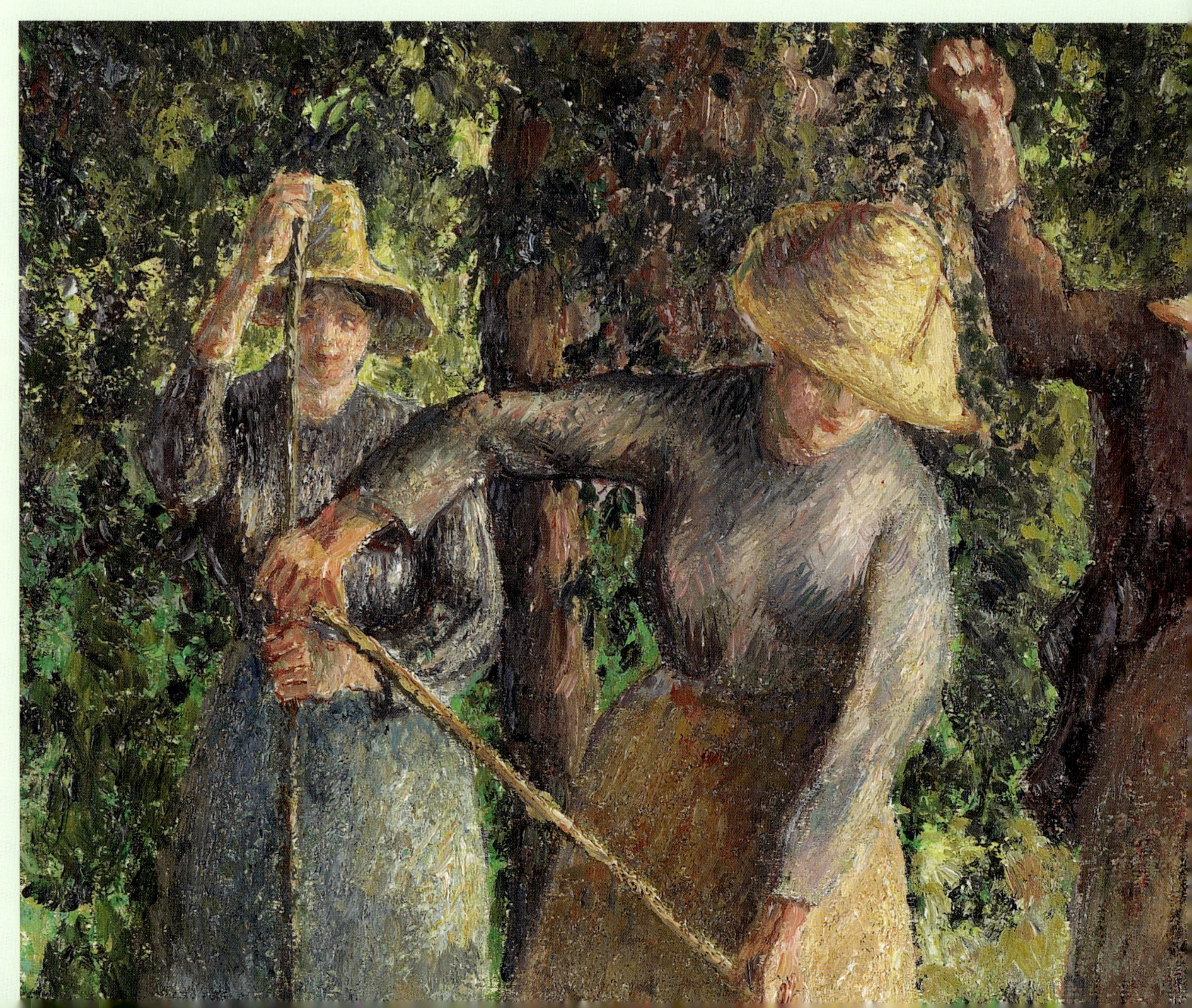

Camille Pissarro presents his ideal of country life in a wide variety of media. He shows women harvesting hay or picking grapes, performing their work easily and rhythmically, as if it were choreographed. At times, they pause for a moment, suggesting the peaceful, fulfilling nature of their activity. Pissarro's stylization of the figures lends them a timeless quality and imbues his carefully developed compositions with universal meaning. The themes evoked by the harvest pictures are continued in lively market scenes in which women offer their agricultural produce for sale. Like the ideal of rural life, the balanced relationship between production and consumption corresponds to Pissarro's anarchist convictions.

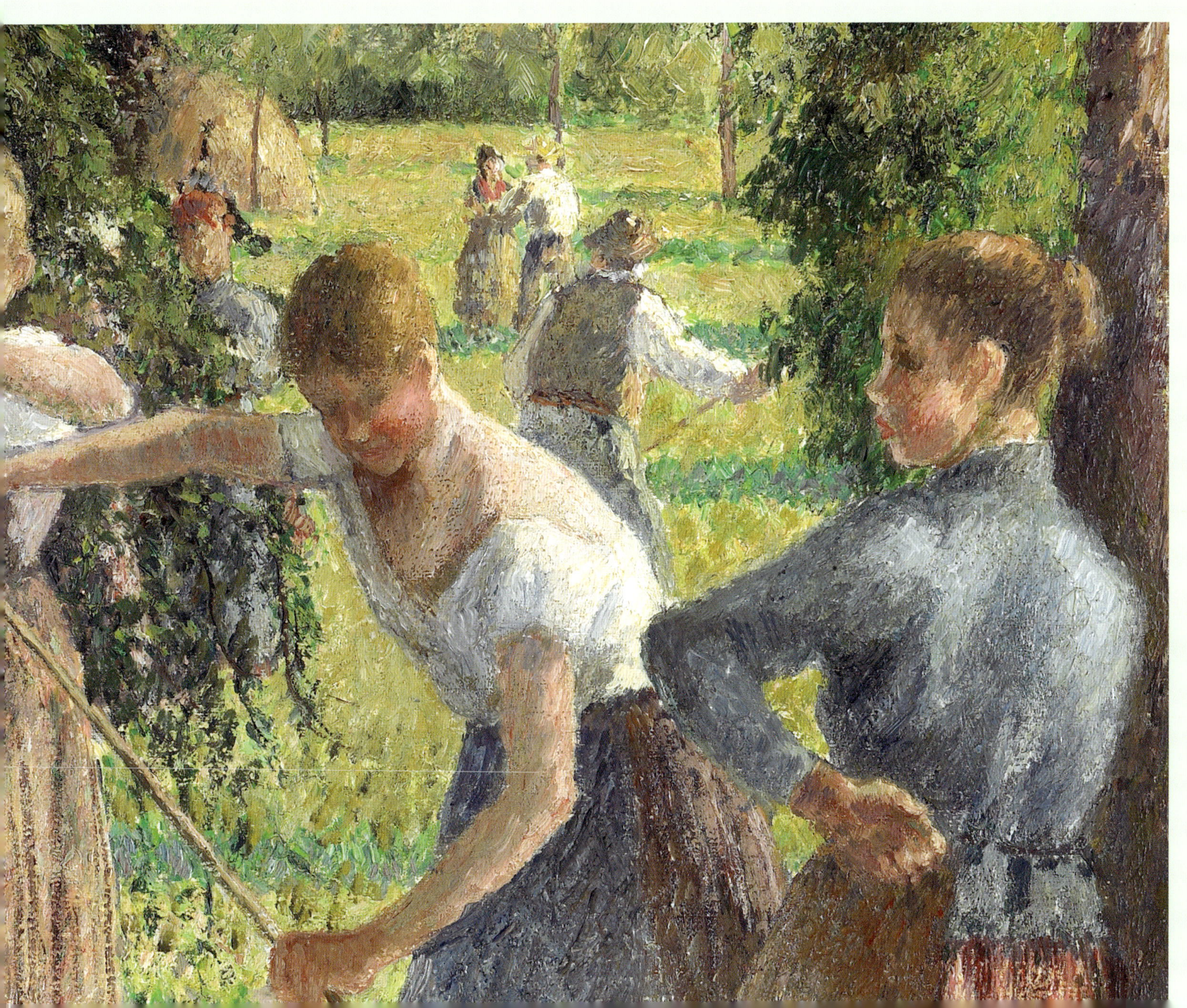

Dressed in simple colored blouses and aprons, wearing large straw hats or headscarves, young women work the fields in harmony (cats. 43, 44, 49). Their facial features are either shielded or generalized, in contrast with the individual portraits that Camille Pissarro depicted in his single-figure paintings (cats. 40–42, see p. 95). Their postures, the tilts of their heads, and the way they hold their rakes set the cadence of their work, their bodies set in motion. Rather than toil or drudgery, this rural labor resembles a dance. Taking cues from Edgar Degas, Pissarro created a visual repertoire of discrete rural movements, in which labor and rest coexist, not unlike his colleague's opera dancers.[1]

Pissarro's rural world contrasts with what was traditionally associated with the peasantry, where labor was often difficult, demeaning, and relentless. Instead, the artist's reading of anarchist thinkers, such as Élisée Reclus and Pyotr Kropotkin, inflected his compositions, giving primacy to the representation of work that is both productive and fulfilling.[2] Indeed, Pissarro's rural images of the 1880s and 1890s show the simple pleasures and ease of life in the countryside. In both *The Haymaker* (cat. 45) and *Gardener Standing by a Haystack, Overcast Sky, Éragny* (cat. 46), a single figure stands in a field, caught in a moment of pause, but without strain or exhaustion. Notably, labor is not confined to a male-dominated field in Pissarro's oeuvre. Quite the opposite, Pissarro's rural world is overwhelmingly governed by women. Scholar Richard R. Brettell suggested that because many men were employed in local industries, rural workers in the artist's vicinity were mostly women.[3] Moreover, his choice of young, vital women laborers as subjects relates to a new type of beauty the artist was searching for, one without the eroticism found in the pastoral tradition that grew out of the legacy of eighteenth-century painters such as François Boucher and Jean-Honoré Fragonard.

Pissarro's complex compositions, in which numerous figures populate a country landscape filled with warmth and light, are based on sketches. *Pea Harvesters* (cat. 47), for instance, demonstrates his working method: he modeled each figure individually, giving a sculptural quality to their rendering. He also tested numerous poses, different scales and placements of figures, and various colors. This prolific graphic production testifies to Pissarro's back-and-forth between working outdoors and in the studio.[4] It also demonstrates his heightened sense of experimentation: using a variety of support, such as fans, where themes range from everyday life in the fields, at home, and on the farm (cats. 50–53) to local fairs and markets (cats. 56, 58). Pissarro was fascinated by the economic interrelationship between work in the fields and the local markets and fairs. In contrast to the peasant imagery by Jean-François Millet and other French Realists and Naturalists, Pissarro balanced depictions of rural labor with the representation of the local marketing and consumption of agricultural products. The motifs are closely interrelated because the peasants first produce and then sell their own products without any intermediaries.[5]

Market scenes exist in a variety of mediums and scales that find no precedent in Pissarro's oeuvre. The artist explored the subject of markets in drawing, watercolor, gouache, tempera, pastel, etching, lithography, and oil paint. Brettell argues that Pissarro's representation of local markets corresponds to a form of pictorial anarchism linked to the anarchist idea of postrevolutionary economic behavior.[6] This included the understanding that there was a balanced relation between production and consumption. In contrast with the heightened anonymity of the large urban markets and the new department stores, small-town markets allowed for a certain intimacy and directness of food shopping. Beyond the contemplative state of some of his market figures, Pissarro crowded his scenes with buyers and sellers alike who chatted, gossiped, jostled, and bargained. It is a world dominated by women—the world of Julie Pissarro more than of Camille Pissarro. The artist's wife prided herself in negotiating good prices, and occasionally credit, in the markets of Pontoise and Gisors to feed the household.

Moreover, Pissarro's market scenes pay homage to his close friend Ludovic Piette, a painter of rural markets and a lifelong anarchist, who died in 1878 at the age of only fifty-one. Piette's panoramic views of regional markets were rather conventional and descriptive. If viewers were knowledgeable, they could likely locate the market based on the painted details. Pissarro, however, emphasized the study of the crowd rather than the place itself. *The Pork Butcher* (cat. 54), for instance, offers a close-up view of a butcher stall in which the central figure, a full-length woman seen in profile, is focused on her task. Some scholars have compared her to Degas's images of laundresses.[7] Pissarro's niece Eugénie Estruc, known as Nini, modeled as the butcher. Behind her, sellers and prospective buyers, of all social classes, crowd the compact composition. Rather than describe a specific, identifiable marketplace, Pissarro highlights female labor in action.

The Poultry Market at Pontoise (cat. 55) depicts the colorful atmosphere of the local open-air market. In this striking close-up, a woman selling eggs from her basket stands with her back to the viewer. Because we don't see her full face, we instead focus on the bustling energy of the market crowd just in front of her. This large-size painting stands out in Pissarro's oeuvre, and the experimental nature of the composition—the main figure's viewpoint, the great number of figures crammed in the background—make it an exceptional painting. Although it was not ready in time to be displayed at the 1882 Impressionist exhibition, where Pissarro made his debut as a figure painter, the painting was included in his first solo exhibition in 1883 at Galerie Durand-Ruel, among a greater number of works representing rural markets.[8] With his market scenes seen from close up, Pissarro immerses his viewer in a sensory world, evoking the tactility of handling produce as well as the smells and sounds of the bustling public space, while at the same time inviting them to participate in this form of market economy.

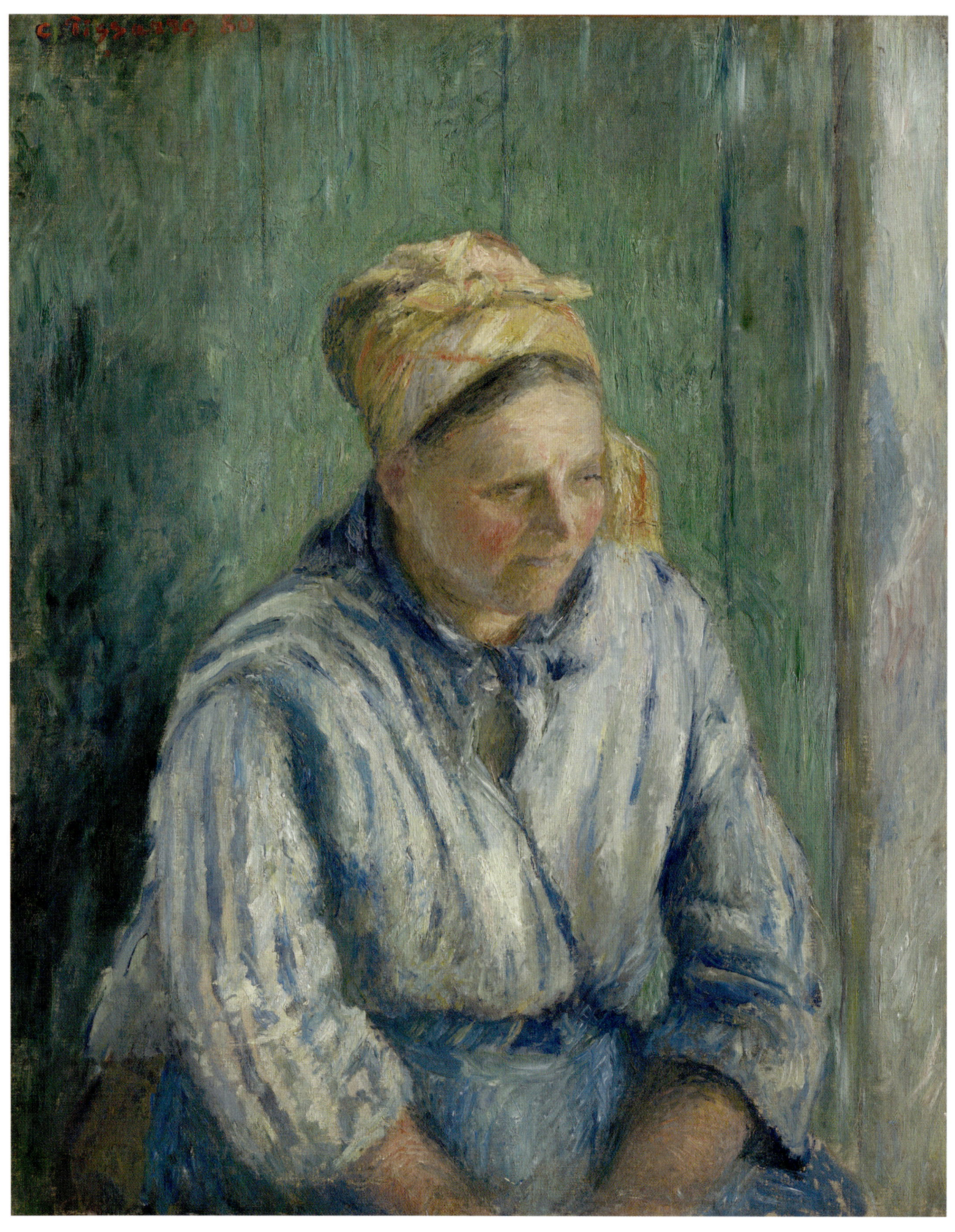

40
Washerwoman, Study, 1880
The Metropolitan Museum of Art, New York, Gift of Mr. and Mrs. Nate B. Spingold, 1956

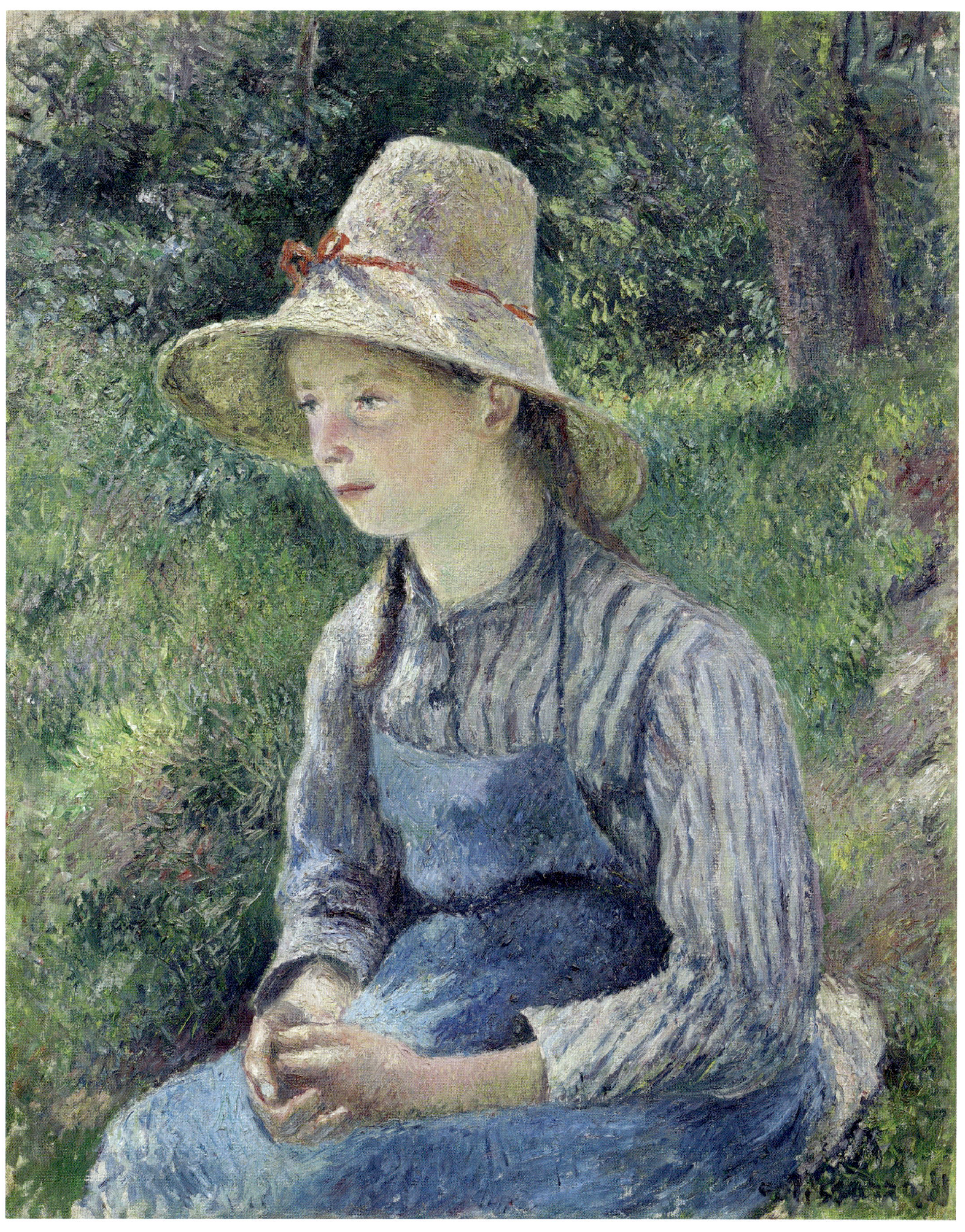

41
Peasant Girl with a Straw Hat, 1881
National Gallery of Art, Washington, Ailsa Mellon Bruce Collection

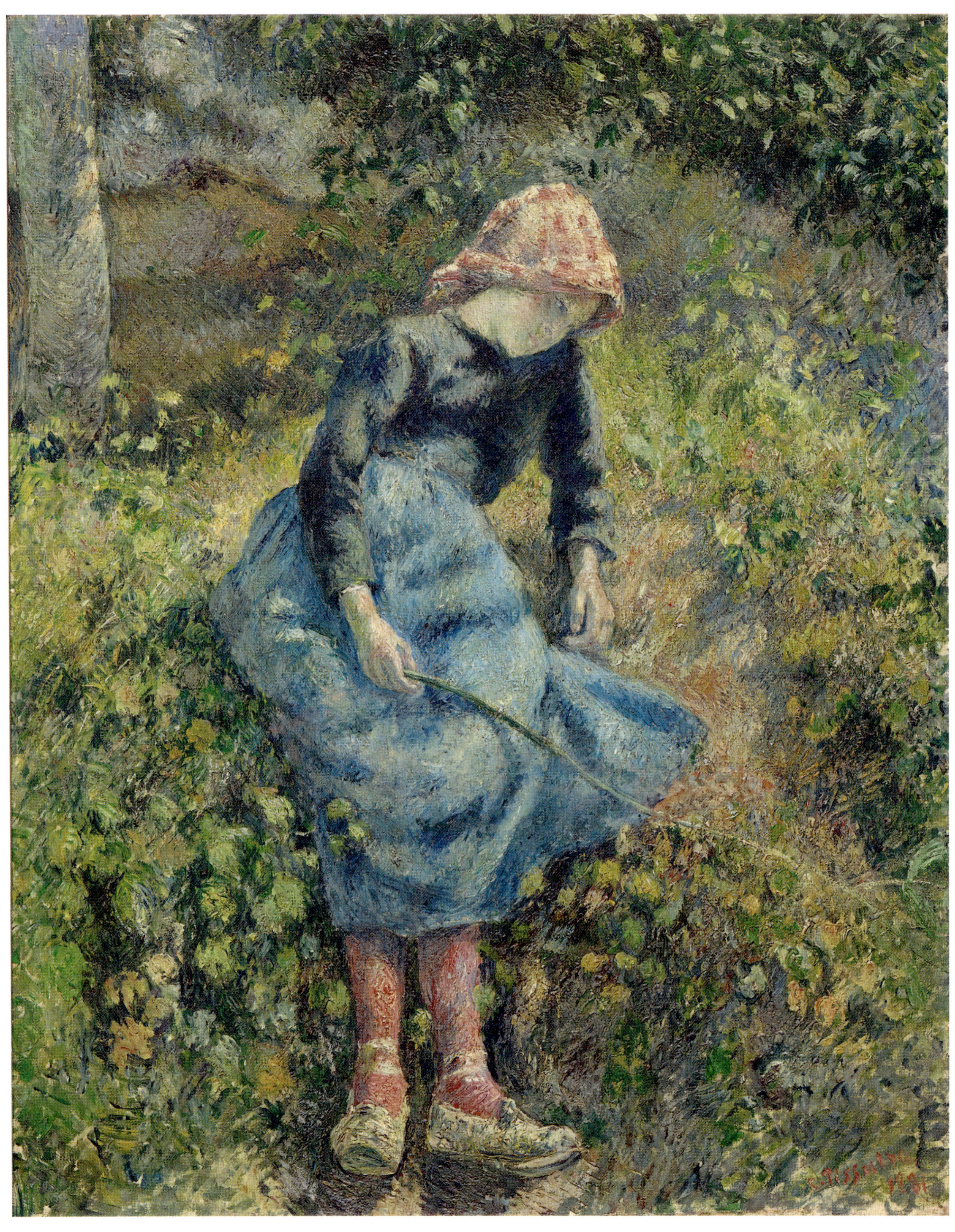

42
The Shepherdess, 1881
Musée d'Orsay, Paris, Bequest of Isaac de Camondo, 1911

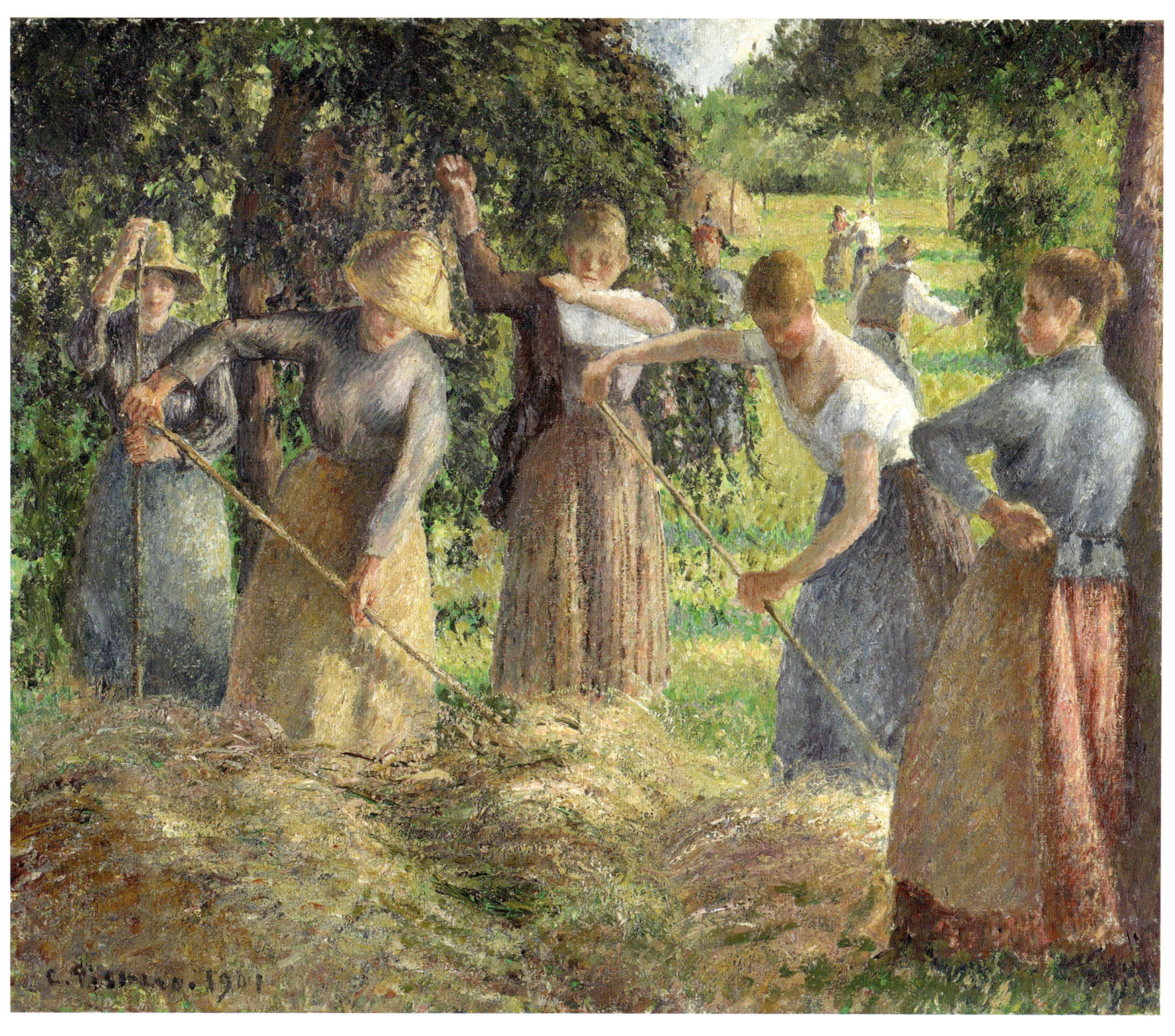

43
Haymaking at Éragny, 1901
National Gallery of Canada, Ottawa, Purchased 1946

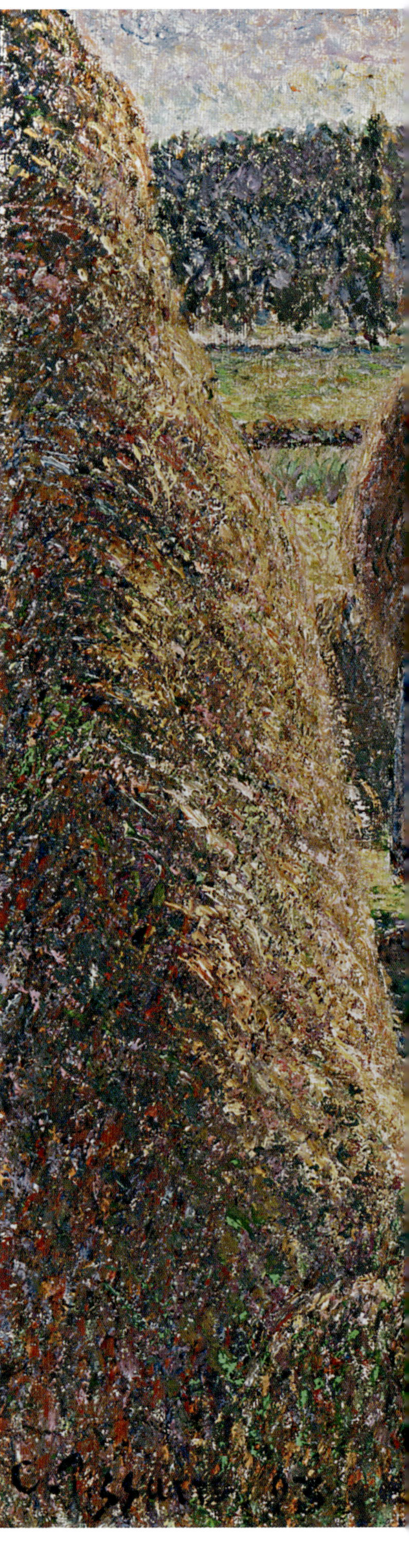

44
Haymakers, Evening, Éragny, 1893
Joslyn Art Museum, Omaha, Nebraska, Museum Purchase

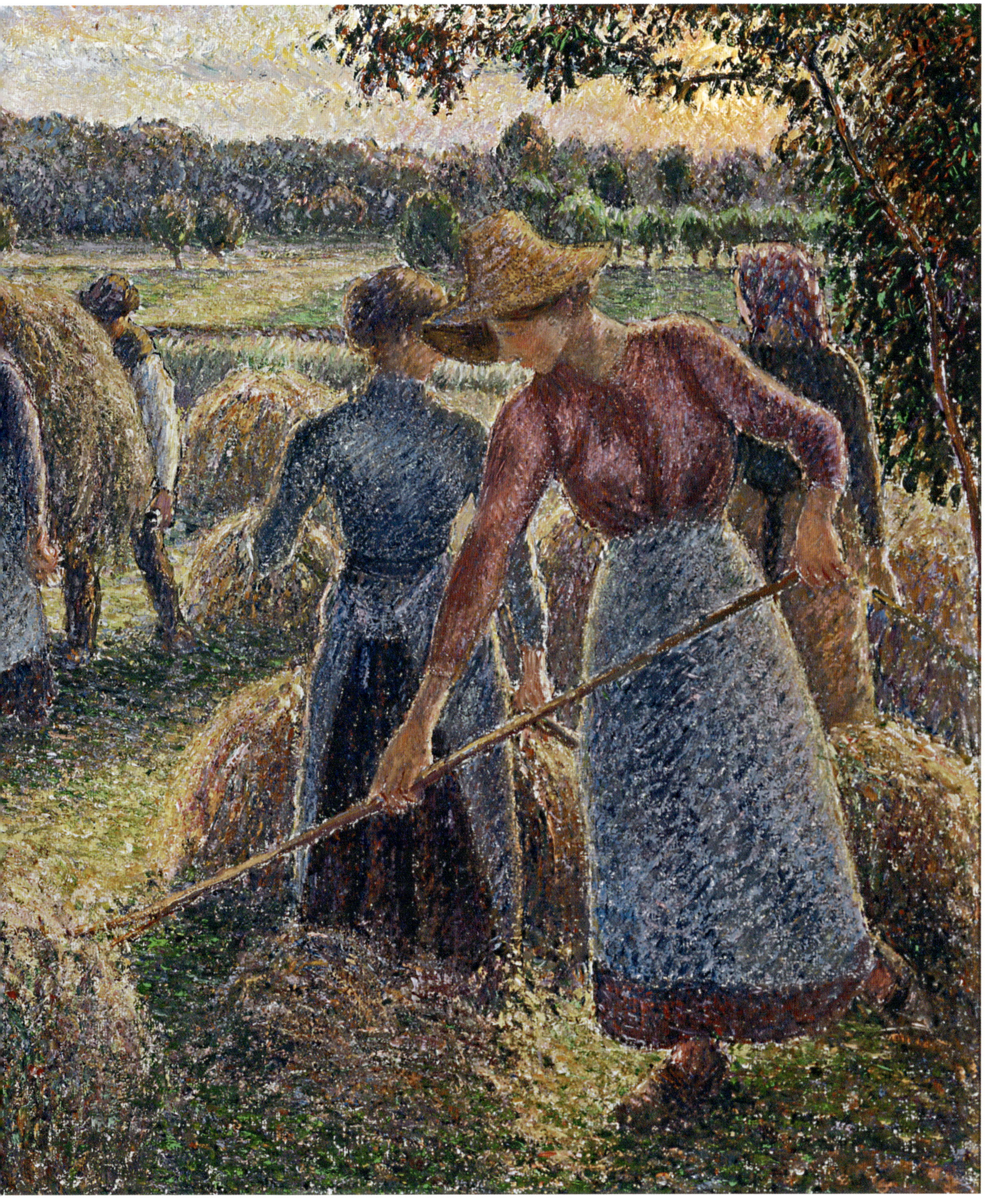

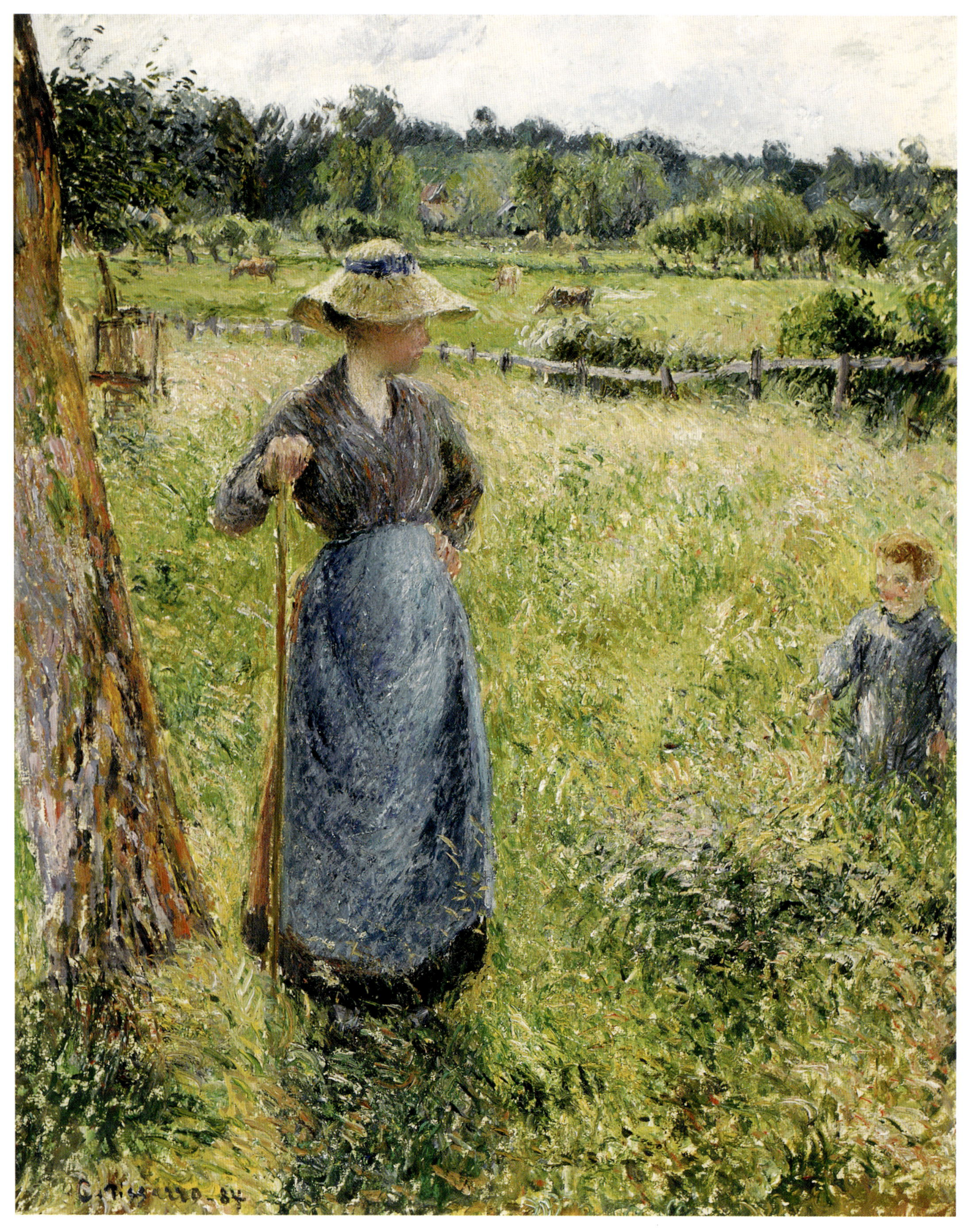

45
The Haymaker, 1884
Colección Pérez Simón

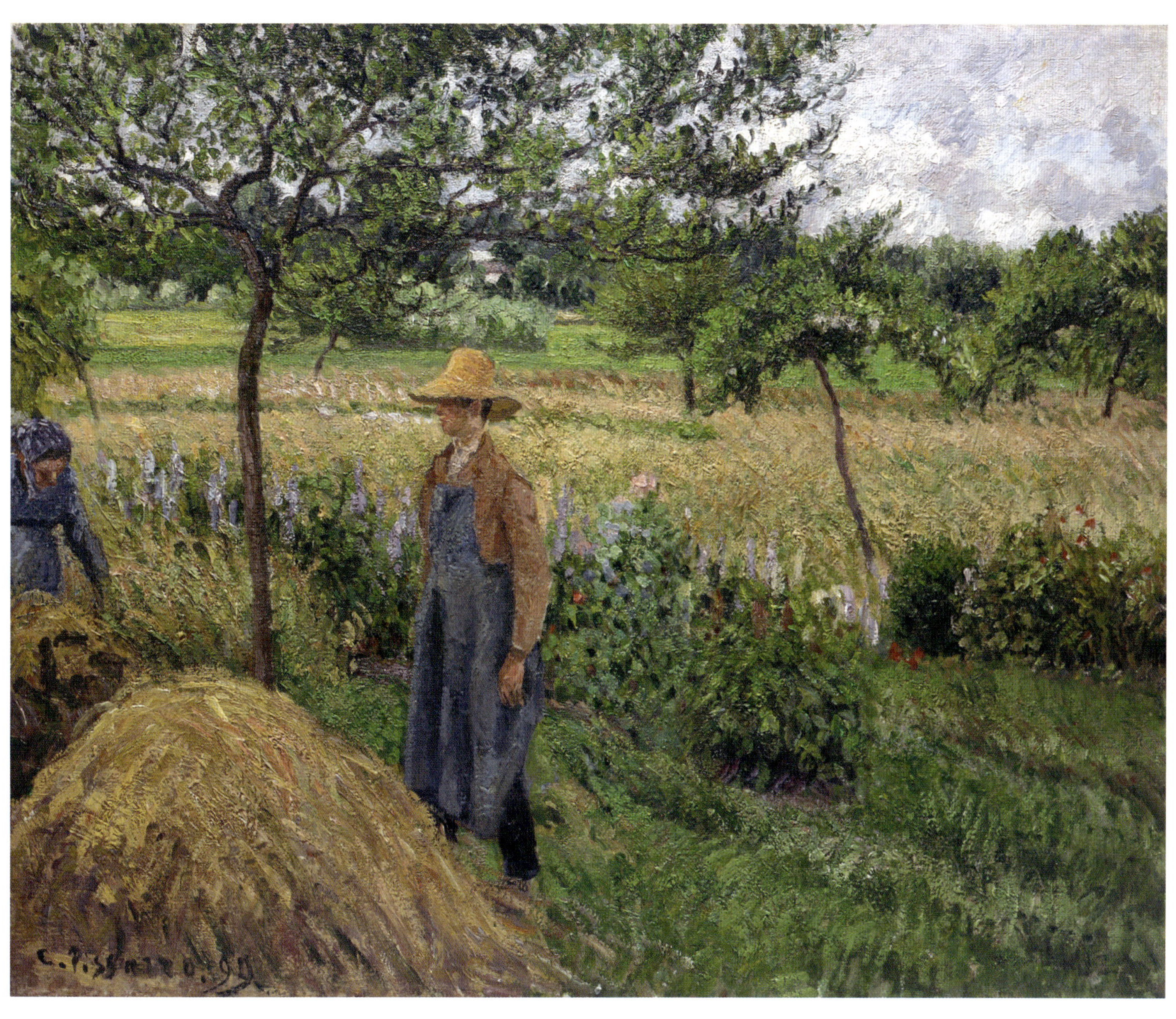

46
Gardener Standing by a Haystack, Overcast Sky, Éragny, 1899
Isabelle and Scott Black Collection

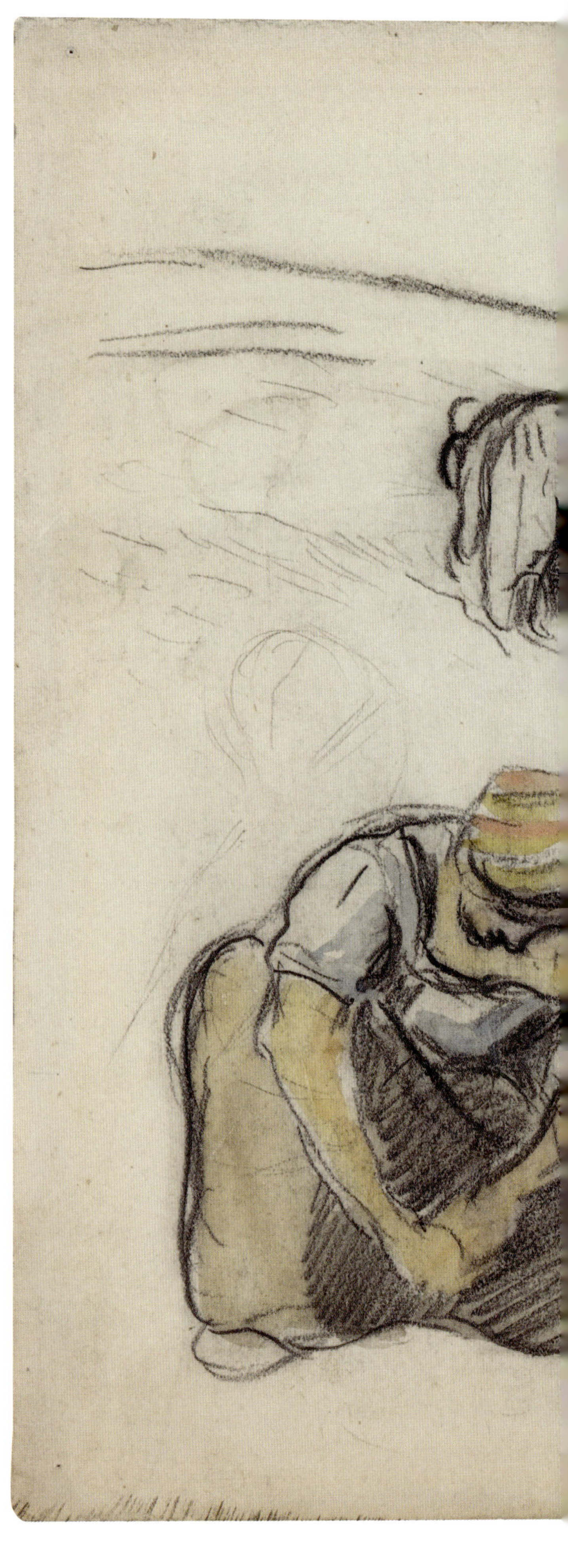

47
Pea Harvesters [recto], ca. 1880
National Gallery of Art, Washington, The Armand Hammer Collection, 1991

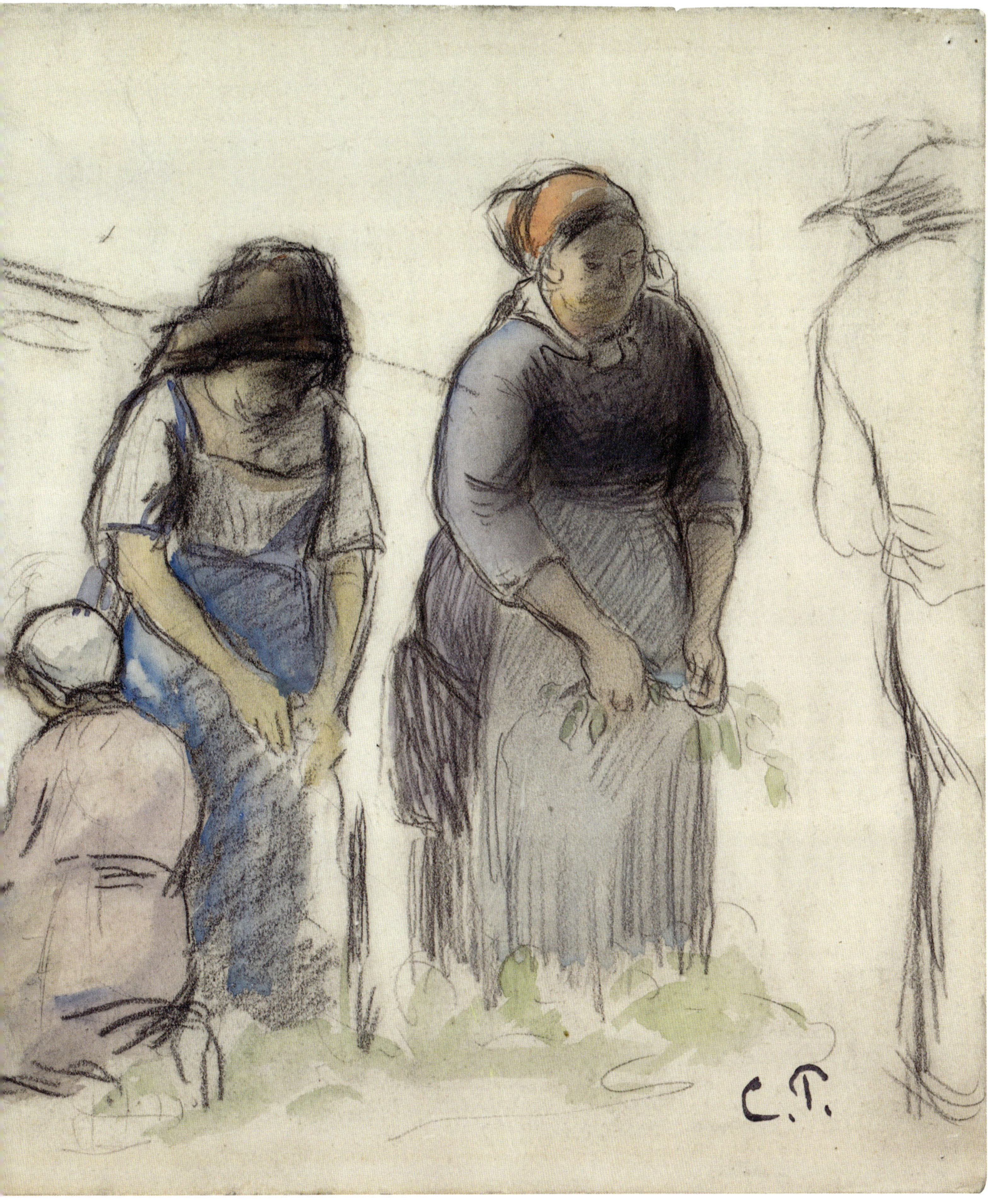
C.P.

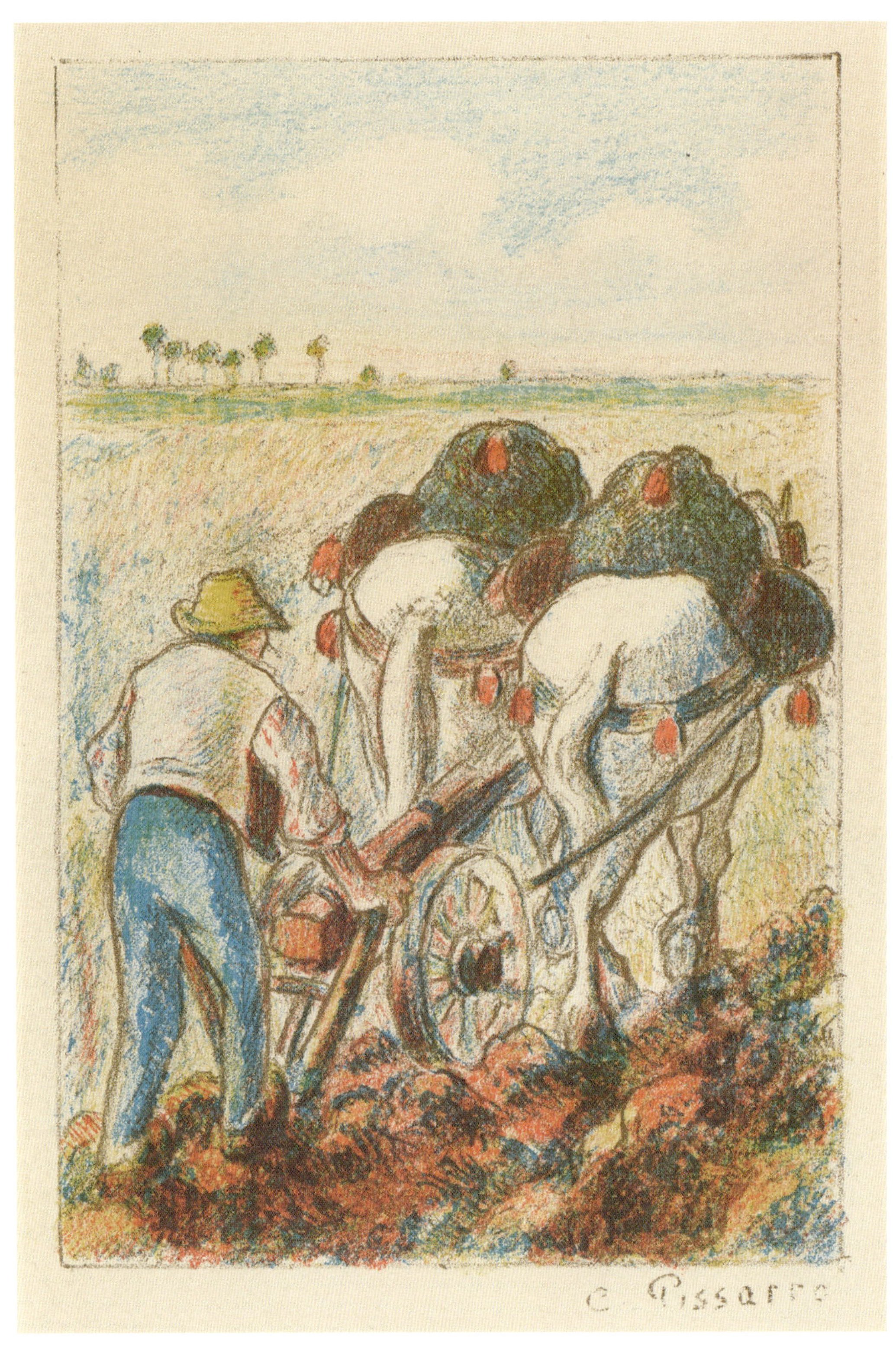

48
The Plow, 1901
Denver Art Museum, Gift of Noëlle and George Beatty

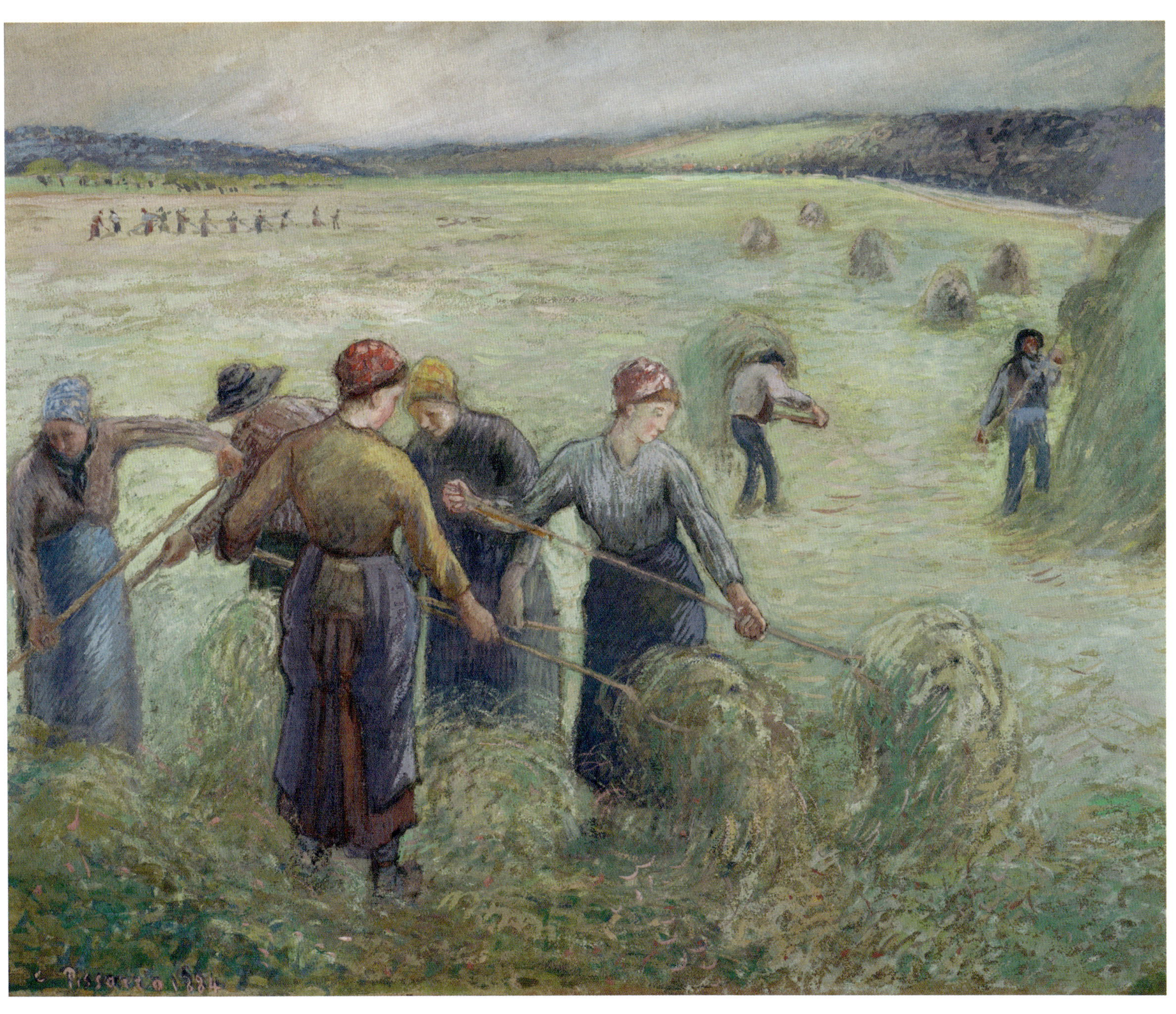

49
Peasants Harvesting Hay, 1884
Denver Art Museum, Anonymous bequest

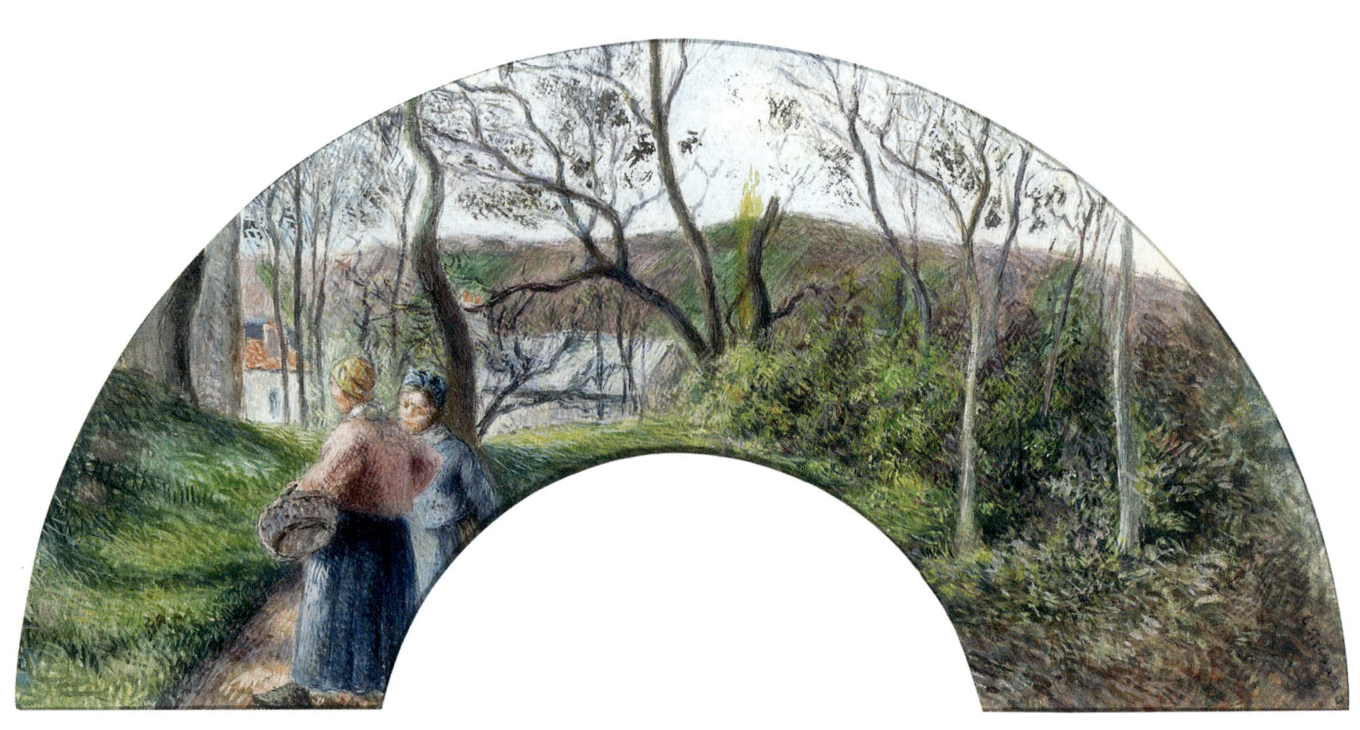

50
Landscape with Two Peasant Women on the Left (fan), 1883
Colección Pérez Simón

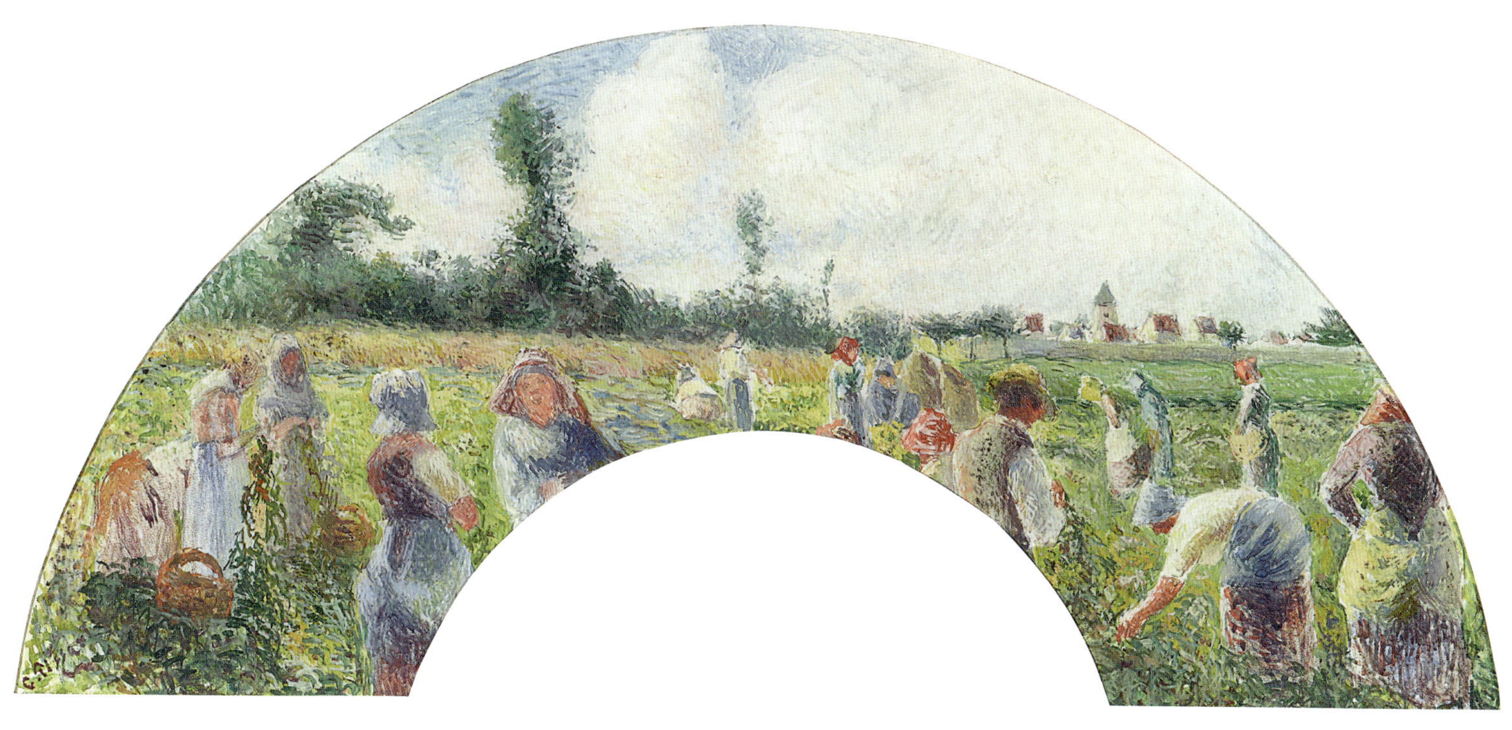

51
Harvest: Peasants Working in the Field (fan), ca. 1880
Private collection

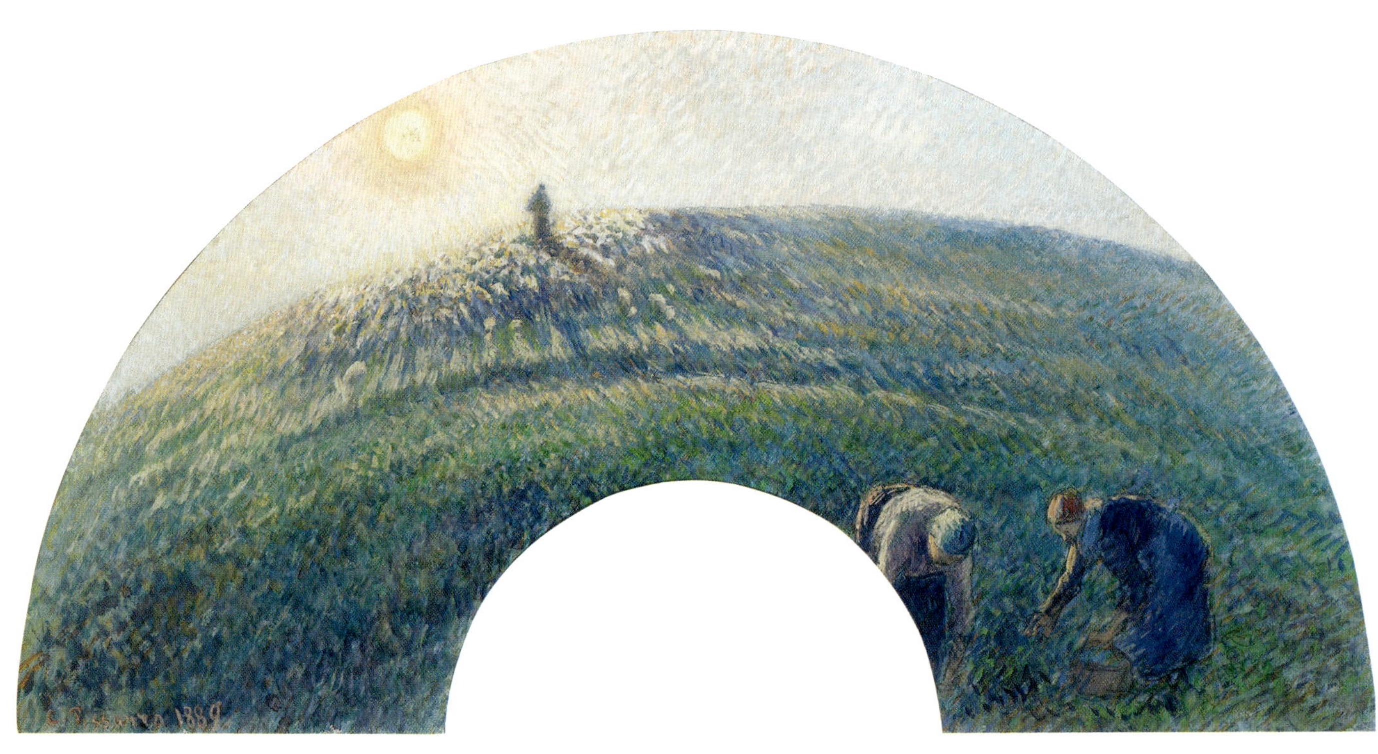

52
Herd of Sheep, Setting Sun (fan), 1889
Colección Pérez Simón

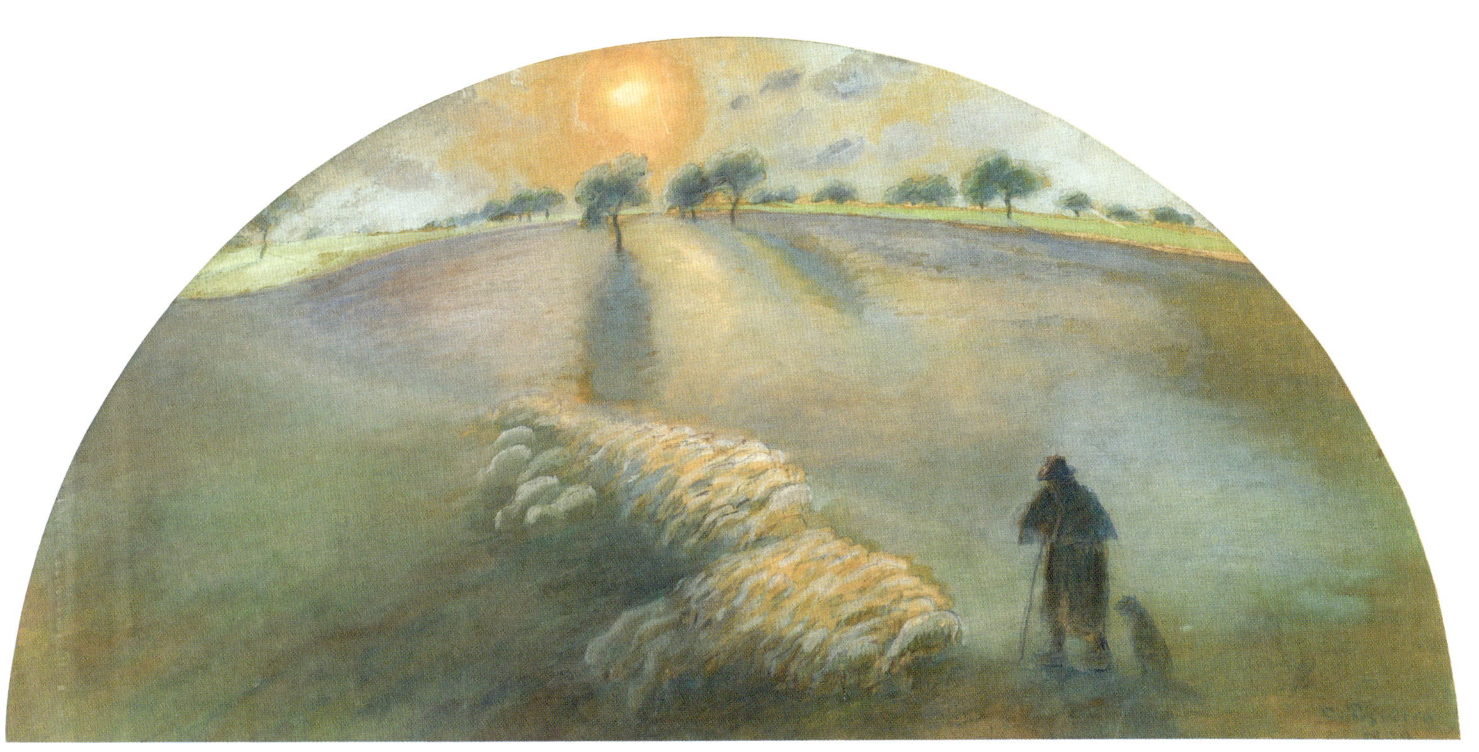

53
Shepherd and Sheep (fan), 1890
Colección Pérez Simón

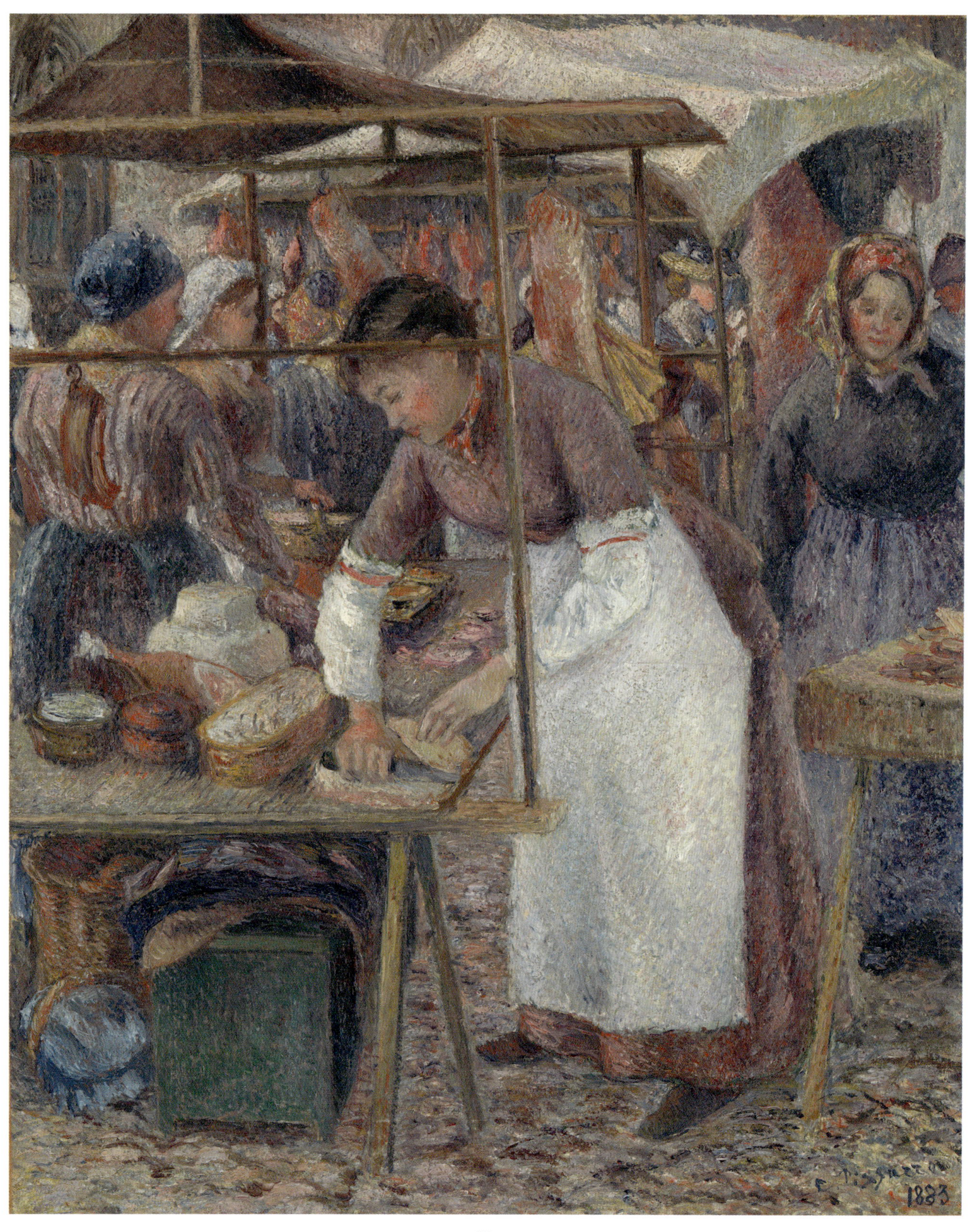

54
The Pork Butcher, 1883
Tate, Bequeathed by Lucien Pissarro, the artist's son 1944

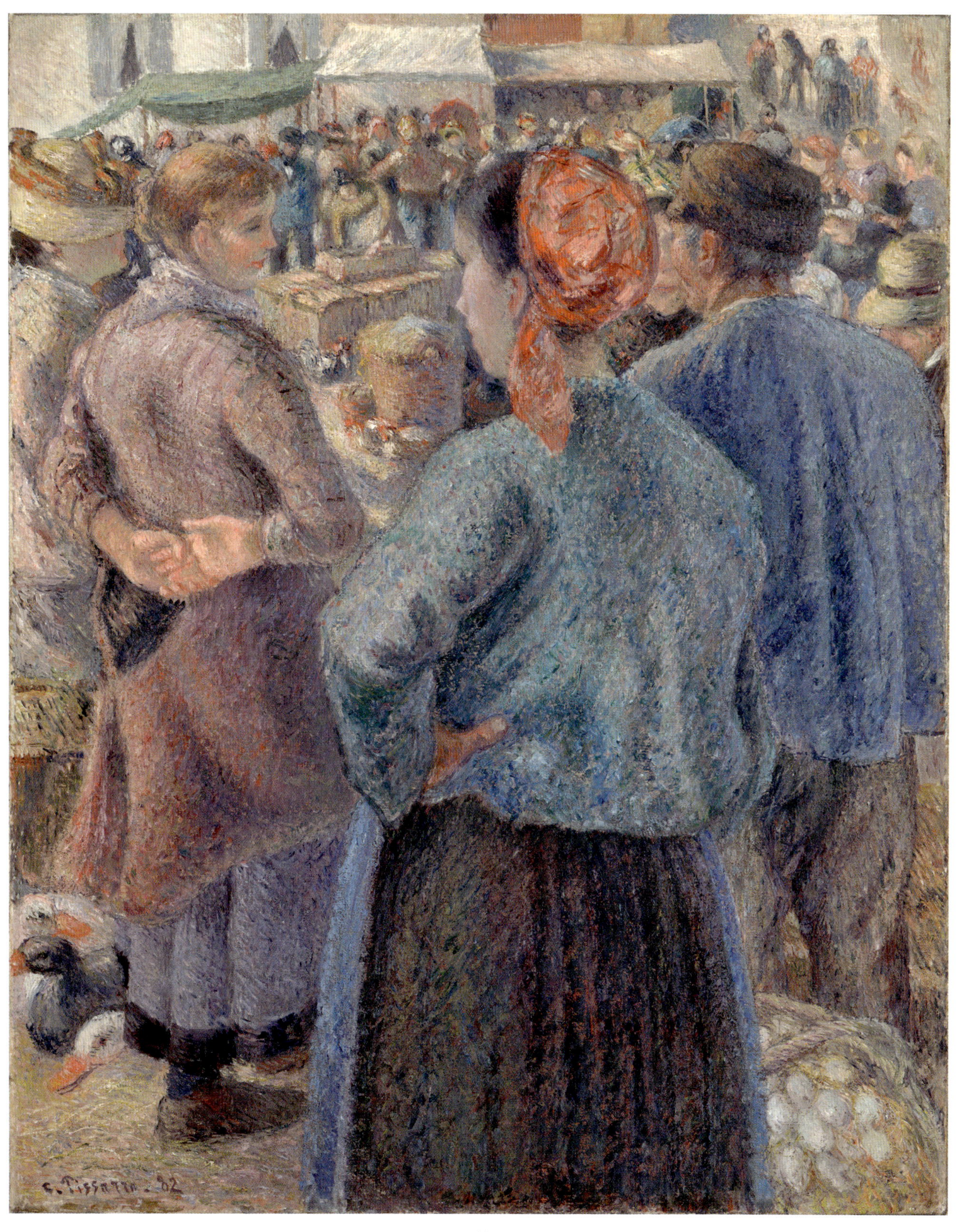

55
The Poultry Market at Pontoise, 1882
Norton Simon Art Foundation, Pasadena, California

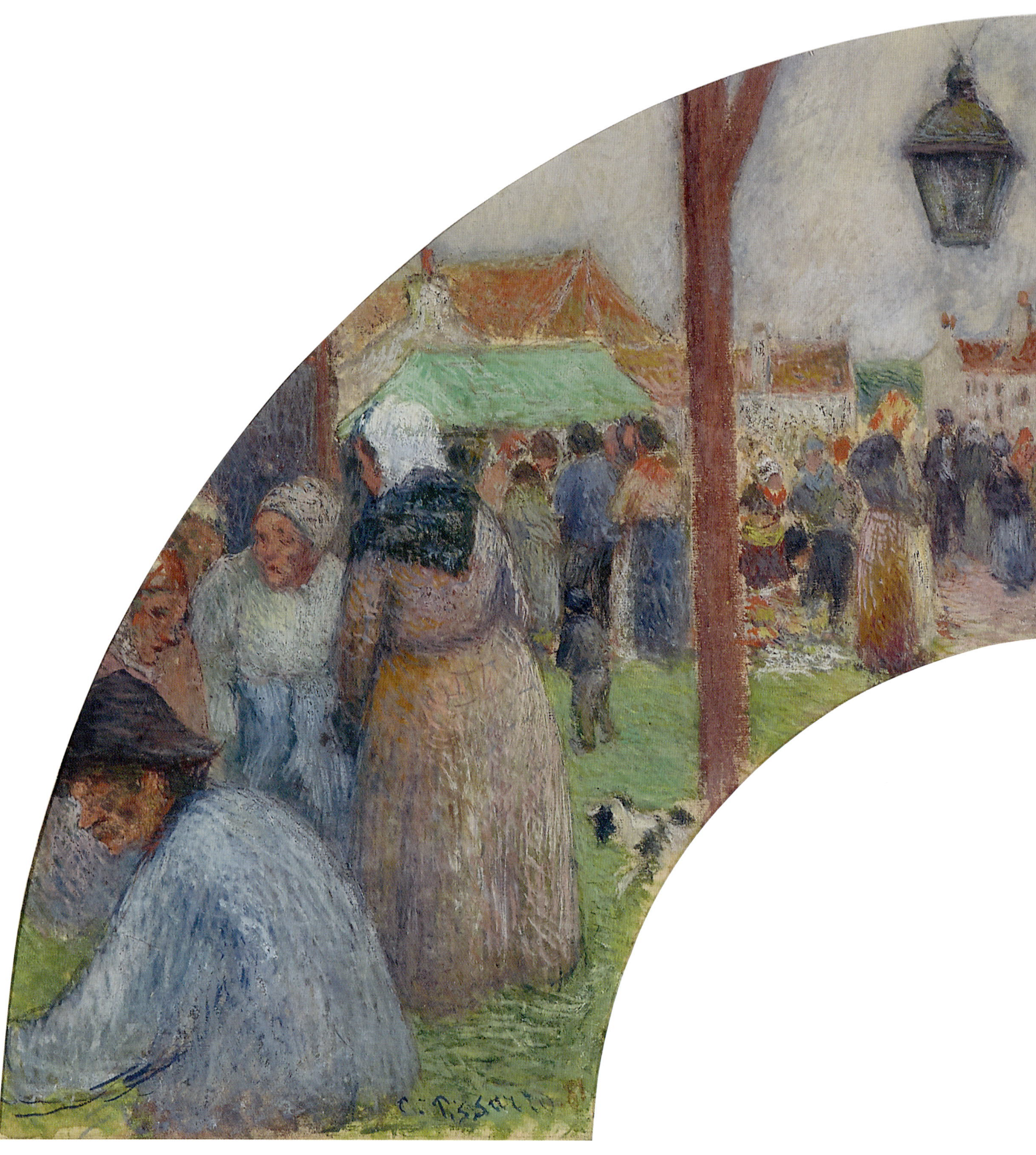

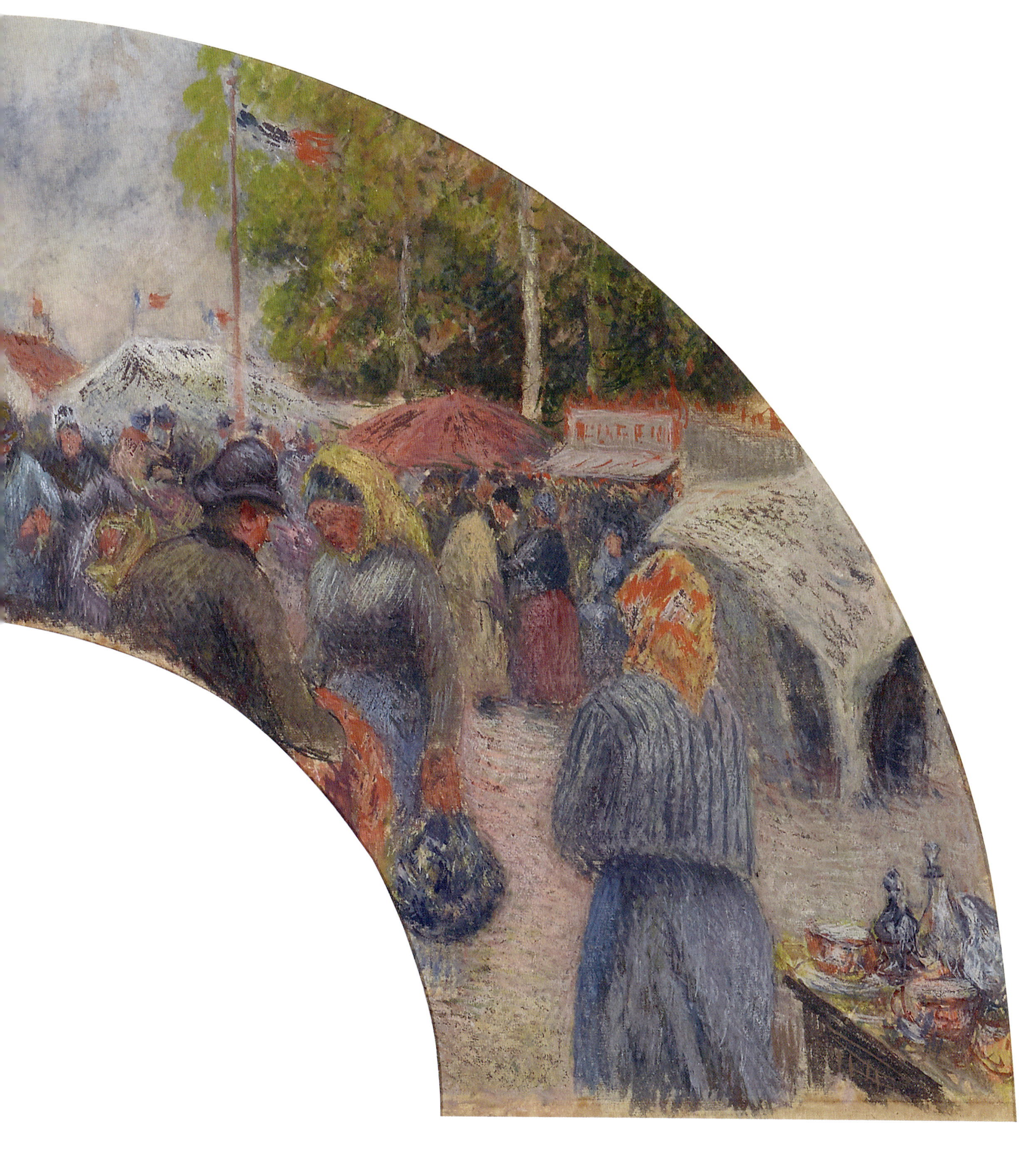

56
Saint-Martin Fair, Pontoise (fan), 1881
Private collection

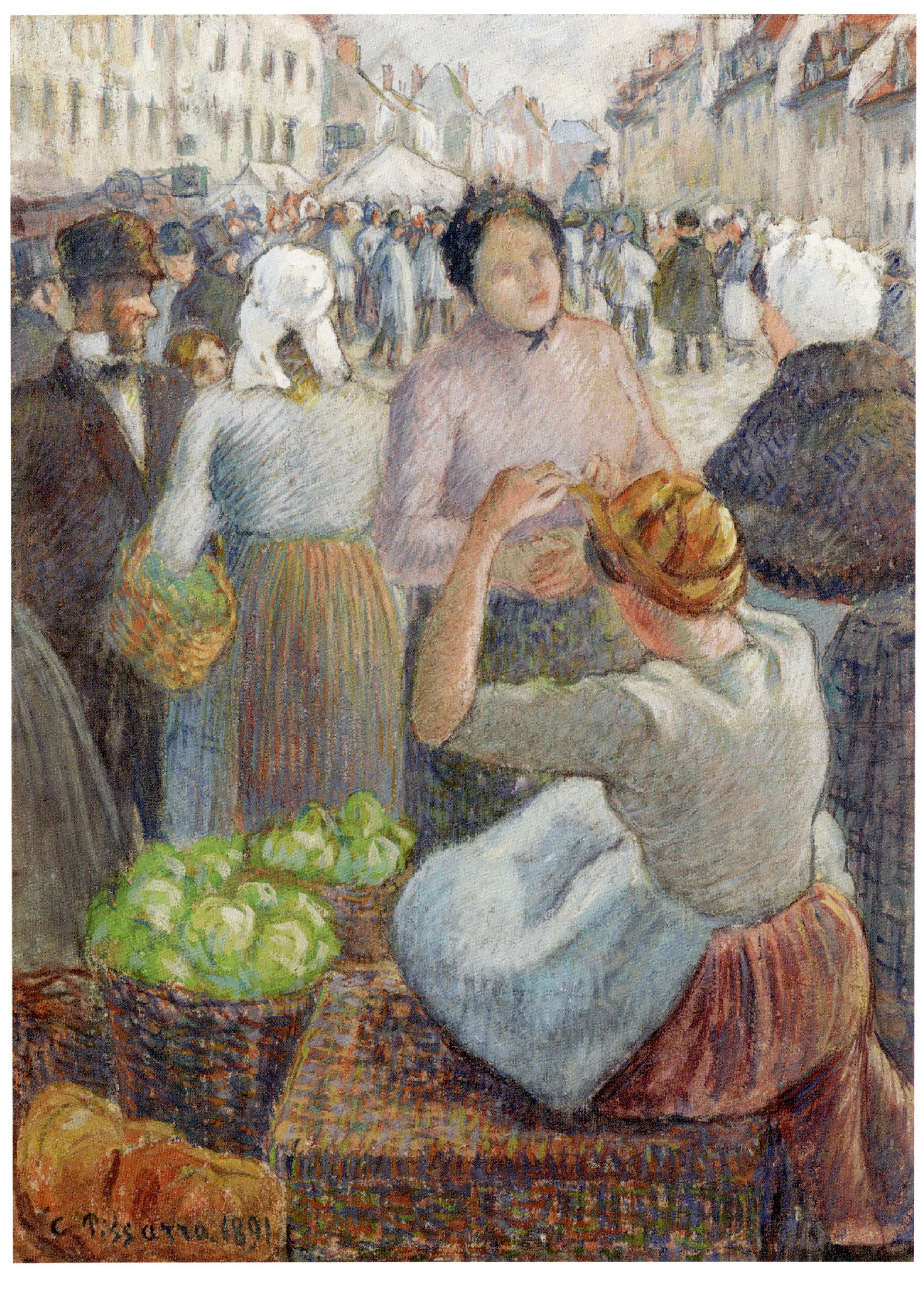

57
The Marketplace, Gisors, 1891
Philadelphia Museum of Art, The Louis E. Stern Collection, 1963

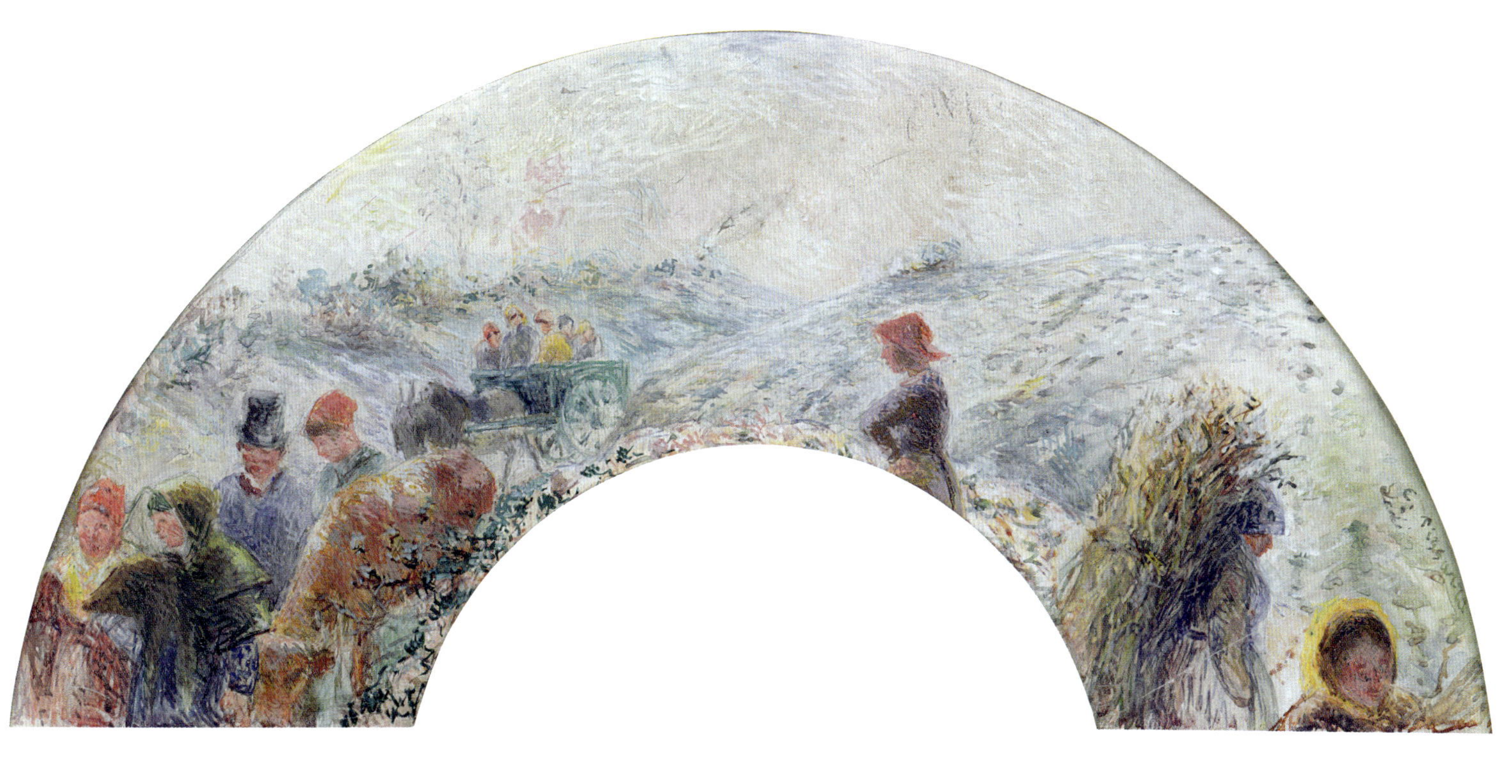

58
Winter, Return from the Fair (fan), ca. 1878
Musée Marmottan Monet, Paris, Bequest of Hauser Roger, 1990

Garden Views
The Studio in Éragny-sur-Epte

Nerina Santorius

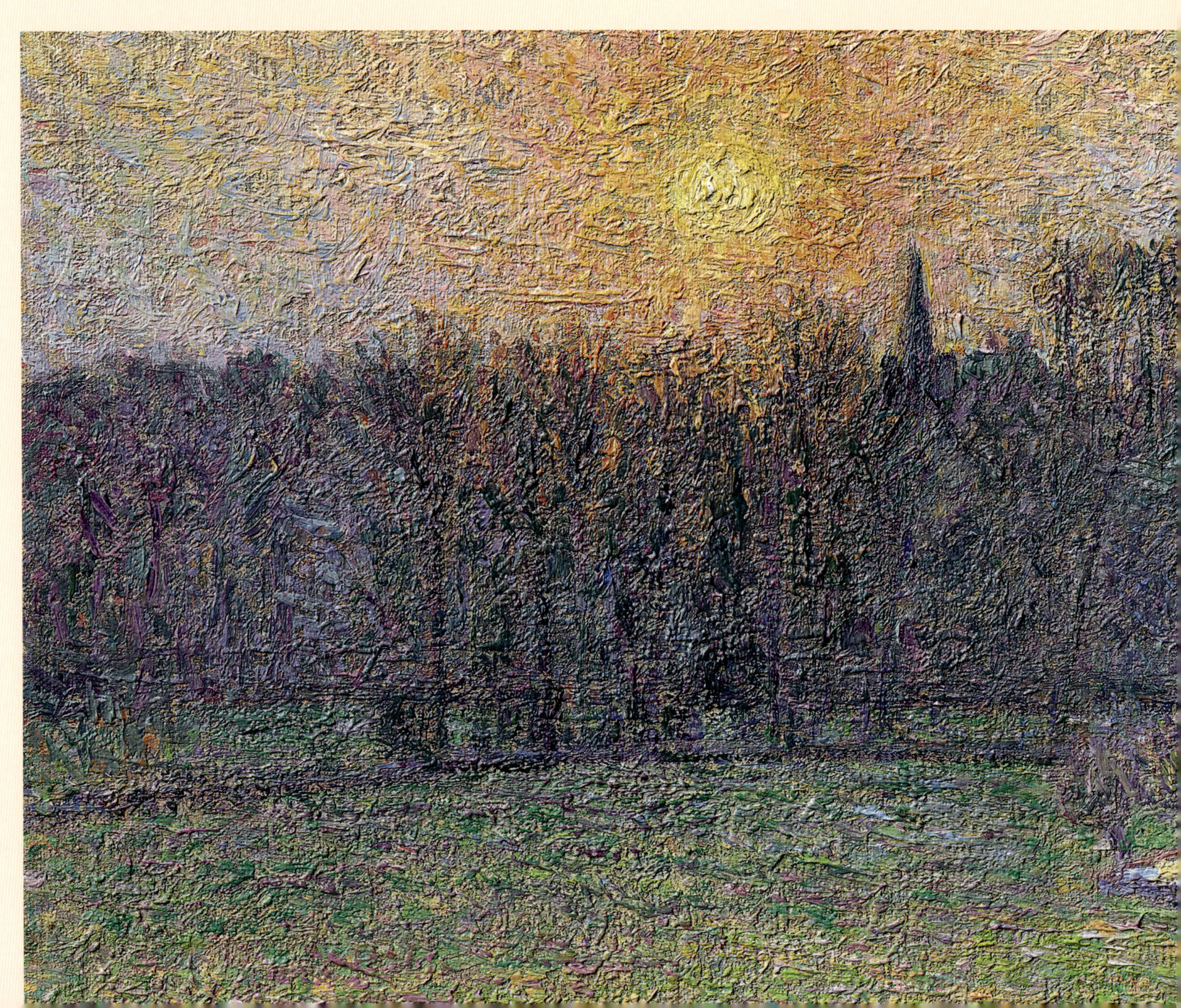

In 1884 Camille Pissarro and his family moved into a house in Éragny-sur-Epte, where he painted not only the surrounding landscape and the neighboring villages but also numerous views of his garden. For years, the vegetable garden cultivated by his wife, Julie Pissarro, was essential to the family's support until they could live from the sale of Pissarro's paintings. After converting the barn into a studio in 1893, the artist frequently painted the garden from the window, often depicting Julie at work. Pissarro's portrayal of the active shaping of nature distinguishes his scenes from the motifs of other Impressionists, who showed the landscape primarily as the site of bourgeois leisure activities and as an object of aesthetic enjoyment.

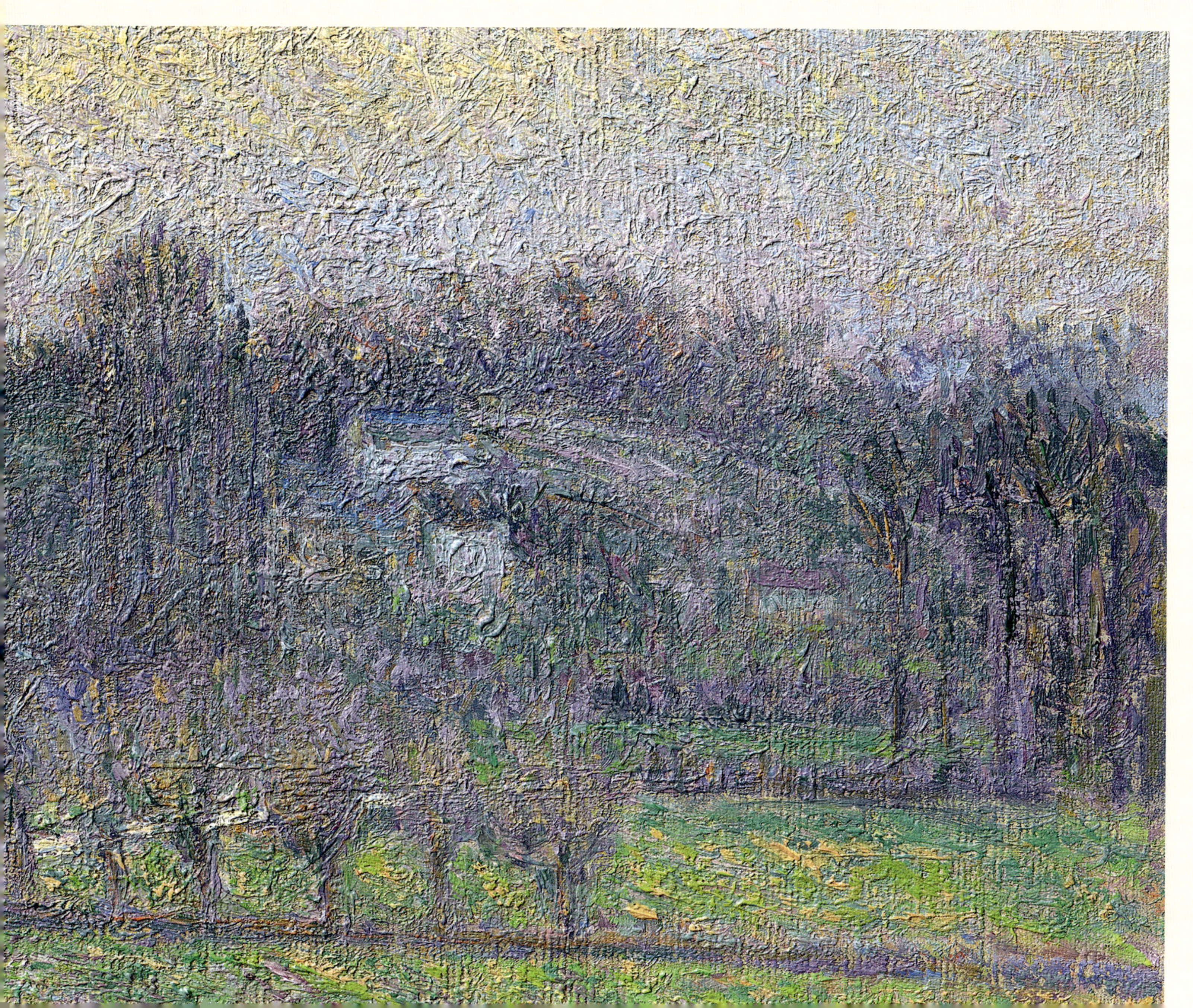

Camille Pissarro "has a deplorable penchant for market gardens [. . .] and does not shy away from any depiction of cabbages or domestic vegetables. But these errors of logic or vulgarities of taste do not alter his fine qualities of execution."[1] These words by critic Jules-Antoine Castagnary, published as early as 1874 in a review of the first Impressionist exhibition, already call attention to one of the singular features of Pissarro's art: while the garden scenes of Pierre-Auguste Renoir or Claude Monet are usually marked by wildly luxuriant or elegant floral growth, Pissarro's canvases show fields, orchards, and vegetable patches.

In 1884 the artist and his family settled in the small village of Éragny-sur-Epte, where he would remain until the end of his life. In 1892, at the instigation of Camille's wife, Julie, and with the financial help of Monet and Paul Durand-Ruel, the Pissarros purchased the house with garden that they had previously rented. In Éragny, the artist painted not only the immediate environs of his home and the neighboring villages (cats. 63, 64) but also numerous views of the garden from differing vantage points and at varying times of the day and year. Often the compositions show simple, less-than-picturesque motifs such as trees in the meadow with the garden wall in the background, shrubbery and garden beds, and the path between the chicken coop and the house (cats. 59–62, 66). Pissarro intentionally chose unpretentious subjects in order to focus on the specific atmospheric effects, joining the pictorial elements into a harmonious whole. This fundamental elevation of "low" pictorial motifs, in defiance of the traditional hierarchy of genres, is a characteristic feature of Impressionist painting and also occurs in the work of Pissarro's colleagues. Yet the countless images of his vegetable garden are still remarkable, and the question arises as to whether the artistic strategy of such works consists only in the rendering of fleeting effects of weather. What conception of nature and the landscape do these paintings convey? How does Pissarro use this group of works to position himself as an artist?

A single tree, covered in delicate spring foliage, occupies the center of the painting *Spring, Gray Weather, Éragny* (cat. 65). Its branches seem to merge with the vegetation behind it, forming a kind of ornamental band. In the foreground, Pissarro emphasizes the horizontals of the garden bed and the fence, while the upper third of the picture is dominated by the verticals of the towering trees. The limited recession in depth makes the scene appear unified, and despite the elevated vantage point—it was probably painted from a window—it has an immersive quality. The two women working in the garden seem one with their environment; like many other figures in paintings by Pissarro, they are actively involved in cultivating nature, which provides them with a habitation and a livelihood. In paintings such as *Plum Trees in Blossom, Éragny* (cat. 59), *A Corner of the Meadow at Éragny* (cat. 60), and *Vegetable Garden, Overcast Morning, Éragny* (cat. 61), a solitary female figure—presumably Julie Pissarro—appears holding pails or a basket, likewise emphasizing the aspect of work. The visible result of these efforts is the carefully tended garden with its variety of thriving, blooming plants. The active, formative role of the human being distinguishes Pissarro's garden scenes from the motifs of other Impressionists, who generally showed the landscape as the setting for middle-class leisure activities and thus as the object of contemplative observation. This aesthetic conception of the landscape had long prevailed in European tradition, a conception in which nature could only become a landscape when the viewer stepped outside it and turned toward it in disinterested contemplation.[2] Here, the focus lay on the human gaze, which elevated nature to the status of landscape. The catalyst for such aesthetic perception was landscape painting, which undergirded this contemplative practice by training the gaze. Painting, in turn, exerted an influence on the design of gardens and parks.[3]

Along with his artistically informed view of the garden, Pissarro also introduced an agrarian perspective such as that of his wife. The daughter of a winegrower, Julie Pissarro was experienced in agriculture, and she cultivated and expanded a domestic garden that was often essential for survival. It would be many years before Pissarro could achieve enough success as a painter to feed his family of eight. Despite these financial difficulties and in contrast to his wife's preoccupation with securing a living, he encouraged his children to pursue artistic training as well. In accord with his anarchist convictions, he sought to establish his home in Éragny-sur-Epte as a place where all the members of his family could ply their own artistic crafts and create a shared *Gesamtkunstwerk.*

According to writer Octave Mirbeau, a longtime comrade-in-arms of the artist, Pissarro believed that "the painter is 'in humanity,' in the same way as the poet, the farmer, [...] the chemist, the worker [...]. For him, the painter contributes, along with all those who do something useful and beautiful, to the work of general harmony, which is to express the universe according to individual aptitudes [...] and to extract from it a piece of strength and beauty."[4] Against this backdrop of the equal value Pissarro attributed to differing activities, both painting and agriculture can be understood as the production of landscape. Within the dynamic framework of the garden, different practices of everyday life came together: while Julie Pissarro cultivated nature, her husband "produced" the landscape by continually exploring a range of vantage points with his portable easel and selecting compositions. He also created new perspectives by remodeling the barn into a studio and by painting from the window.[5] In *Plum Trees in Blossom, Éragny* (cat. 59), the staircase leading to the studio is visible on the left.

A comparison of the views of the neighboring village of Bazincourt that Pissarro painted in 1884 and 1892 (cats. 69–72) shows the aesthetic means by which his specific gaze, increasingly influenced by anarchism from the mid-1880s on, created the landscape in the sense of a contribution to the "work of harmony." For example, in *View of Bazincourt, Clear Sky* (cat. 69), numerous individual elements are identifiable, from fruit trees in the foreground and grazing cows to the buildings of the town. The painting from eight years later (cat. 70), by contrast, omits the orchard and animals and reduces the composition to three horizontal bands: the green meadow, the violet-toned village, and the sky glowing with the colors of the sunset. All the individual details dissolve into the unity of the overall atmosphere, while the unified impression is further strengthened by the diffusion of the colors of sky and village into other areas of the picture.

Pissarro's paintings of Éragny-sur-Epte show the landscape as a dynamic space in which human beings appear not as a contemplative audience but as active participants; the landscape appears as an evolving relationship between humans and nature. Just as the moving crowds of people on the streets and bridges of the artist's views of Paris represent the constitutive element of a cityscape (cats. 97–109), so also the space of the garden is experienced as the landscape of daily life, whose meaning derives from the persons who shape, interact with, and use it.[6] Viewed in light of the earlier function of landscape painting as a model for garden and landscape architecture, Pissarro's images of vegetable gardens may even be interpreted as a tireless artistic effort to realize a social ideal in which the life of his family in Éragny serves to exemplify a harmonious relationship with nature.

Translated from German by Melissa M. Thorson

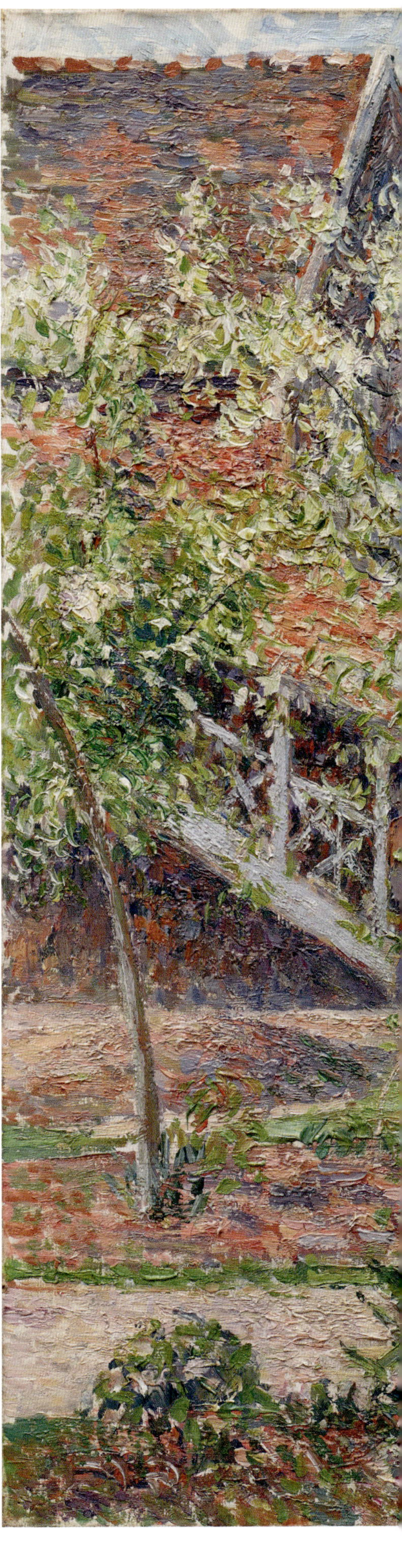

59
Plum Trees in Blossom, Éragny, 1894
Ordrupgaard, Copenhagen

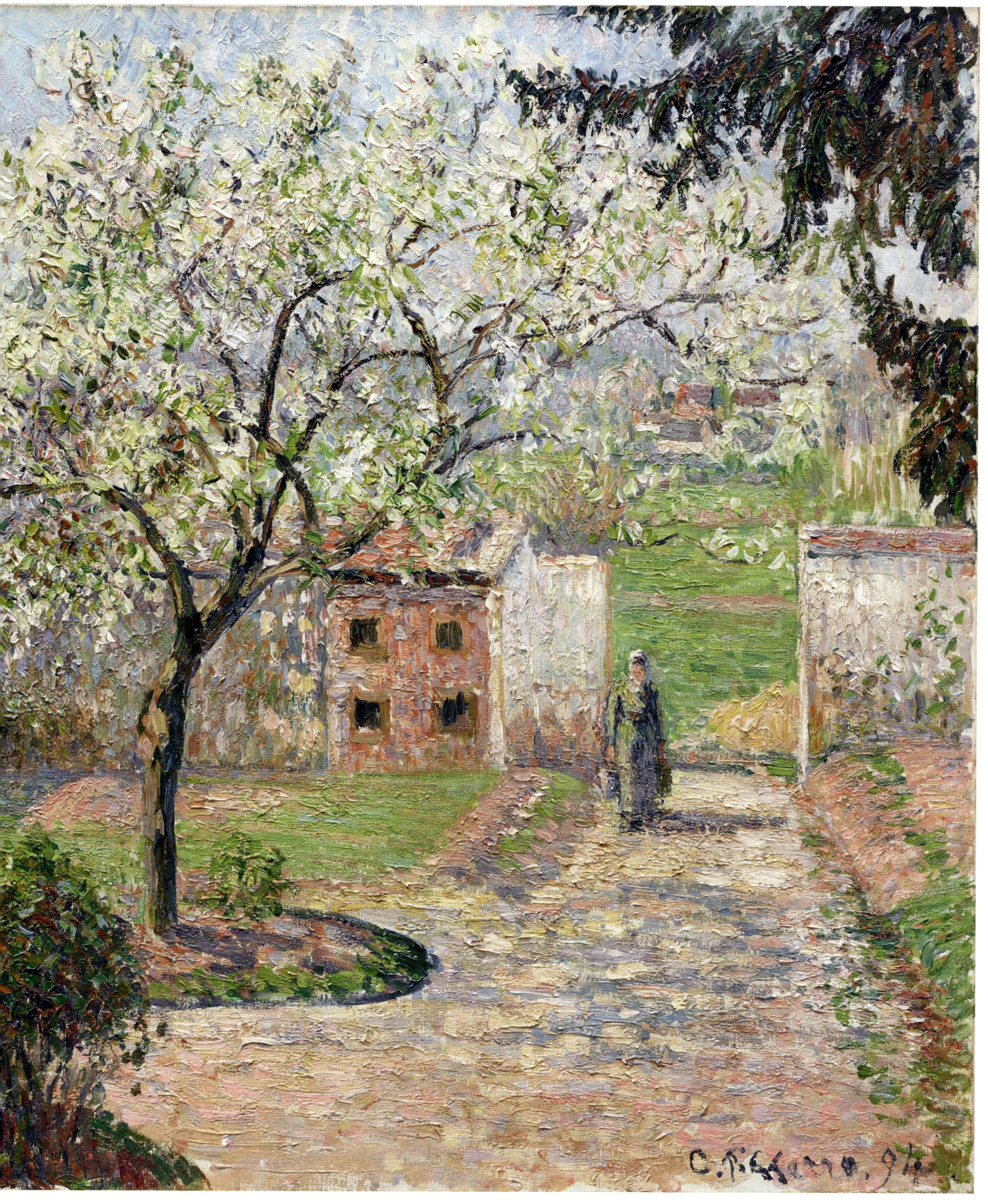

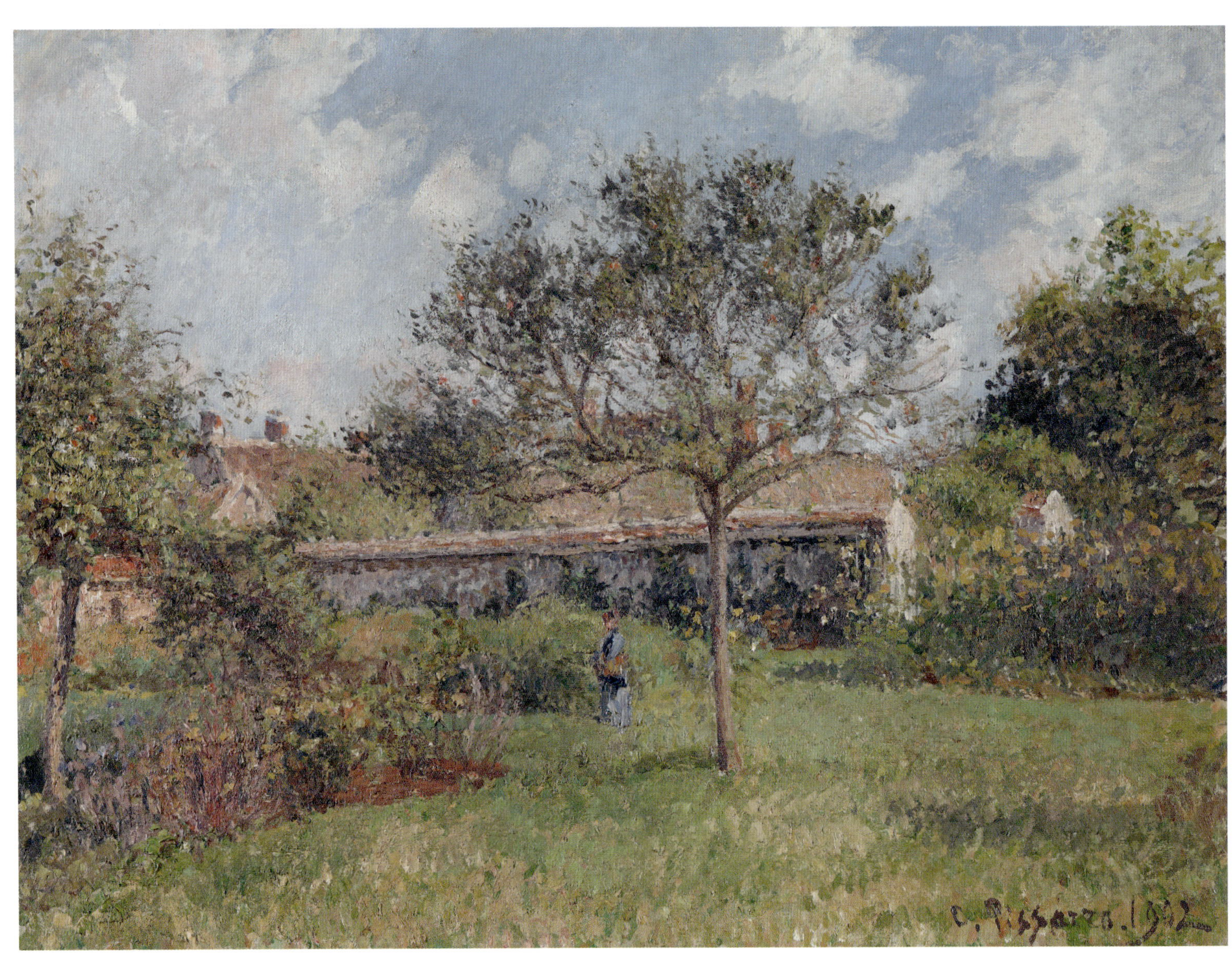

60
A Corner of the Meadow at Éragny, 1902
Tate, Presented by Mrs. Esther Pissarro, the artist's daughter-in-law 1951

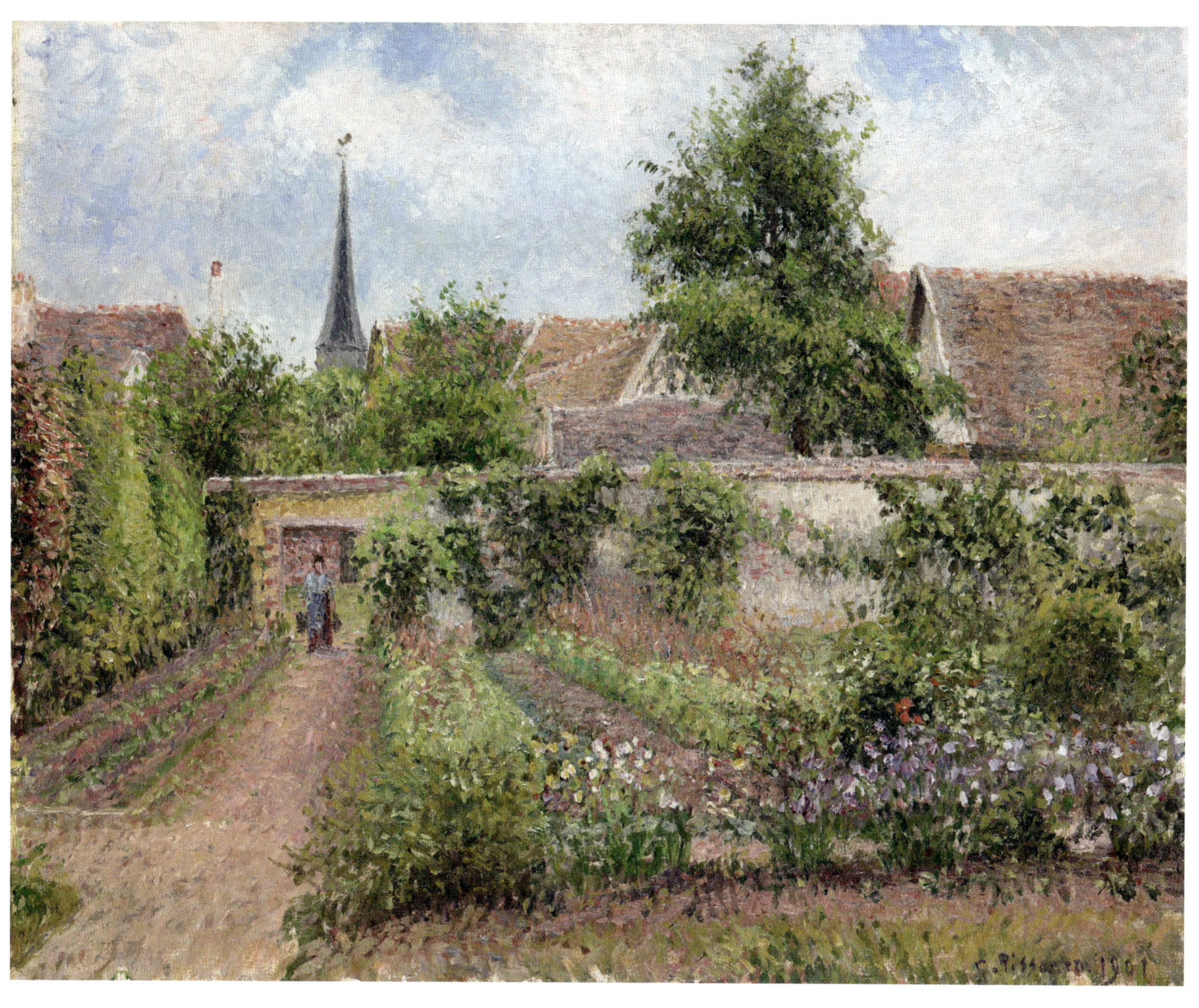

61
Vegetable Garden, Overcast Morning, Éragny, 1901
Philadelphia Museum of Art, Bequest of Charlotte Dorrance Wright, 1978

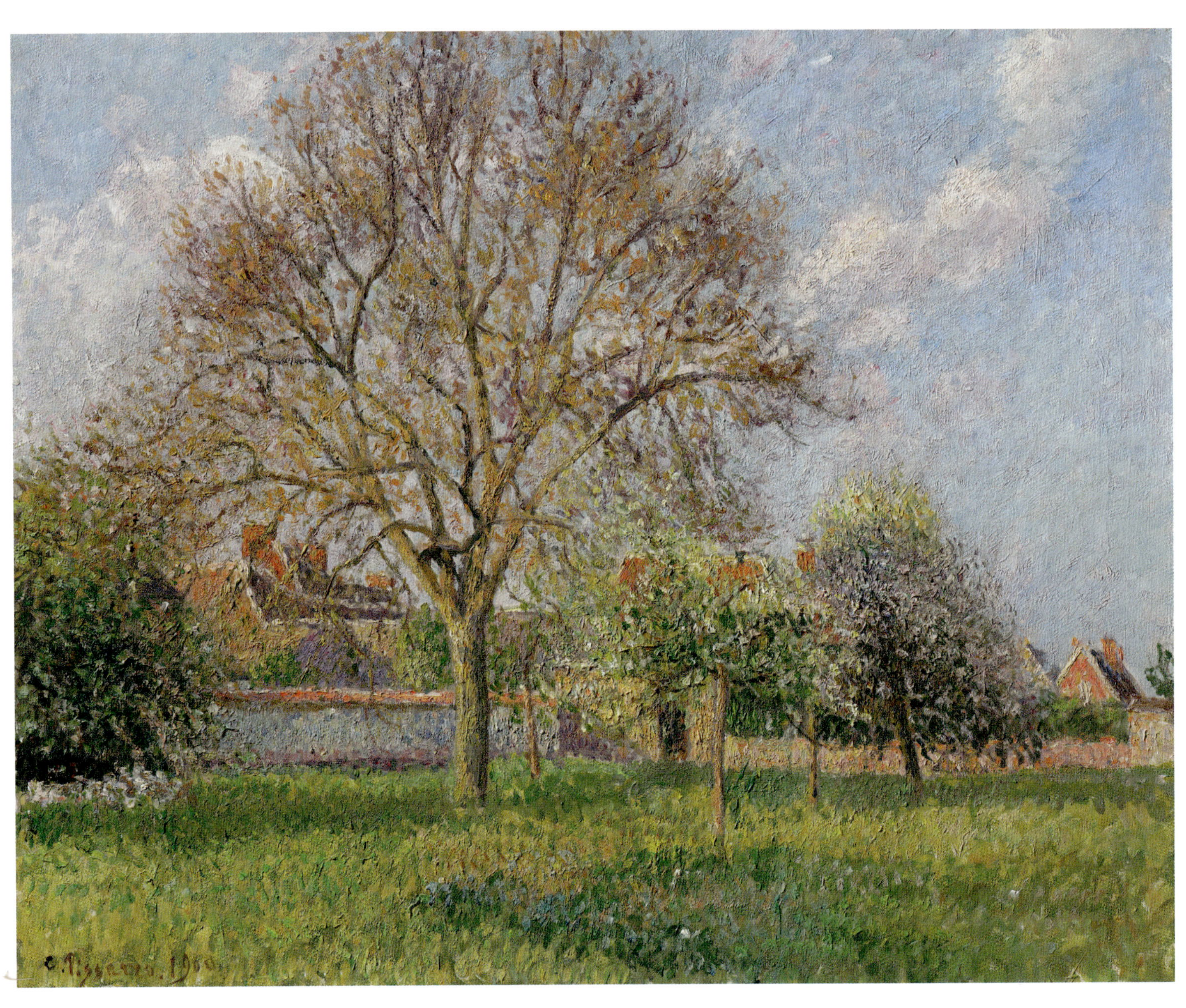

62
The Large Walnut Tree, Éragny, Afternoon, 1900
Private collection, UK

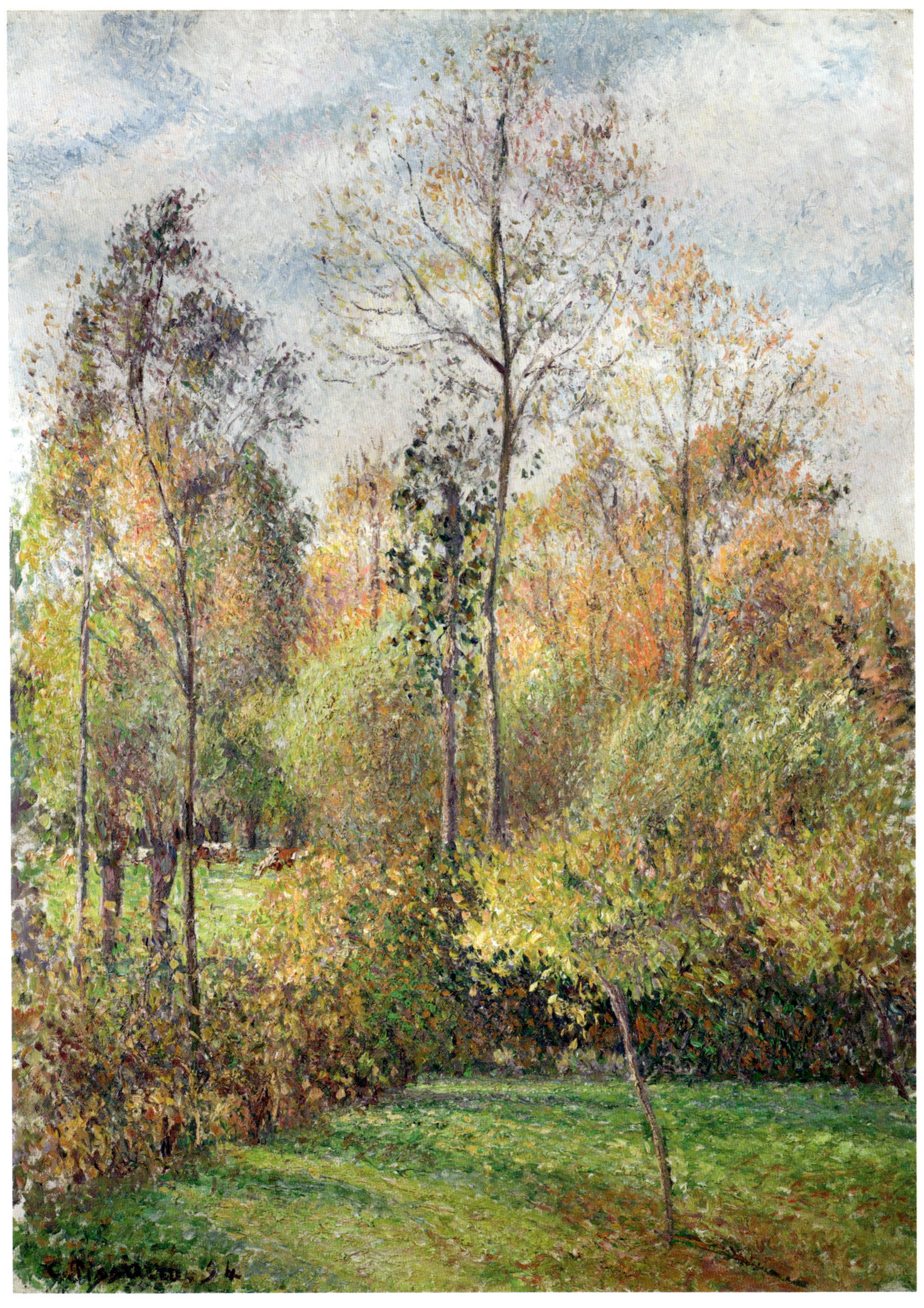

63
Autumn, Poplar Trees, Éragny, 1894
Denver Art Museum, Funds from Helen Dill bequest

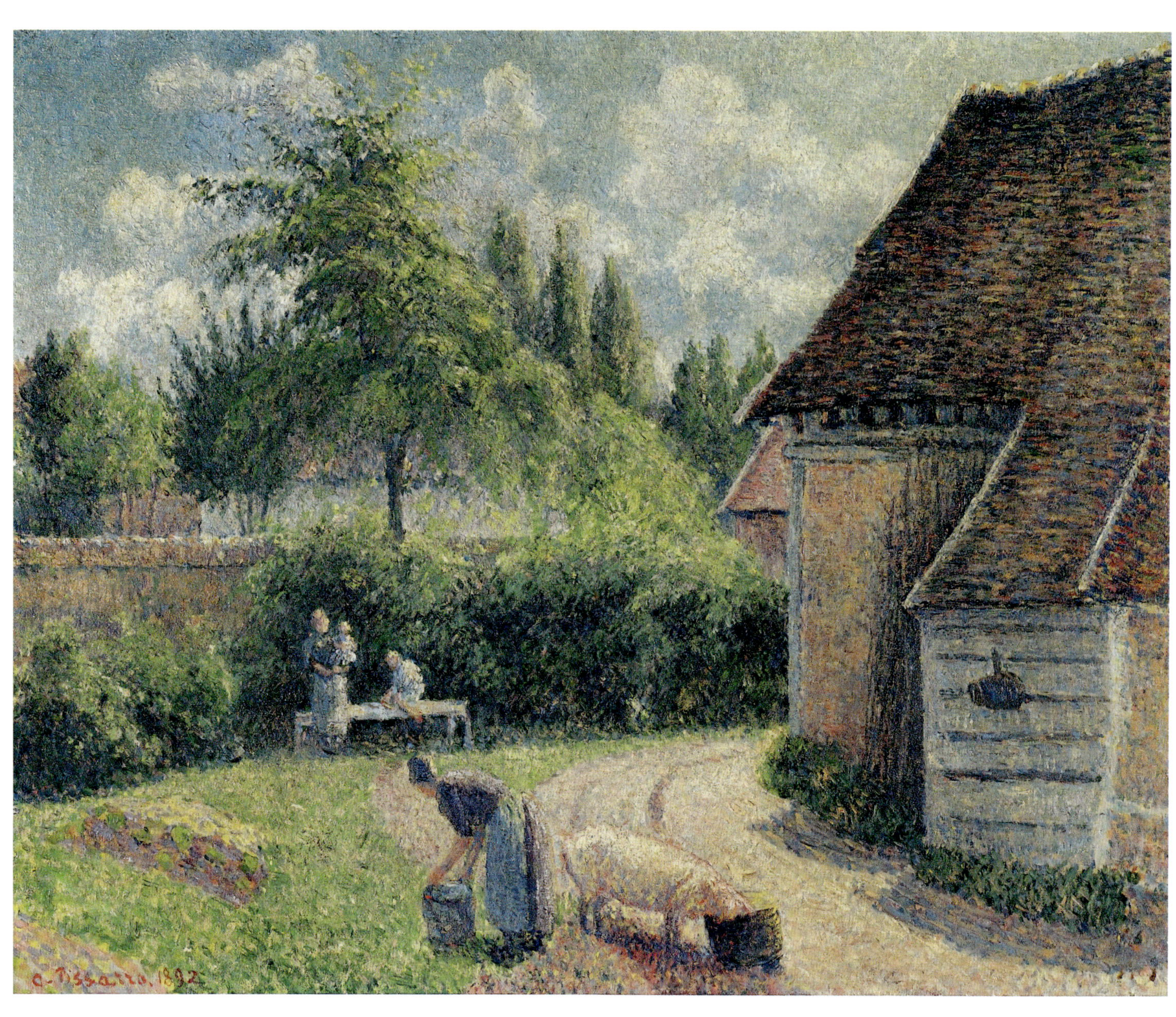

64
Peasant House, 1892
Collection of Prof. Mark Kaufman, Monaco

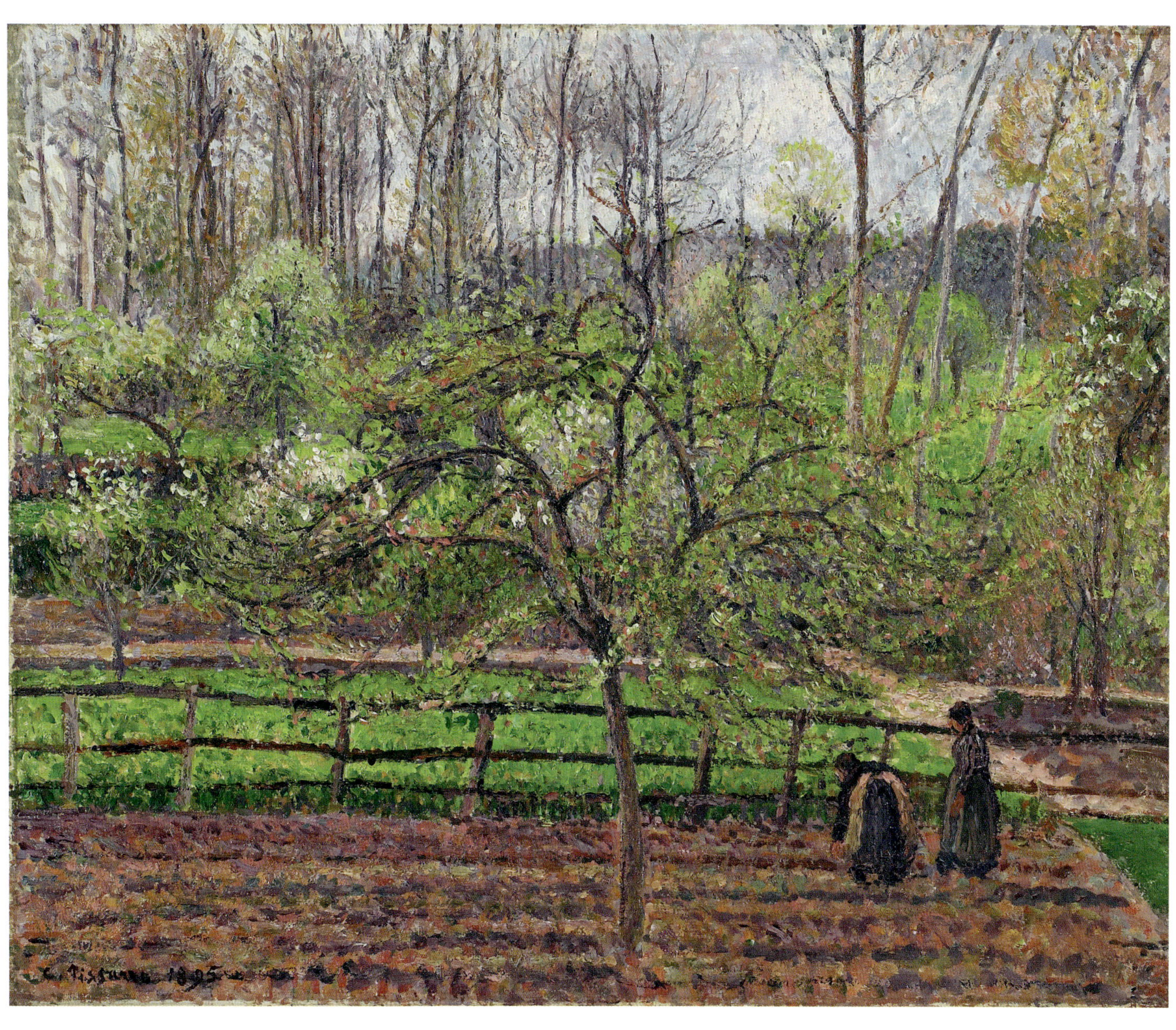

65
Spring, Gray Weather, Éragny, 1895
Collection Art Gallery of Ontario, Toronto, Purchase, 1933

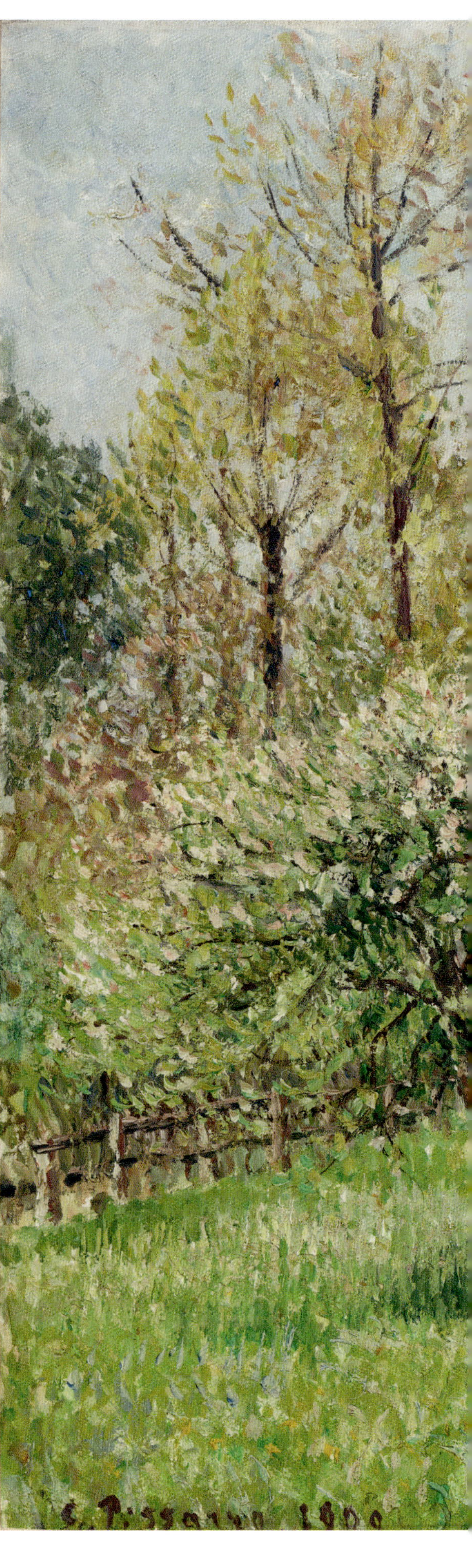

66
Spring at Éragny, 1900
Denver Art Museum, Frederic C. Hamilton Collection, bequeathed to the Denver Art Museum

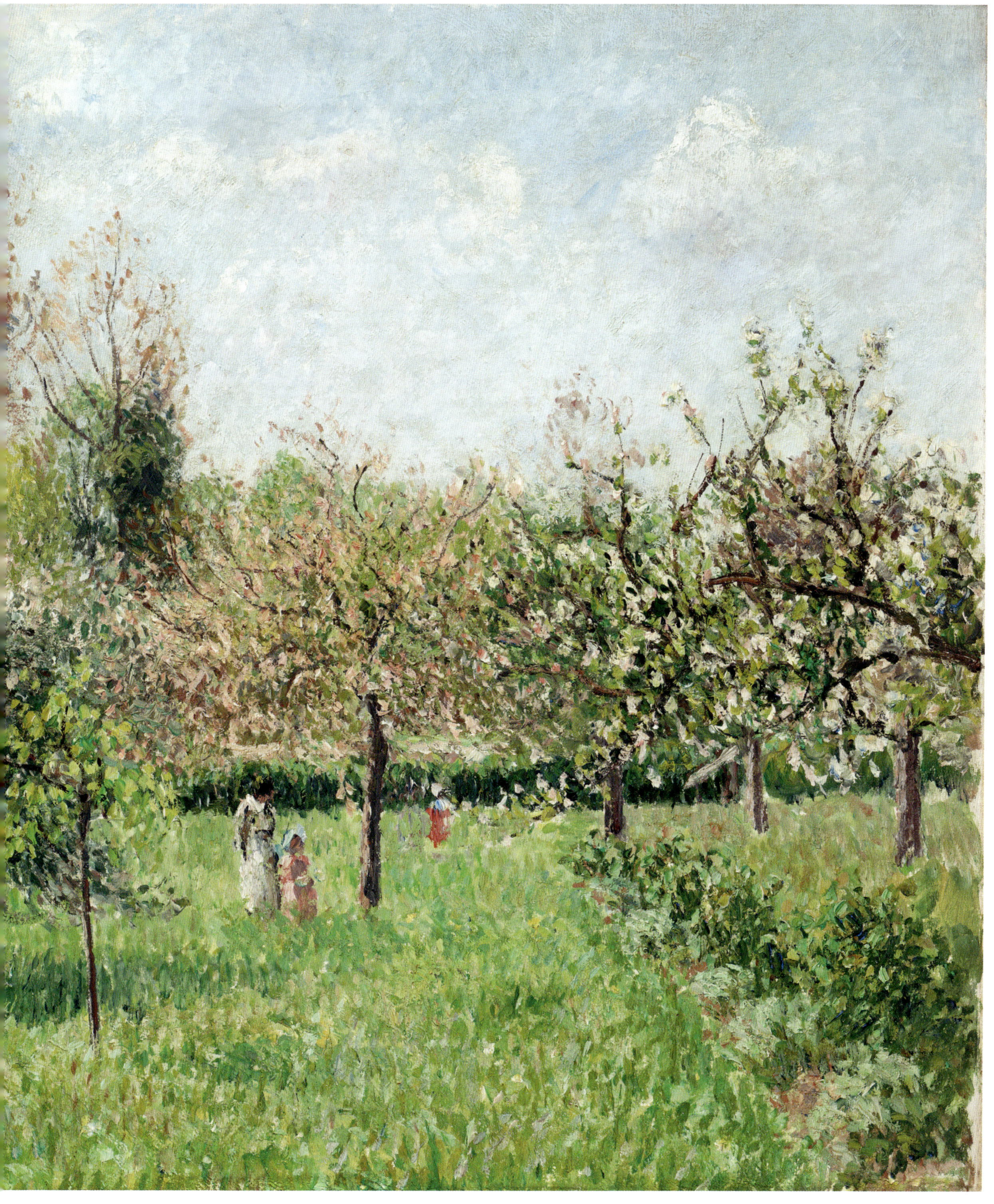

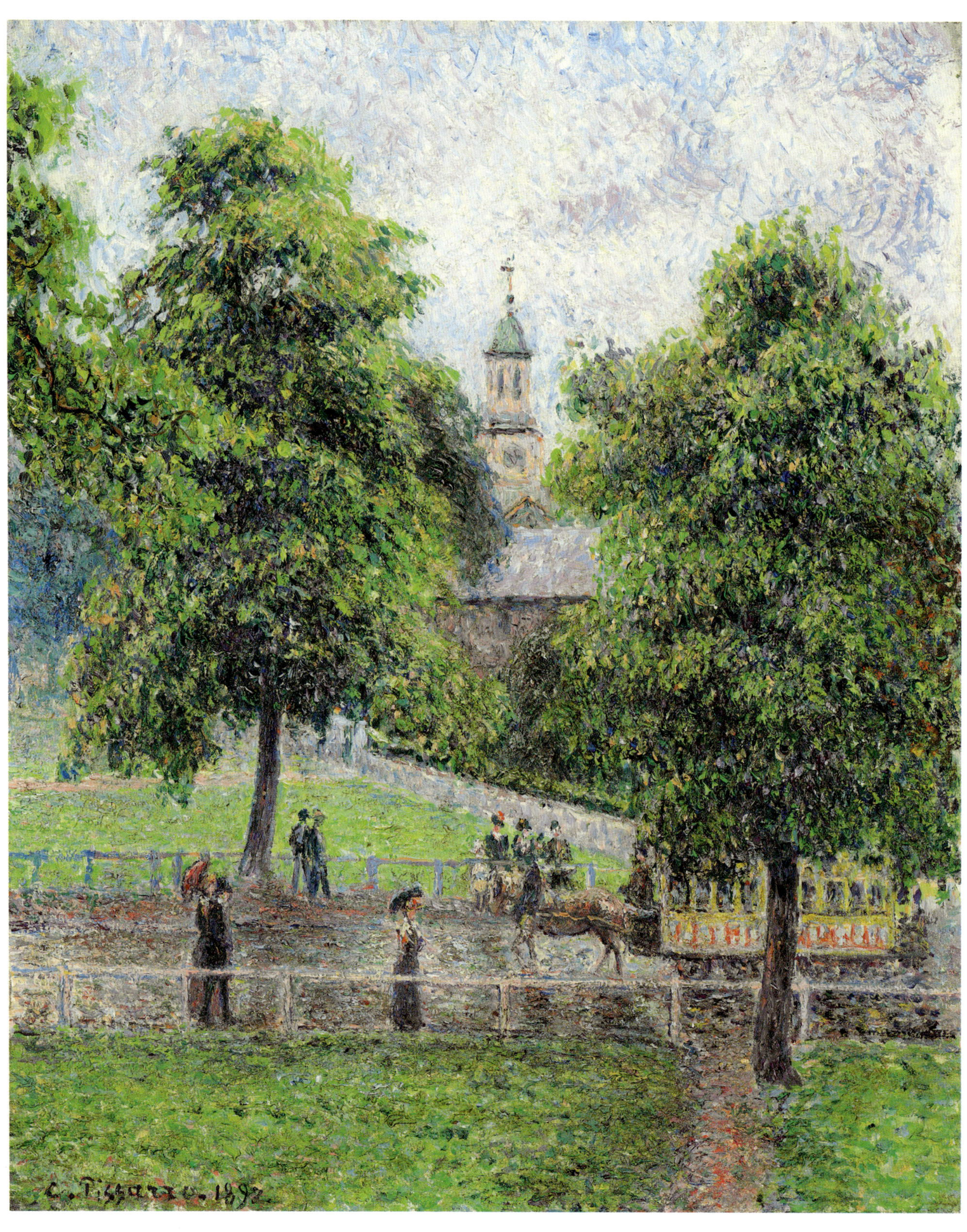

67
Saint Anne's Church in Kew, London, 1892
Collection of Prof. Mark Kaufman, Monaco

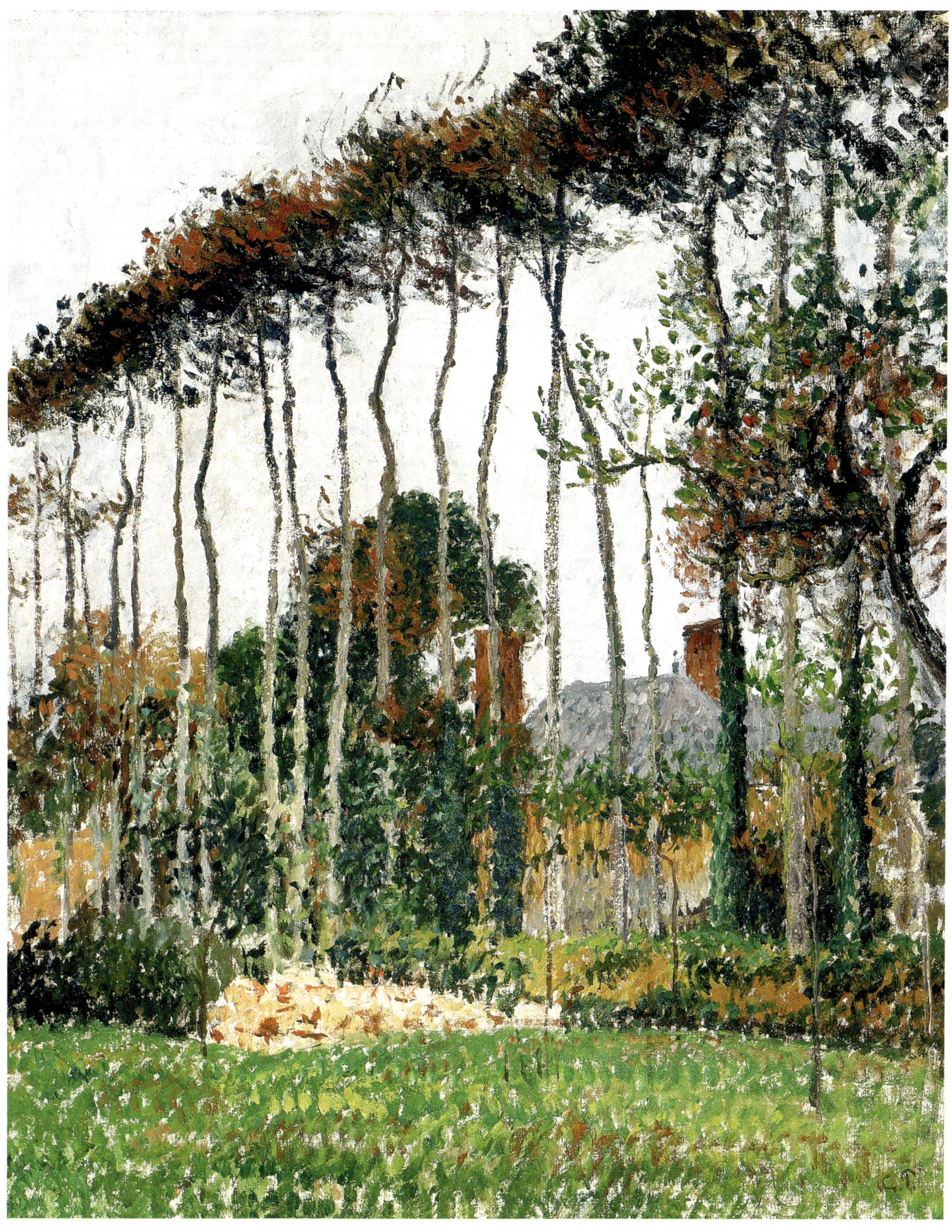

68
The Tall Beech Trees, Varengeville, ca. 1899
Colección Pérez Simón

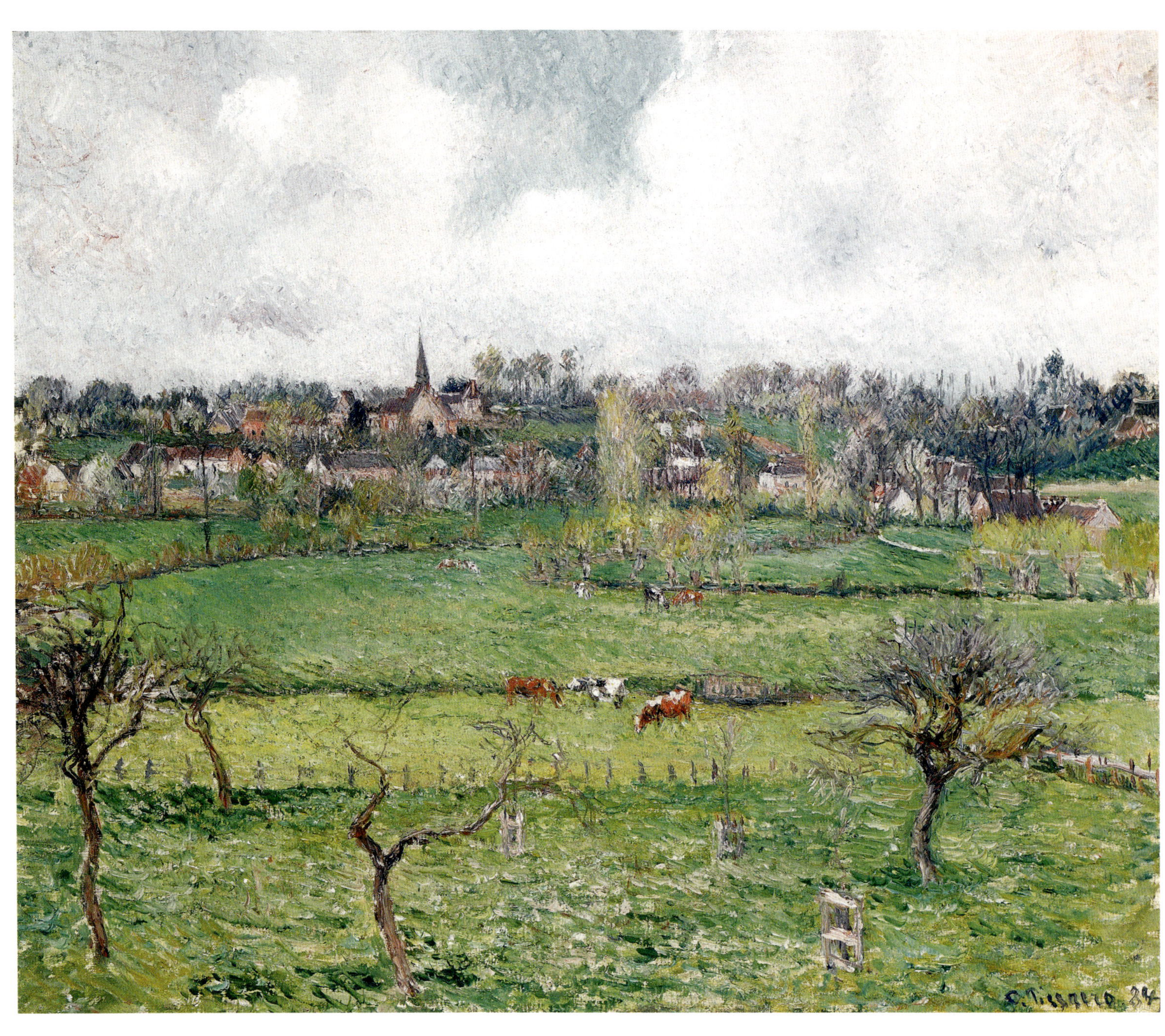

69
View of Bazincourt, Clear Sky, 1884
Colección Pérez Simón

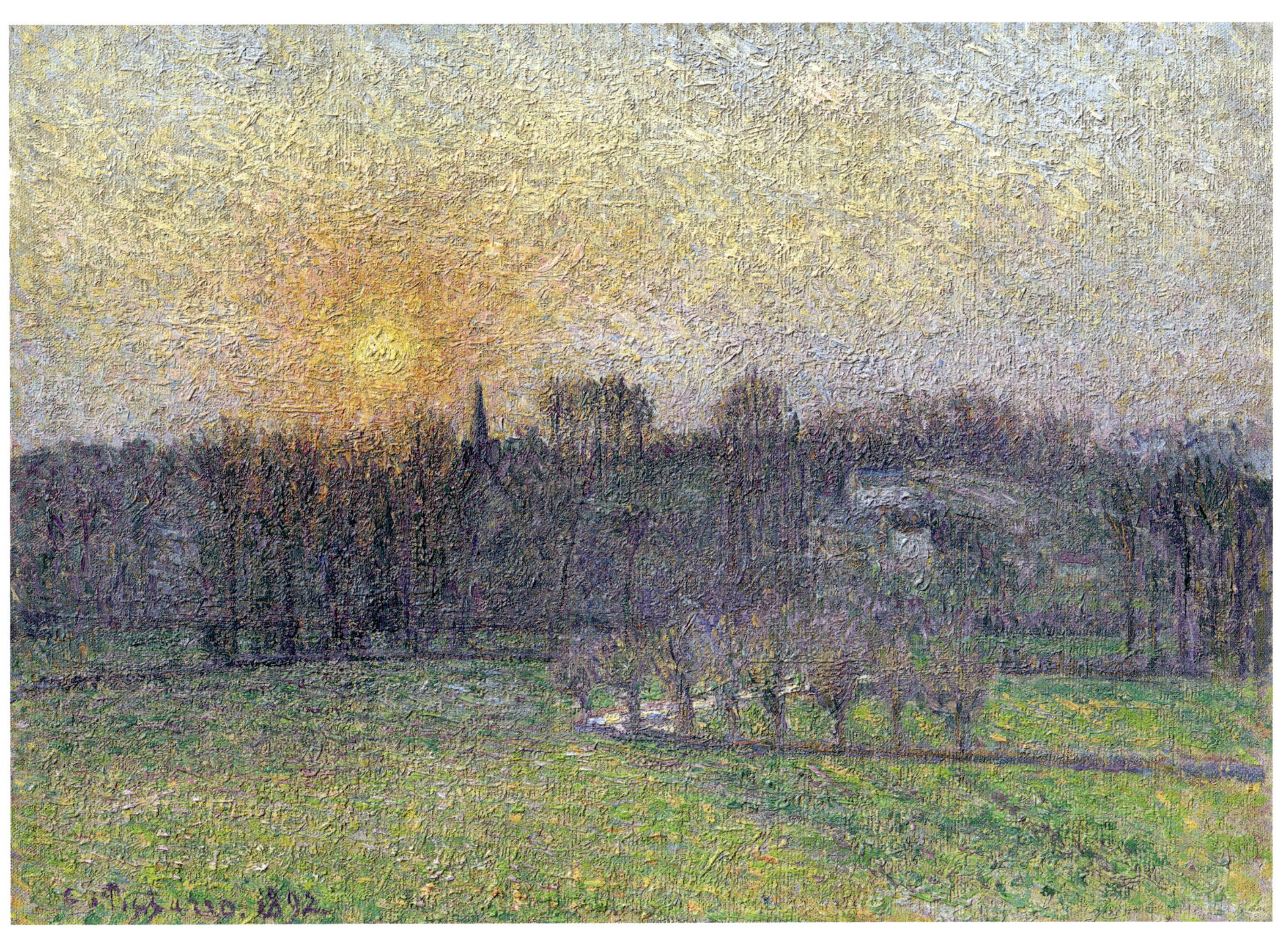

70
View of Bazincourt, Sunset, 1892
Hasso Plattner Collection, Museum Barberini, Potsdam

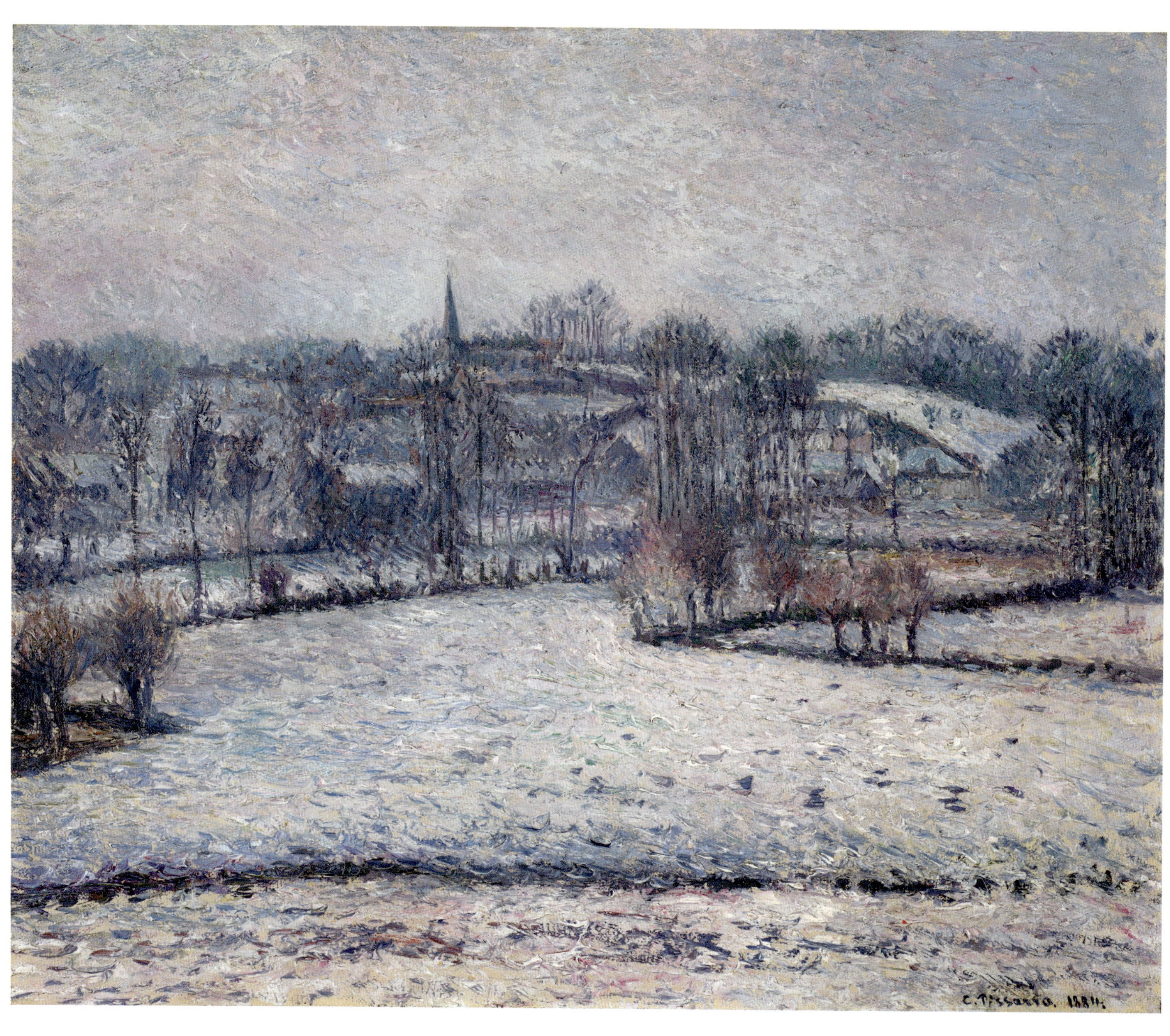

71
Snow Scene at Éragny (View of Bazincourt), 1884
Fine Arts Museums of San Francisco, Gift of Mrs. Renée M. Bransten

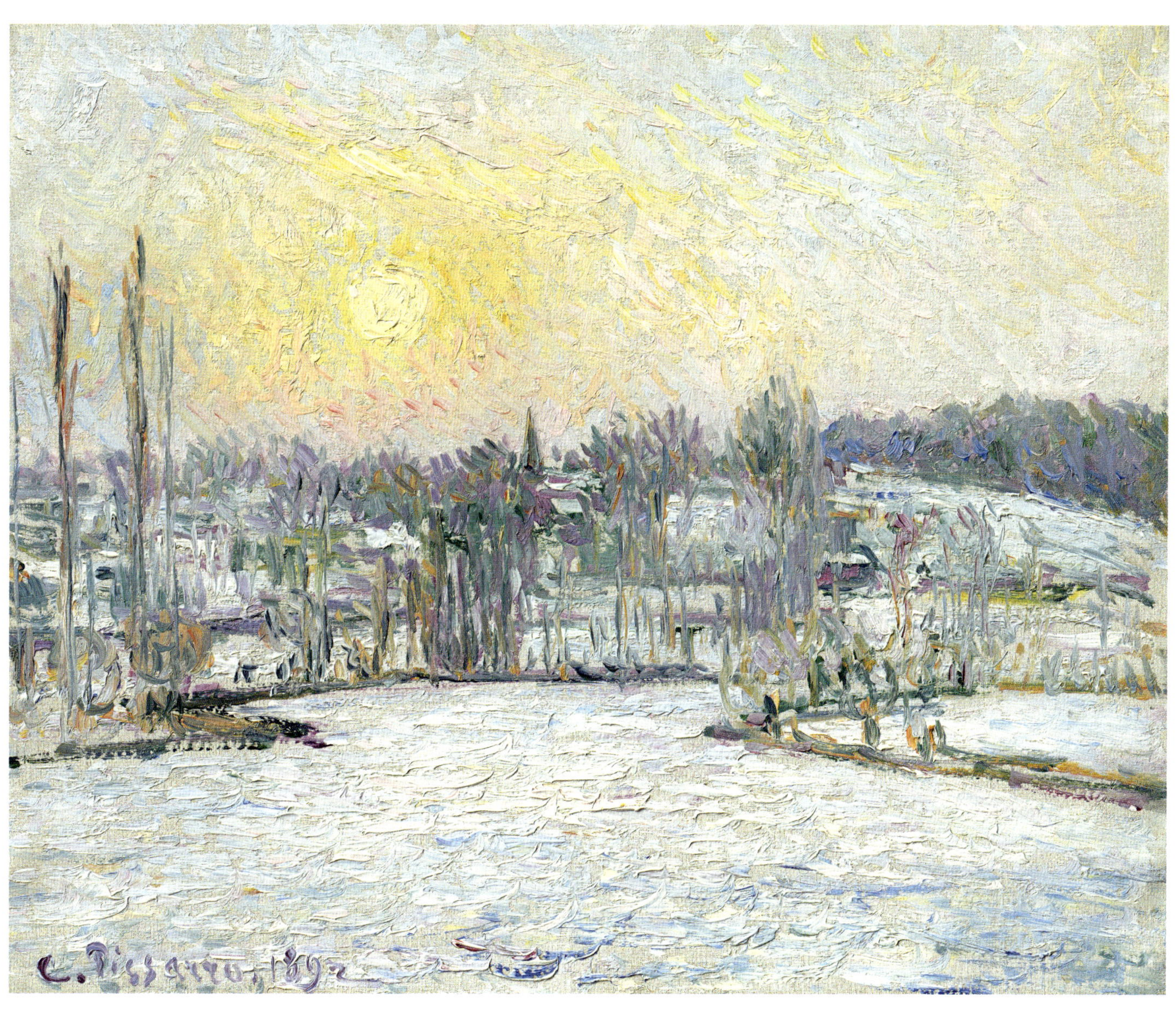

72
View of Bazincourt, Snow Effect, Sunset, 1892
Hasso Plattner Collection, Museum Barberini, Potsdam

A Harmony of Opposites
Neo-Impressionist Paintings

Nerina Santorius

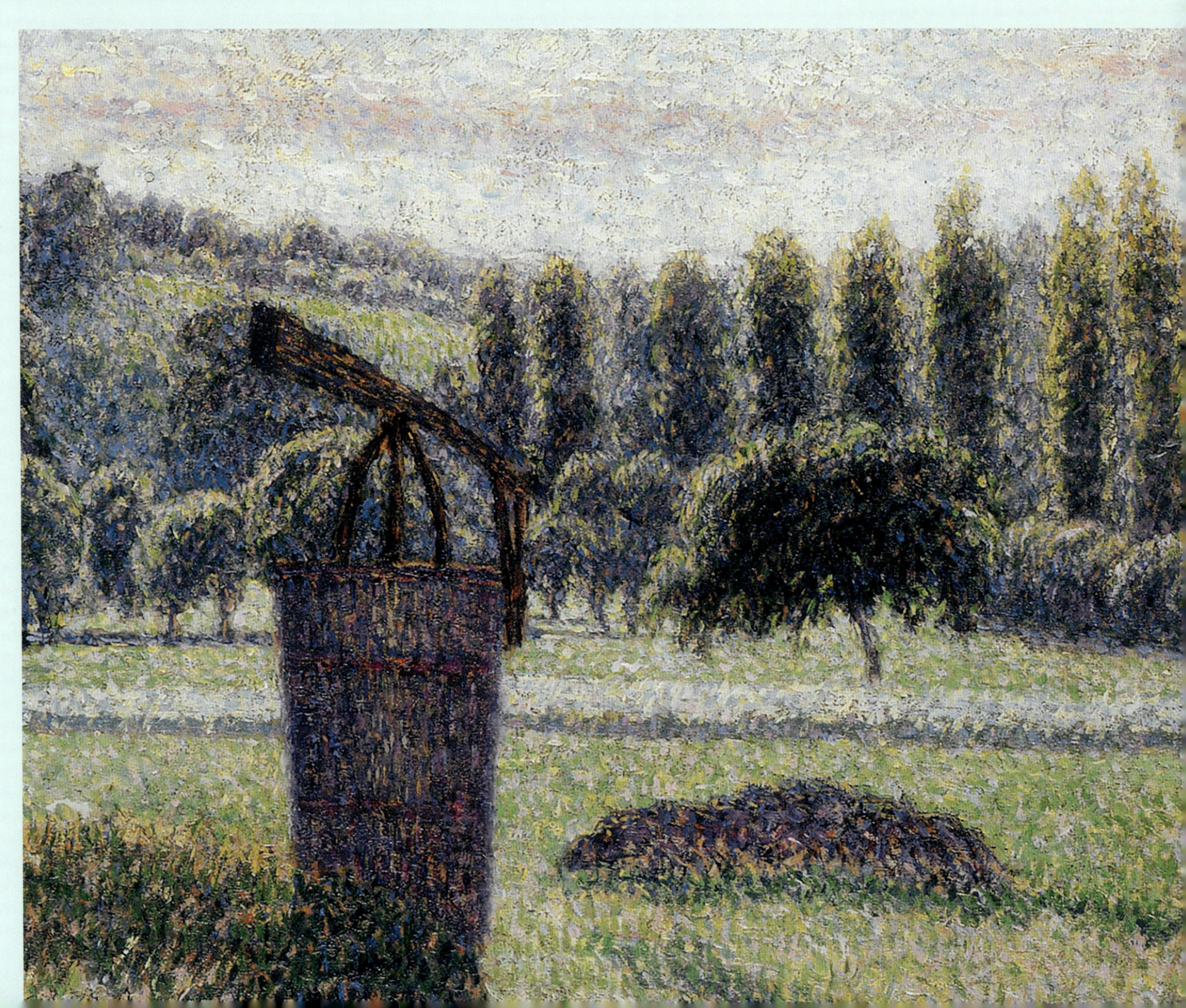

After the encounter with his younger fellow painters Georges Seurat and Paul Signac in 1885, Camille Pissarro adopted their technique, which was based on the newest developments in color theory. The paint was applied to the canvas in small dots, allowing the colors to mix not on the palette but in the eye of the beholder, thereby evoking a greater sense of luminosity. In his paintings, Pissarro sought to unite opposites such as warmth and cold or light and shadow into a harmonious whole in accord with the Neo-Impressionist quest for "a modern synthesis." Due to its laborious nature and unsuitability for the rapid rendering of an immediate impression, however, Pissarro abandoned the technique around 1890.

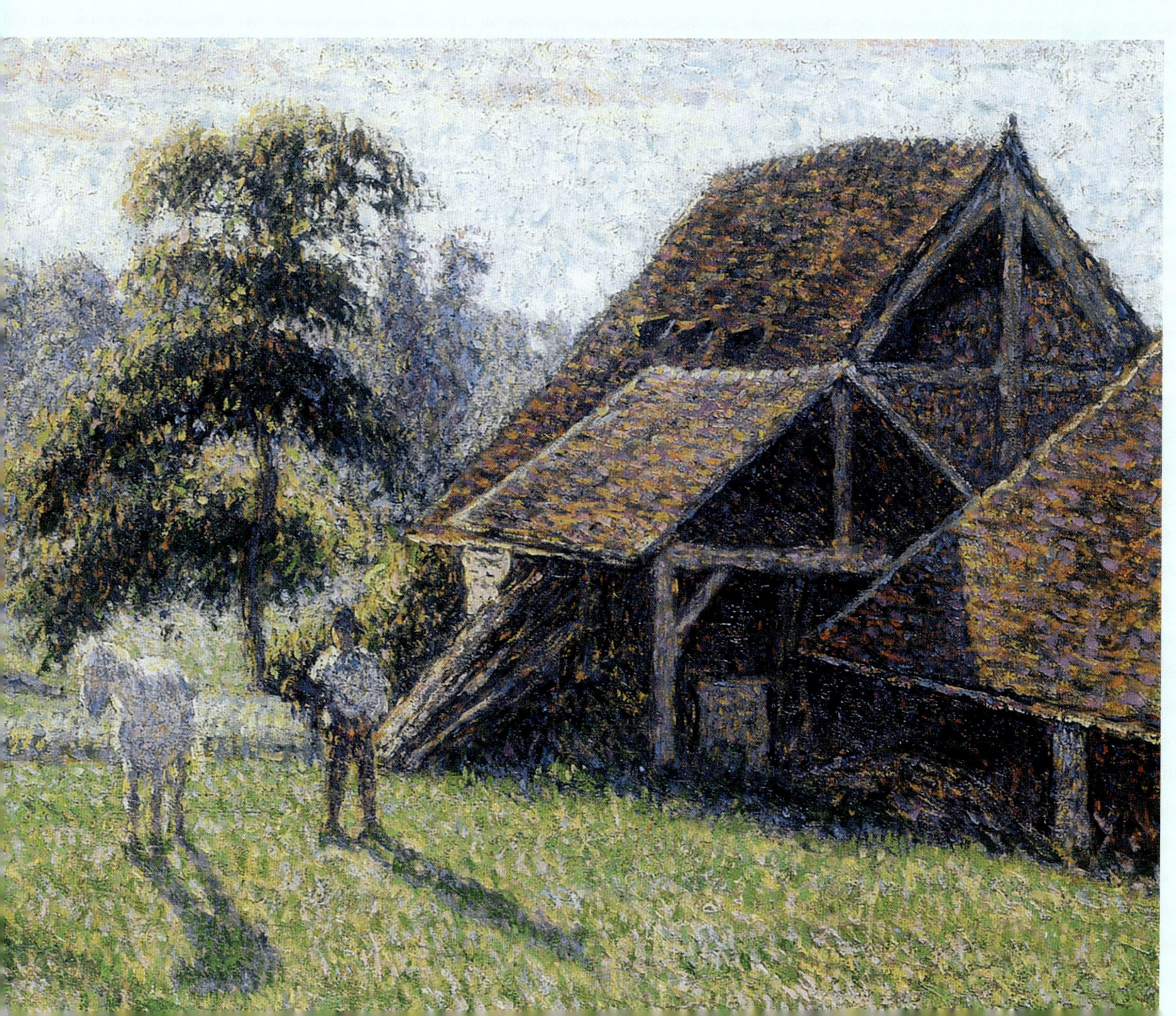

On a windy winter day, a young woman has kindled a fire in a field lined with trees, where a younger companion also warms himself (cat. 74). By applying short brushstrokes of yellow and orange to the green of the grass, Pissarro evokes the sensation of the sun's warmth, while daubs of complementary blue—in the hoarfrost on the meadow, the clothing and shadow of the peasant woman, and the smoke from the fire—convey the impression of cold. When Pissarro exhibited another version of the picture in a gallery in 1890, a critic complained, "In my opinion, the weakness of the painting lies above all in its brilliant monotony. Whether summer or winter, all the seasons appear to be painted in the same colors."[1] But Pissarro's juxtaposition of the conflicting phenomena of warmth and cold—which the reviewer interpreted as a deficit—is in fact programmatic: the picture is also characterized by other contrasts, such as light and shadow, dampness and dryness, the nearby figures in the active foreground and the distant trees and cows in the static background, and the tension between the branch the peasant woman holds in her hands and the unconstrained flickering of the fire. Pissarro's aim was to combine all of these elements into a harmonious whole—using short brushstrokes in pure hues that mingled not on the palette but in the eye of the beholder. His adoption of this new technique of color separation (Divisionism) was inspired by his younger colleagues Georges Seurat and Paul Signac, whom he had met in 1885. Pissarro played a decisive role in the style's propagation in the years that followed.[2] In 1886 the term *synthesis* first occurs in Pissarro's correspondence. In a letter to his dealer Paul Durand-Ruel, he explained the new theory of Neo-Impressionism: "To seek a modern synthesis through methods grounded in science, based on the color theory discovered by M. Chevreul and after the experiments of Maxwell and the measurements of N. O. Rood. To substitute optical mixing for the mixing of pigments; in other words, the decomposition of tones into their constituent elements. Because optical mixing evokes much more intense luminosity than the mixing of pigments."[3] The intensification of color was also intended to produce a concentration of expression that transcended mere sense experience.

Despite certain ephemeral elements, Pissarro's painting *Hoarfrost, Peasant Girl Making a Fire* is not a momentary snapshot. The woman's grip on the branch seems ill-suited for breaking the wood but establishes a compositional link to the trees in the background. This visual relationship invites the viewer to trace the path from the living tree to the warmth-giving firewood. The cloud of billowing smoke also suggests the peasant woman's ability to start a fire, even with damp wood—thus spinning a narrative about the cycle of nature and rural life that imbues the picture with universal meaning.

In 1887 critic Félix Fénéon wrote, "What the Neo-Impressionists are trying to do is synthesize the landscape into a definitive appearance that perpetuates the sensation. [. . .] For them, objective reality is simply a motif for the creation of a superior and sublimated reality into which their personality is transfused."[4] Pissarro's painting *The Flock of Sheep, Éragny* (cat. 75) can also be interpreted in this sense. The center of the picture is dominated by a cloud of dust as tall as the houses, stirred up by the animals on the main street of the town where the artist resided. Within a clear composition articulated by diagonals and horizontals, the foreground remains empty, making the sheep seem like protagonists on a stage while the shepherd in the shadows to the left plays only a supporting role. Here, Pissarro took figures traditionally associated with the genre of the pastoral—scenes of shepherd life in an idyllic landscape—and transplanted them to the world of everyday reality, imbuing it with a sense of timelessness. Once again, the artist synthesized opposites such as light and shadow, fullness and emptiness, visibility and invisibility, bringing them into a harmonious unity. While painters such as Claude Monet were fascinated by London fog or the steam of modern ships and locomotives, Pissarro elevated a cloud of dust kicked up by sheep to the status of a primary motif—in keeping with his preference for humble objects from a rural context, traditionally shunned as pictorial subjects.

Such paintings of ordinary, "unattractive" motifs, combined with the technique of Divisionism, were difficult to sell. Pissarro's dealer Durand-Ruel warned the artist that no one was interested in works such as *View from My Window* (cat. 78), with its chicken coop and prominent red tile roof—which the artist later overpainted in the foreground. Yet for Pissarro, it was precisely these elements that gave the work its character.[5] The clear geometric composition with numerous horizontals that convey a peaceful atmosphere and the complementary contrast of red and green, employed to heighten the intensity of the color, are typical features of Neo-Impressionism.

Art critics of the day frequently compared the artistic strategy of division and synthesis to chemical processes. In chemistry, the term *analysis* describes the separation of compounds into their constituent elements, while *synthesis* refers to the opposite: the combination of two or more elements into a new, more complex substance. This scientific understanding already resonates in Fénéon's assertion that the synthesis of Neo-Impressionist landscape paintings was intended to create a sublimated reality. With regard to Pissarro's works, Fénéon remarked that they were "scrupulously conceived and executed by the process of division into molecules of color."[6] The chemical metaphor also figured prominently in anarchist theories of the time, which the Neo-Impressionist artists endorsed and to which Pissarro also turned his attention. His friend Jean Grave, an anarchist and editor of the journals *La Révolte* and *Les Temps nouveaux,* saw parallels between the concerns of an anarchist and the work of a chemist: in analogy to the latter, the former contributes to the realization of a new and better society by creating an environment conducive to the development of the human "components."[7]

Although Pissarro shared the political views of the anarchists, he usually avoided explicit references to such views in works intended for the public. His album *Turpitudes sociales* (Social Disgraces, cats. 83–86) of 1889–90, however—a collection of twenty-eight satirical drawings created for the political education of his nieces Esther and Alice Isaacson—represents a clear attack on capitalism. In pages such as *Study for "The Temple of the Golden Calf"* (cat. 85) or *Study for "The Asphysia"* (cat. 86), the artist castigates corrupt bankers and the exploitation of the proletariat in an extremely pointed manner, which even made use of anti-Semitic clichés. The completion of the album more or less coincided with his turn away from Neo-Impressionism: the combined disadvantage of greater effort, fewer sales, and the impossibility of rapidly capturing an immediate impression with this technique weighed too heavily in the balance. However, the boundaries of Pissarro's Divisionist phase were fluid: his initial exploration of the new approach developed out of earlier experiments, and later, too, he sometimes used short brushstrokes and daubs of paint to lend his landscapes a lively, flickering atmosphere and harmonize the pictorial elements (cats. 81, 82). For Pissarro, there was no such thing as an anarchist motif, per se: "All the arts are anarchist when they are beautiful and good!"[8] Nevertheless, against the backdrop of his political persuasions, his synthesized images of the surrounding landscape echo the anarchist ideal of social concord. They reflect a model of society defined by an independent life in harmony with nature.

Translated from German by Melissa M. Thorson

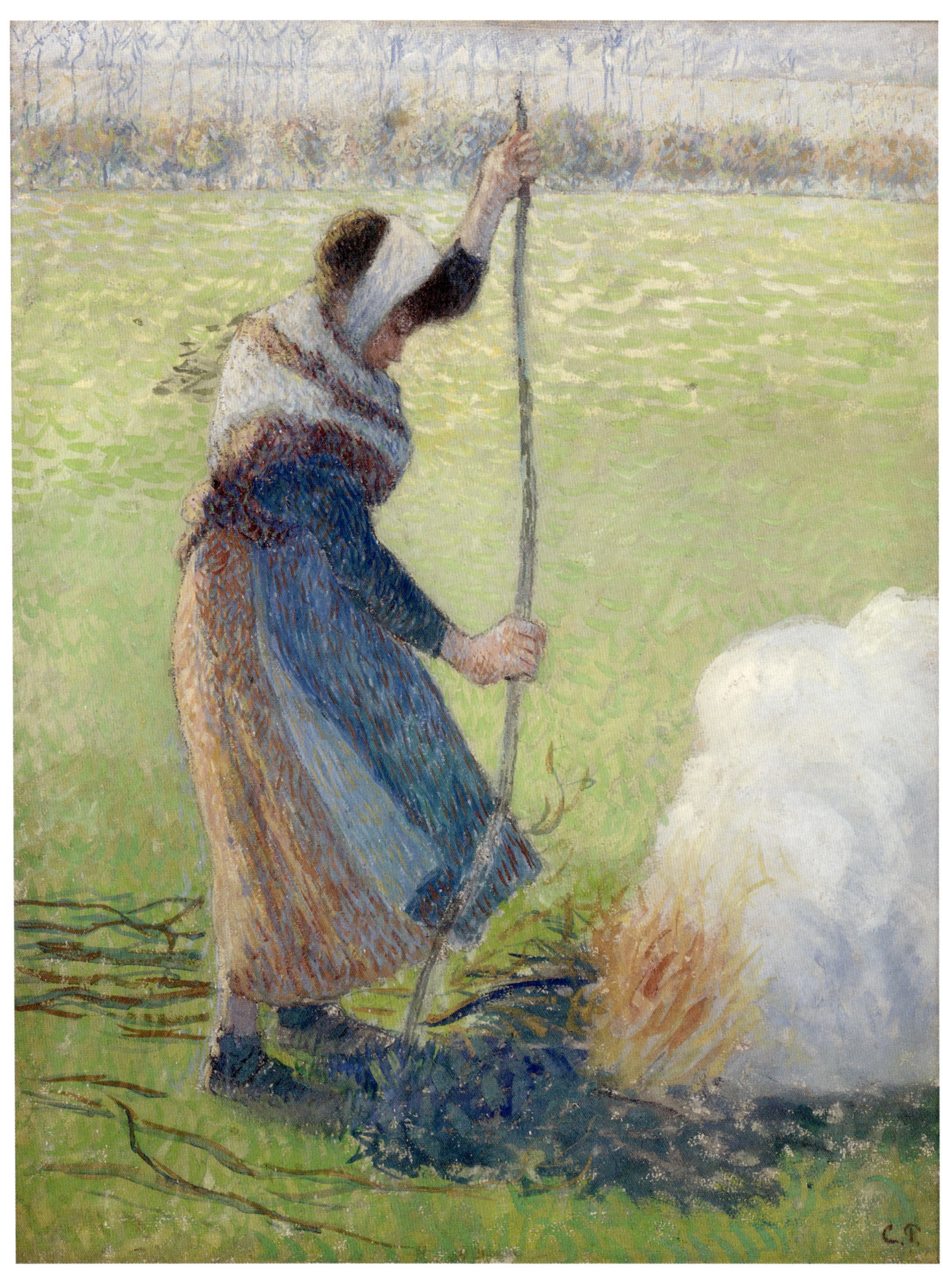

73
Woman Breaking Wood, ca. 1890
Private collection, courtesy of Pissarro & Associates Fine Art

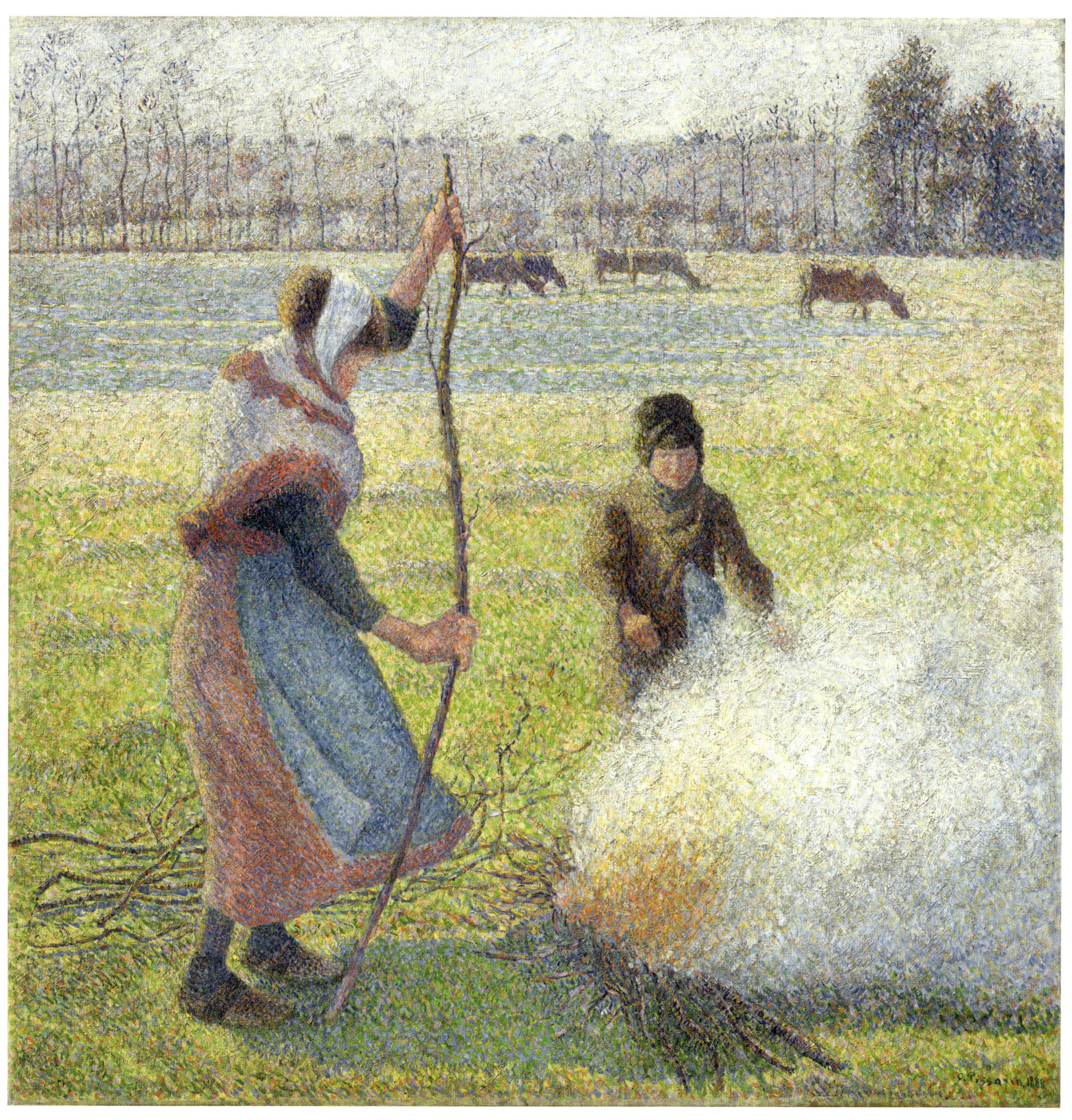

74
Hoarfrost, Peasant Girl Making a Fire, 1888
Hasso Plattner Collection, Museum Barberini, Potsdam

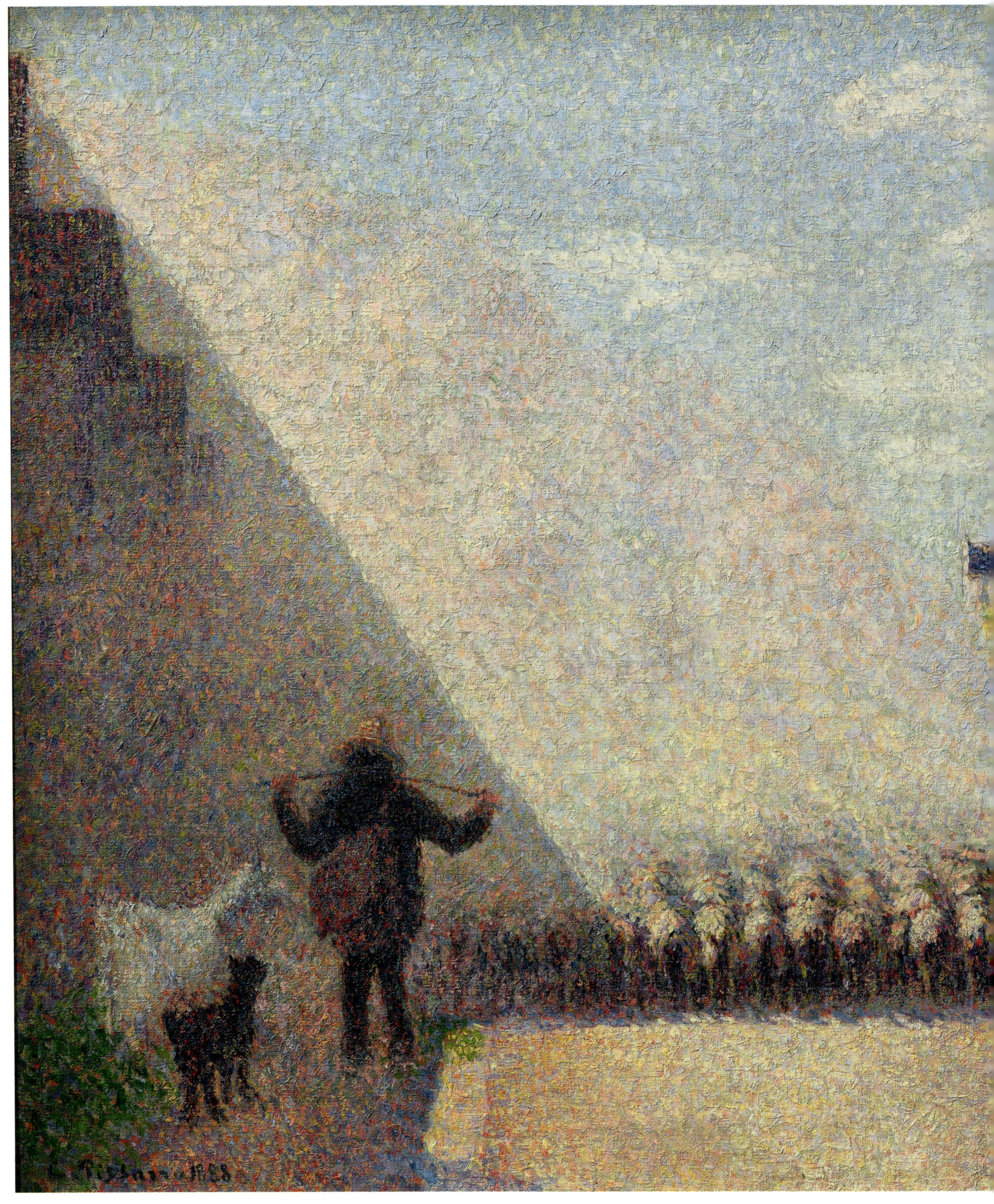

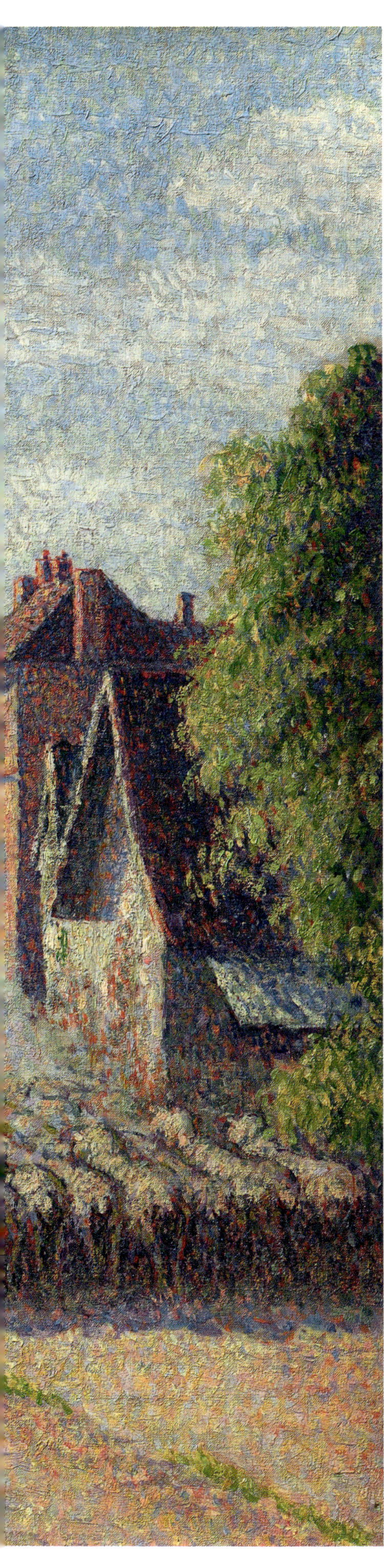

75
The Flock of Sheep, Éragny, 1888
Private collection

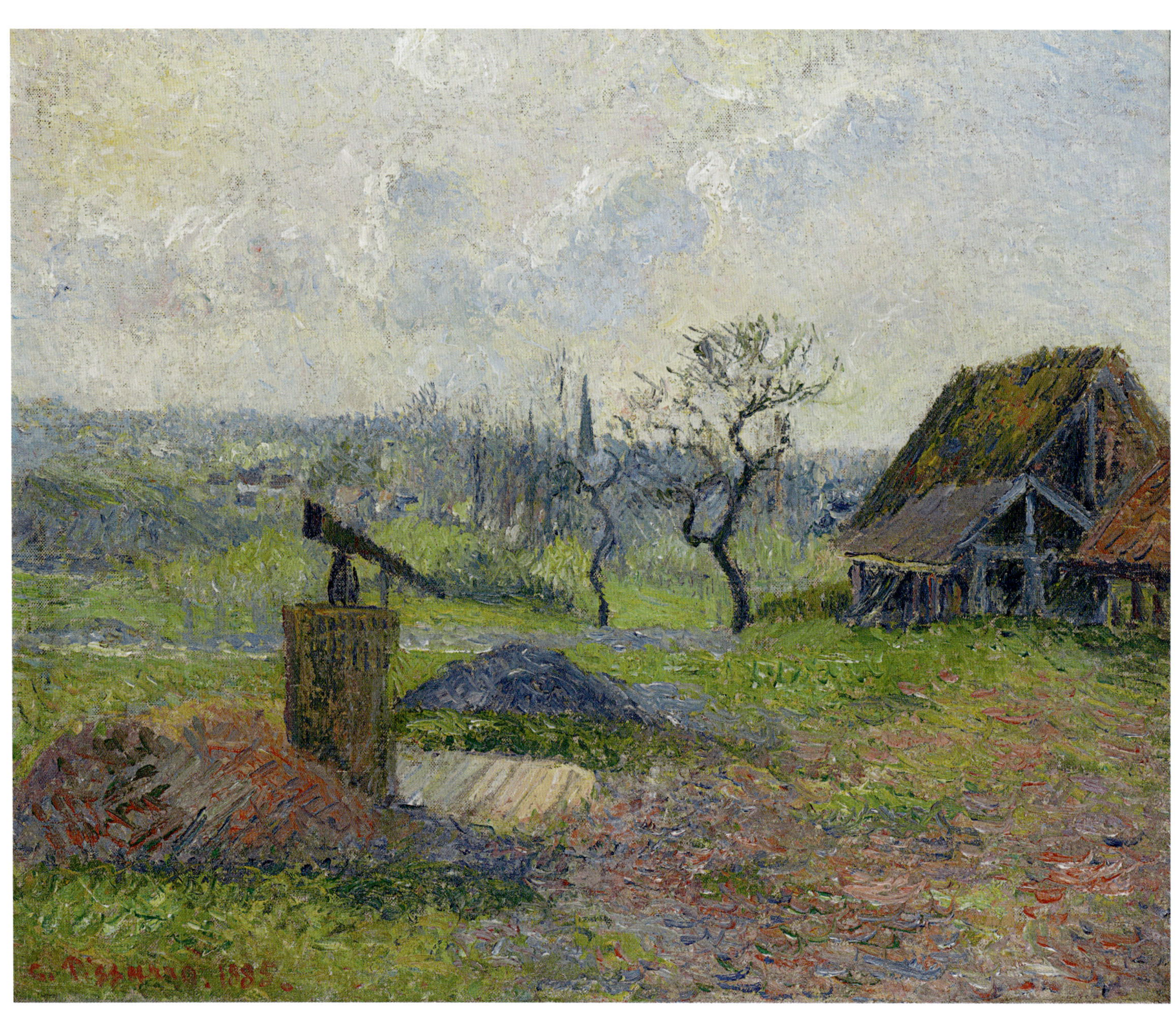

76
The Delafolie Brickyard, Éragny, 1885
The Ashmolean Museum, University of Oxford, Bequeathed by Frank Hindley Smith, 1939

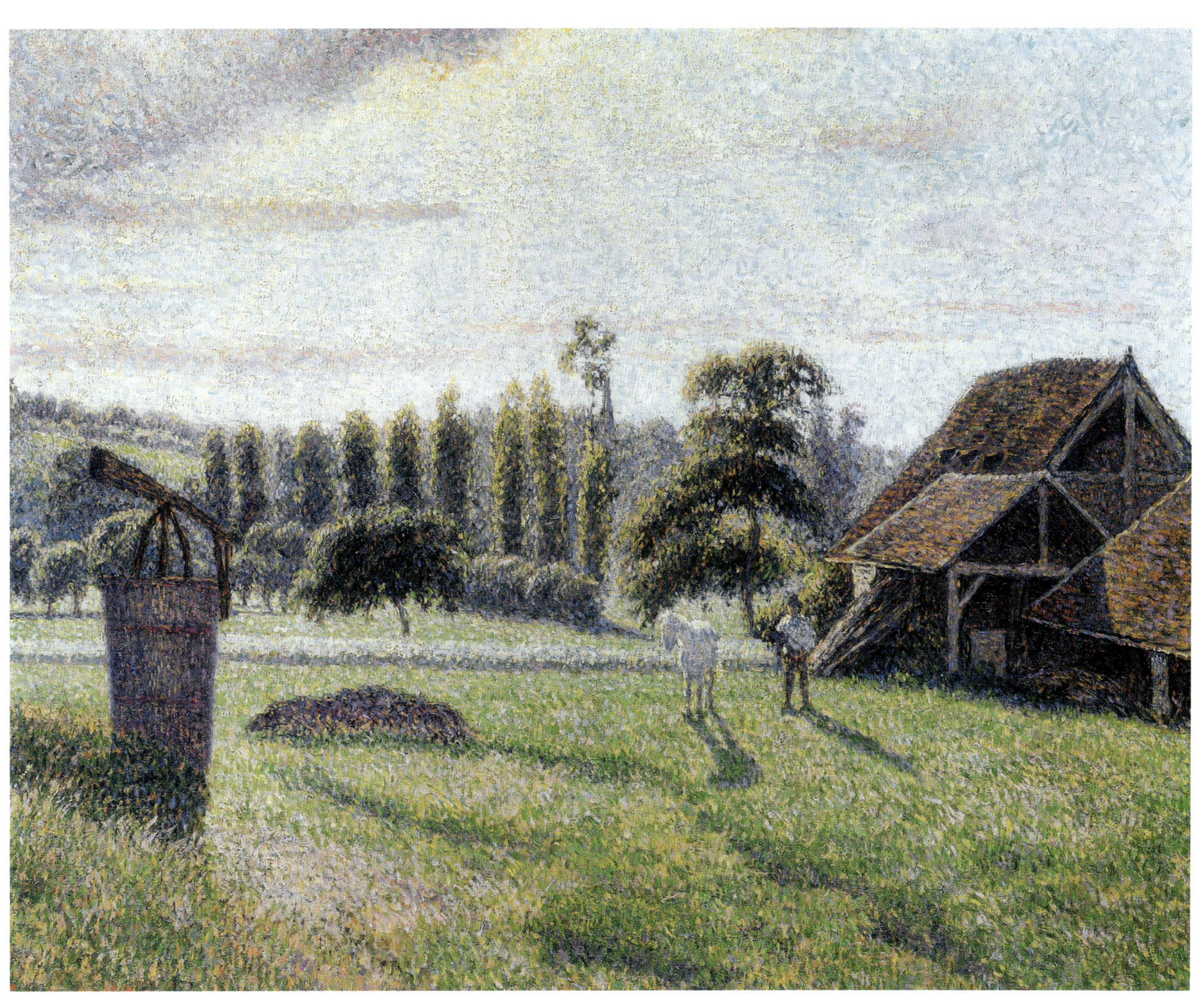

77
The Delafolie Brickyard at Éragny, 1886
Private collection

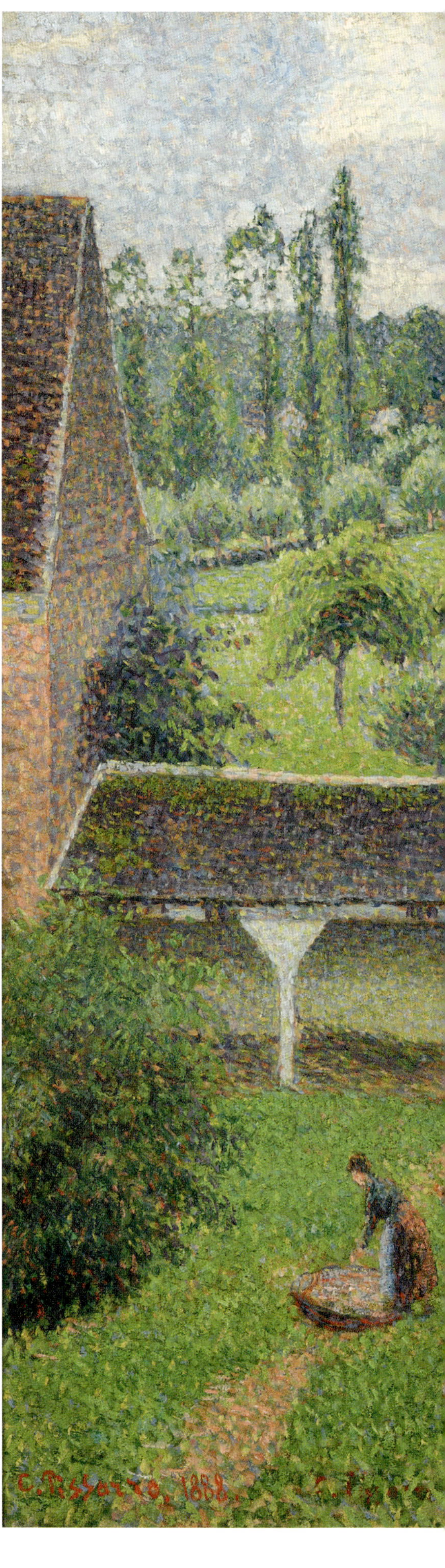

78
View from My Window in Cloudy Weather, 1886–88
The Ashmolean Museum, University of Oxford, Presented by Mrs. Lucien Pissarro, 1950

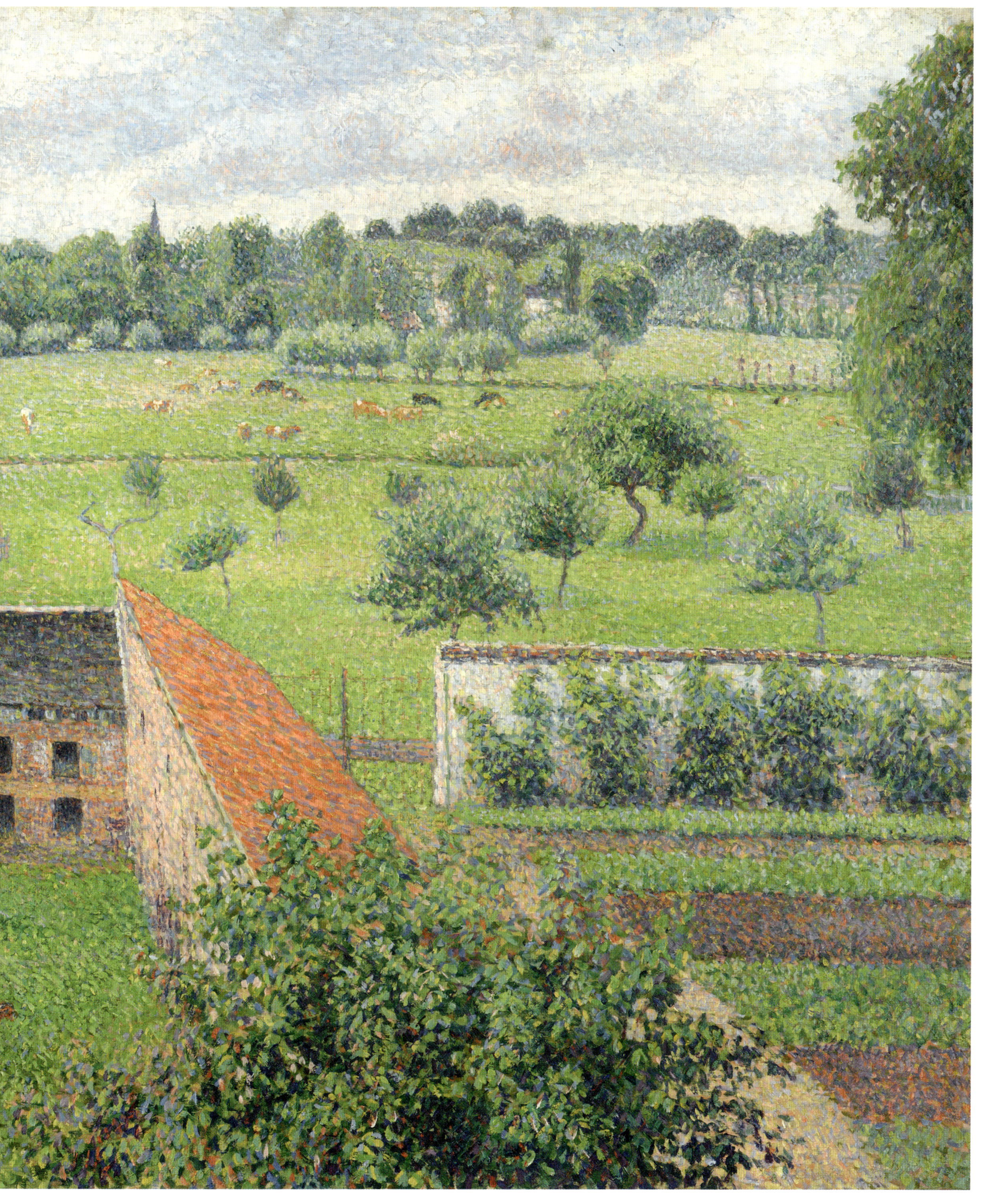

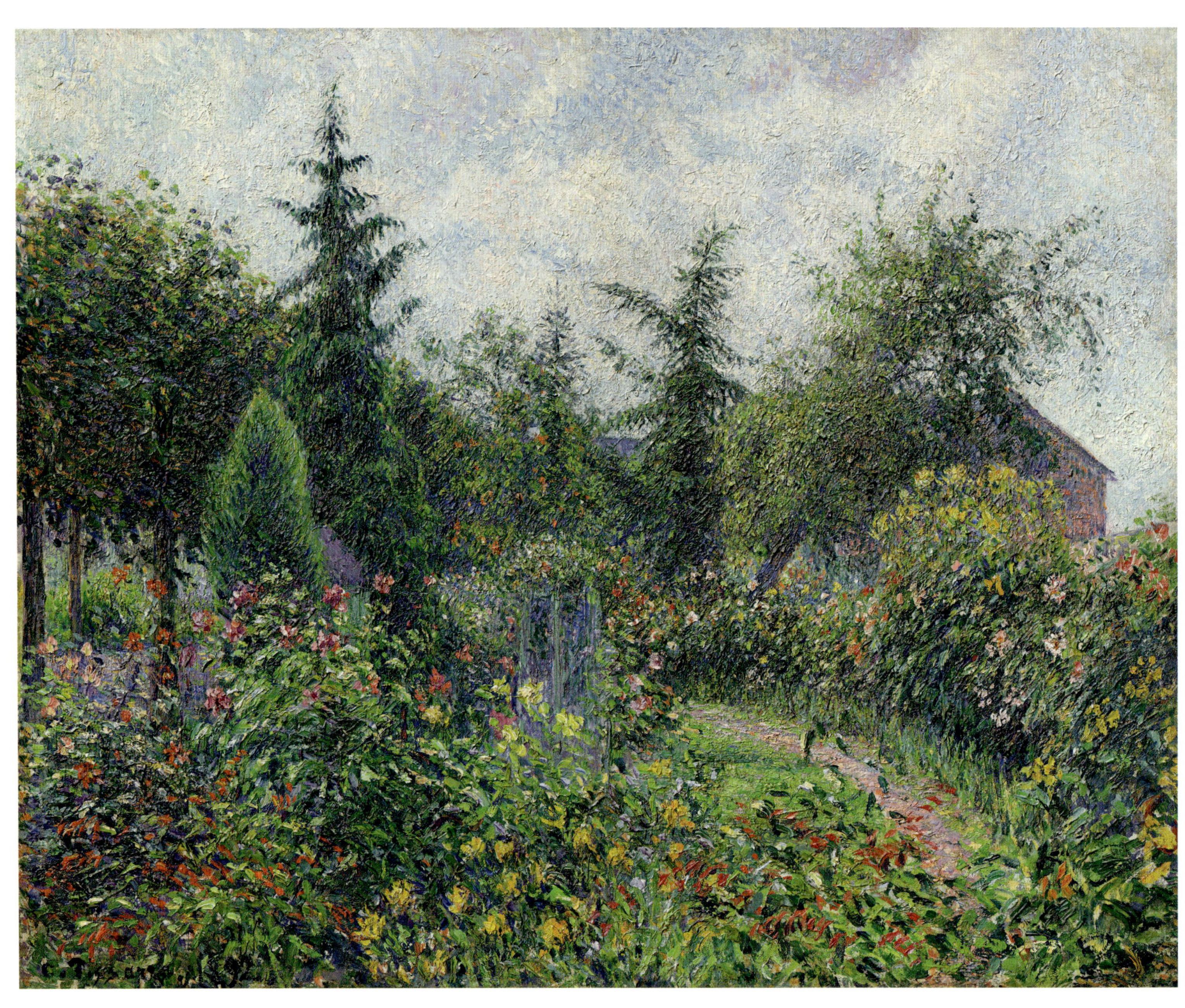

79
The Garden and Henhouse at Octave Mirbeau's, Les Damps, 1892
Hasso Plattner Collection, Museum Barberini, Potsdam

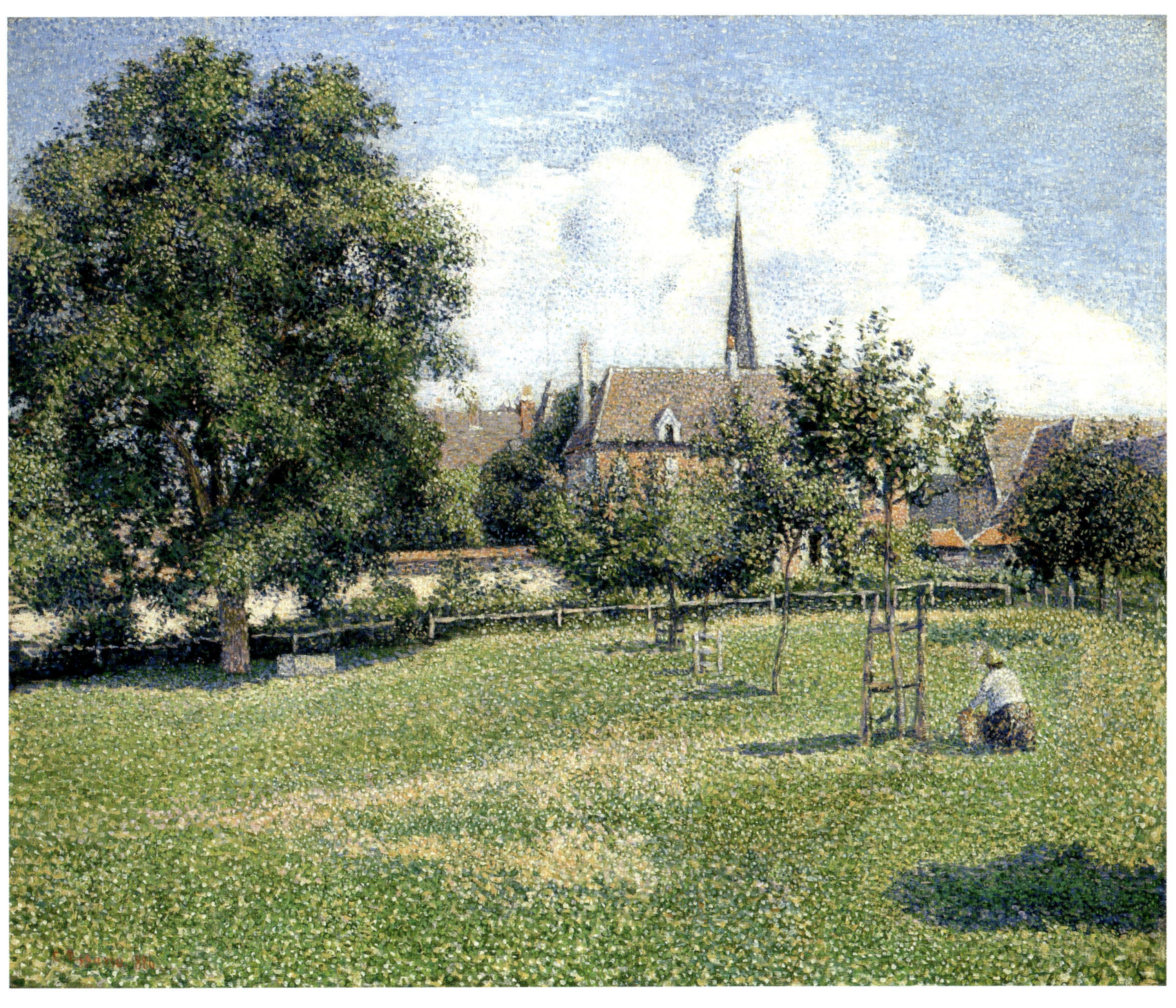

80
The House of the Deaf Woman and the Belfry at Éragny, 1886
Indianapolis Museum of Art at Newfields, Anonymous gift

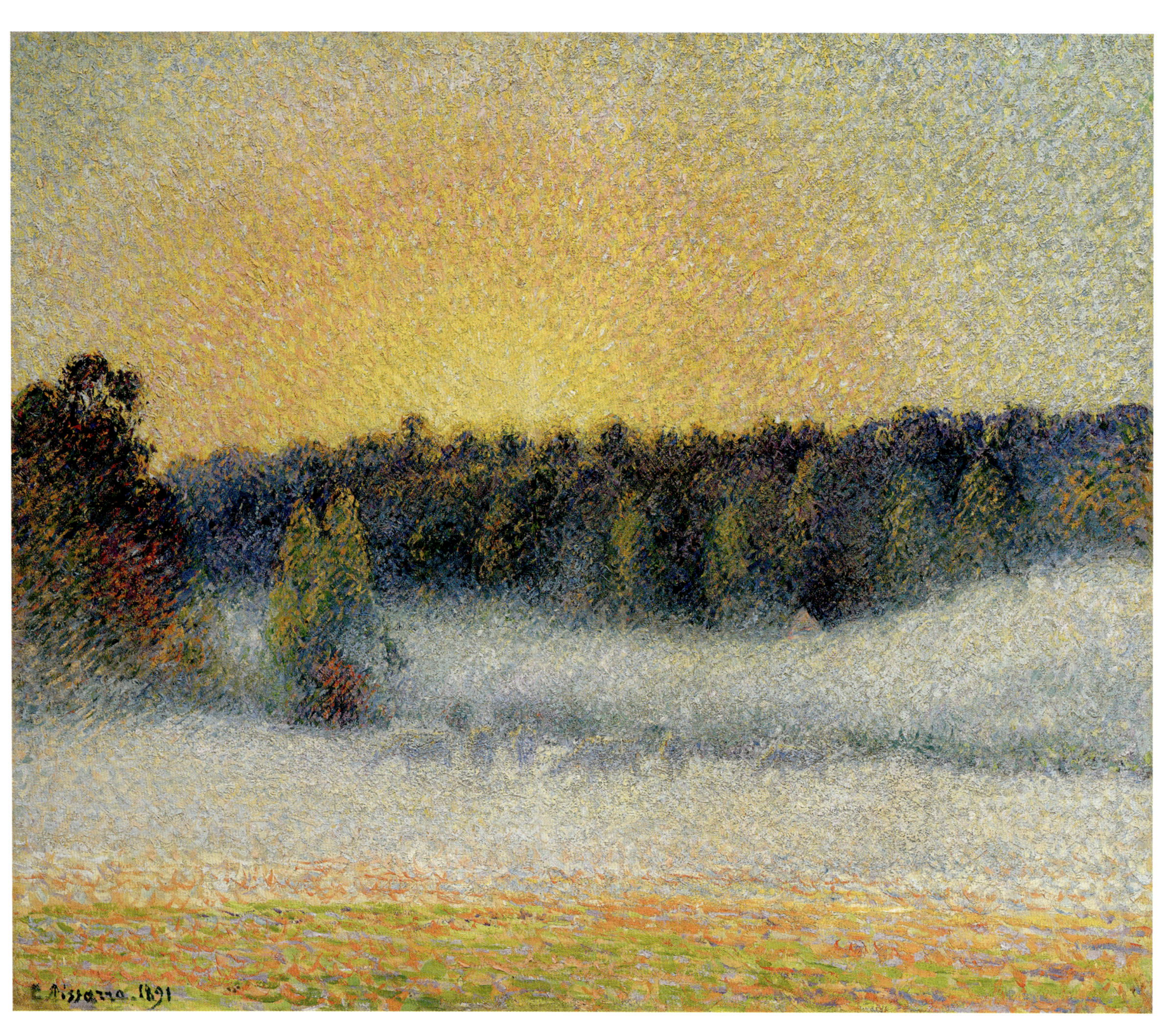

81
Meadow at Éragny with Cows, Fog, Sunset, 1891
Private collection, Switzerland

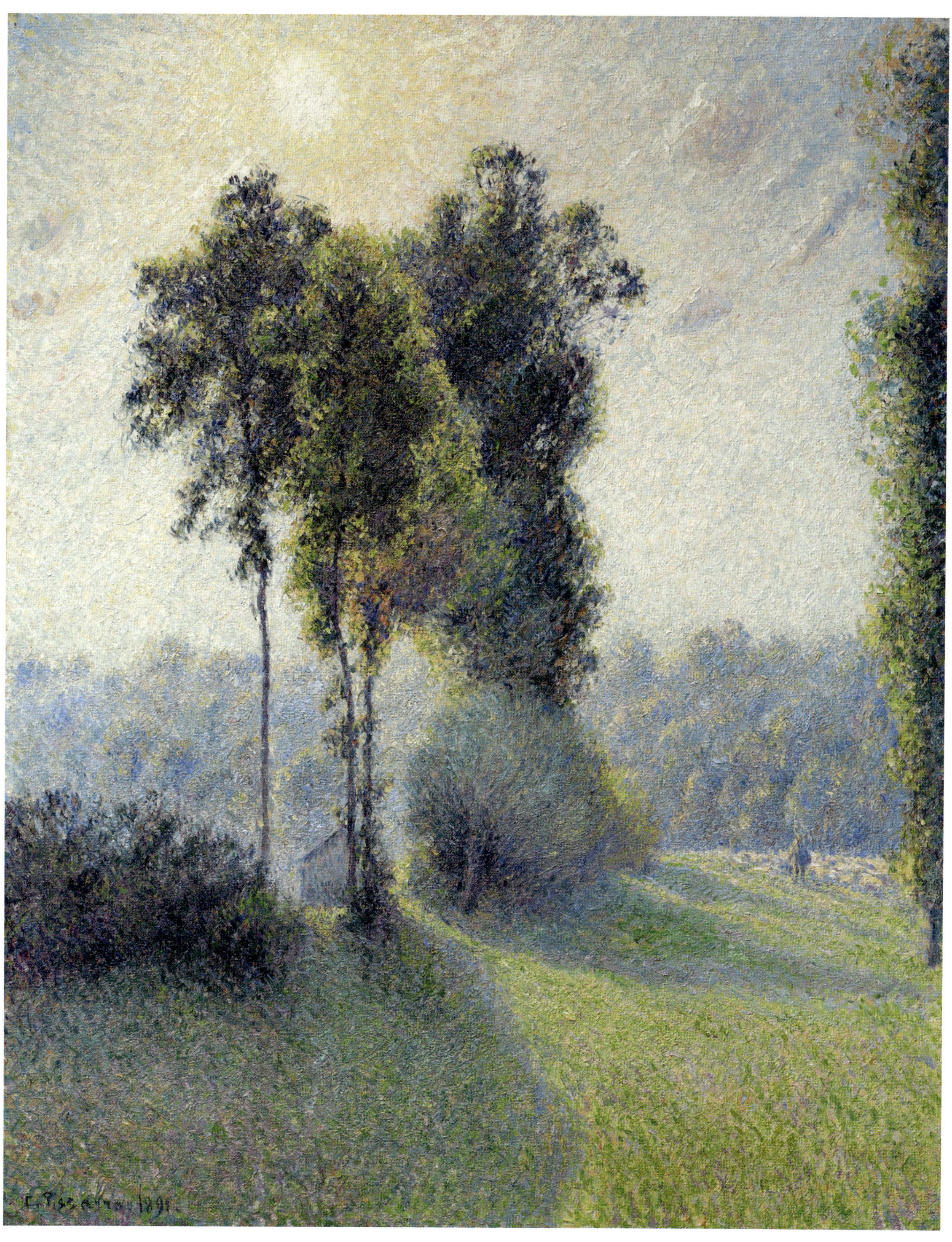

82
Landscape at Saint-Charles, Near Gisors, Sunset, 1891
Clark Art Institute, Williamstown, Massachusetts

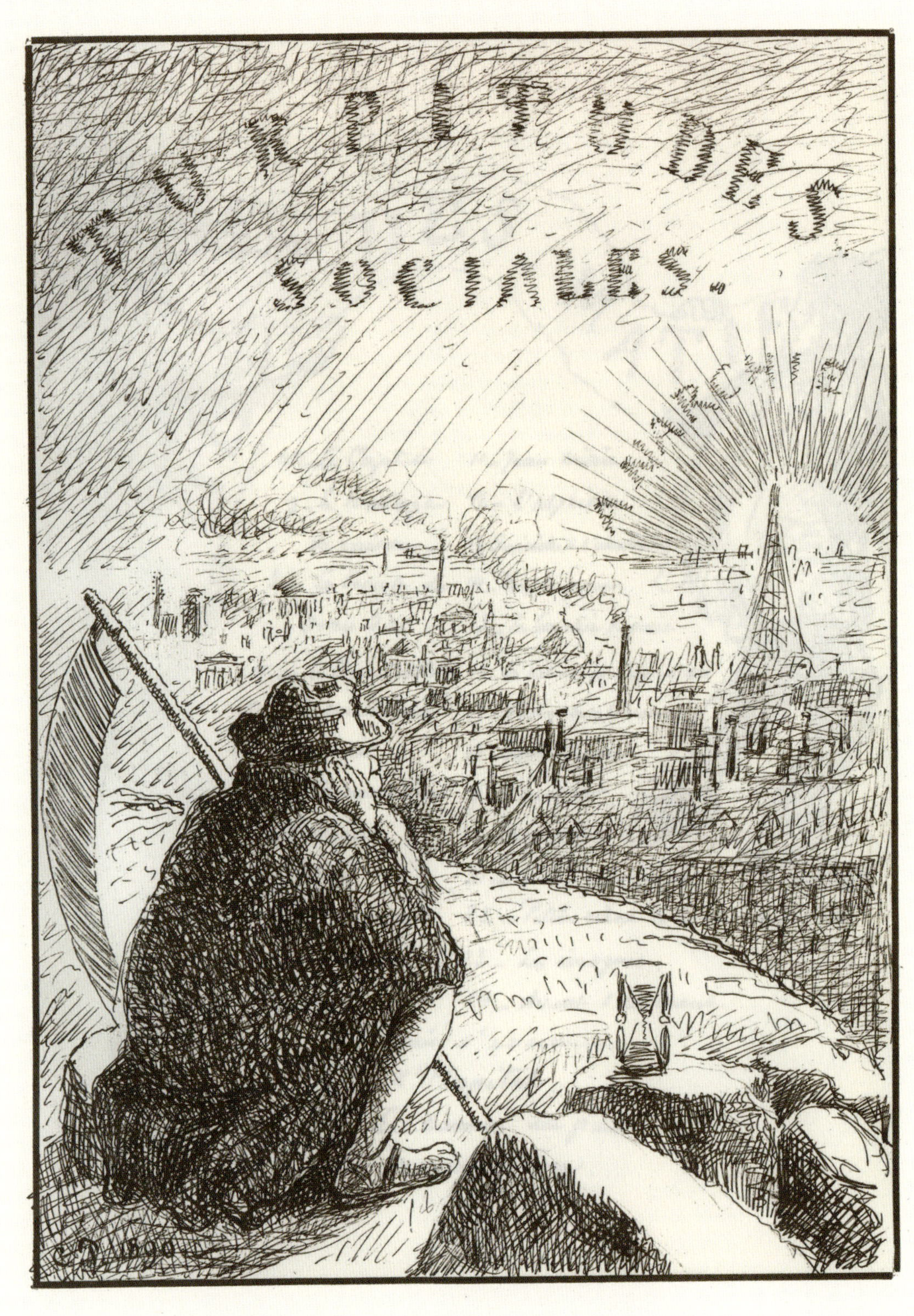

83
Turpitudes sociales, 1889–90 (frontispiece)
Facsimile, Geneva 1972
Private collection, courtesy of Pissarro & Associates Fine Art

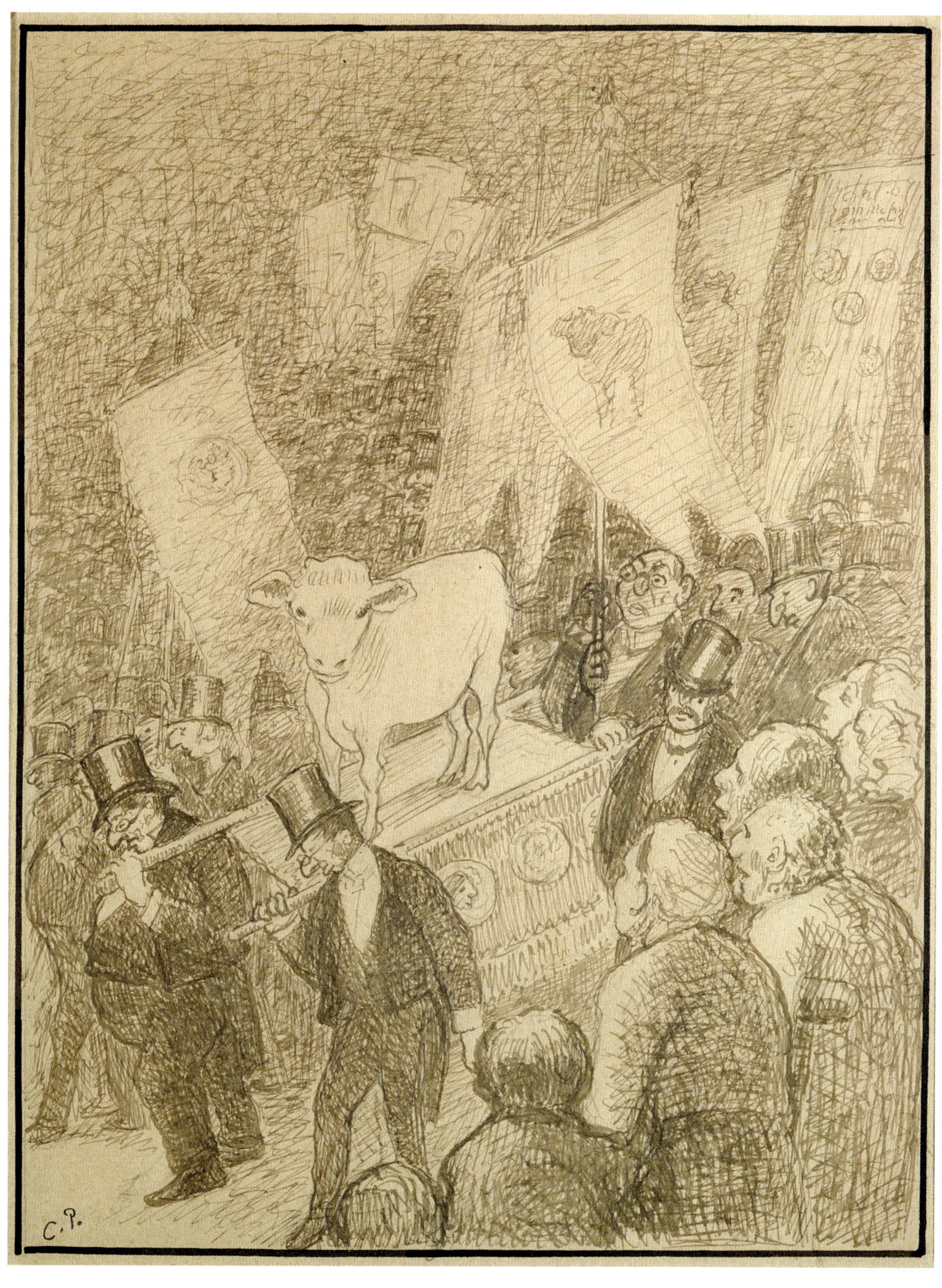

84
The New Idolators (for *Turpitudes sociales,* omitted), 1889
Denver Art Museum, The T. Edward and Tullah Hanley memorial gift to the people of Denver and the area

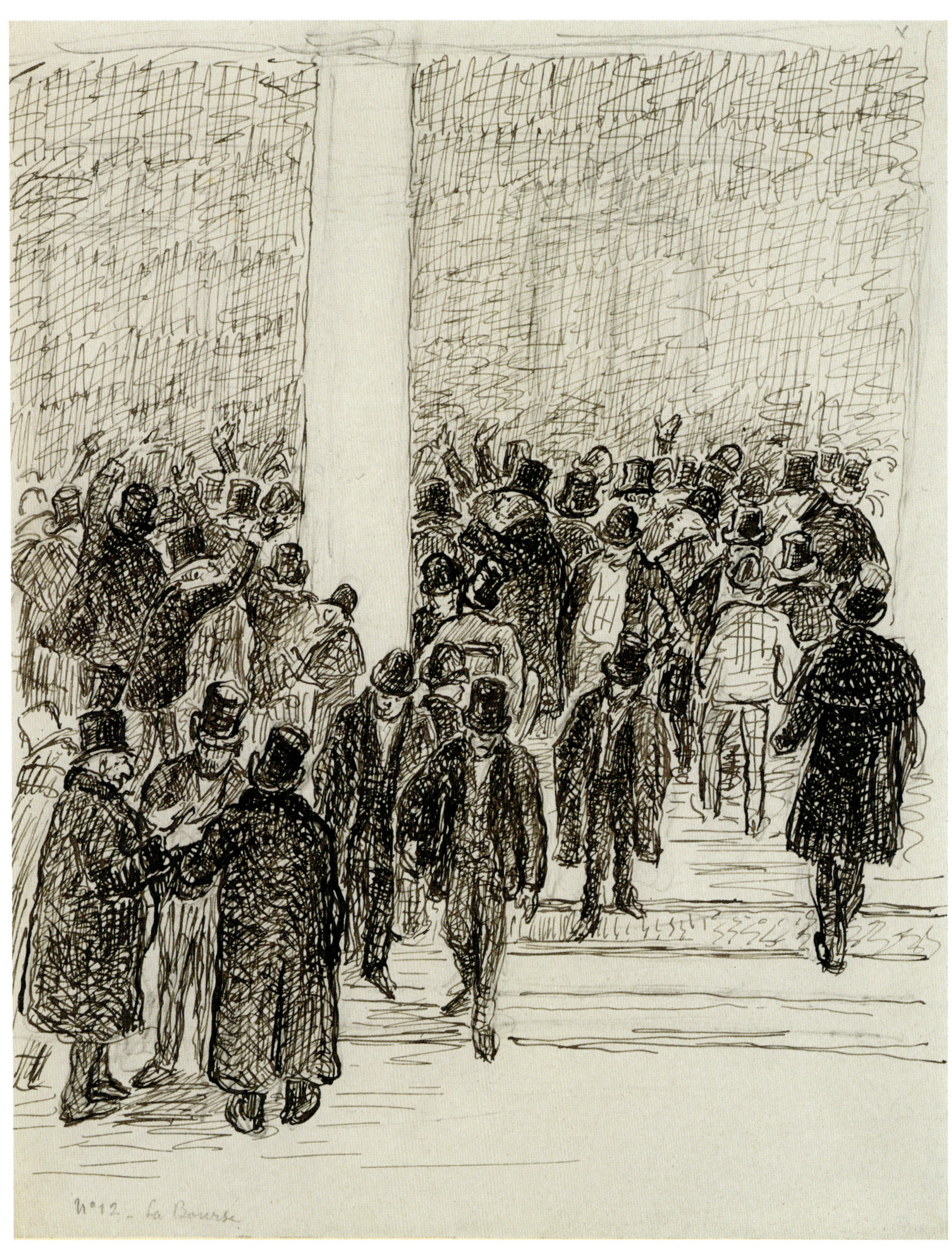

85

Study for "The Temple of the Golden Calf" (for *Turpitudes sociales*), 1889

The Ashmolean Museum, University of Oxford, Presented by the Pissarro Family, 1952

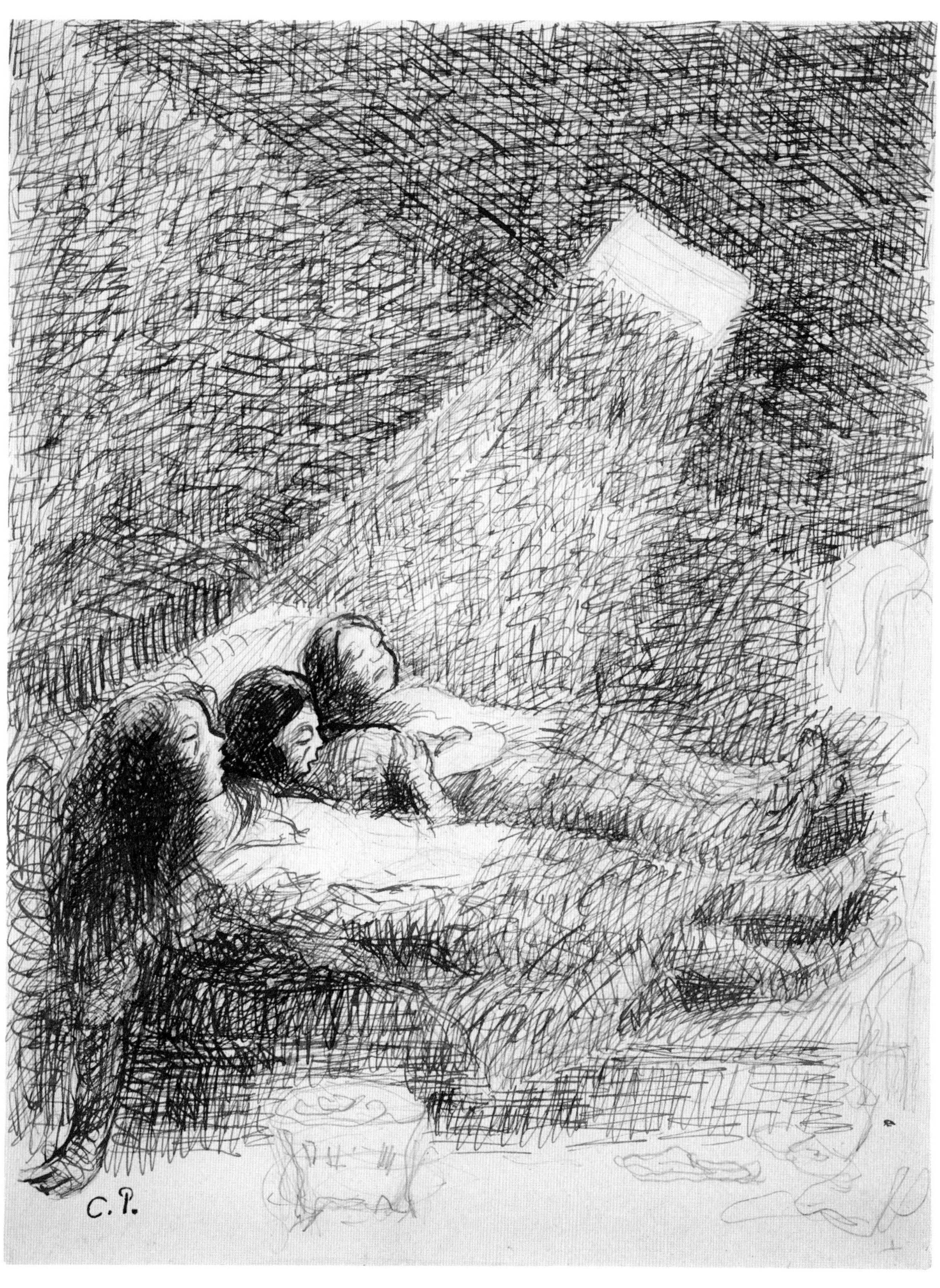

86
Study for "The Asphysia" (for *Turpitudes sociales*), 1890
The Ashmolean Museum, University of Oxford, Presented by the Pissarro Family, 1952

Motors of Progress *Normandy Port Series*

Claire Durand-Ruel Snollaerts

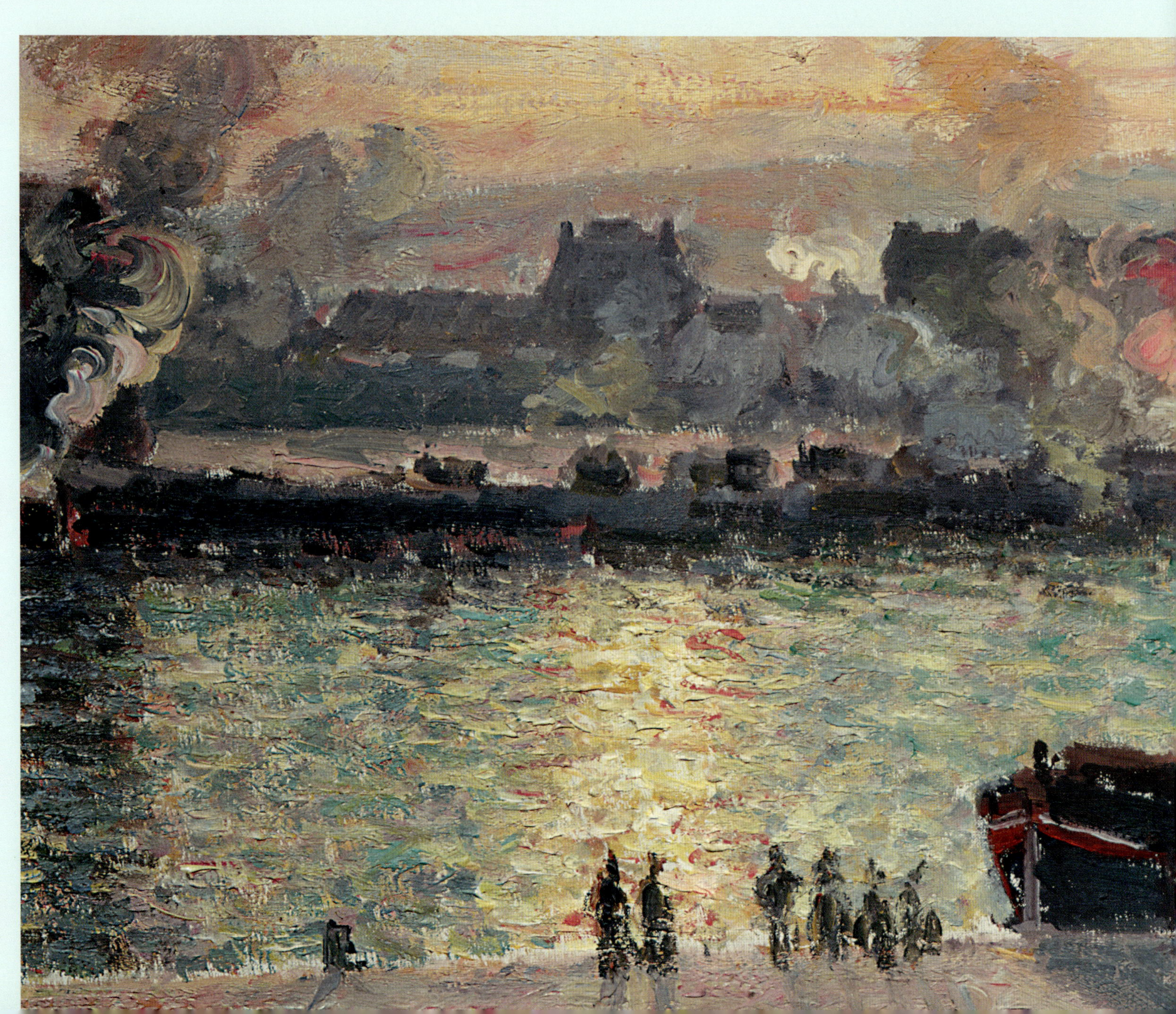

In the final years of his life, Pissarro painted multiple series showing ports in Normandy. In Rouen, Dieppe, and Le Havre, he rented rooms in portside hotels in order to paint the bustle of travelers and sightseers from the window, as well as the workers loading and unloading the ships. Under changing weather conditions, he captured the lively atmosphere and distinctly poetic qualities of the modern industrial landscape. The theme of international trade resonates in these images, bringing us full circle to Pissarro's artistic beginnings on Saint Thomas, where his double perspective as a merchant's son and aspiring painter formed his unique awareness of the harbor as a place.

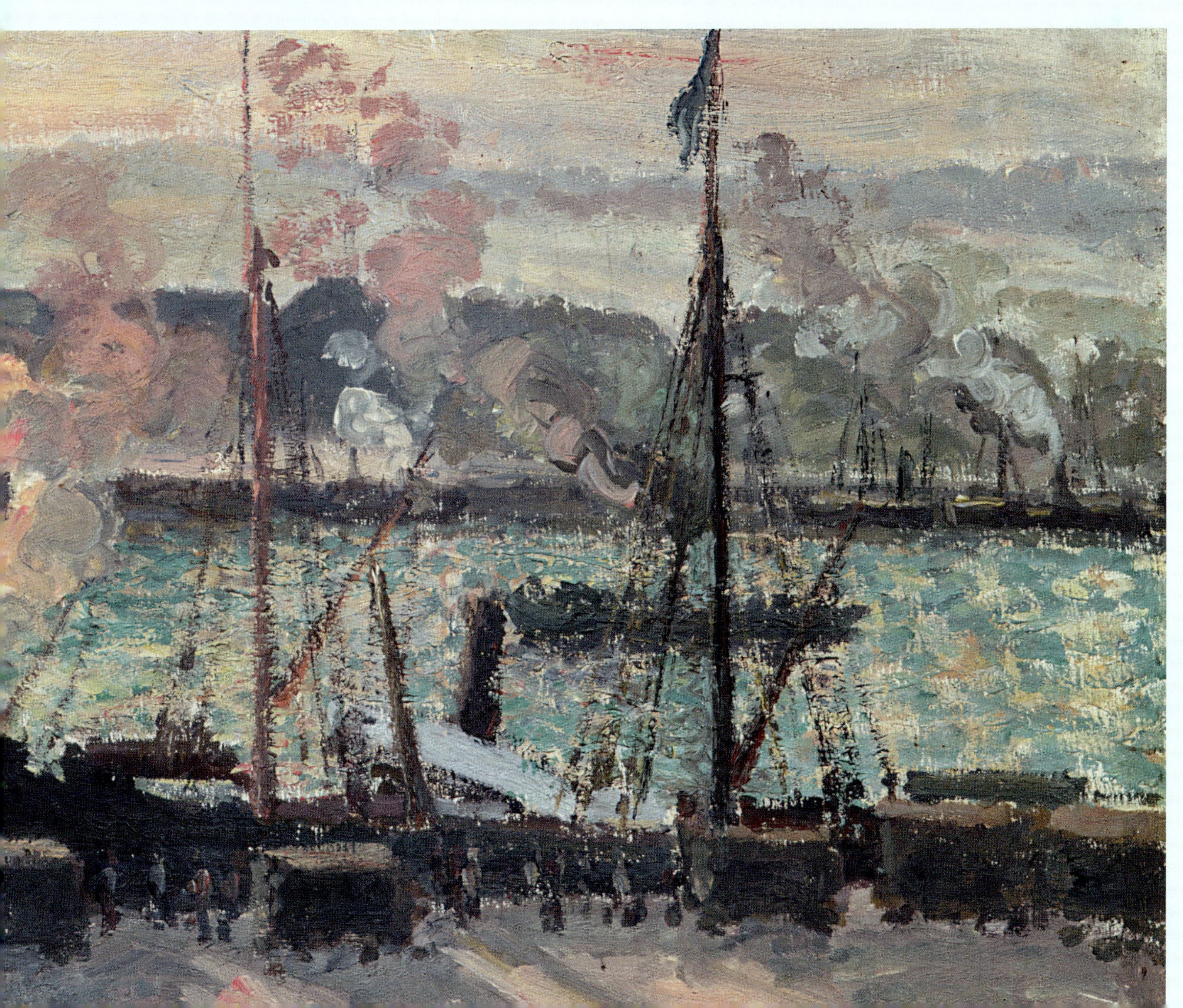

Art critic Gustave Geffroy, a friend of Camille Pissarro's, wrote in 1898, on the occasion of an exhibition of the artist's views of Paris, that the latter "sought to address the spectacle of urban existence: the streets teeming with crowds, the stone and iron bridges thrown across rivers, the heavy boats laden with goods, the masses of houses that signify social drama. Cities have a distinctive physiognomy—transient, anonymous, bustling, mysterious—that must tempt the painter."[1] However, Geffroy, who was well acquainted with Pissarro's work, was alluding to the artist's views of the port of Rouen, painted in 1896. Although the Rouen views were not included in the exhibition, he evoked them to draw attention to parallels in the artist's new pictorial process: painting the city in series from a fixed, elevated position, specifically a window. Whether Pissarro was painting in Paris or the Norman ports of Rouen, Dieppe, and Le Havre, he consistently used the same approach.

Pissarro first encountered the city as subject in Rouen in the fall of 1883. At the time, he was preparing to leave Pontoise and the environs, his home for more than a decade. He had begun to feel that his art was stagnating. Claude Monet, who knew Rouen well, urged him to visit the city before moving to Éragny-sur-Epte, believing that it would provide fresh inspiration. The artist explored both banks of the Seine in France's busiest river port on foot in search of motifs and painting *en plein air*. For this reason, the pictures created in 1883 during this first urban sojourn cannot be considered part of the urban series he would begin producing some ten years later, but his stay did spark a deep attraction to the city as a motif that would intensify over the following decades.

Pissarro returned to Rouen during the winter months in early and late 1896. His fourth and last sojourn extended from the summer to the early fall of 1898. He stayed in hotels across from the quays, facing the Seine. It was in this space that Pissarro, painting with great intensity, produced more than forty views of the Seine and the port, capturing varied effects of light and atmosphere. From his window, he could see the modern aspects of the city: the quays on the right bank in the foreground (cats. 92, 93), the Seine crossed by three bridges—Boieldieu, Corneille, and Chemin de Fer—in the middle distance (cats. 89–91), and beyond them the buildings on the left bank and the docks. Confined behind a window, he had little choice but to paint the same subject over and over again. Working on this series required an intense daily effort. In a letter to his son Lucien, he described his occasional fatigue.[2] In his correspondence, he described working on as many as a dozen paintings at once, with "effects of fog, mist, rain, a sunset, gray weather, bridge motifs from various angles, quays with boats."[3] This passage reveals much about his new artistic approach. Like Monet, Pissarro aimed to capture elusive nuances of light in the landscape. In Rouen, Monet worked on a fixed motif—the cathedral—while Pissarro engaged with a motif in perpetual motion: the busy and sprawling industrial port, which he painted over and over again. Pissarro had to come to terms with the changeable and ephemeral effects of the weather, while simultaneously depicting the port's constant activity. On one occasion, however, the artist produced two paintings of the roofs of old Rouen from the back of his hotel, one with the towers of Saint-Ouen and Saint-Maclou (cat. 87), the other depicting the south side of the cathedral (cat. 88).

Encouraged by the success of his Rouen views, Pissarro began to look for new places to set up his easel each year. He now traveled mostly in the summer, taking his family with him, so the children could enjoy the seaside. They went to Varengeville-sur-Mer in 1899 (cat. 68), to Berneval-le-Grand in 1900, and finally to Dieppe in 1901. The following summer, in 1902, he rented a *chambre-atelier* in a hotel overlooking the port of Dieppe. The vast panorama provided material for a new series: "My motifs are very beautiful, the fish market, the outer harbor, Port Duquesne, the village of Pollet . . . in rain, sun, smoke, etc."[4] Having transcribed onto his canvases the changes of light throughout the day, he returned from the port of Dieppe with twenty-one views (cat. 94).

After spending two summers in Dieppe, Pissarro chose Le Havre for his third and last port series. He stayed there from early July to mid-September 1903. Located in the estuary of the Seine, it was France's second-largest port and the place of transshipment for goods from the United States. As in Dieppe, he chose a hotel room in Le Havre overlooking the jetty, where he could watch the transatlantic steamships, which must have reminded him of arriving in France in 1855, following his passage from Saint Thomas. The years he spent as an apprentice in the firm of his parents as well as his artistic beginnings were also linked with the port.

In Le Havre, Pissarro found material for twenty-four paintings. The city had begun construction to widen the port entrance in August 1902, and work was still underway when Pissarro arrived. His paintings document the appearance of the port before its transformation—a selling point that he certainly intended to use to attract potential buyers for his paintings in Le Havre. This feature prompted the city's museum to buy two of his paintings (cats. 95, 96)—the first purchase of his work by a French art institution.

Although Pissarro's port paintings were created indoors, they challenged the plein-air painter: "Nothing is more difficult than trying to capture the light and the air."[5] A sudden spell of bad weather had interfered with the sun effects that he was working on, forcing him to wait while "keeping a lookout, watching from my window the abrupt changes in effects."[6] These urban stays were vital for enriching Pissarro's work. Satisfied with his painting campaign in Le Havre, he returned to Paris in late September, ready to begin another urban series.

Translated from French by Helge R. Dascher

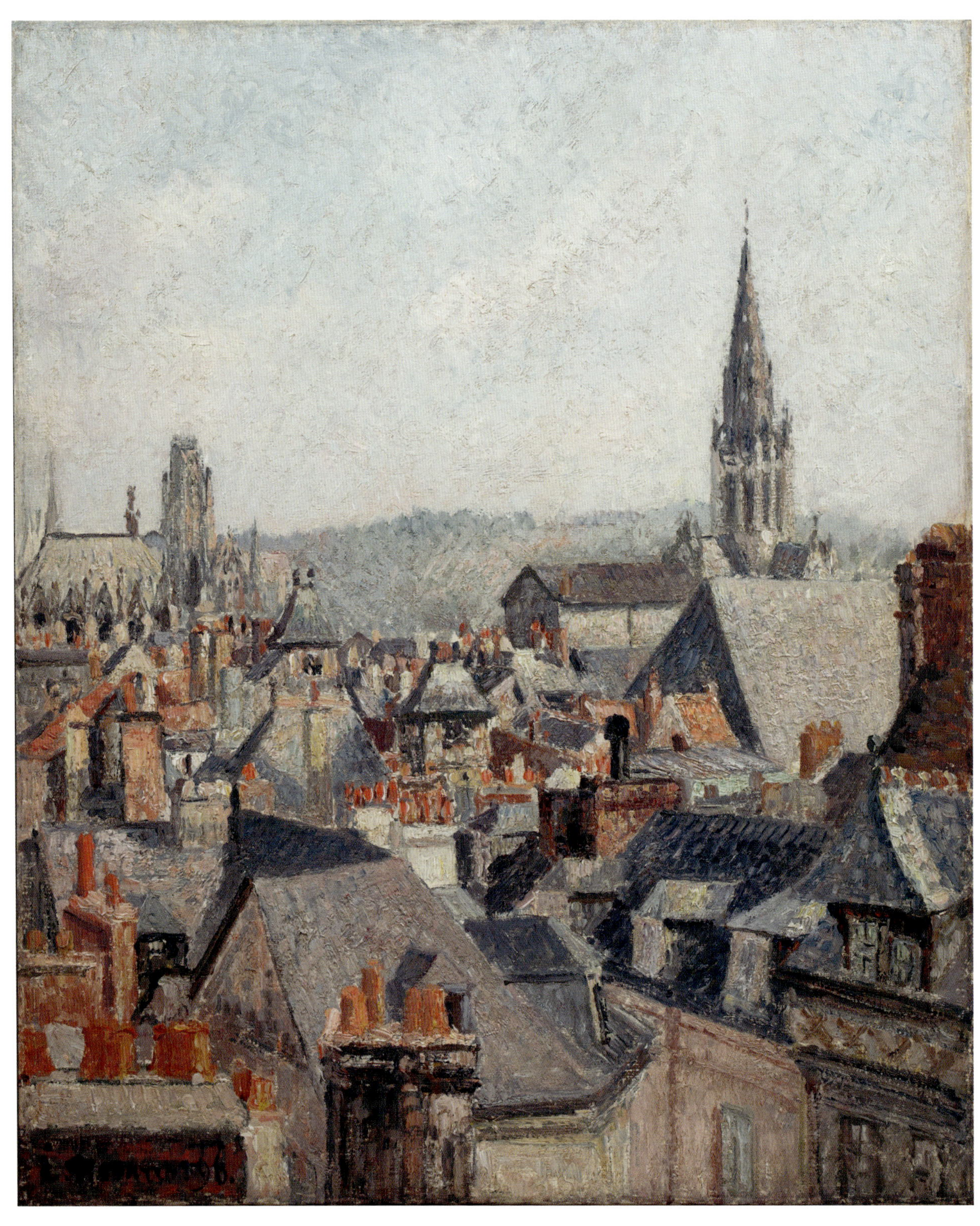

87
The Roofs of Old Rouen, Sunshine, 1896
Private collection

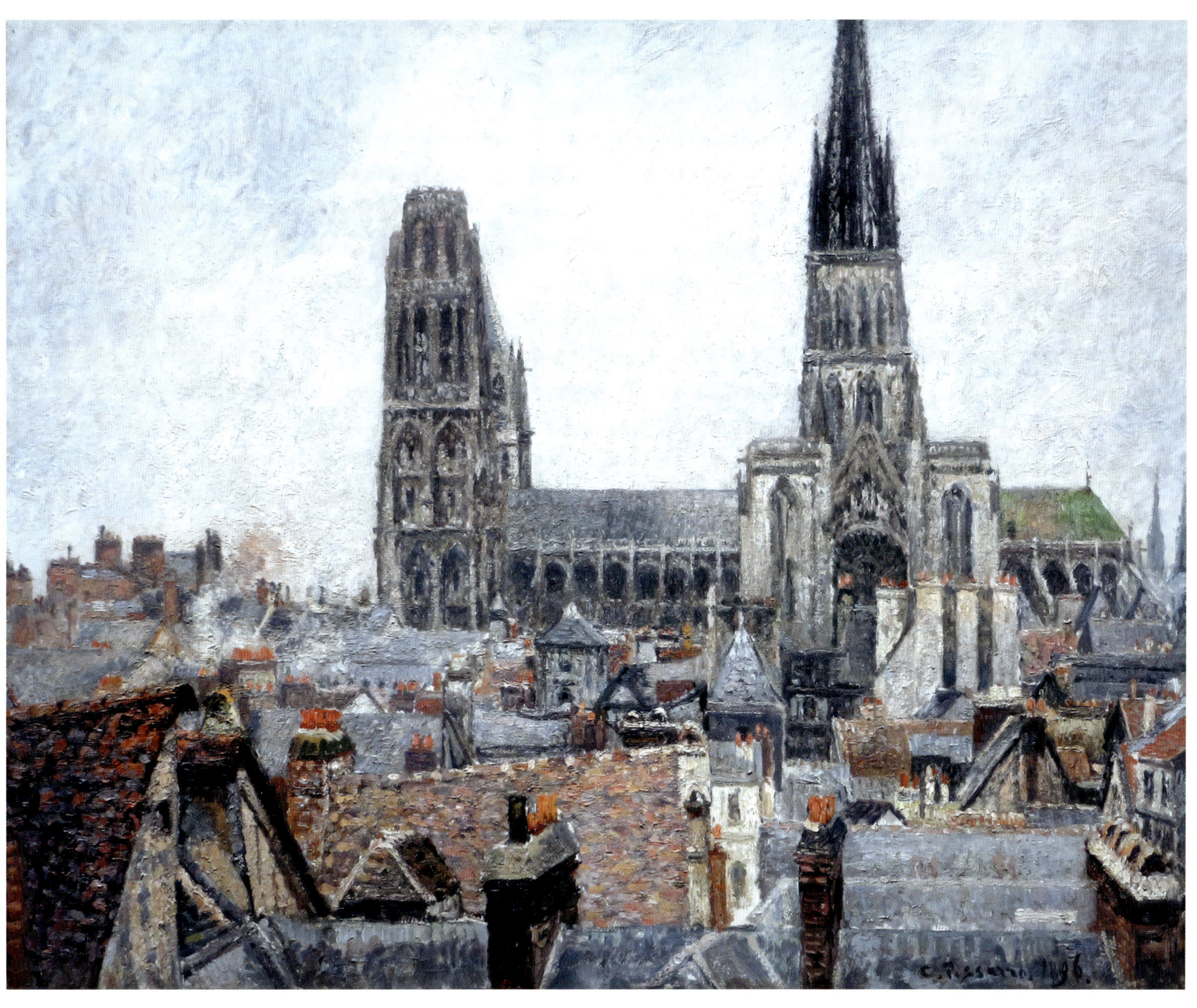

88
The Roofs of Old Rouen, Gray Weather, 1896
Toledo Museum of Art, Purchased with funds from the Libbey Endowment, Gift of Edward Drummond Libbey

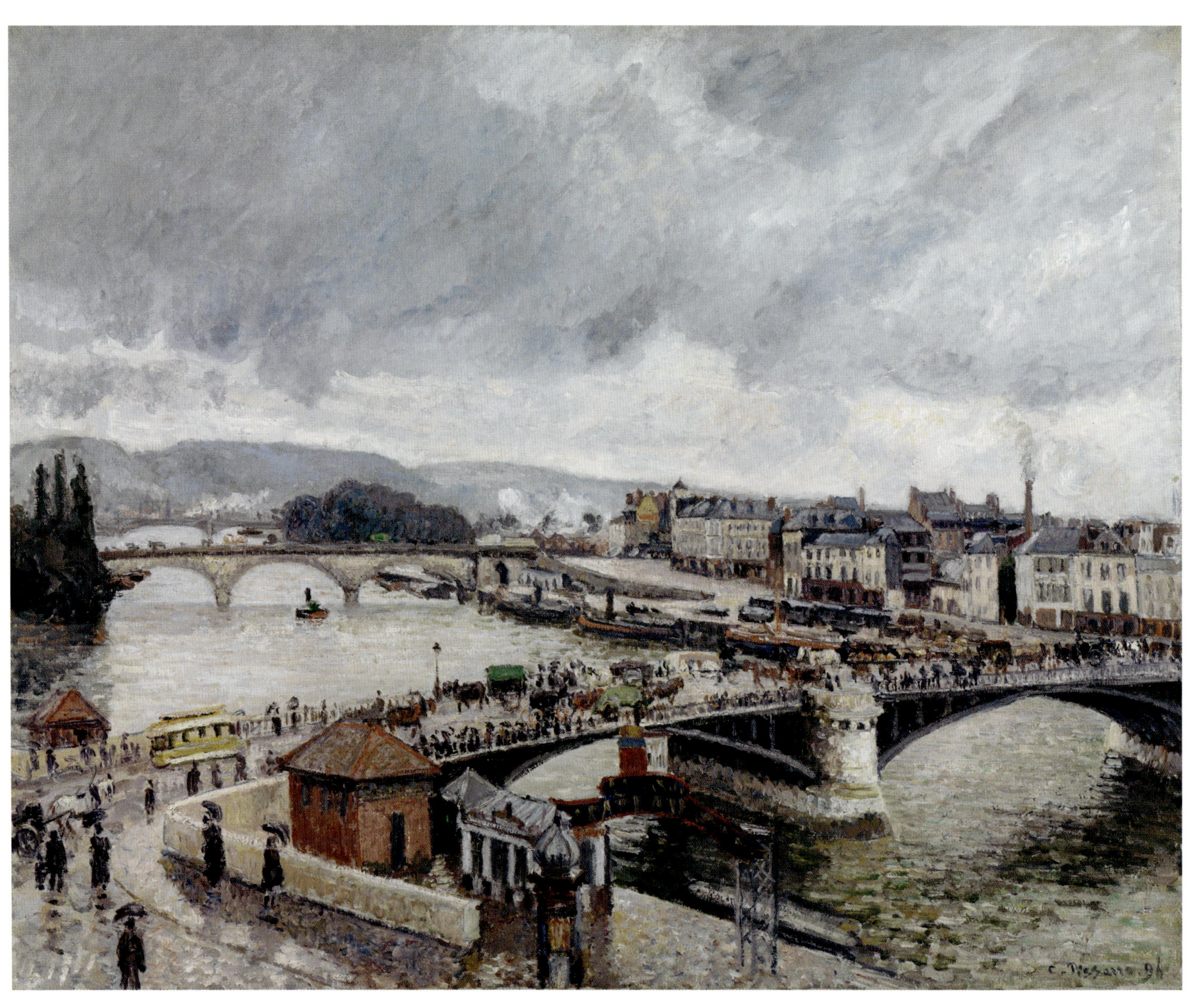

89
The Great Bridge in Rouen, Rainy Weather, 1896
Staatliche Kunsthalle Karlsruhe

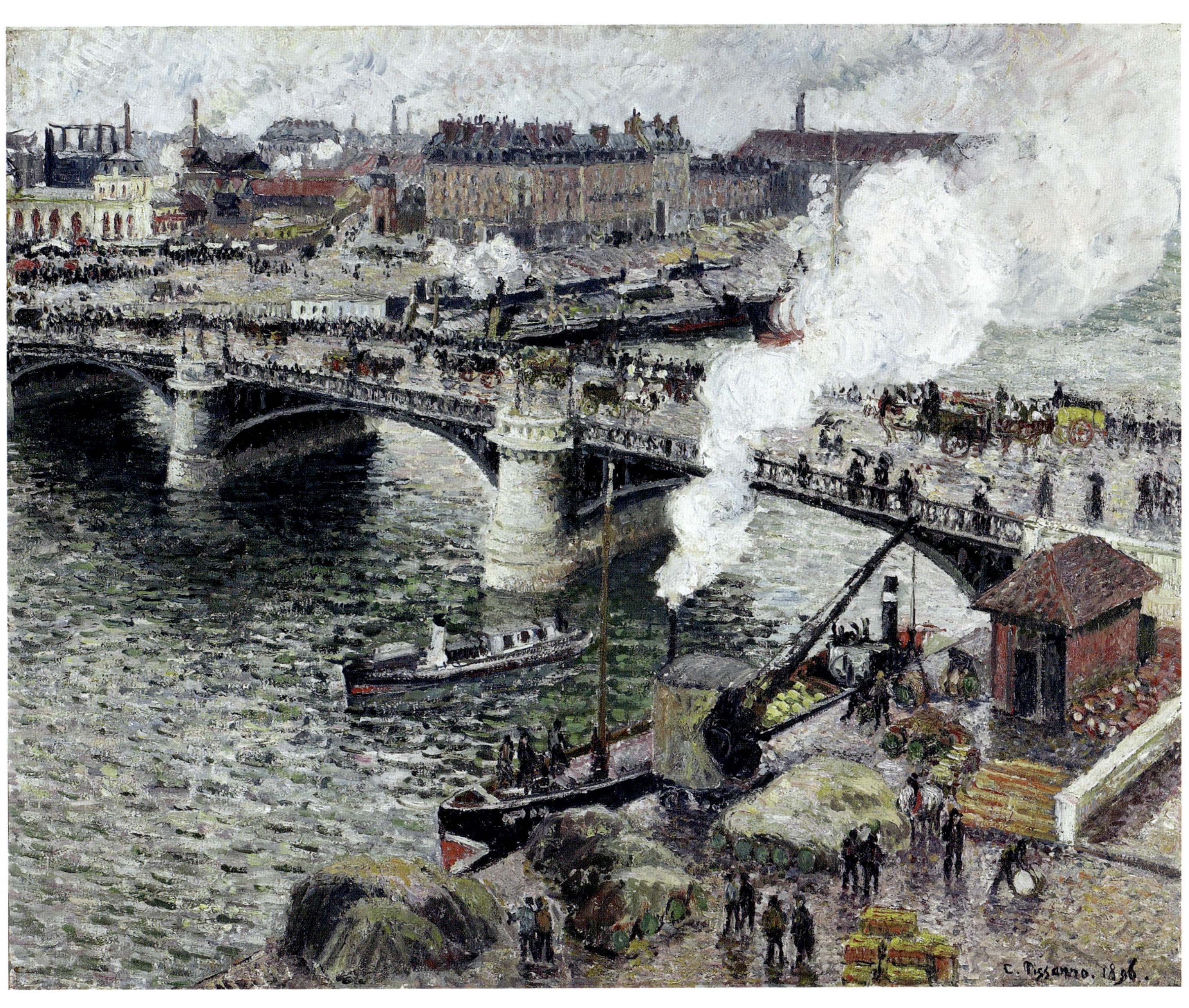

90

Pont Boieldieu, Rouen, Rainy Weather, 1896

Collection Art Gallery of Ontario, Toronto, Gift of Reuben Wells Leonard Estate, 1937

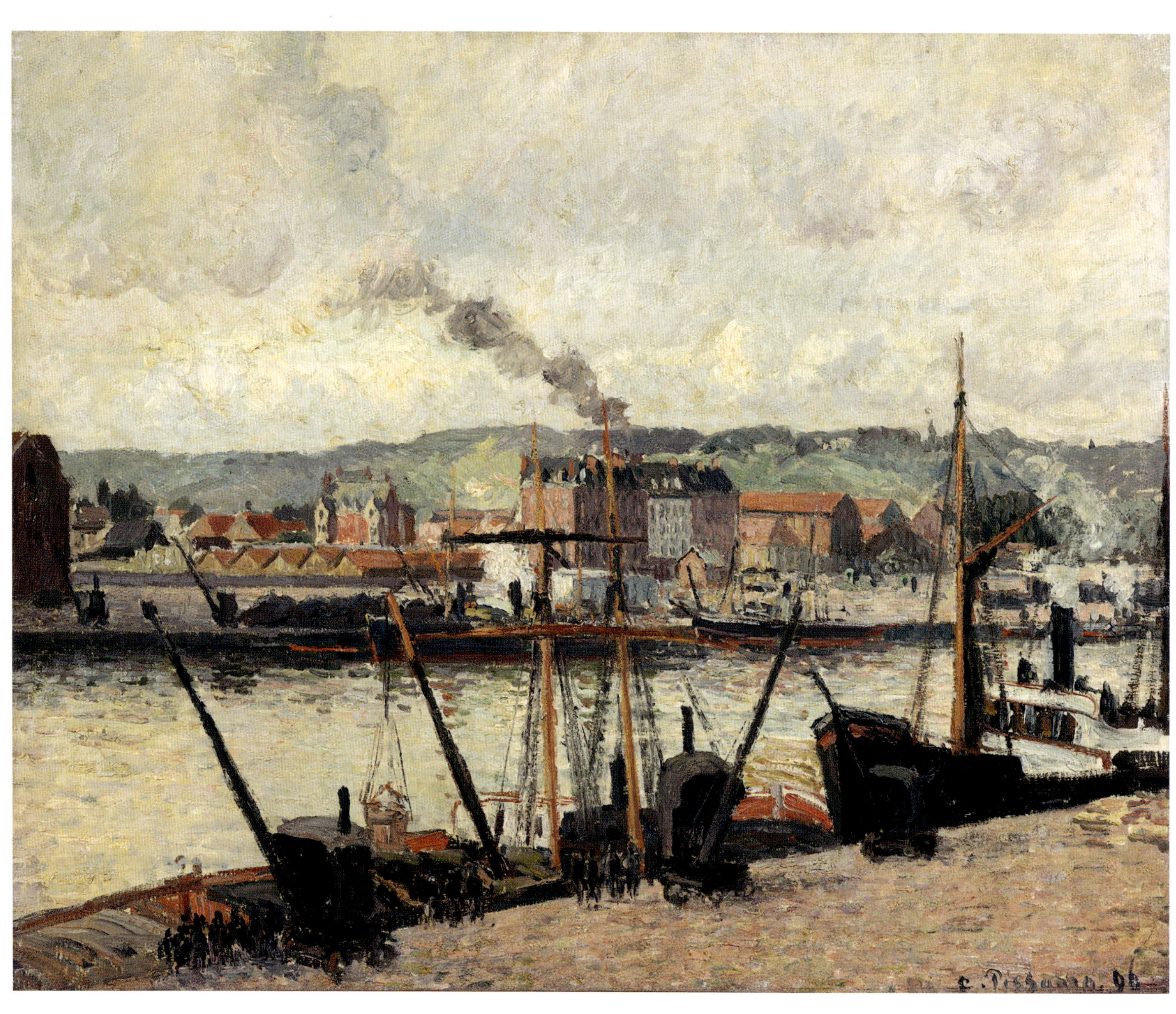

92
View of the Quai Cavelier-de-La-Salle, Rouen, 1896
Private collection

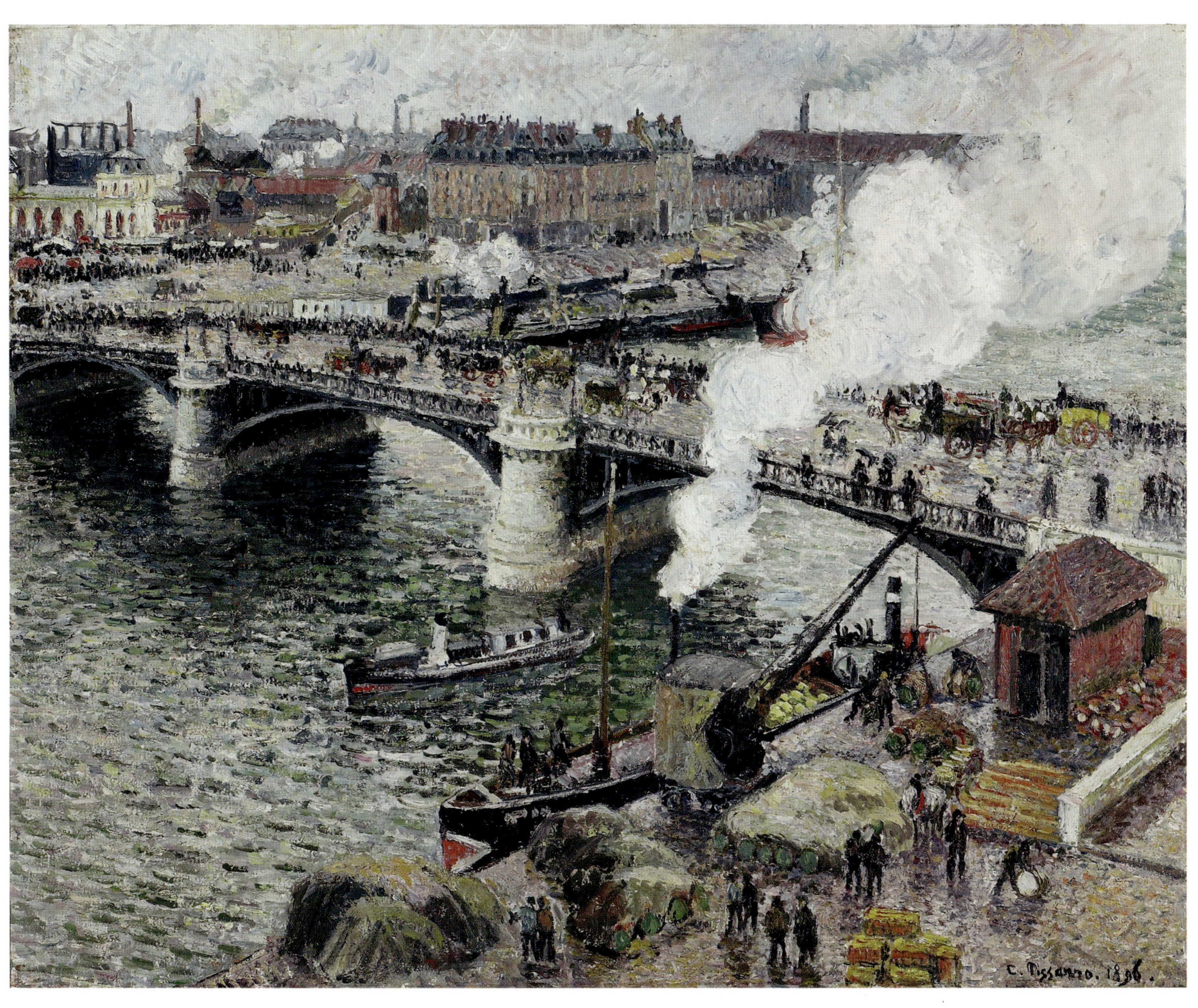

90
Pont Boieldieu, Rouen, Rainy Weather, 1896
Collection Art Gallery of Ontario, Toronto, Gift of Reuben Wells Leonard Estate, 1937

91
Pont Boieldieu, Rouen, Effect of Fog, 1898
Colección Pérez Simón

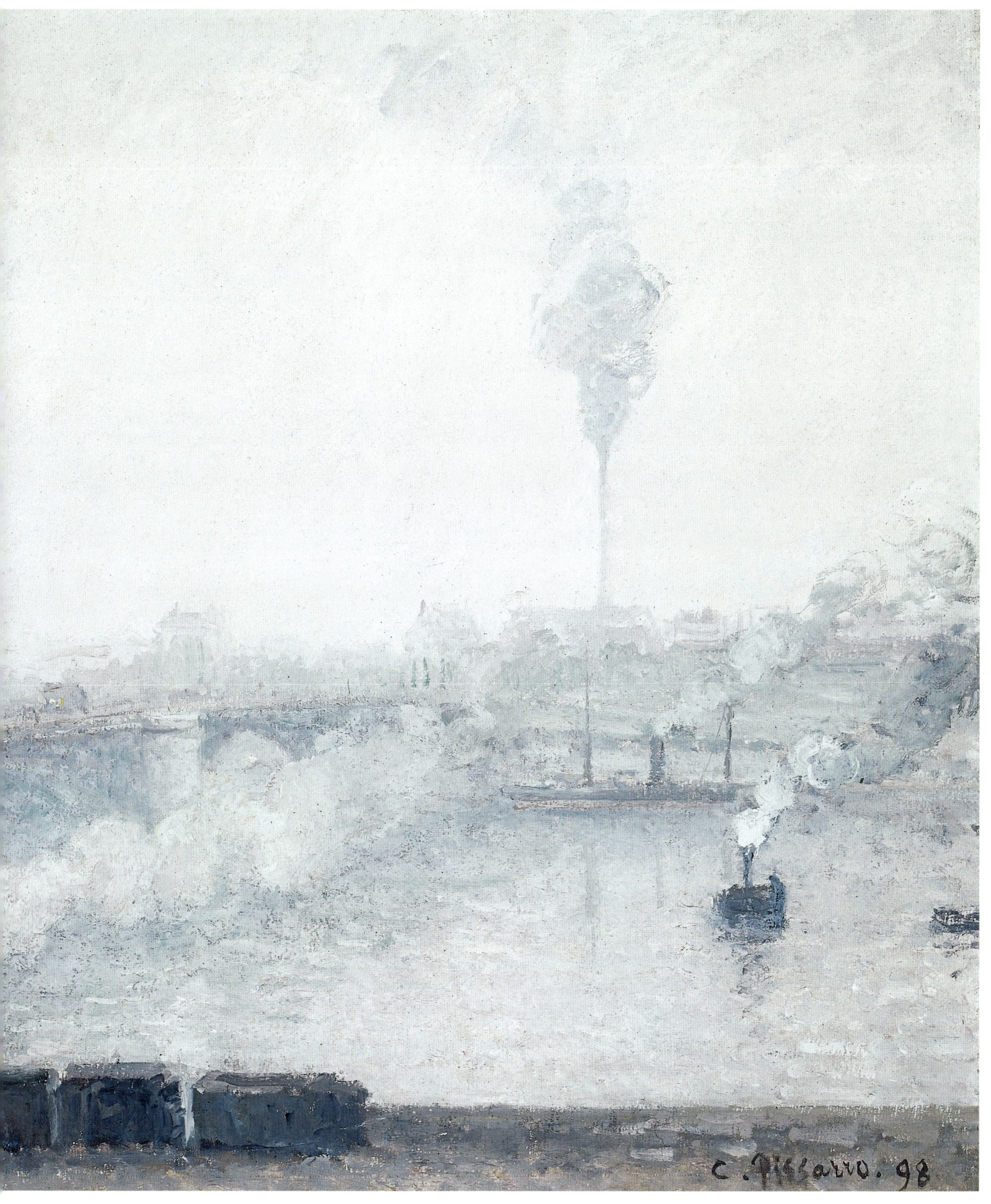
C. Pissarro. 98

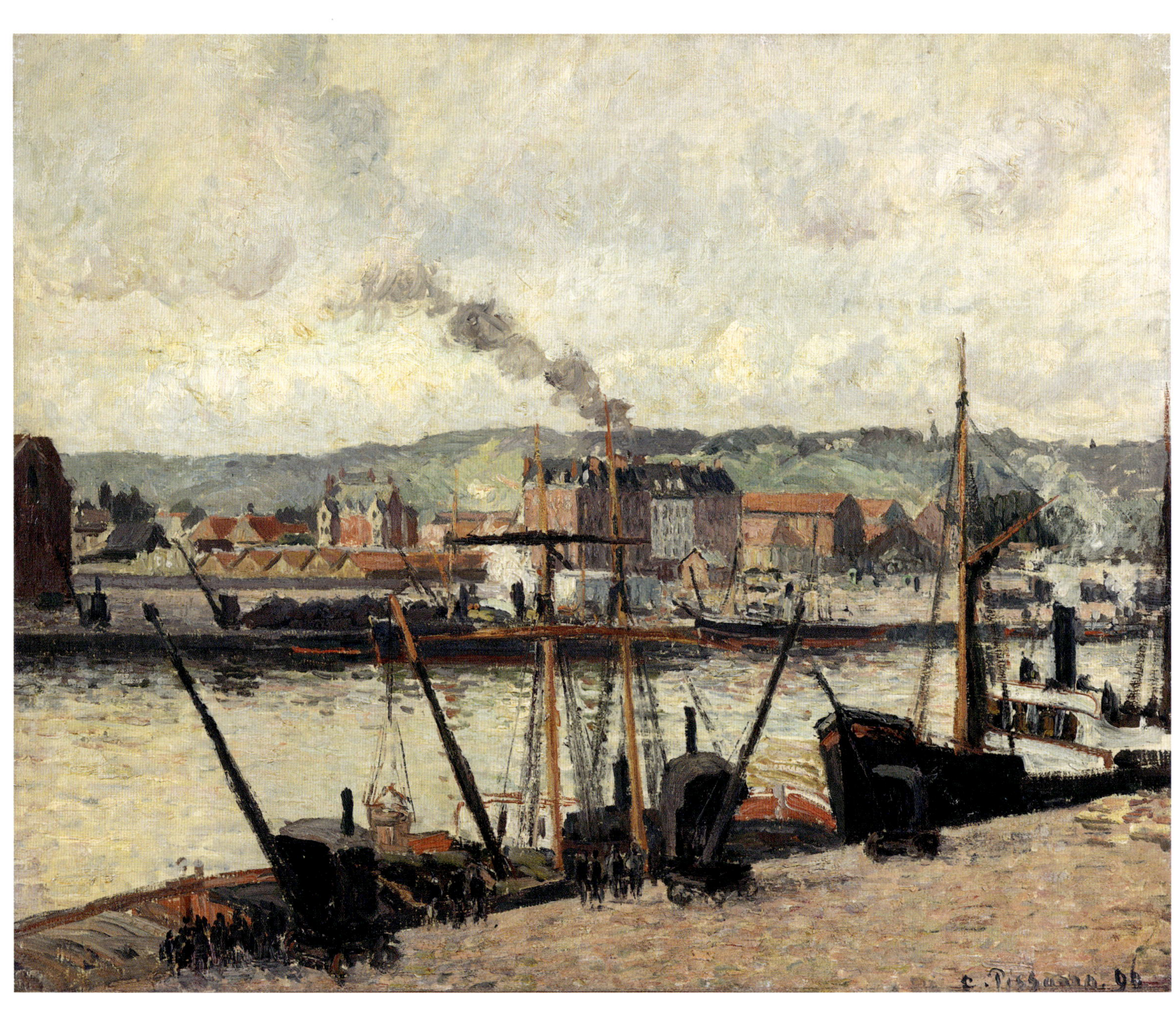

92
View of the Quai Cavelier-de-La-Salle, Rouen, 1896
Private collection

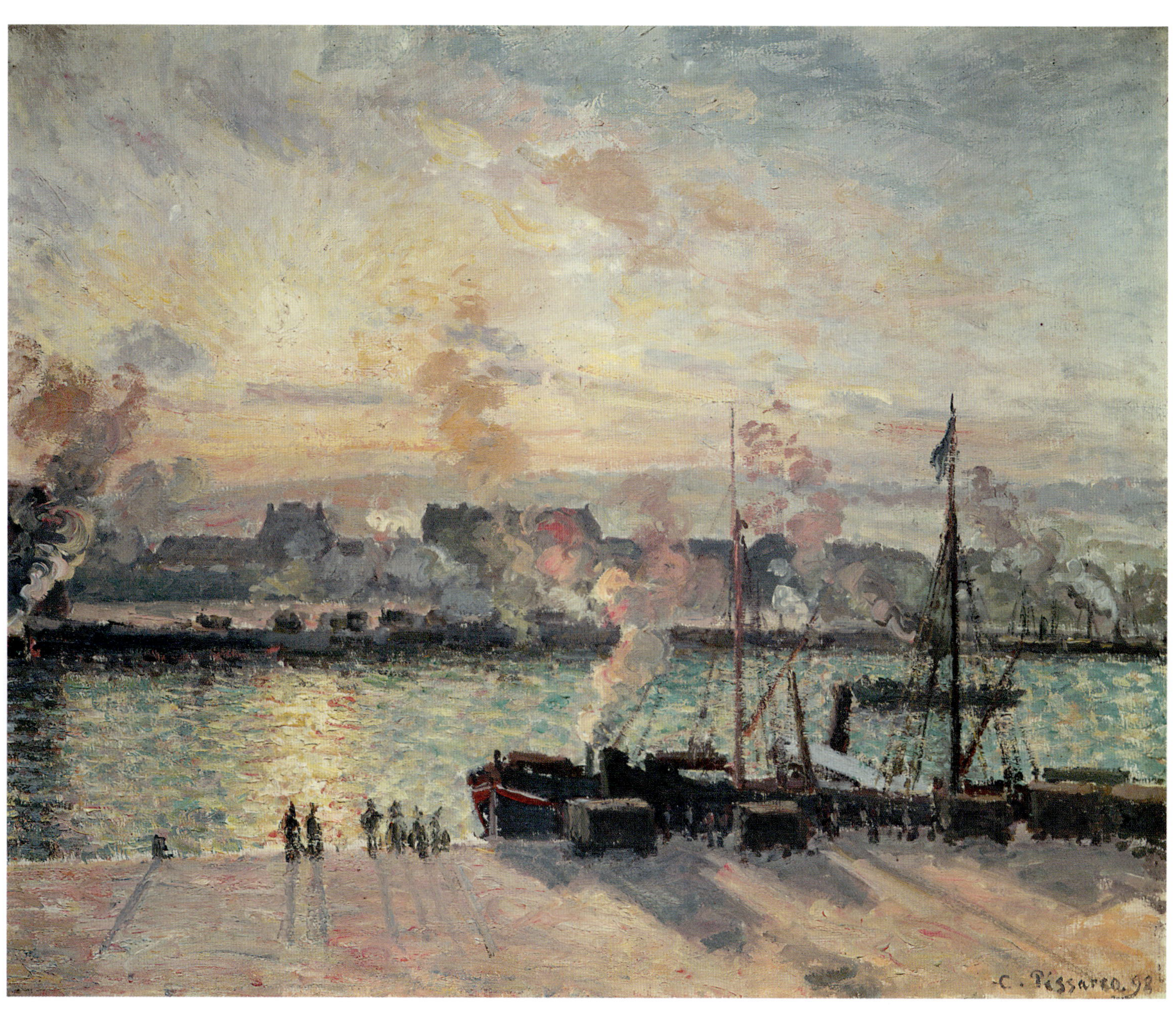

93
Sunset, Port of Rouen (Steamboats), 1898
Amgueddfa Cymru—Museum Wales, Bequeathed by Margaret Davies, 1963

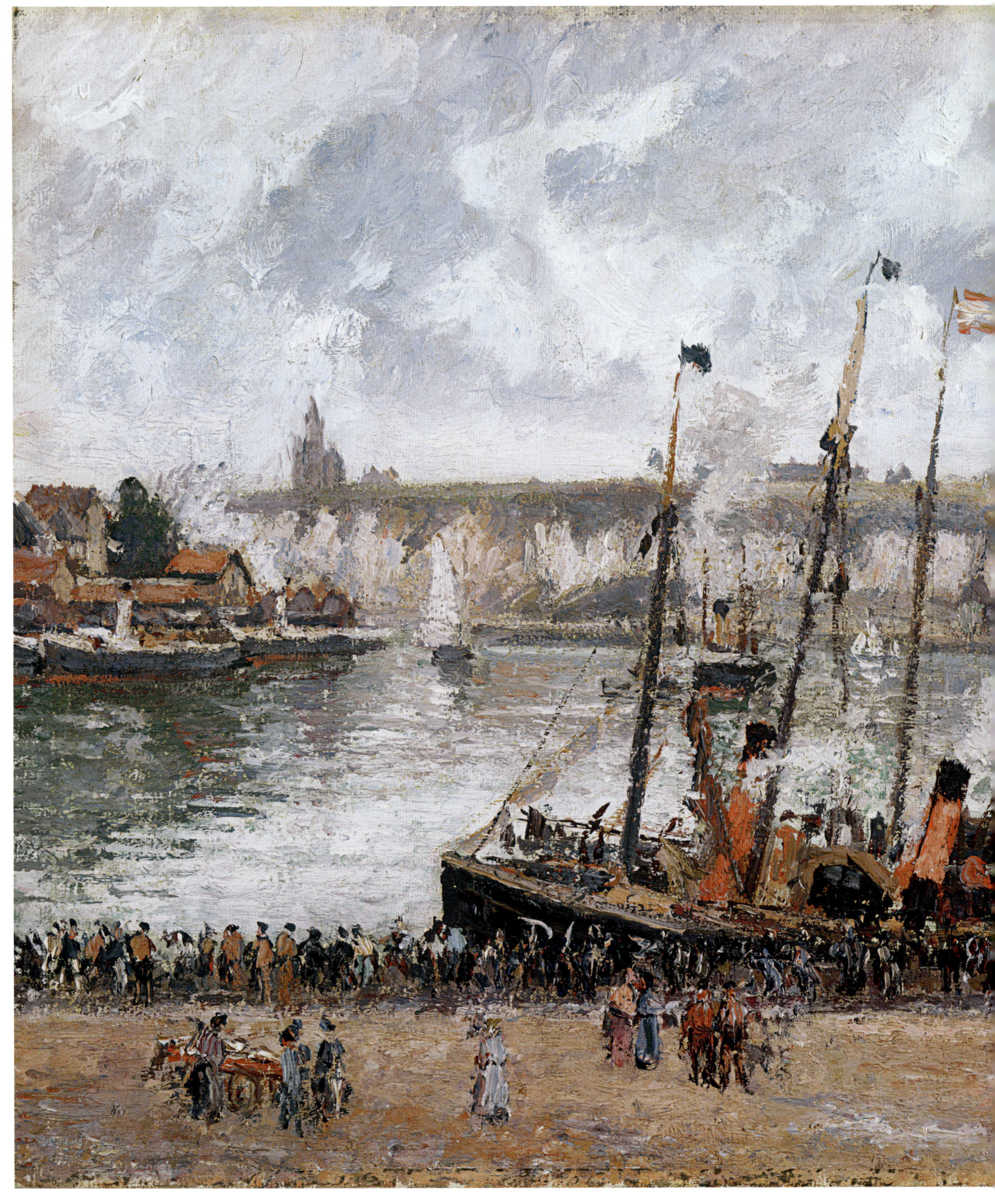

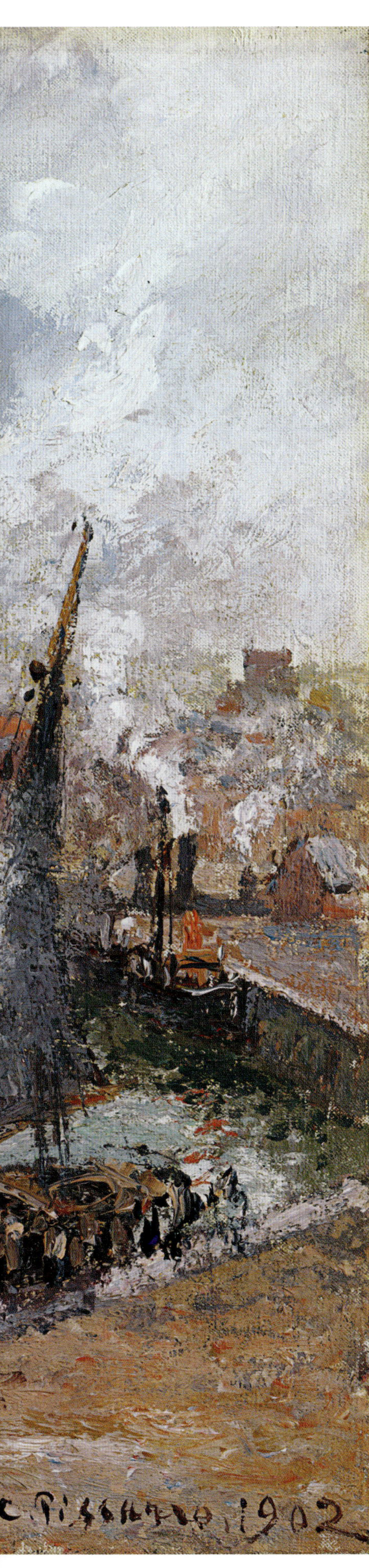

94
Harbor at Dieppe, 1902
Fine Arts Museums of San Francisco, Mildred Anna Williams Collection

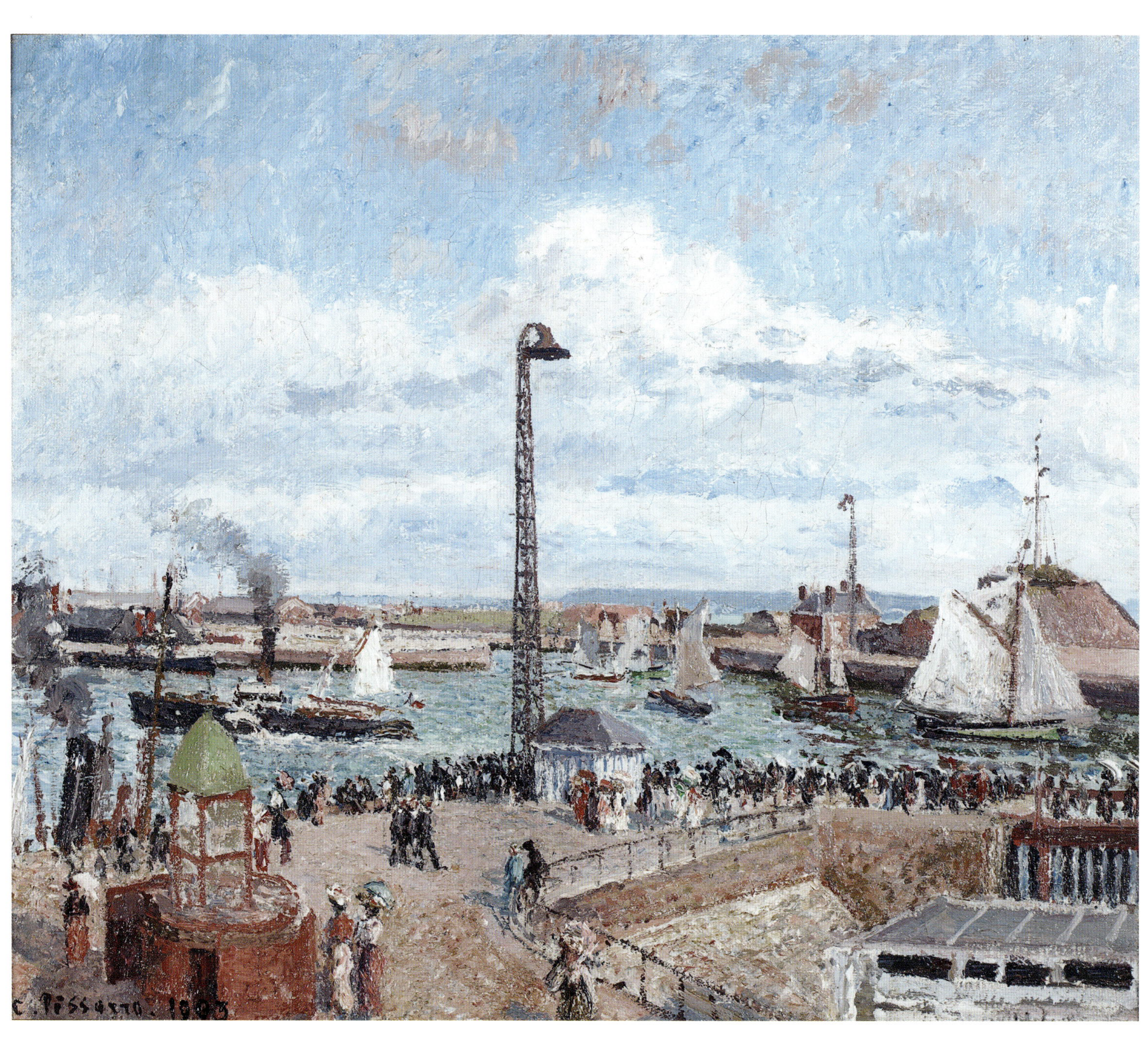

95
The Anse des Pilotes and the East Breakwater, Le Havre, Afternoon, Sunny Weather, 1903
Musée d'art moderne André Malraux, Le Havre

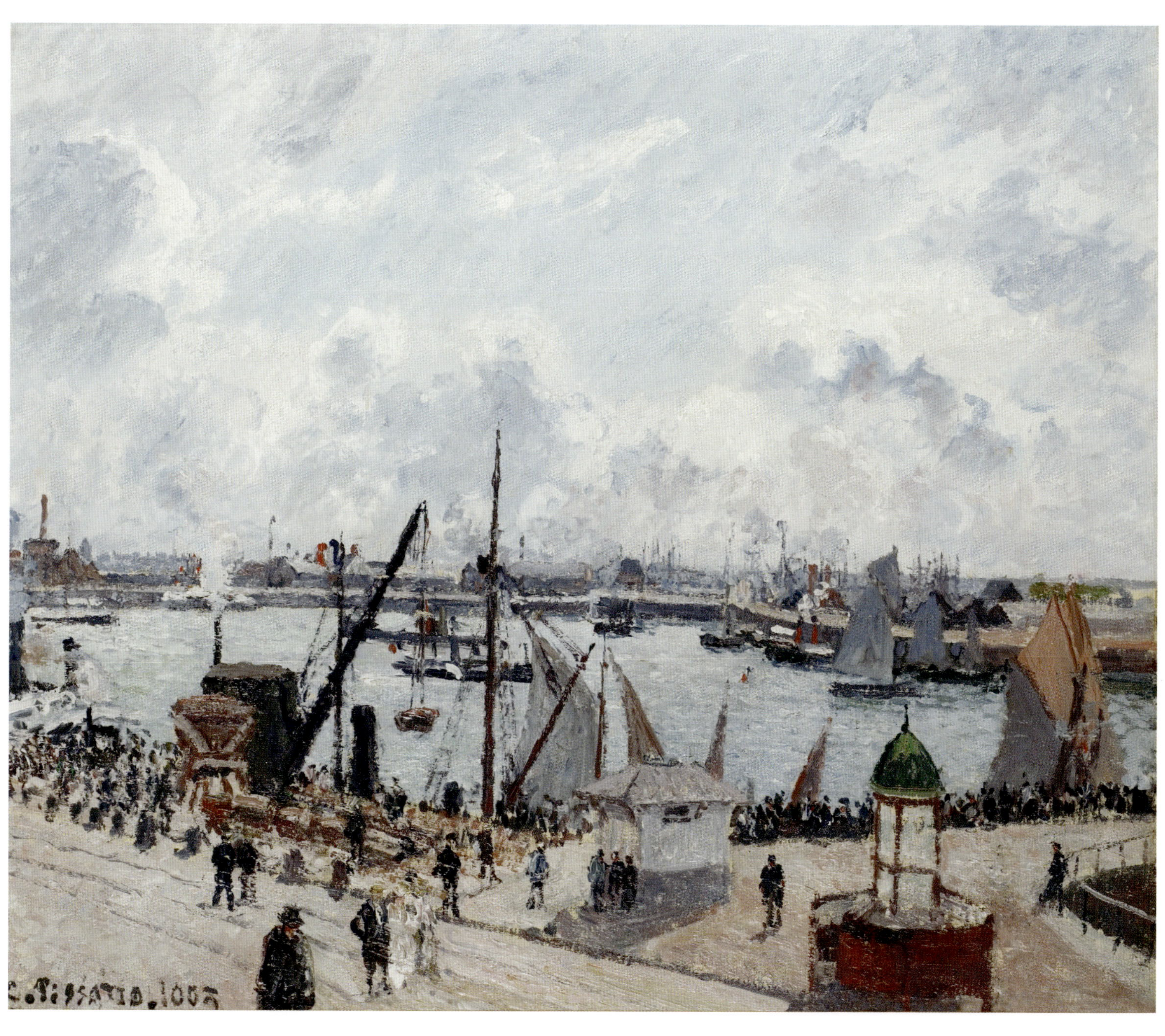

96
The Anse des Pilotes, Le Havre, Morning, Sunshine, Tide Rising, 1903
Musée d'art moderne André Malraux, Le Havre

City People
Paris Series

Claire Durand-Ruel Snollaerts

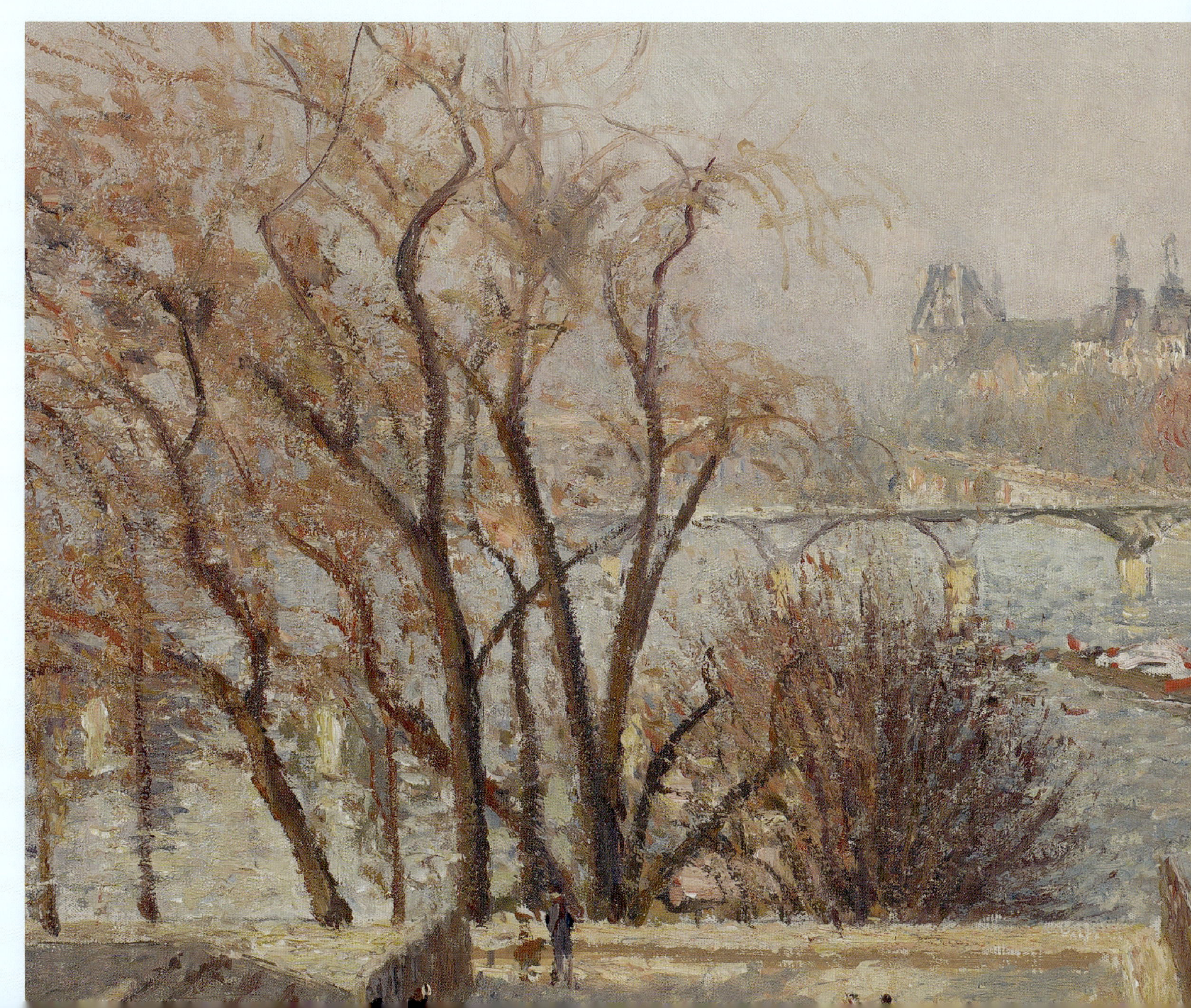

In Camille Pissarro's images of Paris, all is in flux: crowds of people of different social classes, moving along on foot and in carriages, are a central element of his cityscapes. The series the artist created in the capital city between 1893 and 1903 show panoramas viewed from an anonymous distance. Pissarro understood himself as an observer of the metropolis, not as an inhabitant. In varying atmospheres of light, he depicted motifs such as the Boulevard Montmartre, the Pont Neuf, and the Place du Théâtre Français—which some considered ugly, but which for Pissarro was the epitome of modernity—as well as the Seine and the Louvre. His dealer Paul Durand-Ruel encouraged him to paint such scenes, which became popular among progressive collectors.

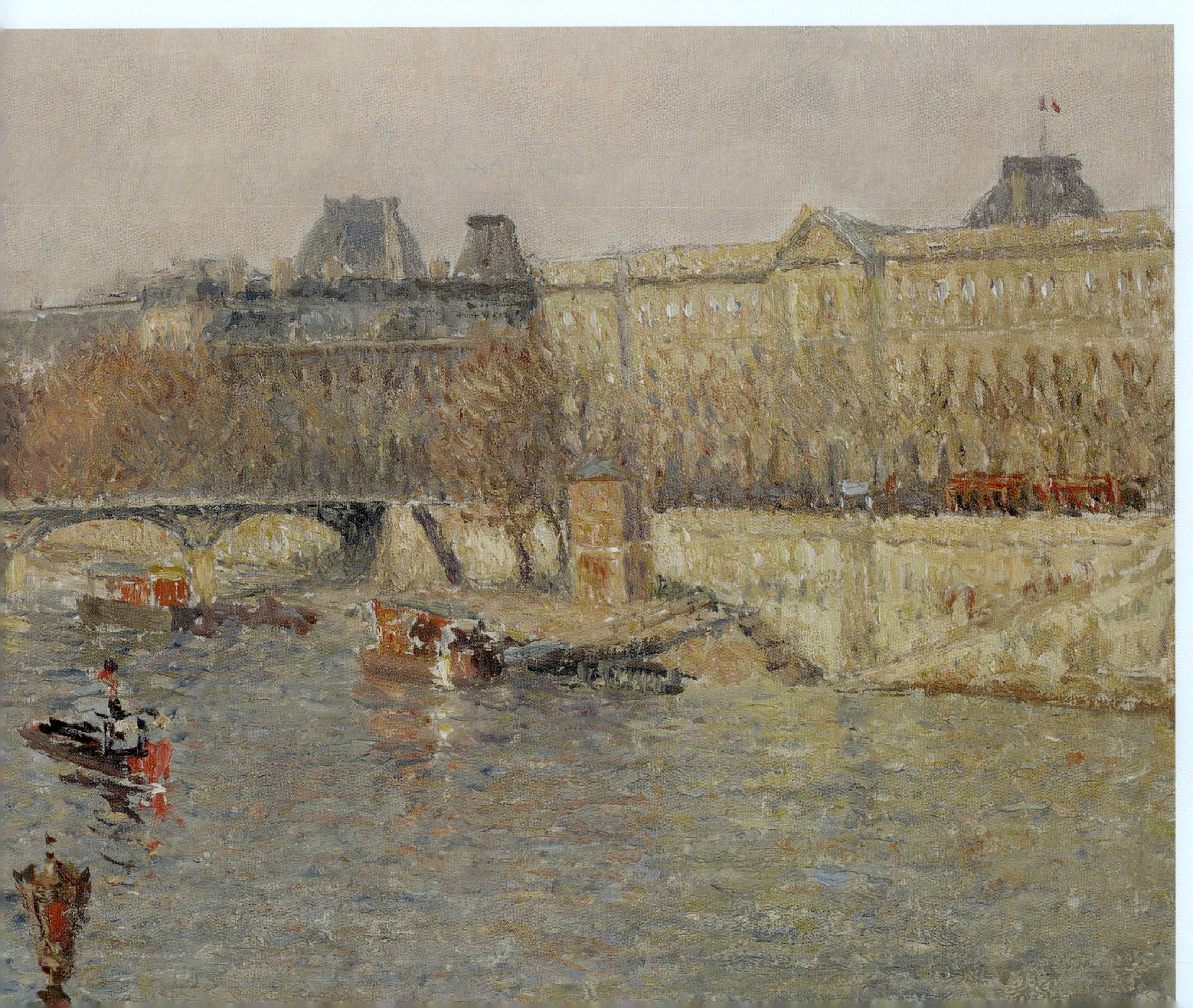

It was precisely when his Impressionist friends were leaving the city that Camille Pissarro chose it as his subject. From 1893 to his death in 1903, he produced nearly 300 urban views, including 125 of Paris. Pissarro had painted his first view of Paris in 1879 (cat. 35). Although the depiction of a snow-covered street on a winter's day recalls later paintings such as *Boulevard Montmartre, Hazy Morning* (private collection) from his Boulevard Montmartre series of 1897, it remained an isolated experiment.

In February 1893, Pissarro visited the capital on business and took a room at the Hôtel Garnier, opposite the Gare Saint-Lazare, the station he used to travel to and from his home in Éragny-sur-Epte. What should have been a short visit turned into an extended stay when Pissarro came down with the flu and an eye infection. His ophthalmologist advised him to avoid the dusty streets and stay in his hotel. Confined to his room, the artist had no distraction but the view from his window of the constant traffic of pedestrians and horse buses below. To occupy his time, he painted four bird's-eye views of the Place du Havre. These cannot be called a series as such, as each represents a very different perspective on the subject. However, they marked the beginning of a new approach for Pissarro—painting from a window. He continued this practice until the end of his life, partly because his recurring eye infections forced him to work indoors during winter to avoid drafts. Painting the outside world from the inside became his new way of working.

In 1895 Pissarro attended the exhibition of Monet's series of *Cathedrals* at Galerie Durand-Ruel. "I am struck by this extraordinary mastery," he wrote to his son Lucien on May 26. "It is the work of a deliberate, determined person, pursuing the elusive nuance of effects that no other artist I know has achieved."[1] As a result, he also studied the myriad variations of light on a given motif in his urban views. But while Monet focused more strongly on inanimate motifs—grainstacks, poplars, Rouen Cathedral—Pissarro depicted vast urban panoramas, full of activity, seen from above, and captured from different angles and under the effect of different seasons and times of day.

In January 1897, Pissarro returned to the motif of the Parisian views, again from the Hôtel Garnier. During a month-long stay, working from the same hotel window, he painted "six small canvases that will cover the month's expenses," as he wrote to Lucien on February 3.[2] He depicted the Rue Saint-Lazare in three different weather conditions: sun, fog, and snow. The principle of the series was now established in his work. His first views of Paris from the Quartier Saint-Lazare gained the immediate approval of his dealer, Paul Durand-Ruel, who encouraged him to continue in this direction, advising him to "paint boulevards—big ones, of course," as Pissarro told his son Georges.[3] Inspired by this new artistic challenge, Pissarro continued working in series and from windows, with the distance of an impartial observer, painting no fewer than six different Parisian sites during this period.

The second site was the Boulevard Montmartre, where the artist worked intensively for two and a half months, until April 1897. His son Lucien supported the idea of painting Paris: "This will increase your success in the eyes of the Parisians, who really only love their city, not to mention the pleasure this completely new series will give you."[4] The series consisted of sixteen paintings of a single subject—the long, monotonous boulevard, created under Baron Haussmann, teeming with pedestrians and carriages (cat. 97)—yet each work was distinct. By depicting a single subject under various atmospheric conditions, at different times of day and across the seasons, Pissarro could reproduce it endlessly without appearing repetitive. Even the Mardi Gras floats that passed by his hotel, the Grand Hôtel de Russie, along with the celebrating crowd and the masses of paper streamers, found their way into the series (cat. 98).

In December 1897, the artist began a series depicting the Place du Théâtre Français and the Avenue de l'Opéra from the Hôtel du Louvre. "Very nice to do!" he wrote to Lucien. "I am delighted to attempt these Parisian streets that are generally thought of as ugly, but which are so silvery, so luminous, and so alive—so fully modern!!!"[5] He sometimes placed his easel overlooking the Rue Saint-Honoré (cat. 99) and other times overlooking the Avenue de l'Opéra (cat. 100). In total, he created fifteen works.

Encouraged by Durand-Ruel, who purchased nearly his entire output, Pissarro sought out a new location. He rented an apartment on the Rue de Rivoli, where he painted the Louvre and the Jardin des Tuileries from his window in the first half of 1899. The spectacular view so captivated him that he returned at the end of the year. He distinguished the two campaigns as "first series" and "second series"—a clear indication that the term *series* had taken root in his vocabulary. Painted under sunshine, snow, and rain (cat. 109), and at all hours of the day, the group of both series comprised twenty-eight paintings.

In March 1900, having exhausted the panorama of the Louvre and the Tuileries, Pissarro noted that he had "found an apartment on the embankment of the Pont-Neuf, with a magnificent view."[6] He rented it starting in November of that year. Once again, it was a choice intended to entice buyers. The apartment on the Place Dauphine on the Île de la Cité did indeed offer a breathtaking vista: from his window, Pissarro could see the Square du Vert-Galant, the Seine, and the Louvre (cats. 104–08), to his right the Pont-Neuf (cats. 101–03), and to his left the Hôtel de la Monnaie and the dome of the Institut de France. He remained there for three years, until 1903, producing three series, totaling sixty documented works. For his final Parisian series, painted between March and May 1903, he stayed in the same neighborhood, in a hotel on the Quai Voltaire, to capture the Louvre and the dome of the Institut from a different angle, producing fourteen paintings in all.

Although Durand-Ruel amassed a significant stock of Pissarro's Parisian views, he rarely exhibited them. In June 1898, he presented twenty-one of the artist's paintings of the Boulevard Montmartre and the Avenue de l'Opéra to critical acclaim.[7] In 1901 the dealer exhibited sixteen views of the Louvre and the Jardin des Tuileries. A critic was captivated by the series, stating that the artist "has carved out from this space paintings that are among the best he has ever painted, possessing a unique and infinite allure. Before them, you will relive exquisite impressions of morning, afternoon, and twilight. [. . .] Surely few artists have expressed the truth of light and atmosphere with such power."[8] In other words, Pissarro, it appeared, was considered the preeminent painter of Paris by his contemporaries.

Translated from French by Helge R. Dascher

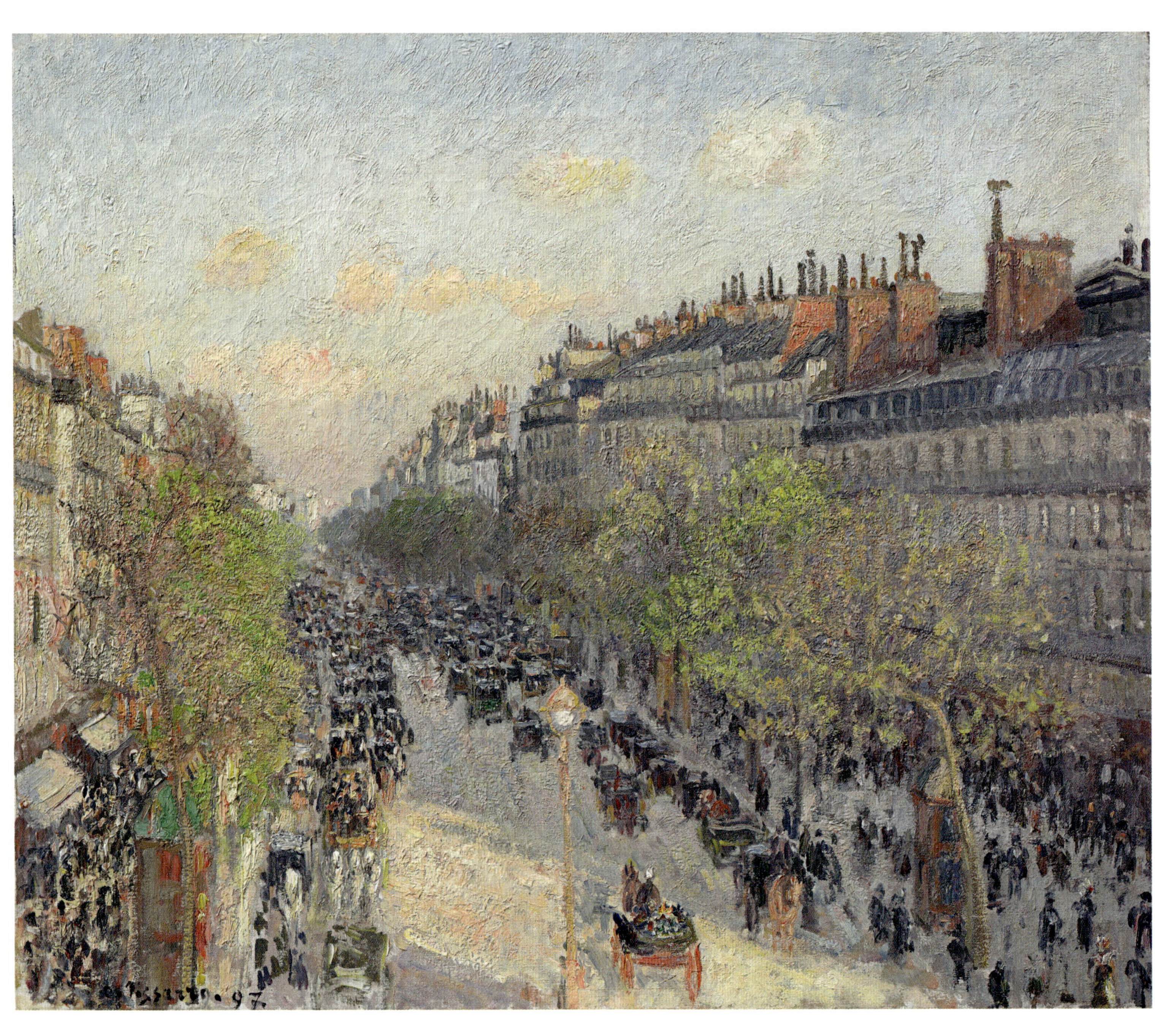

97
Boulevard Montmartre, Twilight, 1897
Hasso Plattner Collection, Museum Barberini, Potsdam

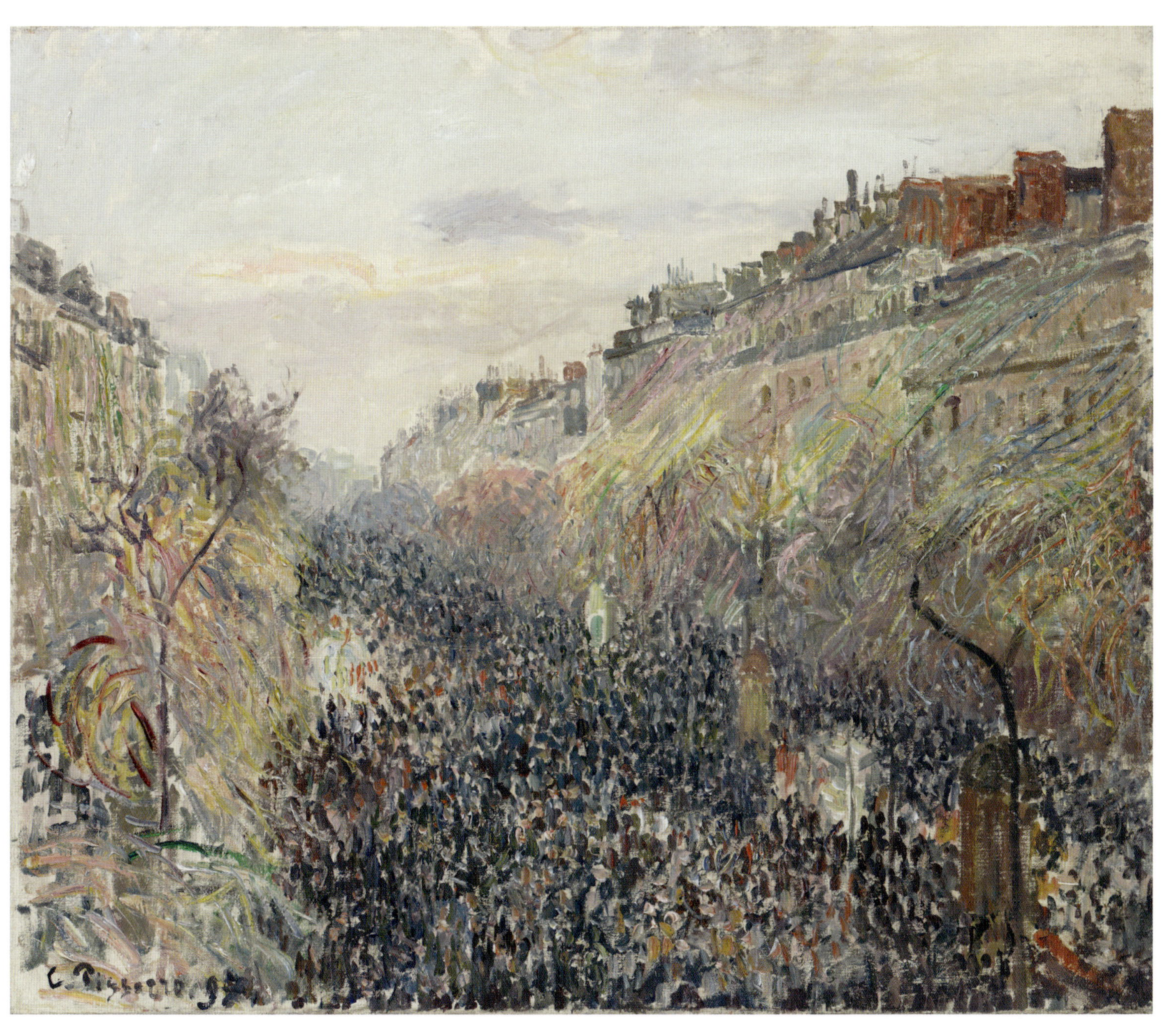

98
Boulevard Montmartre, Mardi Gras, Sunset, 1897
Kunst Museum Winterthur, Purchase, 1947

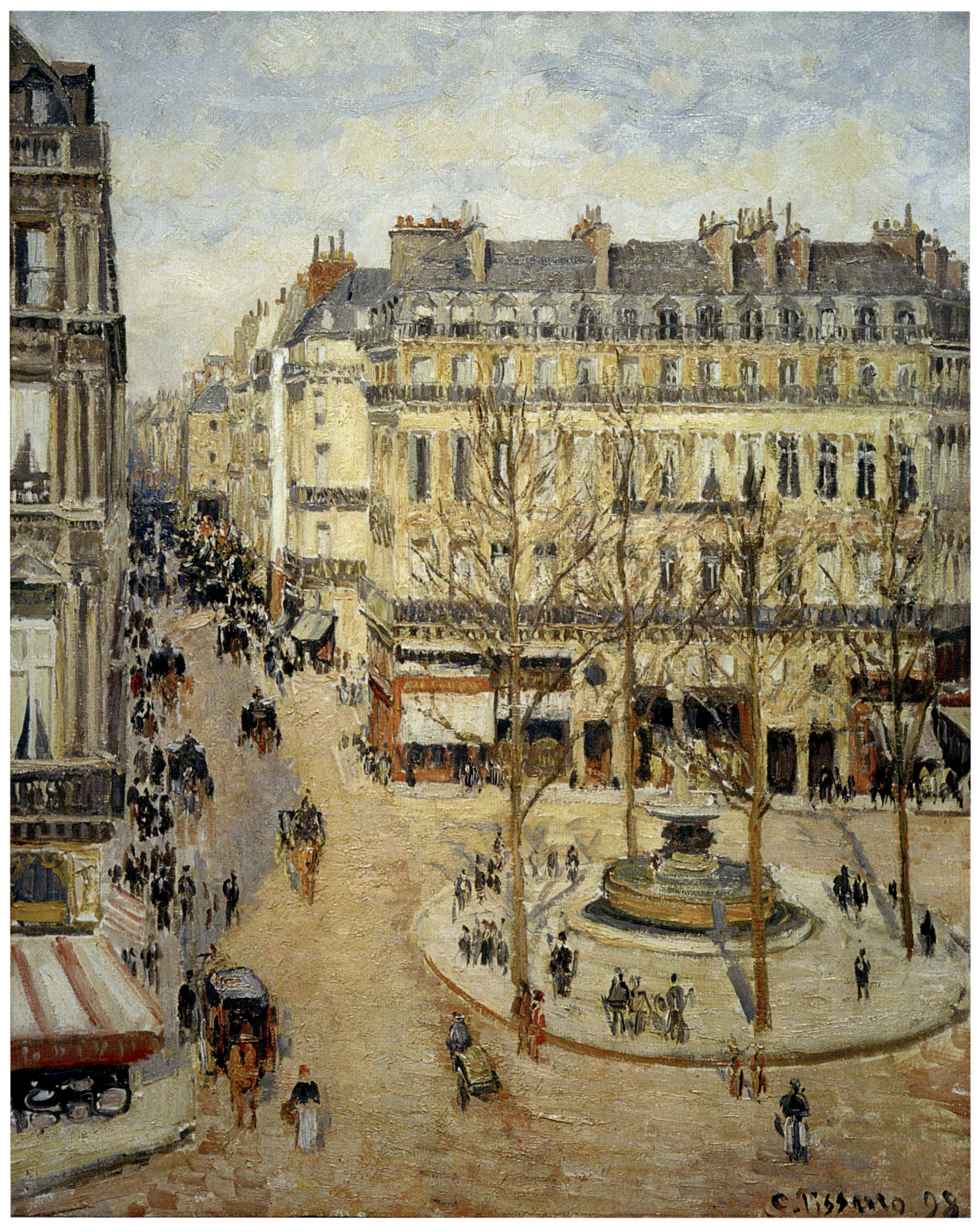

99
Morning Sun in the Rue Saint-Honoré. Place du Théâtre Français, 1898
Ordrupgaard, Copenhagen

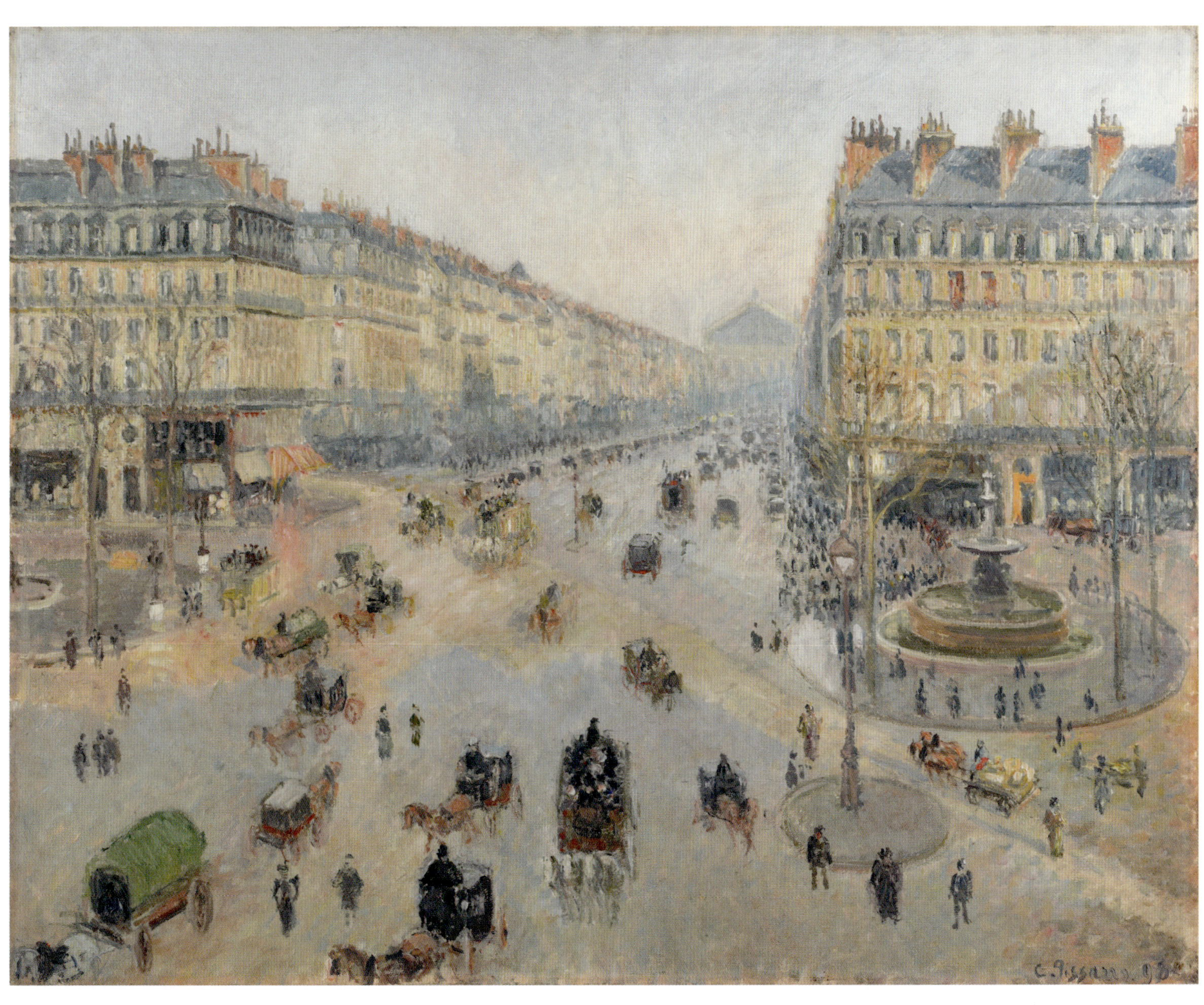

100
Avenue de l'Opéra, 1898
Musée des Beaux-Arts de la Ville de Reims, Bequest of Henry Vasnier, 11/1907

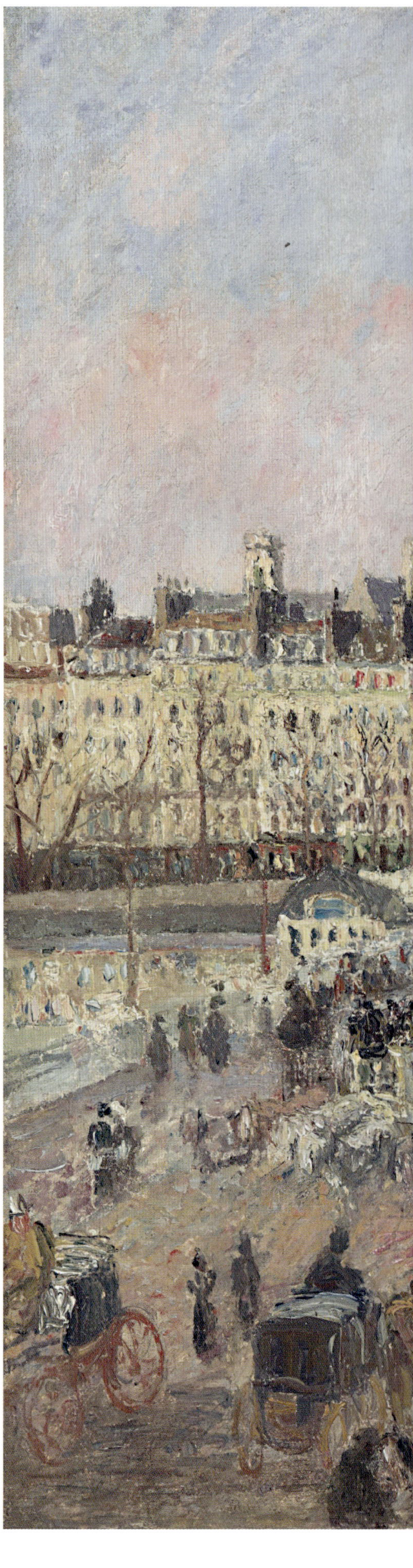

101
Afternoon Sunshine, Pont Neuf (first series), 1901
Philadelphia Museum of Art, Bequest of Charlotte Dorrance Wright, 1978

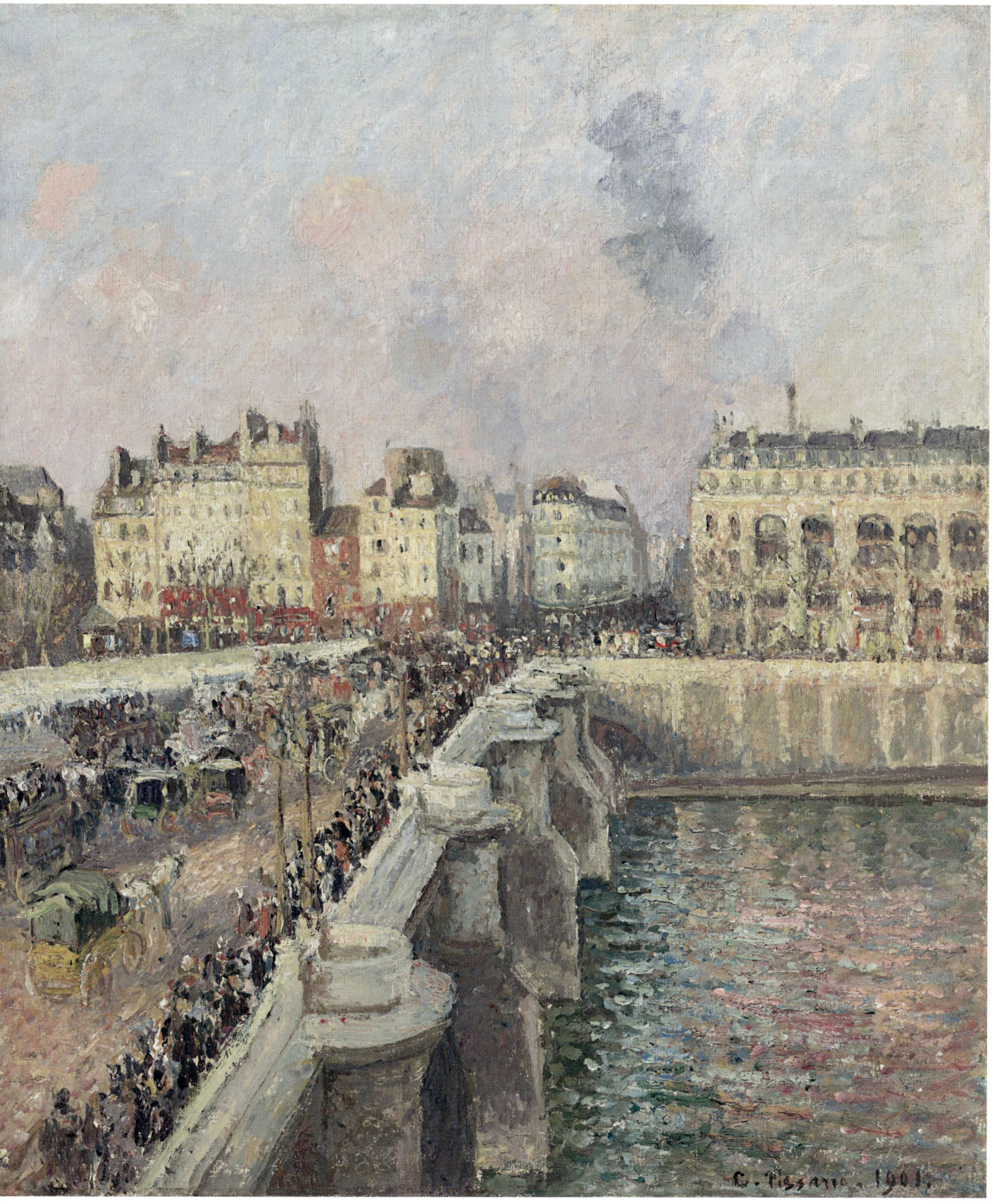
C. Pissarro. 1901

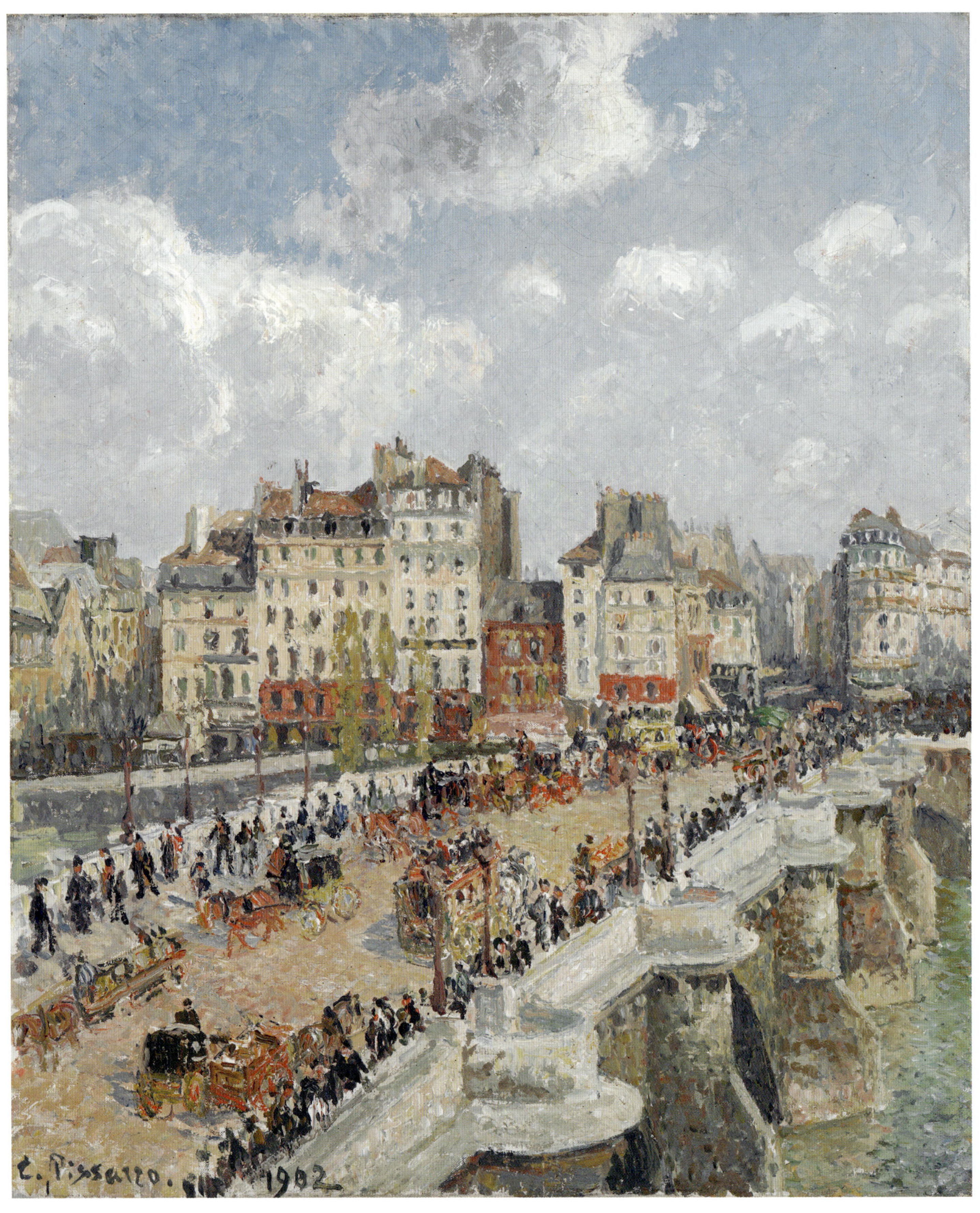

102
The Pont Neuf (second series), 1902
Szépművészeti Múzeum / Museum of Fine Arts, Budapest

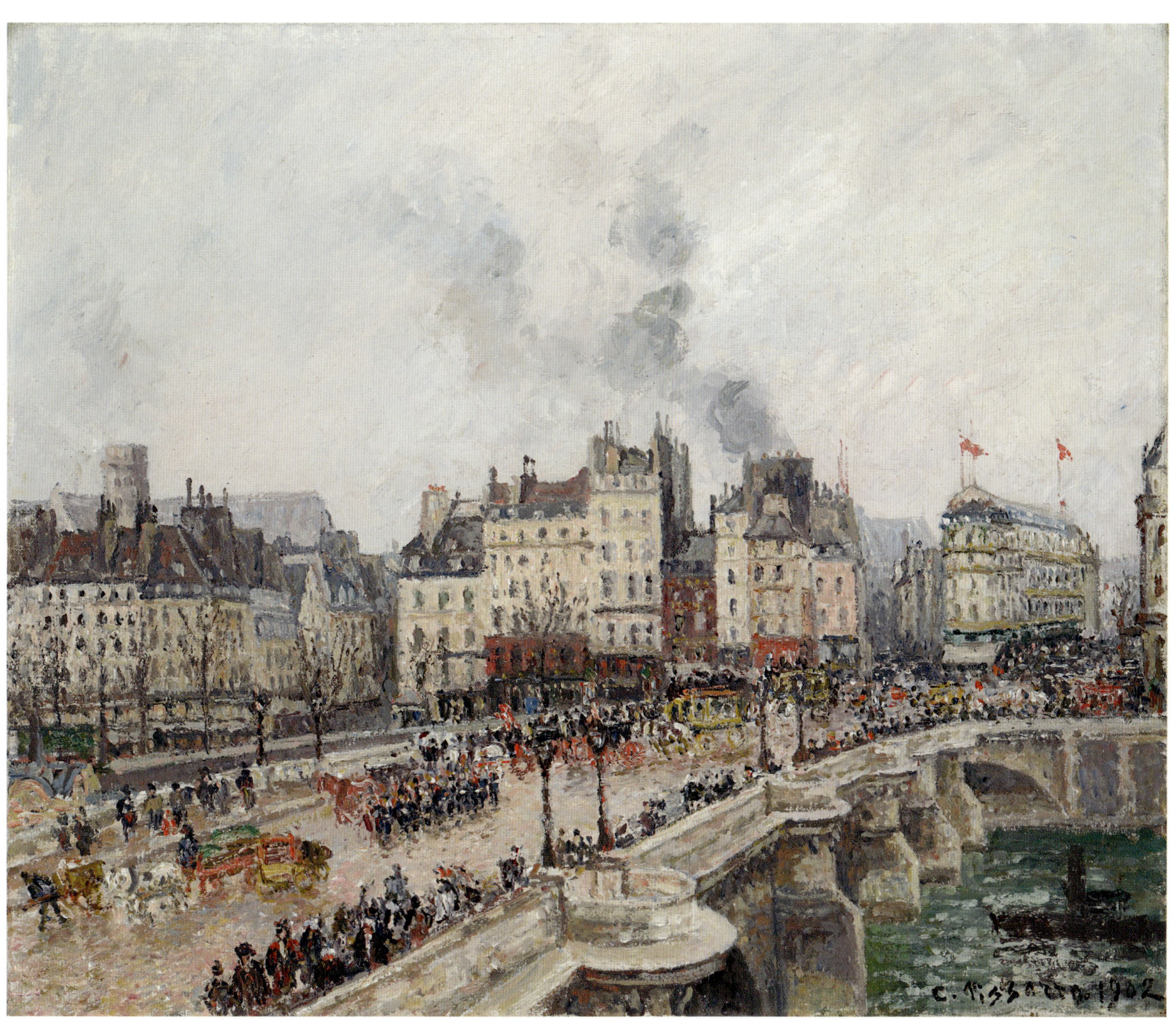

103
The Pont Neuf (second series), 1902
Musée des Beaux-Arts de Lyon

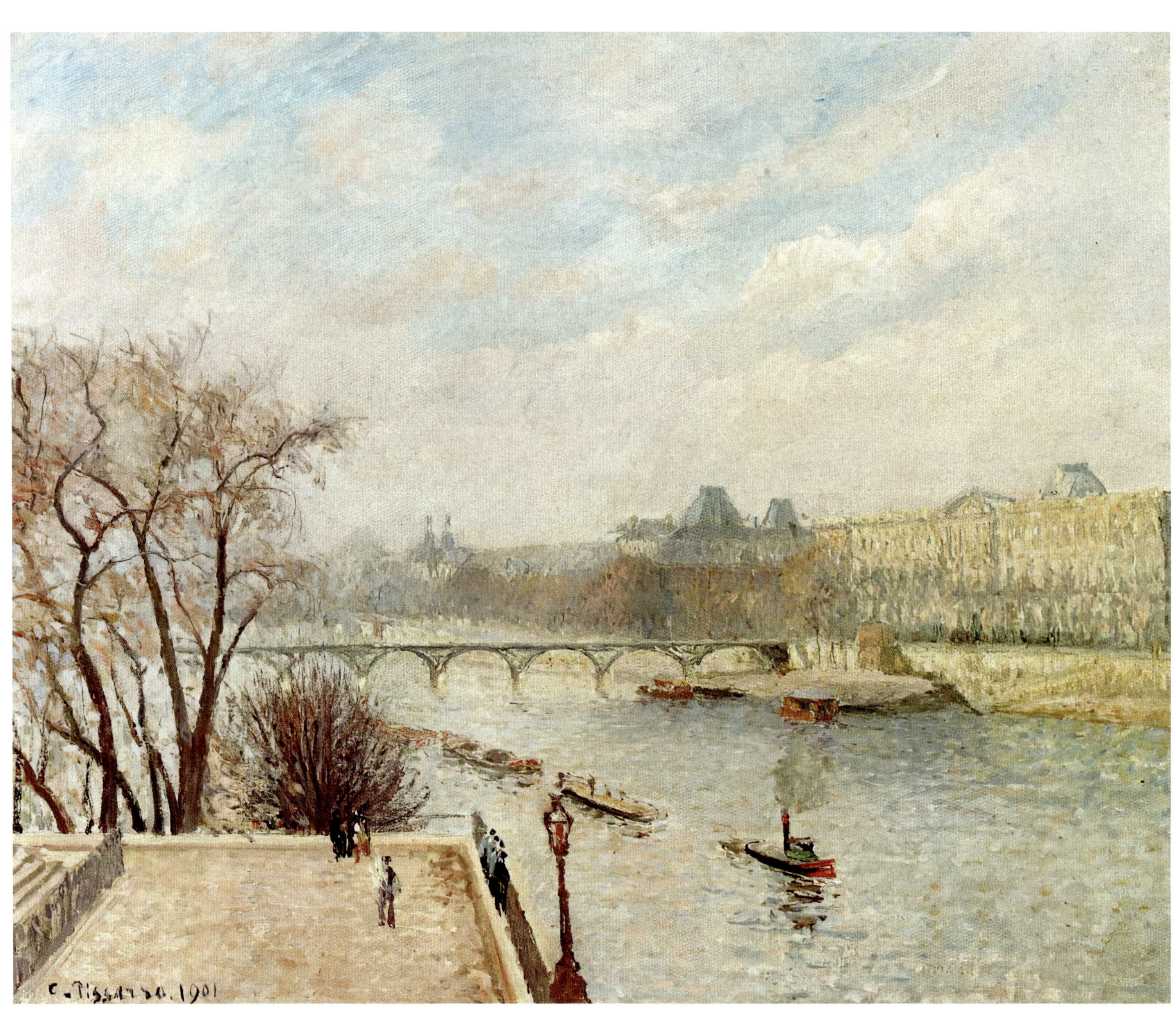

104
The Louvre, Winter Sunlight (second series), 1901
Isabelle and Scott Black Collection

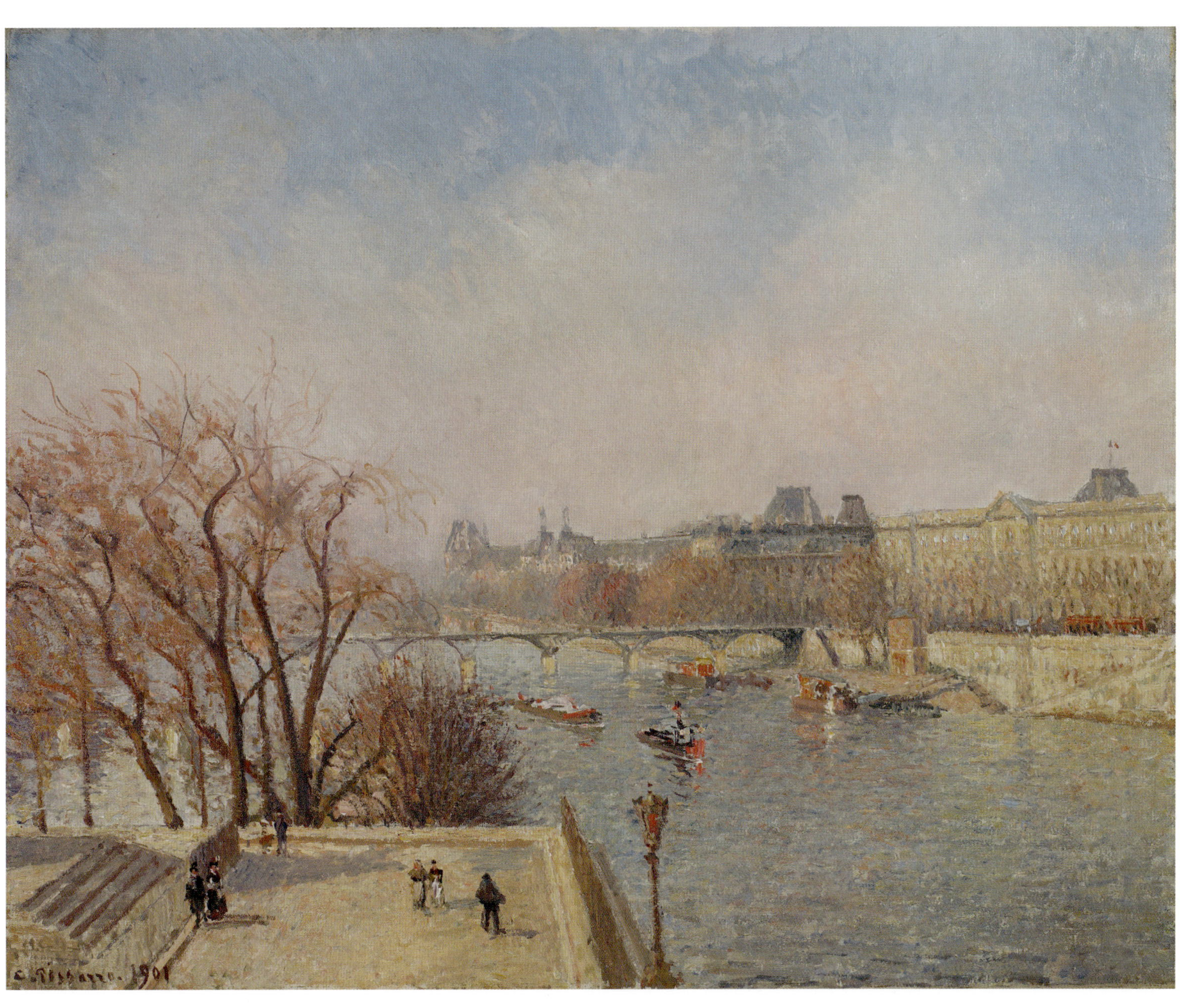

105
The Louvre, Morning, Sunlight (second series), 1901
Saint Louis Art Museum, Museum purchase

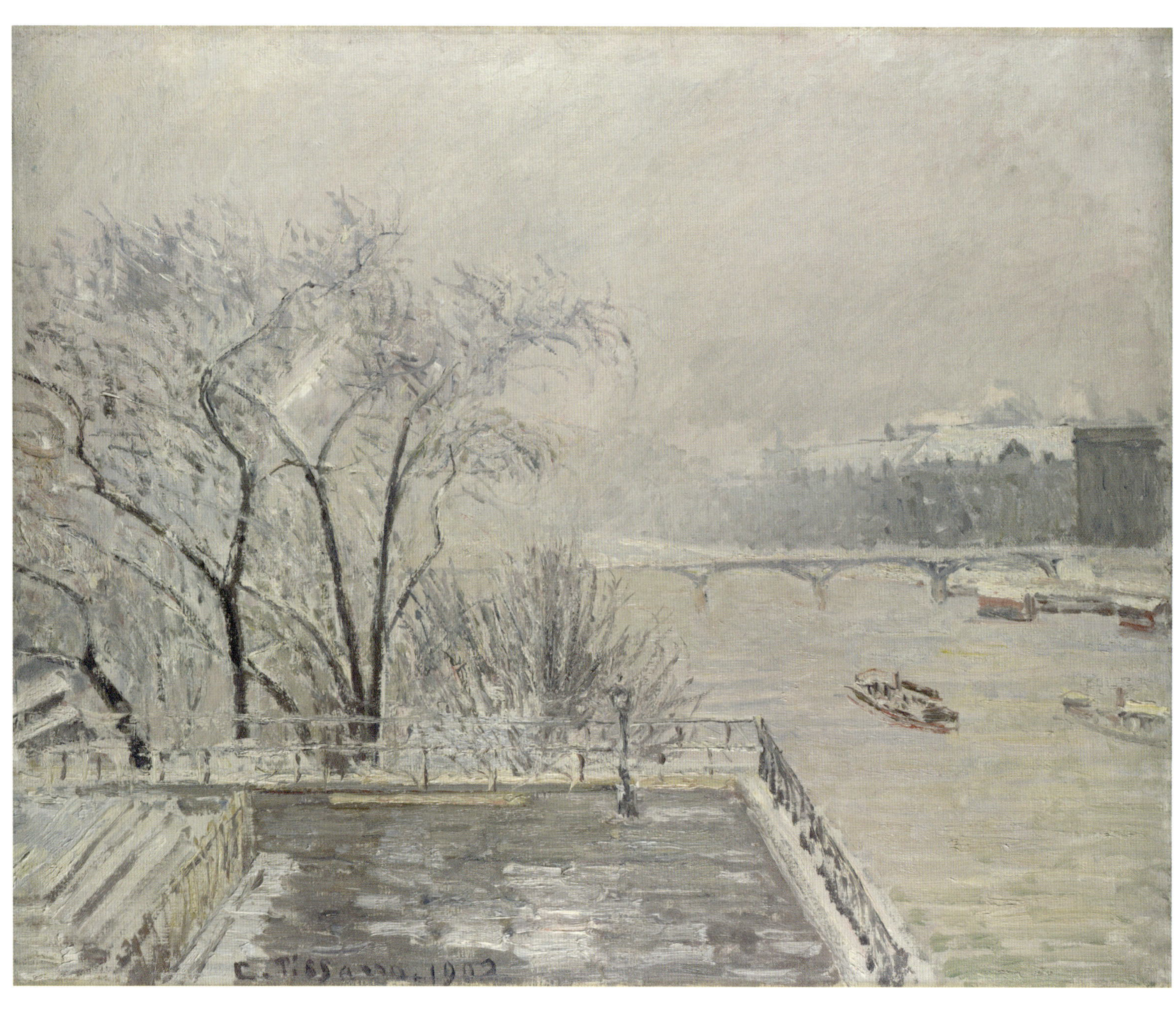

106
The Louvre Under Snow (second series), 1902
The National Gallery, London, Bought 1932

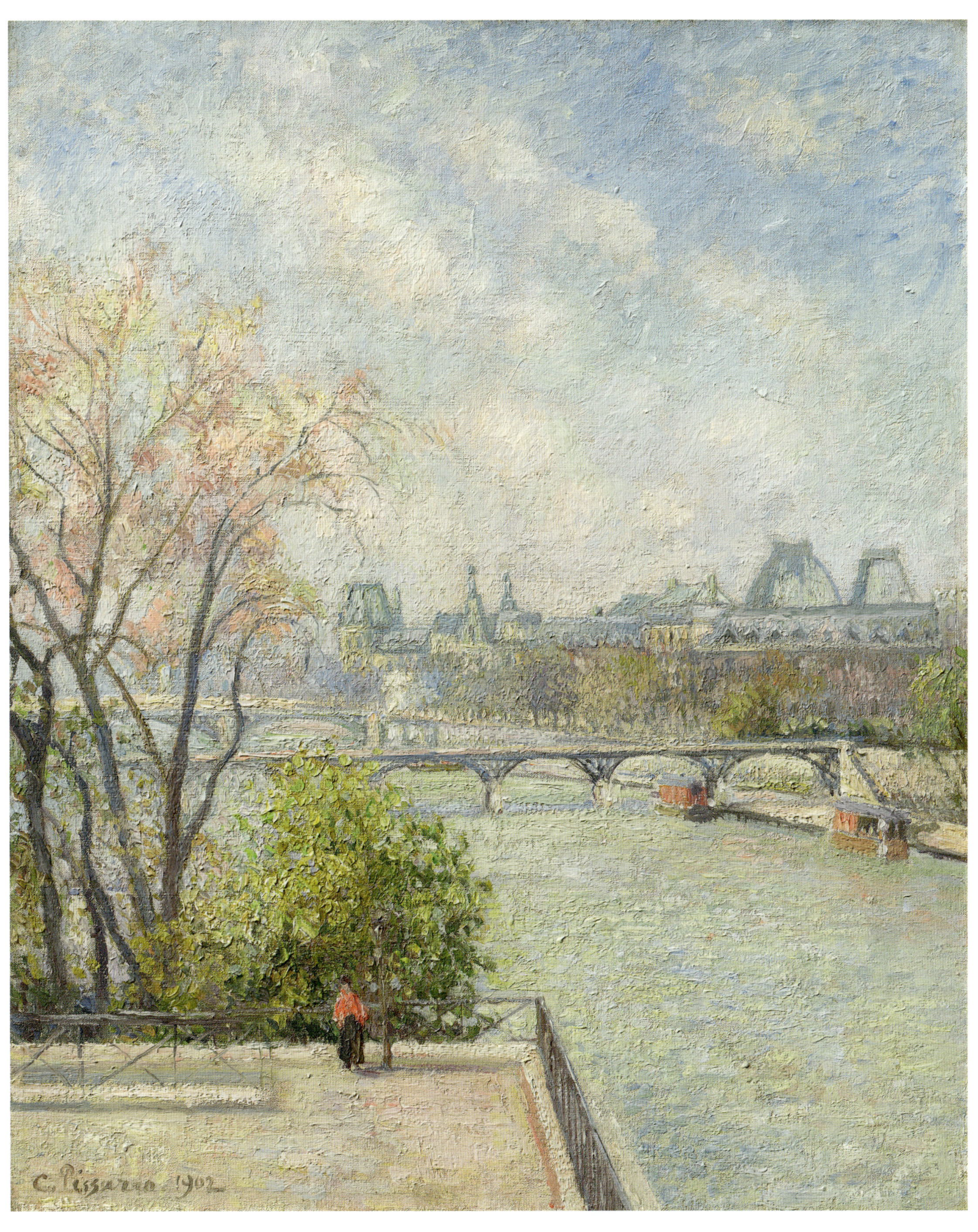

107
The Louvre, Morning, Spring (second series), 1902
Hasso Plattner Collection, Museum Barberini, Potsdam

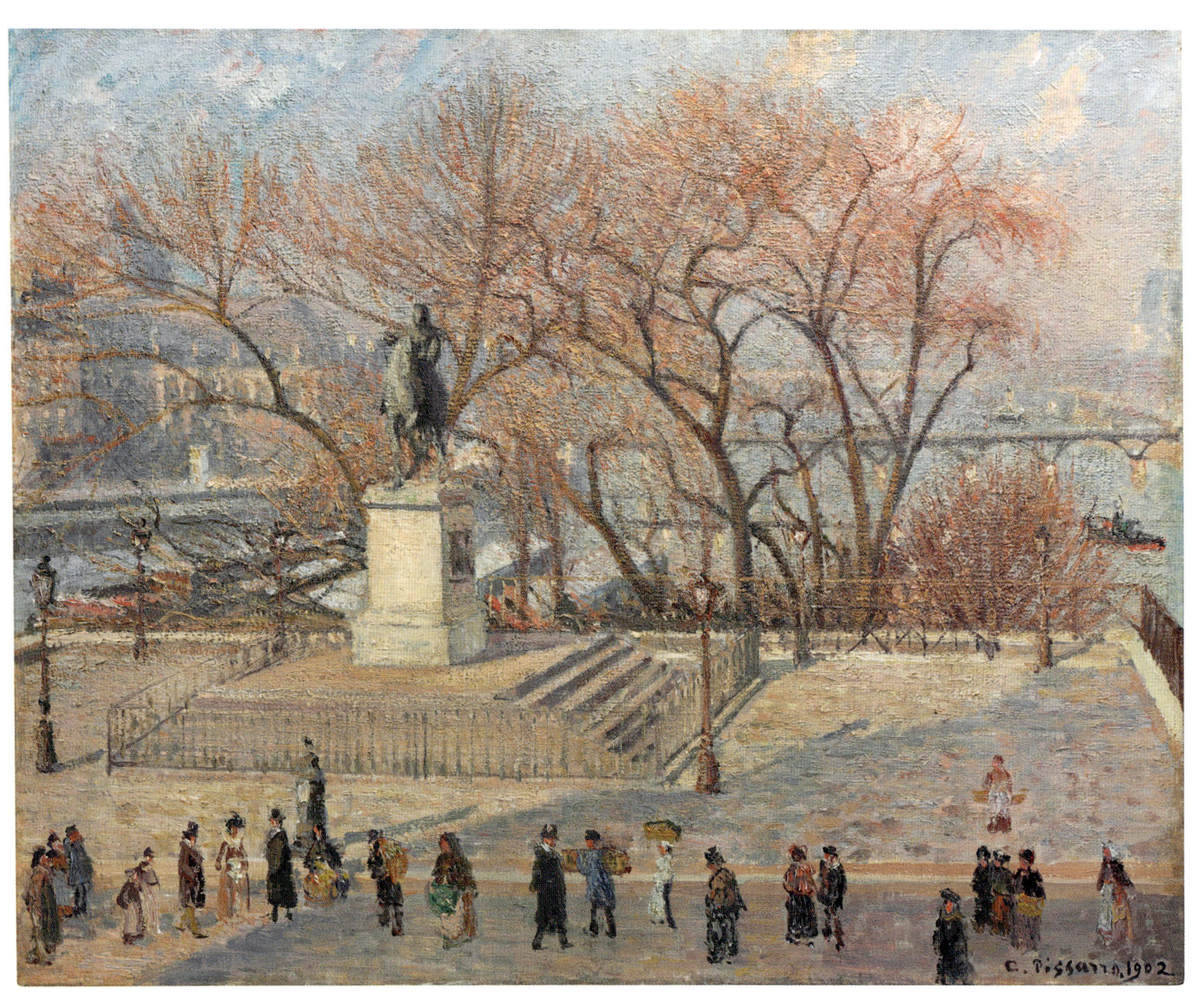

108
Statue of Henri IV, Morning, Sunlight (second series), 1902
Private collection

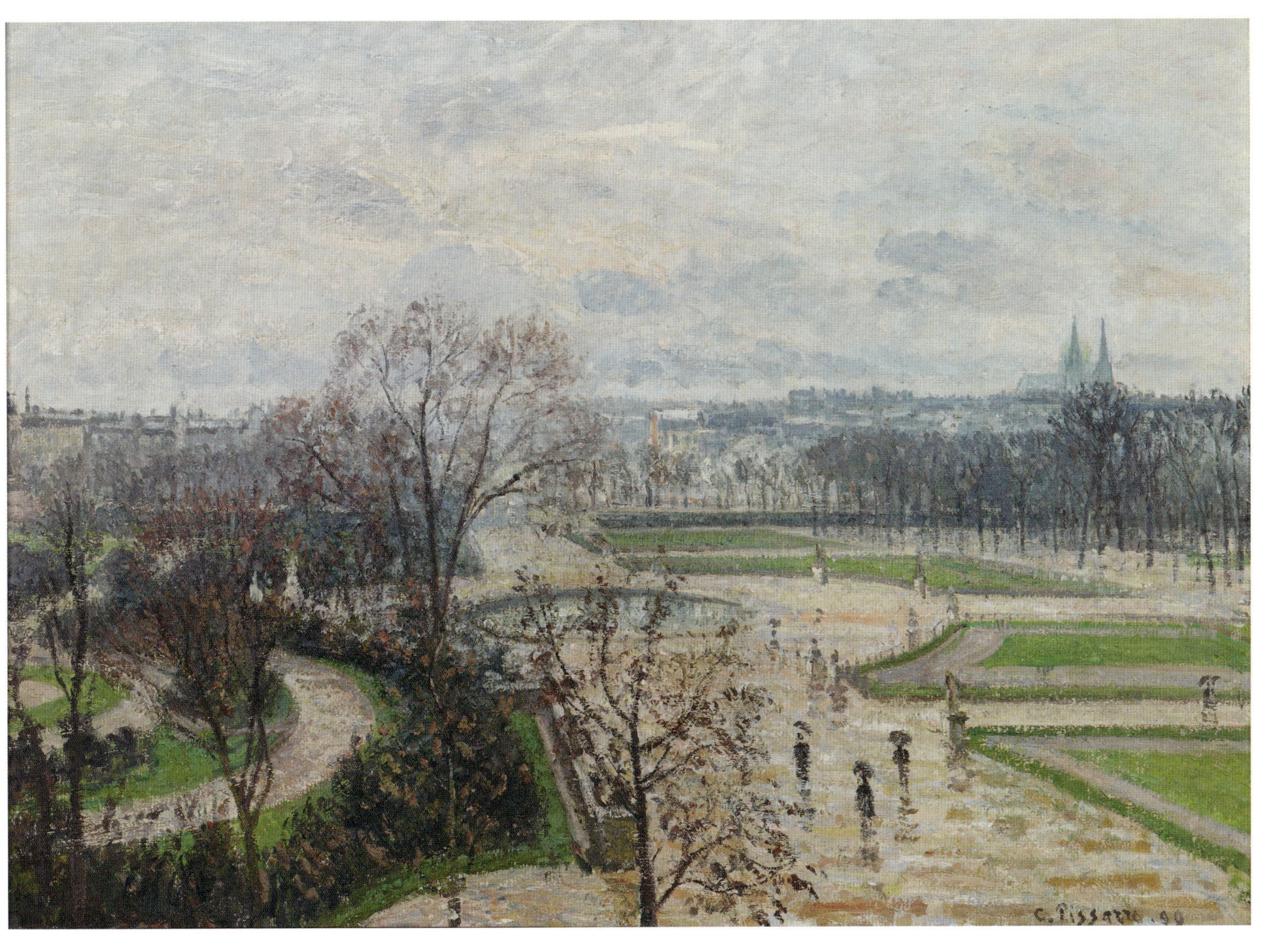

109

The Tuileries Gardens, Rainy Weather, 1899

The Ashmolean Museum, University of Oxford, Bequeathed by Mrs. W. F. R. Weldon, 1936

Chronology

Emily Willkom

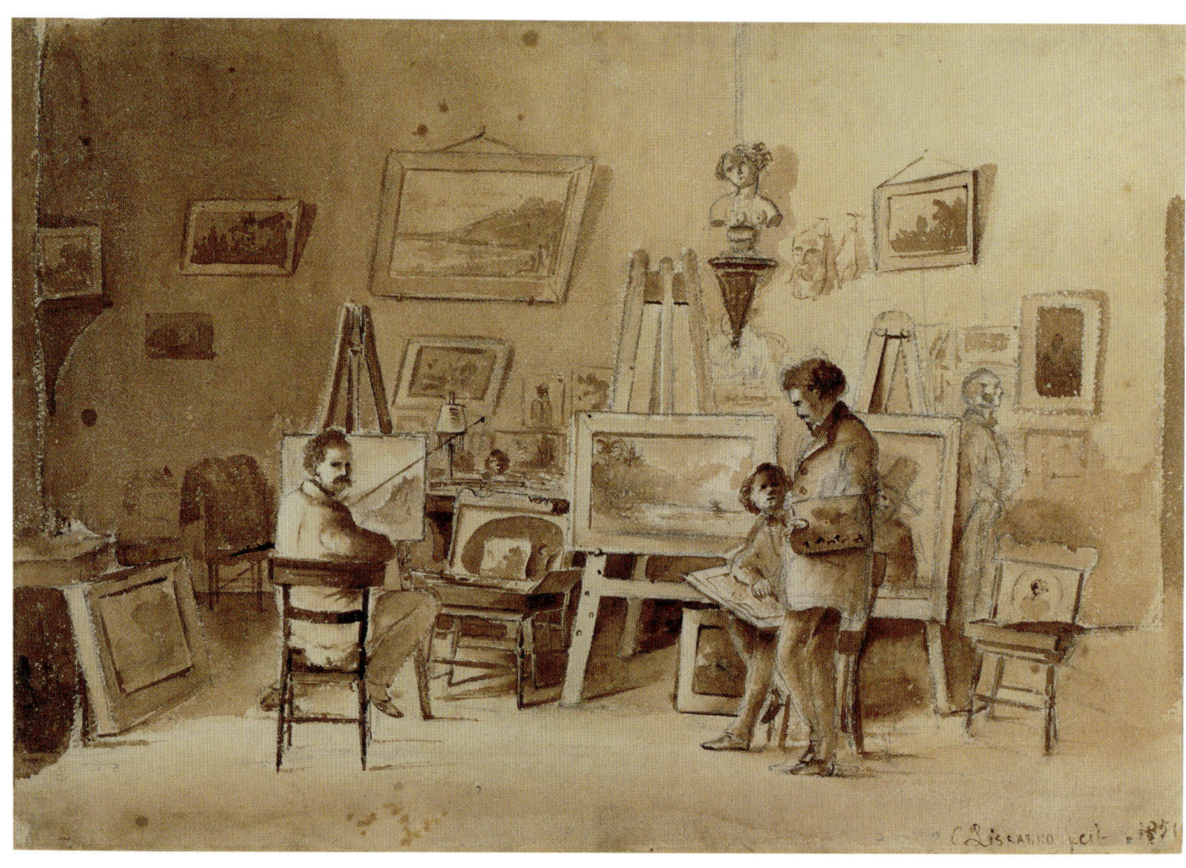

Melbye and Pissarro in Their Studio in Caracas, ca. 1854, Banco Central de Venezuela, Caracas

1830

July 10: Frédéric Pissarro and Rachel Manzana-Pomié welcome their third son, Camille Pissarro, into the world. He is born in Charlotte Amalie, Saint Thomas, in the Danish West Indies (now the US Virgin Islands) and is recorded as Jacob Abraham Camille Pizarro in the register of the local synagogue. His parents are Sephardic Jews; Pissarro will later decide to no longer practice the faith.

1842–48

At the age of twelve, Pissarro is sent to the Savary boarding school in France, located in Passy, which at the time is on the outskirts of Paris. His parents are hopeful this education will prepare him to enter the family business, a hardware shop and haberdashery, but his early interest in drawing will soon defy their expectations.

At the age of seventeen, Pissarro returns to Saint Thomas to work with his oldest brother, Alfred, in the family business. He sketches the native landscapes and draws from nature.

July 3, 1848: Slavery is abolished in the Danish colonies.

1850

Pissarro meets Danish painter Fritz Melbye, who is known for his marine paintings. Melbye plays an important role in Pissarro's early artistic development. They begin to work together and become close friends.

1852–54

Without informing his family, Pissarro travels with Melbye to Venezuela, staying at the port of La Guaira for a few months. They then settle in Caracas, setting up their own studio.

Pissarro focuses full time on his paintings and drawings for the first time, observing and capturing local landscapes and market scenes (cats. 1–6). Pissarro and Melbye make numerous trips around the Caracas region.

March 24, 1854: Slavery is abolished in the Republic of Venezuela.

Pissarro returns to Saint Thomas, having previously agreed with his father to run the family store for a few months. In exchange, his father accepts Pissarro's move to France to pursue a career in art.

1855

Pissarro boards a steamship for his passage to France on September 16. He arrives in Le Havre, a city he will later depict in his paintings (cats. 95, 96).

Reaching his destination in Paris, Pissarro visits the Exposition Universelle, where he discovers the work of French painters Camille Corot and Eugène Delacroix, as well as Gustave Courbet's autonomous exhibition space, the Pavillon du Réalisme.

1856

Pissarro's father agrees to financially support him on the condition that he enroll at the École des Beaux-Arts, hoping his son will receive proper academic training there to ensure his success as an artist. Rejecting this instruction, Pissarro prefers to draw from life and takes private classes from individual teachers at the École. He studies first with François-Édouard Picot, then with Isidore Dagnan, and lastly with Henri Lehmann, not staying with any one studio for very long. While in Paris, Pissarro meets Anton Melbye, brother of Fritz Melbye, and his circle of Danish artist friends and colleagues.

Pissarro spends the summer in Montmorency Forest, just north of Paris, painting outdoors.

1857–58

Pissarro enrolls at the Académie Suisse, a large, independent drawing school in Paris. There, he later meets Armand Guillaumin, Antoine Guillemet, Claude Monet, and Ludovic Piette.

On the recommendation of Fritz Melbye, Pissarro pays a visit to Corot, who emboldens him to continue painting surrounded by nature. Corot proves to be a great mentor for Pissarro stylistically, as is reflected in his early works.

Pissarro spends the summers of 1857 and 1858 at La Roche-Guyon in the Département du Val d'Oise, northwest of Paris.

1859

Pissarro's first submission to the Paris Salon, his painting *Landscape at Montmorency* (fig. p. 12), is accepted for exhibition, while those of several of his contemporaries, such as Henri Fantin-Latour, Édouard Manet, Jean-François Millet, and James Abbott McNeill Whistler, are rejected. Pissarro lists himself as a student of Anton Melbye.

1860

In Paris, Pissarro meets Julie Vellay, age twenty-one, from Burgundy, who is employed by his mother as a maid following his parents' relocation to France in 1859. She and Pissarro will marry in 1871 and have eight children together—five of whom will go on to become artists.

Julie Pissarro in the Garden, 1874, Petit Palais—Musée des Beaux-Arts de la Ville de Paris

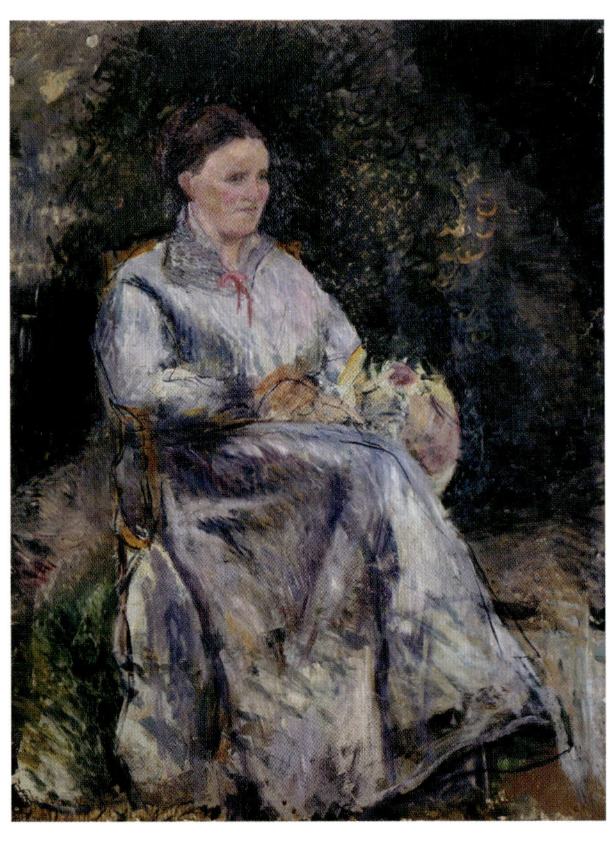

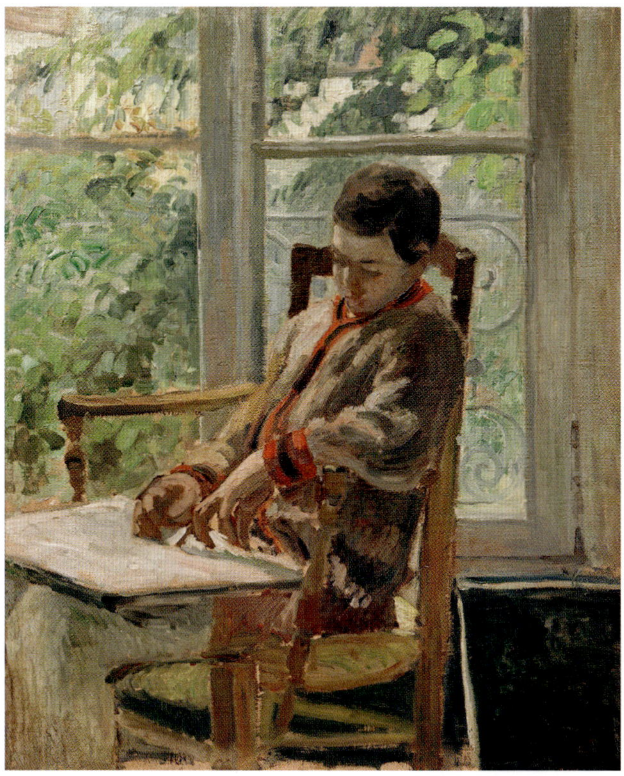

Portrait of Lucien Pissarro, 1875, private collection

1861

At the Académie Suisse, Pissarro meets Paul Cézanne, whom he encourages to move away from his dark palette and paint outdoors. Pissarro registers as a copyist at the Musée du Louvre.

1863

Monet introduces Pissarro to his friends Frédéric Bazille, Pierre-Auguste Renoir, and Alfred Sisley.

February 20: In Paris, Julie Vellay gives birth to their first child, a son, Lucien.

At the newly established Salon des Refusés, Pissarro exhibits three canvases previously rejected by the Paris Salon.

Pissarro and his family spend the summer in La Varenne-Saint-Hilaire on the outskirts of Paris so that he can paint the village.

Pissarro begins experimenting with etching and joins the Société des Aquafortistes, an artist association founded in 1862 to encourage etching. After its dissolution in 1867, Pissarro will pause his practice of printmaking until 1873.

Pissarro moves back to Paris with his family for the winter.

1864

Pissarro submits two canvases to the Paris Salon, listing himself as a pupil of both Corot and Anton Melbye.

In the fall, Pissarro brings his family to Montfoucault in the Département de la Mayenne, bordering Normandy, to visit his dear friend, painter Ludovic Piette, and paint the small village. For the winter, they return to La Varenne-Saint-Hilaire.

1865

Pissarro reads the anarchist writings of Pierre-Joseph Proudhon and, feeling a great connection with his philosophy, shares it with friends and family.

Two of Pissarro's paintings are accepted at the Paris Salon, where he lists himself again as a pupil of Corot and Anton Melbye.

May 18: In La Varenne-Saint-Hilaire, Julie Vellay gives birth to their second child and first daughter, Jeanne-Rachel "Minette."

1866

Pissarro moves with his family to Pontoise, a provincial town just northwest of Paris, in the spring.

One canvas, *The Banks of the Marne in Winter* (cat. 13), is accepted to the Paris Salon; this time Pissarro cites himself only as a pupil of Anton Melbye. Author Émile Zola sees his work and sings its praises.

1867

Pissarro's submission—along with those by Bazille, Manet, Cézanne, Manet, Monet, Renoir, and Sisley—is rejected by the Paris Salon.

1868

Struggling to sell his works, Pissarro takes on odd jobs, including painting store blinds and shop signs (fig. p. 30).

Two canvases of Pontoise are accepted to the Paris Salon. Zola continues to write favorably, producing a lengthy and praiseworthy article on Pissarro's work.

1869

In the spring, the Pissarro family moves to Louveciennes, a village west of Paris that is closer to the capital than Pontoise is.

Only one canvas by Pissarro is accepted to the Paris Salon. He sends an angry letter to the administration contesting the placement of his painting. Having been hung high over a doorway, critics make no mention of his work, presumably because they did not see it.

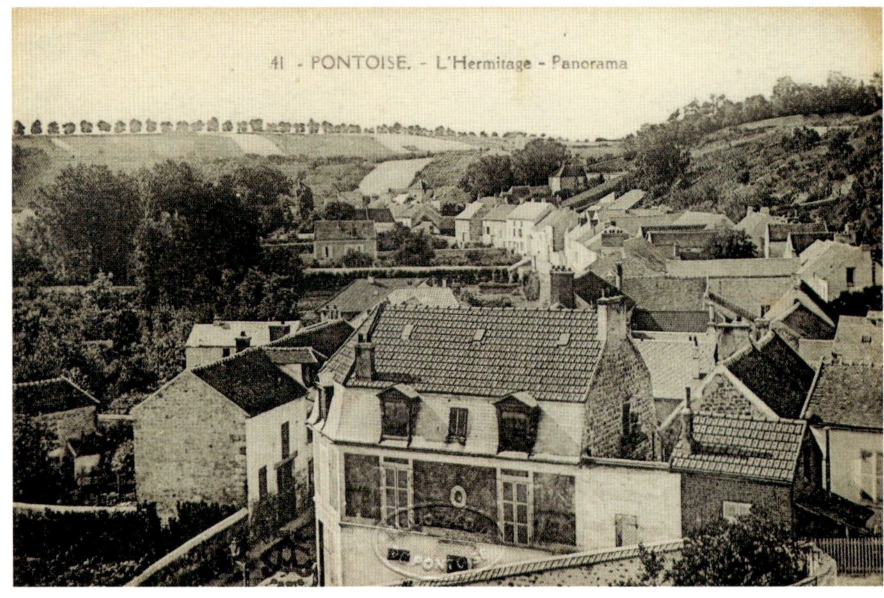

Postcard with a view of the neighborhood of L'Hermitage in Pontoise, undated, Musée d'Art et d'Histoire Pissarro—Pontoise

1870

Pissarro submits two paintings to the Paris Salon, both of which are accepted. Art critic Théodore Duret takes notice of his work.

July 19: The Franco-Prussian War begins.

In September, the Pissarro family departs Louveciennes quickly, leaving most of their belongings behind at the advance of the Prussian army. They take on lodging with Piette in Montfoucault.

October 21: Julie Vellay gives birth to their third child, Adèle-Emma. The girl dies two weeks later, on November 5, from an intestinal infection.

On December 2, the Pissarro family flees Montfoucault and seeks refuge from the war in London.

1871

Pissarro connects with art dealer Paul Durand-Ruel through fellow artist Charles-François Daubigny. Durand-Ruel, who had also fled to London because of the war, becomes Pissarro's primary gallerist. Durand-Ruel requests several canvases of Pissarro to sell, of which he buys two views of London for himself.

Pissarro submits a canvas to the Royal Academy in London but is rejected. Disappointed, he turns to the International Exhibition of Fine Art in South Kensington, organized by Durand-Ruel, and is accepted.

May 10: The Franco-Prussian War ends.

In Croydon, on June 14, Pissarro and Julie Vellay marry in a small civil ceremony without family in attendance, as his parents do not approve of the marriage.

Julie and Camille Pissarro in Pontoise, ca. 1877 (photomontage), private collection

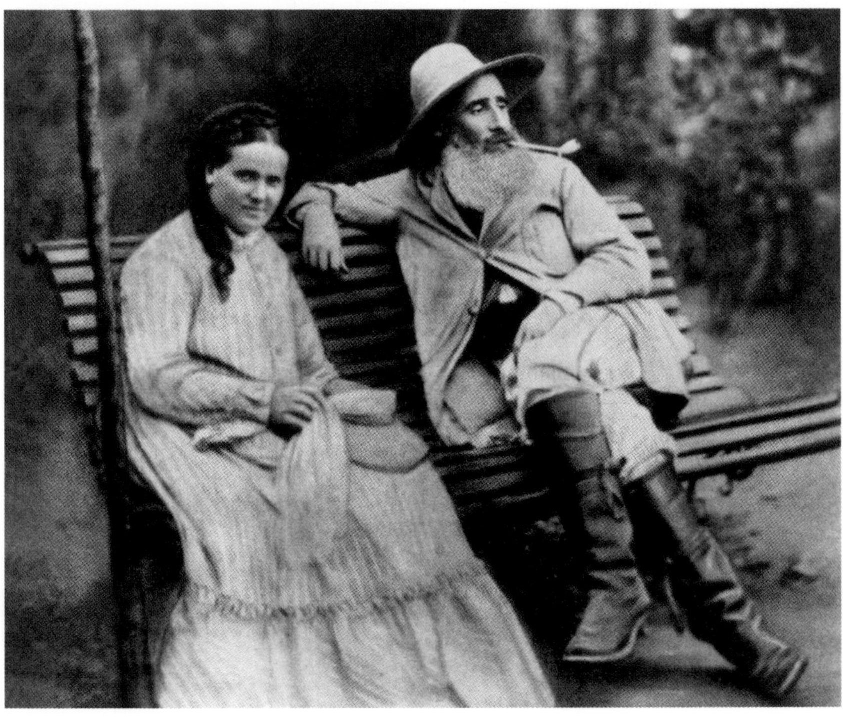

After the withdrawal of the Prussian troops, the Pissarro family returns to what is left of their house in Louveciennes. The studio is destroyed, and twenty years of work is lost. Only a few paintings were spared, having been kept safe by the neighbors. The Pissarro family moves next door while repairs are made on their home.

November 22: Julie Pissarro gives birth to their fourth child, Georges.

1872

With regular purchases from Durand-Ruel, Pissarro is finally able to support his family through the sale of his artwork alone, establishing his financial independence. Despite this relief, Julie Pissarro will continue to keep animals and a vegetable garden to help minimize household expenses.

Durand-Ruel holds regular exhibitions of the Society of French Artists at his German Gallery in London. By the time he closes the gallery in 1875, he will have shown a total of twenty-one works by Pissarro.

After a four-year reprieve, the Pissarro family returns to the countryside of Pontoise, renting a house so that Pissarro may paint. A number of Pissarro's friends visit him, including Édouard Béliard, Paul Cézanne, Armand Guillaumin, and Francisco Oller. Cézanne's is the first of several visits in which the artists exchange advice and views on painting over a ten-year working relationship.

1873

Pissarro has difficulties with his grocery bill and negotiates payment through the barter of his paintings. Durand-Ruel purchases eight canvases from him this year, and Pissarro finds growing support among collectors.

Tired of the judges' biases at the Paris Salon, Pissarro and Monet establish the Société Anonyme des Artistes Peintres, Sculpteurs, Graveurs, etc. (Anonymous Society of Painters, Sculptors, Engravers, etc.) to hold its own annual exhibitions, in which members may show an unlimited number of works without jury approval. This group launches the Impressionism movement, although it will not officially use this name until 1877.

Pissarro rekindles his interest in printmaking when his friend Dr. Gachet purchases a printing press, allowing the artist to use it at his leisure. Between 1873 and 1874, Pissarro makes six etchings and twelve lithographs.

1874

April 6: Jeanne-Rachel Pissarro, just shy of nine years old, dies from a respiratory illness.

The inaugural exhibition of the Société Anonyme des Artistes Peintres, Sculpteurs, Graveurs, etc. takes place, and Pissarro exhibits five of his landscapes—including *Hoarfrost* (cat. 33). The show is attended by 3,400 visitors and accompanied by lively discussions in the press; however, some of the more strident critics are unimpressed with the sketchy quality and fleeting brushstrokes. In spite of the financial failure and the subsequent dissolvement of the society, the group members will continue to exhibit together in changing constellations.

Durand-Ruel, who at this point is also struggling financially, stops buying Pissarro's work and will continue to abstain from buying until 1880.

July 24: In Pontoise, Julie Pissarro gives birth to their fifth child, Félix "Titi."

The Pissarro family returns to Montfoucault to live with Piette in October, which helps ease their financial burden. They stay through the beginning of February.

1875

Pissarro is introduced to collector Eugène Murer through his friend Guillaumin, who is one of a few making purchases from him during this time.

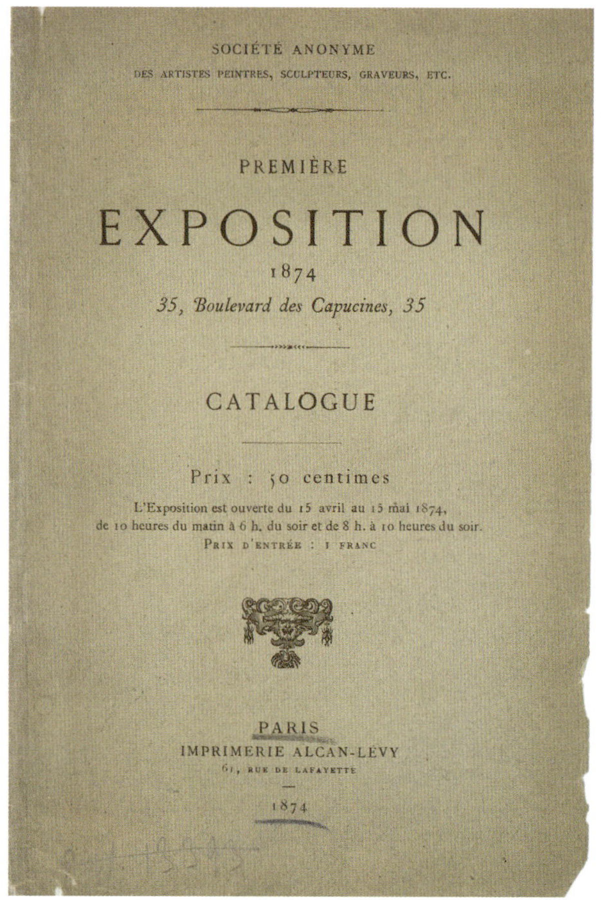

SOCIÉTÉ ANONYME
DES ARTISTES PEINTRES, SCULPTEURS, GRAVEURS, ETC.

PREMIÈRE
EXPOSITION
1874
35, Boulevard des Capucines, 35

CATALOGUE

Prix : 50 centimes
L'Exposition est ouverte du 15 avril au 15 mai 1874,
de 10 heures du matin à 6 h. du soir et de 8 h. à 10 heures du soir.
PRIX D'ENTRÉE : 1 FRANC

PARIS
IMPRIMERIE ALCAN-LÉVY
61, RUE DE LAFAYETTE

1874

Catalog of the first exhibition of the Société Anonyme des Artistes Peintres, Sculpteurs, Graveurs, etc. (first Impressionist exhibition), 1874, Bibliothèque Nationale de France, Paris

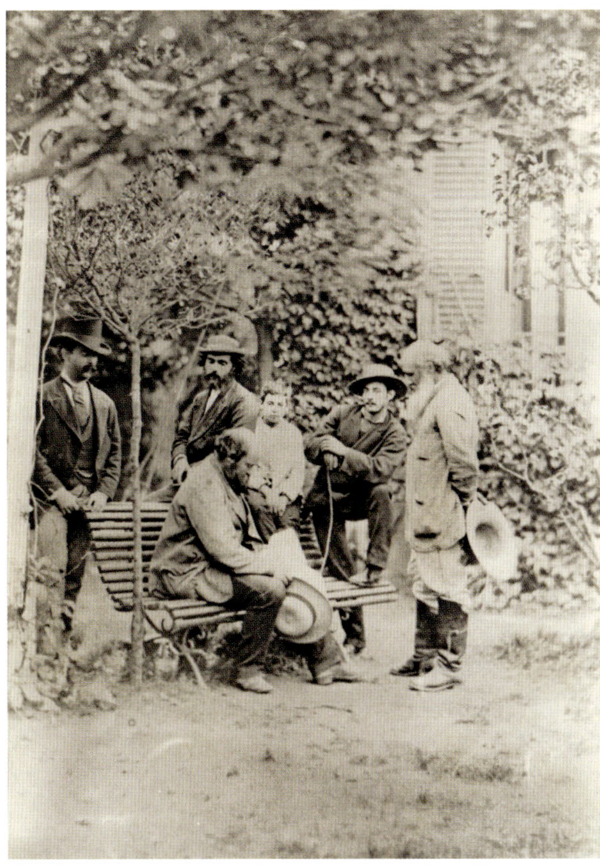

Friends in Pontoise (from left to right): photographer Martinès (standing), medical student and painter Alfonso, Lucien Pissarro, Dr. A. Aguiar, Camille Pissarro, and Paul Cézanne (sitting on the bench), ca. 1873 (photo: Martinès), The Ashmolean Museum, University of Oxford

1876

The second exhibition of the group of Impressionists takes place in Durand-Ruel's newly opened galleries at 11, Rue Le Peletier, Paris, where Pissarro shows twelve paintings. The exhibition is a failure, with critics again giving brutal reviews, although Zola comes to the defense of Pissarro and the Impressionists. Pissarro's submissions fail to generate the much-needed revenue that he is desperate for. Forced to give up their apartment in Paris, the Pissarro family continues to live with Piette.

Edmond Duranty publishes *La Nouvelle Peinture,* a thirty-eight-page booklet that comes to the defense of the Impressionists and argues for the significance of the art movement.

1877

Gustave Caillebotte buys several of Pissarro's paintings to spare him from a forced sale of his works to pay his creditors. Pissarro begins making faience tiles for steady income.

Caillebotte is determined to bring together friends and colleagues to organize another Impressionist exhibition. He sees Pissarro's inclusion as essential to its success. The third exhibition of the group takes place, showing 241 works by eighteen artists. Pissarro exhibits twenty-two works. Their exhibitions continue to shock and bewilder the public, as critics call out their departure from tradition, one-point perspective, and naturalistic color palettes.

1878

Pissarro continues to solicit collectors and any potential buyers in hopes of expanding his client base to bring in more income.

Duret writes a pamphlet in support of the Impressionists, *Les Peintres impressionnistes: Claude Monet, Sisley, C. Pissarro, Renoir, Berthe Morisot,* proclaiming his admiration for the movement and the significance of Pissarro's canvases.

The Exposition Universelle takes place in Paris and attempts to showcase France's recovery following the Franco-Prussian War. However, no living artists are invited to exhibit for the Fine Arts section.

November 21: Julie Pissarro gives birth to their sixth child, Ludovic-Rodolphe "Rodo," named in honor of their friend Ludovic Piette, who had died in April.

1879

Pissarro and Caillebotte, with the support of Edgar Degas, organize a fourth Impressionist exhibition, exhibiting fifteen painters, including the newly invited Mary Cassatt and Paul Gauguin. Pissarro exhibits an impressive array of media, showing thirty-eight works, including twelve fans, making his contribution the largest. Critics are far more approving of Pissarro than they had been in previous years. With the exhibition seeing more than 15,400 visitors, it is labeled a success and Impressionism finally gains traction among the public.

A self-taught painter, Gauguin comes to Pontoise in September to visit and paint with Pissarro for the first time. Seeking his advice and mentorship, Gauguin is introduced to a lighter palette and Impressionist techniques of handling light and paint.

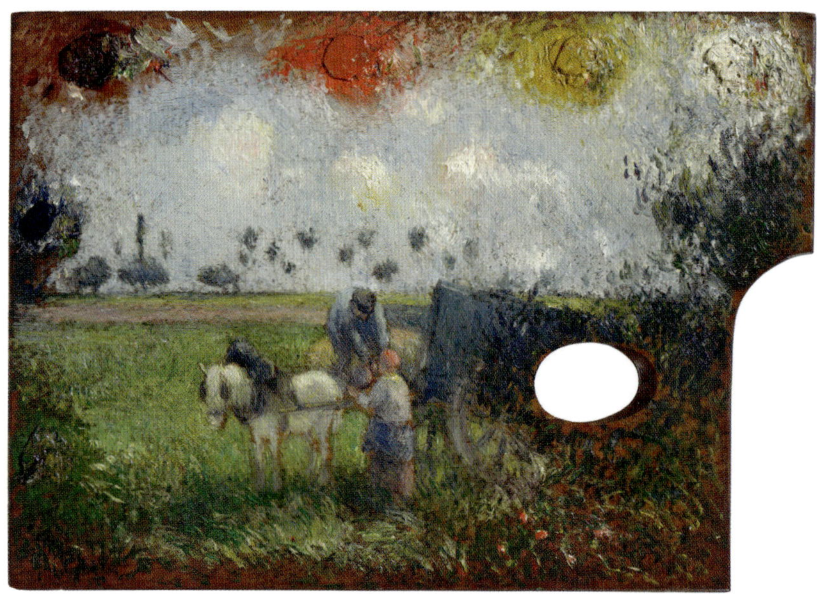

Camille Pissarro's palette with a landscape, ca. 1878–80, Clark Art Institute, Williamstown, Massachusetts

1880

The fifth Impressionist exhibition takes place, although this year several of its important members are absent. Cézanne, Renoir, Sisley, and Monet all decide instead to submit their works to the Paris Salon. Pissarro presents ten paintings, nine etchings, and one fan. The exhibition affords the opportunity for the group to show samples of the work that is being produced for the journal *Le Jour et la nuit* (Day and Night, a play on the dominance of black and white in printing), a project by Cassatt, Degas, and Pissarro, which they intend to be an outlet for Impressionist etching techniques. The journal will never come to fruition; nevertheless, Pissarro continues his experimentation with printmaking.

Pissarro first mentions troubles with his eyes; his eyes will continue to cause issues for years to come.

Through the financial support of the bank Union Générale, Durand-Ruel can buy Impressionist works again.

1881

At the sixth Impressionist exhibition, Pissarro makes one of the largest contributions: twenty-eight works, including fifteen gouaches. Monet, Renoir, and Sisley prefer to send paintings to the Paris Salon, once again. Pissarro's landscapes continue to receive favorable reviews.

August 27: In Pontoise, Julie Pissarro gives birth to their seventh child, Jeanne-Marguerite "Cocotte."

1882

In January, the Union Générale collapses, causing the Paris Bourse, or stock exchange, to crash.

The seventh exhibition of the Impressionists takes place, with Pissarro presenting thirty-six works, eleven of which are gouaches. After years of experimentation with figures, Pissarro shows paintings depicting landscapes with prominent individual figures as well as groupings of figures (cats. 40–42) for the first time.

In December, the family moves from Pontoise to a nearby village, Osny, where the cost of housing is cheaper.

Draner (i.e., Jules Renard), "A Visit with the Impressionists," in *Le Charivari,* March 9, 1882

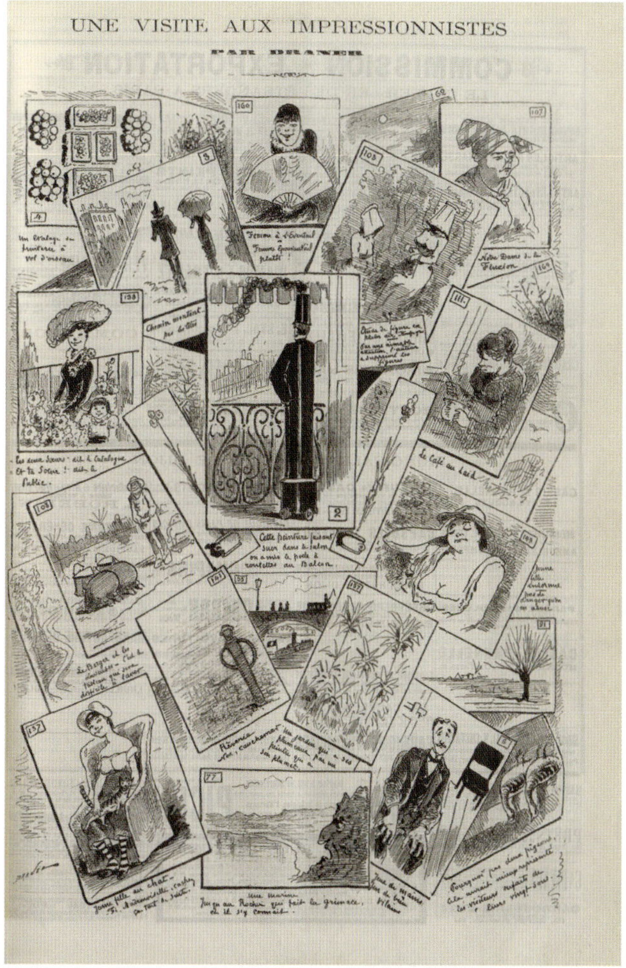

1883

Lucien Pissarro, now twenty years old, travels to England to work on improving his English and to learn a trade. This is the beginning of an extensive correspondence with his father.

Durand-Ruel holds an Impressionist exhibition at Dowdeswell & Dowdeswell's Gallery in London, featuring a few of Pissarro's oil paintings, watercolors, and a gouache. Despite his best efforts, given its poor reception, Durand-Ruel will not hold an Impressionist show in London again until 1901.

Pissarro has his first solo exhibition in Paris with Durand-Ruel, a retrospective comprising seventy works—oils, gouaches, pastels, and watercolors—spanning two periods of his career, combining recent works and early works from the 1870s.

Durand-Ruel sends several Impressionist works, including three oil paintings and three watercolors by Pissarro, to the Foreign Exhibition in Boston, in hopes of launching interest in Impressionism on the US market.

In the fall, Pissarro searches for a new motif and spends two months in Rouen—the first of many trips—painting a series of fifteen canvases of the port.

1884

Eager to leave Osny, Pissarro moves his family into a house in Éragny-sur-Epte, a village located about fifty-six miles to the northwest of Paris, in the Département de l'Oise, bordering the French Vexin region, now much further away from the capital. He finds great inspiration with the move.

Durand-Ruel suffers from the Paris stock market crash of 1882 and can only buy twelve oil paintings and two gouaches from Pissarro this year. Pissarro spends most of May in Paris trying to find buyers for his works, while also producing a few watercolors that he hands off to smaller dealers in hopes that they might sell more easily than his oil paintings.

August 22: Julie Pissarro gives birth to a son, their eighth and last child, Paul-Émile.

1885

Through Durand-Ruel, Pissarro meets Octave Mirbeau, who will become an important reviewer of the artist's career in the 1890s.

After meeting Paul Signac and Georges Seurat, Pissarro begins to work in the Neo-Impressionist style—a movement he will belong to until about 1890 (cats. 73–82). He is invigorated by the development of his work.

1886

Pissarro spends much of his time in Éragny-sur-Epte, immersed in working. Given his lack of income and mounting debts, he limits his costly business trips to Paris.

Durand-Ruel takes three hundred canvases by French artists to New York for an exhibition at the American Art Association. Of these, Pissarro contributes eighteen oil paintings and twenty-two pastels and watercolors. The exhibition receives a positive reception from US collectors.

The eighth and final Impressionist exhibition takes place in Paris. The group lacks unity and stability, and it falls apart as the artists explore different stylistic directions. Pissarro eventually convinces the group that Neo-Impressionists should be included but exhibited in a separate room. Pissarro shows twenty works—nine oil paintings (cat. 78), four gouaches (including one fan), two pastels, and five etchings—and is labeled as a Neo-Impressionist this time. Durand-Ruel is unsure of Pissarro's newest stylistic venture.

Pissarro seeks out new dealers and collectors as Durand-Ruel is unable to provide needed financial support, given his own debts that he is actively trying to overcome.

Jeanne, Called "Cocotte," and Ludovic-Rodolphe Pissarro on a Rug, ca. 1883, private collection

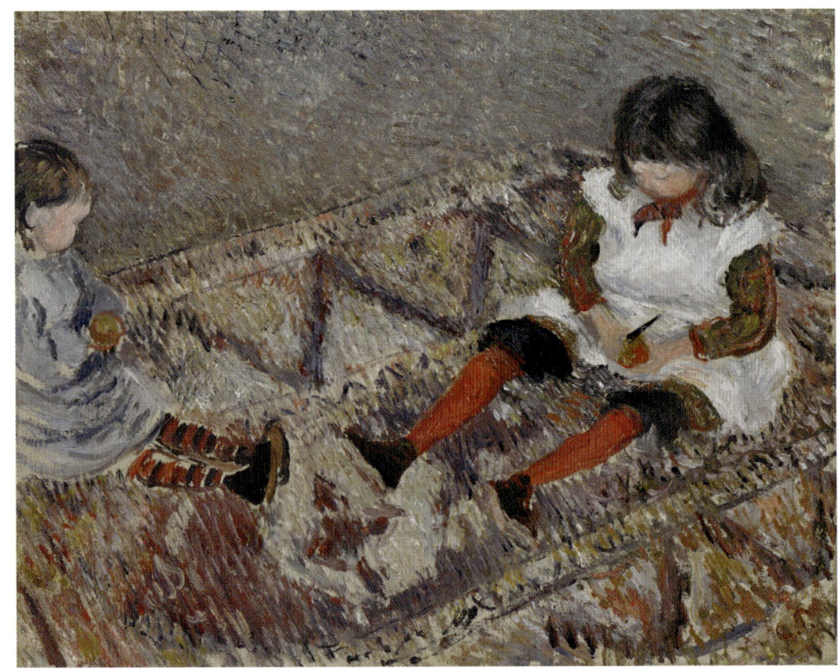

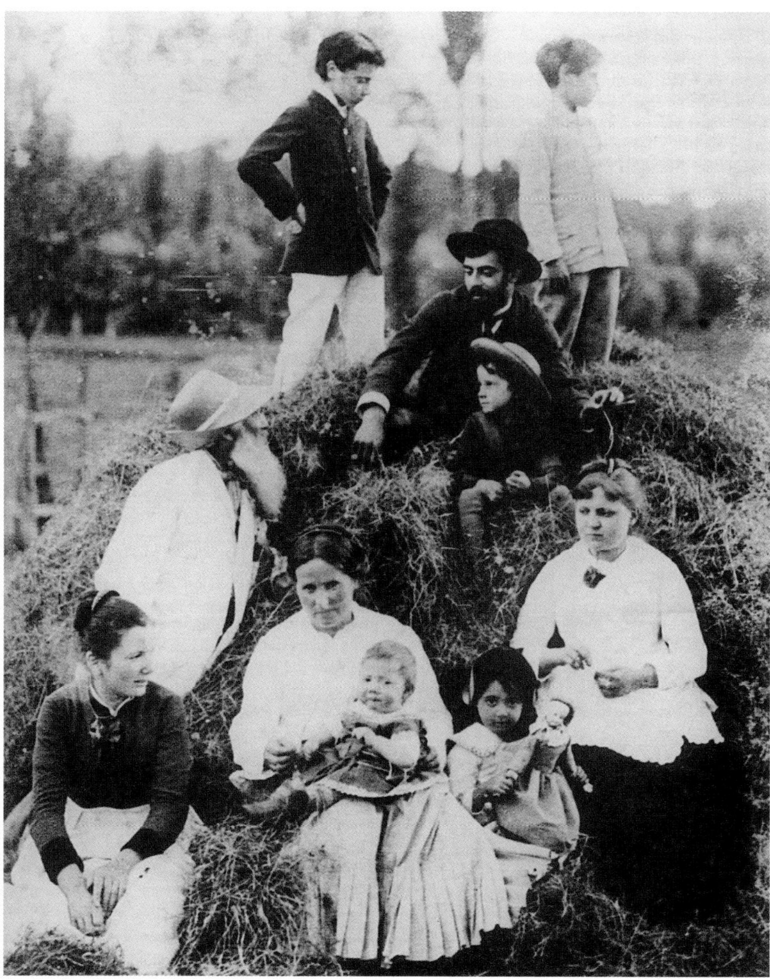

The Pissarro family in the fields of Éragny-sur-Epte (from left to right): a servant, Julie with Paul-Émile on her lap, Jeanne-Marguerite (holding a doll), and Eugénie Estruc (Pissarro's niece) in the front row; Camille, Lucien, and Ludovic-Rodolphe sitting in the middle; Félix and Georges standing on top, ca. 1885 (unknown photographer), Musée d'Art et d'Histoire Pissarro – Pontoise

1887

Pissarro has difficulty finding buyers, as collectors of Neo-Impressionism are few. This leads to a division between himself, the Impressionists, and Durand-Ruel, who all lack confidence and certainty in the movement. Feeling misunderstood by the public, Pissarro finds support from Theo van Gogh, manager of the gallery Boussod, Valadon & Cie. Pissarro later meets his brother, Vincent, as they attend the same artistic discussion groups. Vincent van Gogh seeks his painting advice.

Pissarro receives the first of several invitations to exhibit in Brussels at the society Les Vingt, an avant-garde movement of young Belgian artists. He is also invited to exhibit at the International Society of Painting and Sculpture with Galerie Georges Petit in Paris and submits eight canvases as the only artist showing Neo-Impressionist works.

1888

Under great financial strain, Pissarro imparts more works to Theo van Gogh to sell in his gallery. Van Gogh's support allows Pissarro to focus solely on his painting. Pissarro also directly sells thirty-one works to Durand-Ruel instead of receiving funds only when a sale has been made. Having worked in Neo-Impressionism for the last three years, Pissarro finds the process too slow and stifling, resulting in fewer works.

With finances mostly restored—thanks to his successful organization of exhibitions in New York, where collectors support the Impressionists—Durand-Ruel facilitates an Impressionist exhibition in Paris. Pissarro's earlier works from 1881 to 1885 are shown, including eleven canvases, fifteen pastels, and gouaches.

1889

The Société des Peintres-Graveurs, a society founded in 1889 for the dissemination of etching as an art form, holds its inaugural exhibition at Galerie Durand-Ruel. This revives Pissarro's interest in printmaking, and he submits seven canvases and twenty-five etchings.

May 30: Pissarro's mother, Rachel, dies at the age of ninety-four in her apartment in Paris. Shortly after, Pissarro's son Georges travels to England to work on his English—just as his elder brother, Lucien, had done—and enrolls at the Guild and School of Handicraft.

Pissarro's eye problems persist. He begins working more in his studio, where he completes paintings that he had begun outdoors.

Pissarro offers his London-based nieces, Esther and Alice Isaacson, an album of satirical drawings, *Turpitudes sociales* (Social Disgraces), illustrating his anarchist vision of society (cats. 83–86). He reads several anarchist publications and journals and supports their writing by sending money and offering them drawings.

In May, the Exposition Universelle in Paris opens to commemorate the centennial of the French Revolution. The Eiffel Tower is erected for the occasion. Two paintings by Pissarro are included in the exhibition.

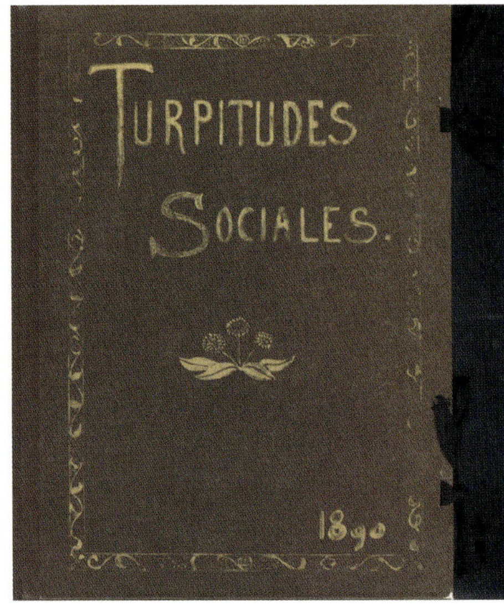

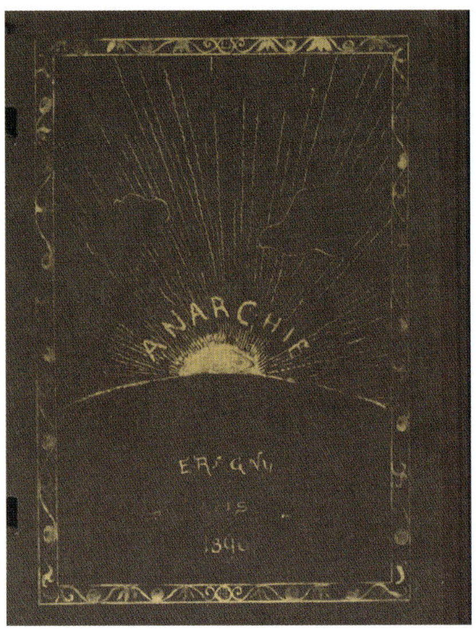

Cover of *Turpitudes sociales* (Social Disgraces), 1889, designed by Camille Pissarro, Jean Bonna Collection, Geneva

1890

Theo van Gogh holds a solo exhibition of Pissarro's work at his gallery, including sixteen oils, seven distempers, and four gouaches in the Neo-Impressionist style. The show receives wonderful reviews from avant-garde journals.

At the second exhibition of Société des Peintres-Graveurs at Galerie Durand-Ruel, Pissarro shows thirteen etchings, two drawings, and a gouache.

In the spring, Pissarro and his son Lucien visit Pissarro's younger son Georges in London, where Pissarro makes studies of the local gardens. Lucien settles permanently in London, hoping to find a future in printmaking and providing drawing lessons.

Three of Pissarro's works are sent to the eighteenth Industrial Exposition in Chicago. Shortly afterward, the St. Louis Exposition and Music Hall Association shows another three of his works.

Durand-Ruel takes a financial hit from the stock market crash in the United States; sales overseas slow rapidly and become unpredictable.

1891

January 21: Theo van Gogh dies after several months of illness—six months after his brother Vincent. Pissarro is devastated, losing both a devoted friend and supporter.

March 29: Seurat dies of diphtheria in Paris at the age of thirty-one.

In April, the Société des Peintres-Graveurs has another exhibition at Galerie Durand-Ruel. After they change their name to the Société des Peintres-Graveurs Français, Pissarro—who is not French—is no longer able to participate in their exhibitions. Durand-Ruel offers him and Cassatt space for their own exhibitions.

Pissarro sends articles from anarchist presses to his son Lucien in London. They continue their conversations about art, its role in society, and life through regular correspondence.

Experiencing more inflammation and irritation of his eyes, Pissarro has an operation in Paris to obliterate the tear gland, in hopes of improving his eyesight.

Although Pissarro sends forty-two etchings to Lucien, wishing that English collectors might buy them, his first major interest in prints comes from the US market.

Pissarro asks Monet for a loan of one thousand francs for household expenses and medical treatment for his eyes. Monet is happy to lend, and Pissarro repays the loan a few months later.

Pissarro receives offers from the galleries Durand-Ruel, Boussod, Valadon & Cie, and Bernheim-Jeune to hold exhibitions of his work.

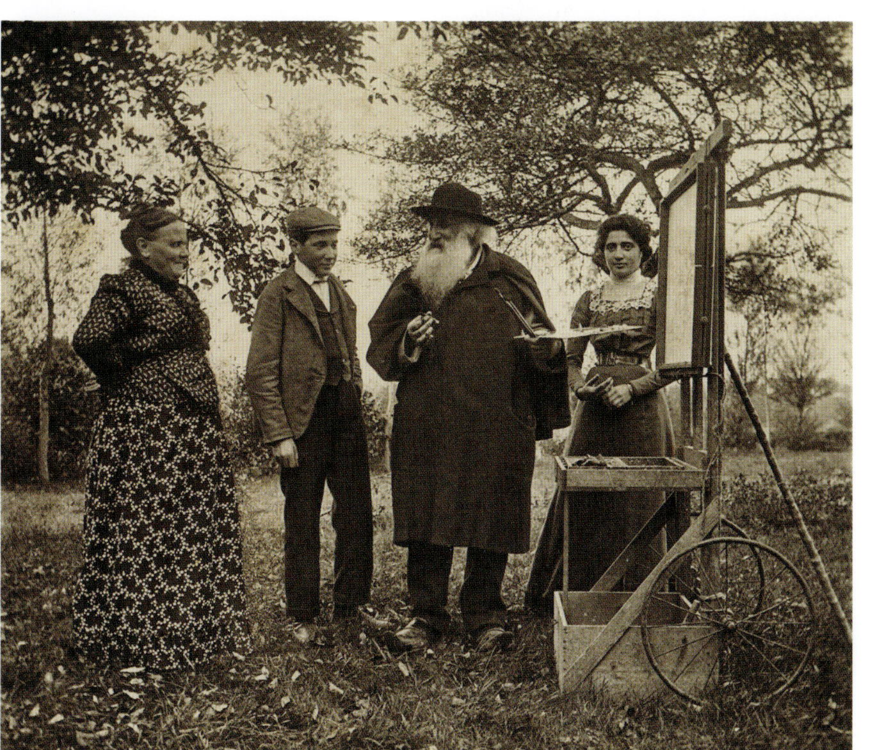

The Pissarro family in Éragny-sur-Epte (from left to right): Julie, Paul-Émile, Camille, and Jeanne-Marguerite, with the artist's movable easel on the right, ca. 1900 (unknown photographer), Musée d'Art et d'Histoire Pissarro—Pontoise

1892

Durand-Ruel holds a second solo exhibition of Pissarro's work, a retrospective. It is a great success, with several glowing reviews from the press. A number of paintings sell at the show, and for the first time in his career, Pissarro is in demand and has the upper hand with dealers—who compete to buy several canvases at a time.

In March and April, Paris is shaken by a series of anarchist bombings.

During the summer, Pissarro and his wife, Julie, purchase the house in Éragny-sur-Epte that their family has been renting for the last eight years, with the help of a substantial loan from Monet and a smaller amount from Durand-Ruel. Julie Pissarro will live there until her death in 1926. Pissarro visits his sons Lucien and Georges in London for two months, looking for new motifs (cat. 67).

Pissarro is invited to Mirbeau's home at Les Damps in the Département de l'Eure, where he makes four paintings of the gardens (cat. 79).

1893

Pissarro spends a large part of the first half of the year at the Hôtel Garnier in Paris painting a series of Parisian cityscapes from his hotel windows: the first Rue Saint-Lazare series.

The Belgian avant-garde society Les Vingt disbands and is replaced with a new artistic group, La Libre Esthétique. Pissarro exhibits regularly in their salon alongside his sons Lucien and Georges.

A drawing of stevedores, dock-workers who are responsible for loading and unloading ships in port, inspired by Pissarro's stay in Rouen in 1883, is featured on the first page of the May issue of the magazine *La Plume,* which focused on the theme of anarchy. Despite his anarchist sympathies, Pissarro does not produce many drawings or lithographs for the anarchist press.

The World's Columbian Exposition opens in Chicago, and while French artists have a presence, Impressionists are not invited. However, through a group of American collectors, a section of foreign works from American collections are exhibited, including three of Pissarro's works.

Pissarro has another eye operation in July and returns to Éragny-sur-Epte at the end of the month. He converts his barn into a studio and installs a large arched window looking out into the garden. This allows him to paint during inclement weather and mitigate any further irritation that his eyes might experience while working outdoors. Durand-Ruel travels to Éragny to buy eighteen canvases from Pissarro.

In response to anarchist efforts following the 1892 bombings, the French government begins to pass laws restricting the freedom of the press and targeting criminal associations. A mass of sweeps, searches, arrests, and prison sentences ensues.

1894

Pissarro buys his first printing press from printer Auguste Delâtre, a purchase he had been wanting to make for some time.

February 21: Caillebotte dies.

May 1, 1893, issue of *La Plume* with Camille Pissarro's drawing *Stevedores Loading Coal on the Dock at Rouen* (1892, Collection Mount Holyoke College Art Museum, South Hadley, Massachusetts) on the cover

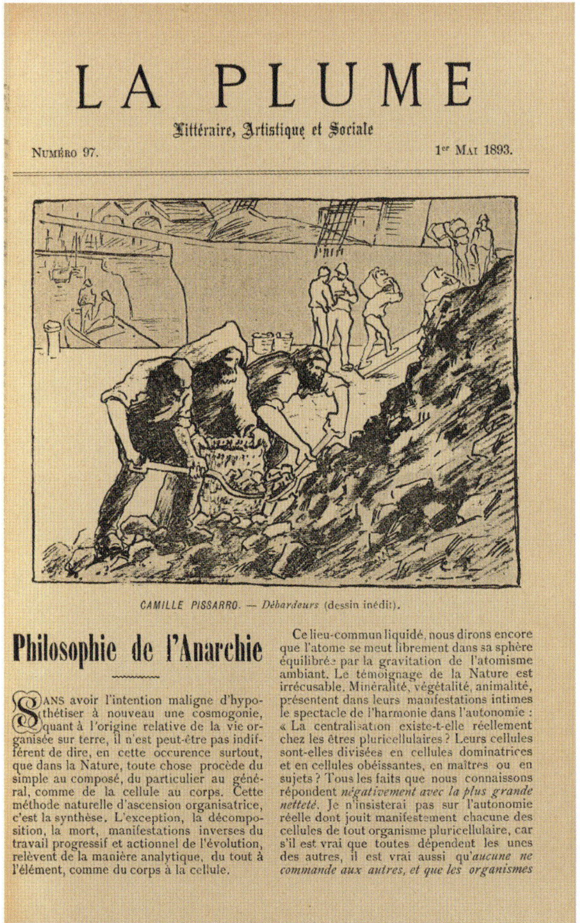

LA PLUME

Littéraire, Artistique et Sociale

Numéro 97. 1er Mai 1893.

CAMILLE PISSARRO. — *Débardeurs* (dessin inédit).

Philosophie de l'Anarchie

Sans avoir l'intention maligne d'hypothétiser à nouveau une cosmogonie, quant à l'origine relative de la vie organisée sur terre, il n'est peut-être pas indifférent de dire, en cette occurence surtout, que dans la Nature, toute chose procède du simple au composé, du particulier au général, comme de la cellule au corps. Cette méthode naturelle d'ascension organisatrice, c'est la synthèse. L'exception, la décomposition, la mort, manifestations inverses du travail progressif et actionnel de l'évolution, relèvent de la manière analytique, du tout à l'élément, comme du corps à la cellule.

Ce lieu-commun liquidé, nous dirons encore que l'atome se meut librement dans sa sphère équilibrée par la gravitation de l'atomisme ambiant. Le témoignage de la Nature est irrécusable. Minéralité, végétalité, animalité, présentent dans leurs manifestations intimes le spectacle de l'harmonie dans l'autonomie : « La centralisation existe-t-elle réellement chez les êtres pluricellulaires ? Leurs cellules sont-elles divisées en cellules dominatrices et en cellules obéissantes, en maîtres ou en sujets ? Tous les faits que nous connaissons répondent *négativement avec la plus grande netteté*. Je n'insisterai pas sur l'autonomie réelle dont jouit manifestement chacune des cellules de tout organisme pluricellulaire, car s'il est vrai que toutes dépendent les unes des autres, il est vrai aussi qu'*aucune ne commande aux autres, et que les organismes*

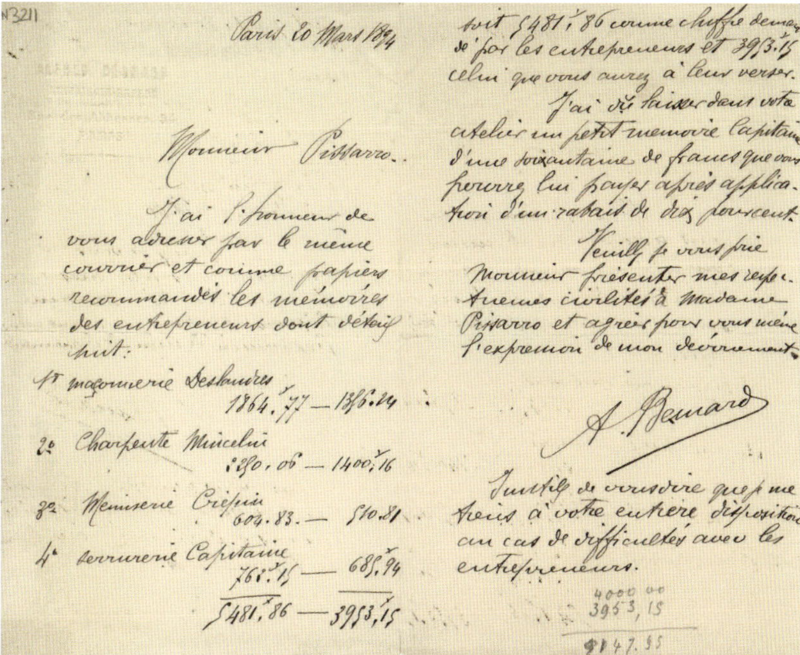

N 3211

Paris 20 Mars 1894

Monsieur Pissarro.

J'ai l'honneur de vous adresser par le même courrier et comme papiers recommandés les mémoires des entrepreneurs dont détail suit:

1° maçonnerie Deslandes 1864.77 — 1356.24

2° Charpente Mincelui 850.06 — 1400.16

3° Menuiserie Crépin 604.83 — 510.81

4° serrurerie Capitaine 768.15 — 685.94

5481.86 — 3953.15

soit 5481.86 comme chiffre demandé par les entrepreneurs et 3953.15 celui que vous aurez à leur verser.

J'ai dû laisser dans votre atelier un petit mémoire Capitaine d'une soixantaine de francs que vous pourrez lui payer après application d'un rabais de dix pour cent.

Veuillez je vous prie Monsieur présenter mes respectueuses civilités à Madame Pissarro et agréez pour vous même l'expression de mon dévouement.

A. Besnard

Inutile de vous dire que je me tiens à votre entière disposition en cas de difficultés avec les entrepreneurs.

4000.00
3953.15
47.85

Letter from architect Alfred Besnard to Camille Pissarro with a list of the workers hired to build the studio in Éragny-sur-Epte, Paris, March 20, 1894, Pissarro Family Archives

Durand-Ruel puts on a solo show of Pissarro's work, his third retrospective, exhibiting thirty canvases, four gouaches, nineteen pastels, and fifty drawings and watercolors. While the exhibition is a critical success, not many works sell.

June 25: Pissarro leaves for Brussels with his son Félix and his wife, Julie. The day before, anarchist violence had erupted, resulting in the death of French president Sadi Carnot at the hands of anarchist Sante Geronimo Caserio in Lyon. Known to the police as an anarchist sympathizer since the seizure of the lists of subscribers to Jean Grave's periodical *La Révolte* that year, Pissarro is relieved to be abroad given the tense political situation. He does not return to Éragny-sur-Epte until October.

1895

From Caillebotte's bequest to the Musée du Luxembourg, the French state accepts only seven of eighteen works by Pissarro. Offended that his work is not being accepted like that of other artists, Pissarro proclaims that Impressionism is coming to an end. Durand-Ruel is the only one buying, and even still, Pissarro has financial difficulties. He begins to dabble in a more fluid and rapid style, creating a number of bathing scenes in addition to his landscapes (cat. 65). In November, he travels to Paris to support Cézanne during his first public exhibition since 1877.

1896

Early in the year, for two and a half months, Pissarro stays in Rouen and paints a series of twelve canvases of the harbor as seen from his hotel room (cats. 89–90). Like Monet, he captures the variations of light and color during different times of day. Pissarro has a successful exhibition at Durand-Ruel, showing thirty-five paintings, including eleven canvases from this trip. The critics' reviews are positive.

In April, Pissarro pays Monet the last installment of the loan on his house and returns to Éragny-sur-Epte, staying for the summer.

Having exhausted his interest in painting Éragny landscapes, Pissarro returns to Rouen toward the end of the year. He seeks a new hotel room so that he may obtain a different viewpoint of the Seine and continue painting the harbor (cat. 92). He produces another twenty-nine paintings.

1897

Pissarro travels to Paris and paints a second series of Rue Saint-Lazare from his hotel room at the Hôtel Garnier. With a positive response from Durand-Ruel for these new works, he follows up with additional series of the Boulevard Montmartre and Boulevard des Italiens (cats. 97, 98).

Durand-Ruel holds his first exhibition of Pissarro's work for an American audience in his New York gallery. On display are thirty-seven paintings, fifteen being recent views of Rouen, and five gouaches and pastels.

In May, Pissarro rushes to Lucien, who appears to have had a stroke. He is partially paralyzed. In late July, Lucien is well enough to travel and goes with Pissarro to the family home in Éragny-sur-Epte for the summer, accompanied by his wife and daughter.

Félix, having been coughing up blood since March, goes into a rapid decline toward the end of September. On November 25, he dies of tuberculosis at the age of twenty-three. His death weighs heavily on the family. Mirbeau publishes a heartfelt obituary and a lengthy article about the Pissarro artist-family.

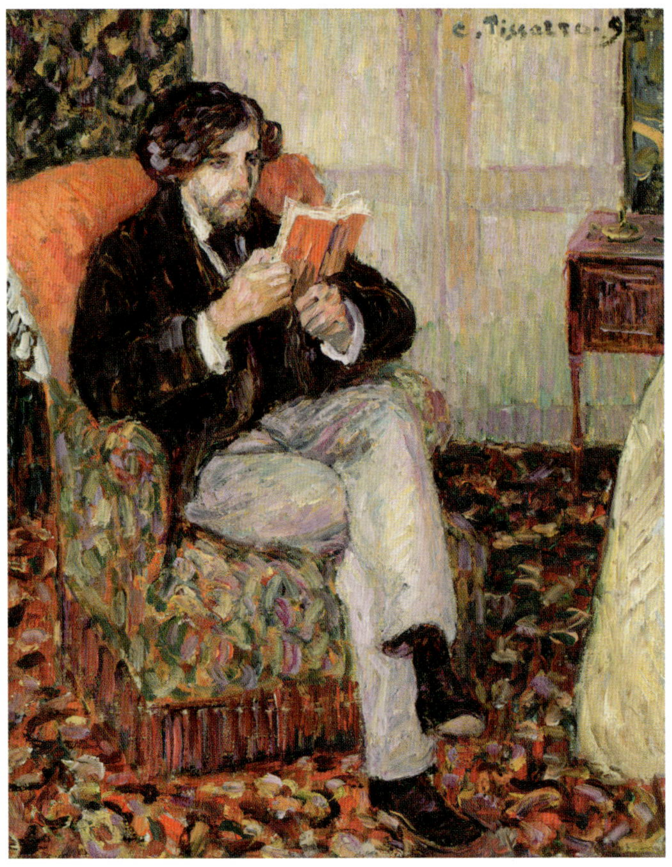

Félix Pissarro Reading, 1893, private collection

1898

To cope with his grief, Pissarro throws himself fully into his work, returning to his city motifs as he paints a series of the Avenue de l'Opéra (cat. 100). This series, along with his Boulevard Montmartre and Boulevard des Italiens series, are shown at Durand-Ruel's gallery in June. Durand-Ruel is very pleased with the work.

After Jewish officer Alfred Dreyfus is falsely accused of treason in 1894 and subsequently banished from France, a rise of nationalism and anti-Semitism grips France. Pissarro worries about those of Jewish faith being expelled. He sides with Dreyfus and with Émile Zola's public defense of the innocent man. Pissarro's friendship with Degas and Renoir is tarnished by the two painters' open anti-Semitism.

With improved finances, Pissarro takes the summer to travel through Burgundy with Julie for three weeks, including a stop at her hometown of Grancey-sur-Ource, before he makes his fourth and final trip in late July to Rouen, where he stays through October to paint a new harbor series of twenty canvases (cat. 93).

Pissarro can also afford to keep a home in Paris again. He and his family winter in the city, while returning to the countryside during the warmer months. The Pissarro family will continue this seasonal migration until his death. Pissarro finds an apartment on the Rue de Rivoli, overlooking the Tuileries Garden, a great location for both his family and his work.

Camille Pissarro in his studio, undated, (unknown photographer), Pissarro Family Archives

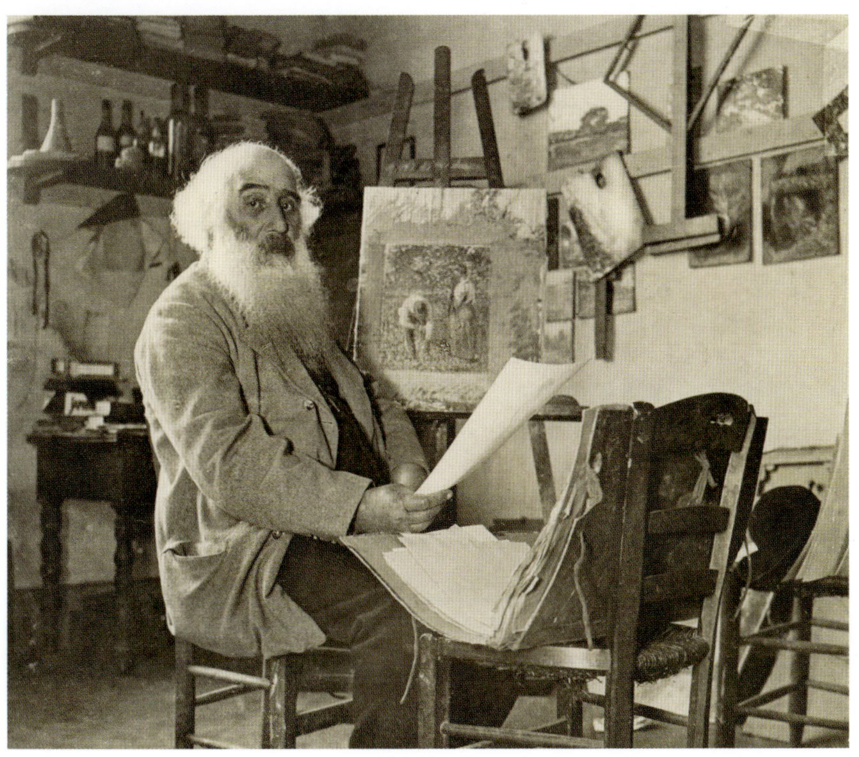

1899

The Pissarro family celebrates New Year's in their new apartment, and Pissarro paints a series of the Louvre and the Tuileries Garden (cat. 109) from the apartment window. By this time, his eyes are doing poorly, and he is unable to spend long periods of time outdoors.

January 29: Fellow Impressionist and longtime friend Alfred Sisley dies. Pissarro is distraught by this profound loss.

During the summer back in Éragny-sur-Epte, Pissarro paints in the pleasant weather and begins to look for new subjects to capture, one being his bountiful garden just beyond the foot of the stairs below his studio.

In the fall, Pissarro visits Varengeville-sur-Mer, west of Dieppe, near the sea, for a month and a half to paint. He is joined by his son Lucien, Lucien's wife and daughter, and Julie with their youngest children, Jeanne-Marguerite and Paul-Émile. They move to Paris in November.

1900

Pissarro paints his second series of the Louvre and Tuileries.

In May, Pissarro donates a complete set of his etchings to the Musée du Luxembourg.

Pissarro spends the summer in Berneval-le-Grand painting eight canvases and the fall in Éragny-sur-Epte painting autumnal scenes, while also creating prints with his son Lucien (figs. pp. 42, 43).

Toward the end of the year, Pissarro moves to another apartment on the Place Dauphine on the Île de la Cité with new views. This location provides breathtaking vistas of the Square du Vert-Galant, the Seine, the Louvre, and the Pont Neuf. Until 1903, Pissarro produces his biggest series: sixty paintings broken down into three campaigns.

The Exposition Universelle in Paris features an Impressionist section, where seven paintings and a drawing by Pissarro are shown. The present-day Carnegie Museum of Art (formerly the Carnegie Institute) in Pittsburgh buys one of Pissarro's Rouen paintings.

1901

During the winter in Paris, Pissarro continues working on the Place Dauphine series (cat. 101), which had begun the previous year. Durand-Ruel is particularly interested in his winter cityscapes.

At the beginning of the year, Pissarro shows forty-two works with Durand-Ruel in another successful solo exhibition.

With continued eye issues, Pissarro undergoes his third and final eye operation.

In the spring, Pissarro travels to Moret-sur-Loing near Fontainebleau Forest to paint with his son Georges; they will return again the following year. These canvases are purchased by the brothers Josse and Gaston Bernheim-Jeune instead of Durand-Ruel, encouraging a bidding war between dealers for the second time. The present-day Staatsgalerie Stuttgart is the second international museum to buy a work by Pissarro.

Pissarro spends the summer in Dieppe painting from his hotel room that overlooks a busy market square, opposite the church of Saint-Jacques. Again, he offers his canvases to Durand-Ruel and the Bernheim-Jeunes concurrently.

After moving back to Paris in October, Pissarro paints his second Place Dauphine series (cats. 102–08).

The Pissarro family in front of the cathedral of Saint-Jacques in Dieppe (from left to right): Georges, Ludovic-Rodolphe, Julie, Esther Pissarro née Isaacson (Pissarro's niece), Tommy (son of Esther and Georges), Camille, and Jeanne-Marguerite, 1902 (unknown photographer), Pissarro Family Archives

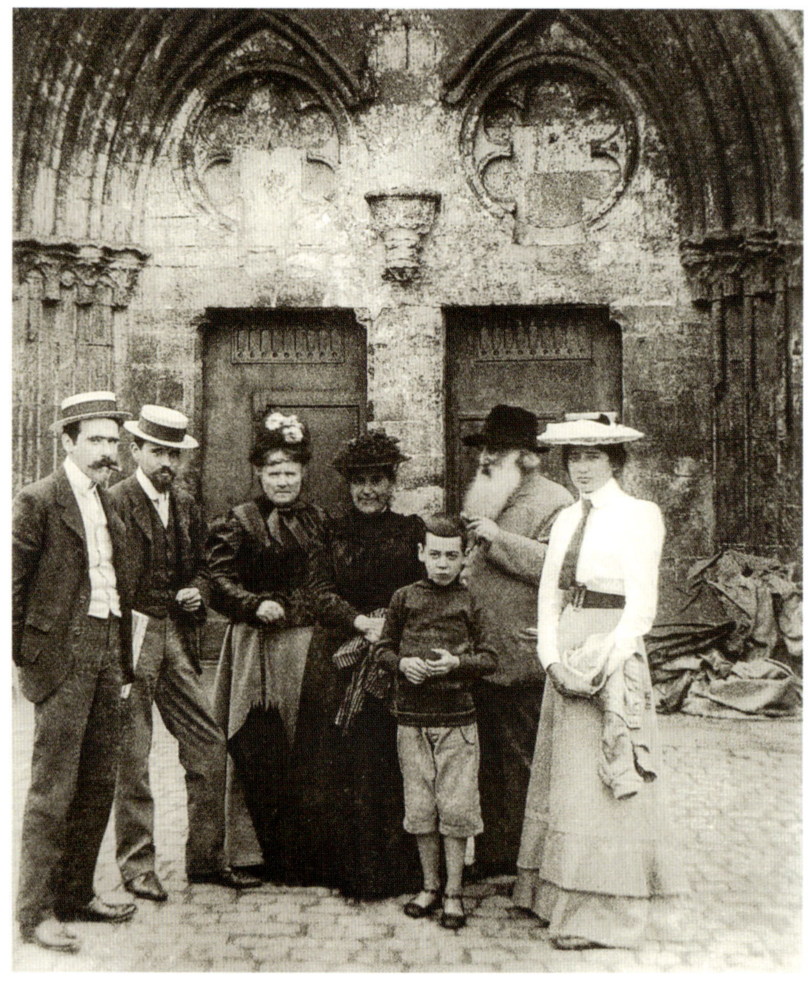

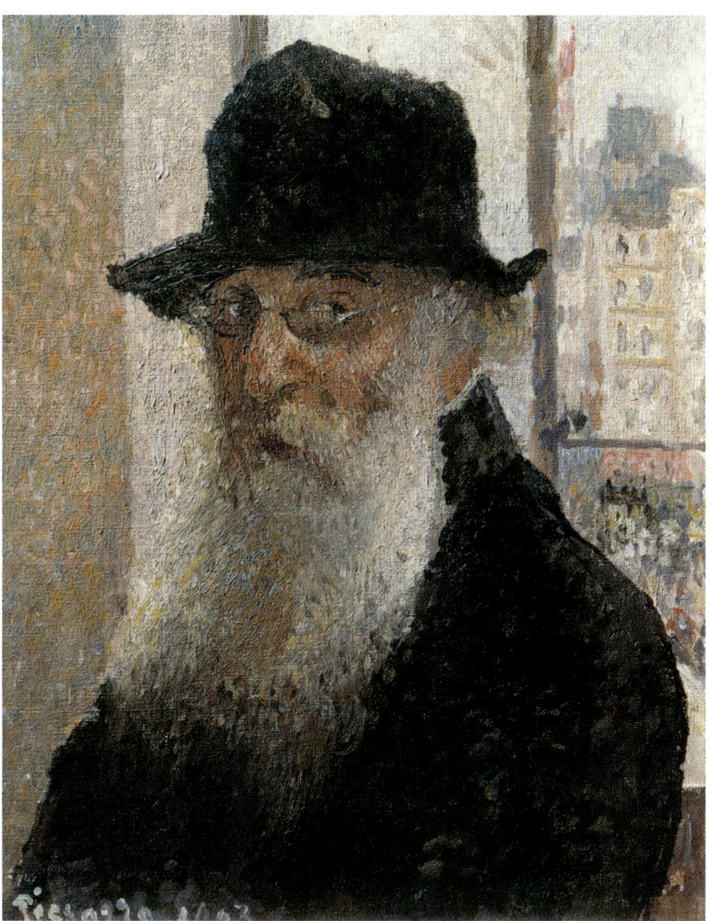

Self-Portrait, 1903, Tate, London

1902

Pissarro exhibits his most recent works—five views of Dieppe and eight of Paris—alongside paintings by Monet at Galerie Bernheim-Jeune in February. Despite Pissarro's uncertainty in being compared to his friend, the show is well received by critics.

Painting in Dieppe again for the summer, Pissarro selects a hotel room overlooking the harbor (cat. 94). Neither Durand-Ruel nor Bernheim-Jeune is interested in these twenty-one canvases. Before leaving the city, Pissarro donates one of the canvases to the Dieppe city art museum.

In Paris for the winter, Pissarro paints a third Place Dauphine series.

September 28: Zola dies.

1903

Pissarro rents an additional room in Paris on the Quai Voltaire, with views of the Quai Malaquais, the Seine, and the Louvre, providing spectacular new views for him to paint.

He spends the summer painting the harbor at Le Havre (cats. 95, 96) and builds friendships with local collectors while also selling two paintings to the local art museum.

Pissarro returns to Paris on September 26, feeling optimistic but tired of the Left Bank and the Place Dauphine. He takes up residence in a new location facing the Bassin de l'Arsenal but falls ill in early October before he is able to start painting. The family doctor is called, but after several treatments without improvement, additional doctors are consulted, who provide various diagnoses.

In early November, the artist's entire family gathers by his side as his condition worsens. On November 13, Pissarro dies from sepsis at the age of seventy-three. He is buried at the Père Lachaise Cemetery in Paris.

Claire Durand-Ruel Snollaerts

Excerpts from Camille Pissarro's Letters

Eragny par Gisors (Eure)

Mon cher Mr Durand-Ruel

Je suis encore sans le sou, pourriez-vous m'envoyer le restant de la somme que vous me devez, vous me rendriez service.

avec mes remerciements anticipés

mes salutations

C. Pissarro.

26 oct. 88.

Letter from Camille Pissarro to his art dealer Paul Durand-Ruel, Éragny-sur-Epte, October 26, 1888 (letter 509), Archives Durand-Ruel, Paris

Camille Pissarro wrote detailed letters almost daily to his family, artist friends, writers, art critics, collectors, dealers, suppliers, his notary, and others. Pissarro's published correspondence dates from 1865 to his death in 1903. His exchange of letters increased markedly in 1883, when his eldest son Lucien moved to London and became his primary correspondent. Day by day, Pissarro chronicled the French art scene. He updated Lucien on current and upcoming exhibitions and reported elaborately on his meetings and various interactions. Lucien's pursuit of his own artistic career in distant England compelled Pissarro to give precise accounts of his works in progress, sharing his creative process, uncertainties, experiments, setbacks, and achievements, along with abundant artistic advice—conveyed with the warmth of a devoted father. He offered the same professional guidance to his other sons, Georges, Félix, and Ludovic-Rodolphe, when they too pursued careers in art.

Janine Bailly-Herzberg undertook the task of editing and publishing Pissarro's letters.[1] This landmark edition contains more than two thousand letters, enhanced by Bailly-Herzberg's annotations and commentary.[2] Available only in French, this edition remains an essential resource for research on Pissarro today.

The following excerpts from letters, published between 1872 and 1903, were selected from Bailly-Herzberg's edition and translated for this exhibition and publication.[3] They provide insight into the life and personality of the painter, as well as his friendships and political views, and are particularly informative about Pissarro's ideas, doubts, and goals as an artist.

- · -

Our Cézanne gives us hope, and I've seen some paintings; I have a painting of remarkable vigor and strength at home. If, as I hope, he stays for a while in Auvers,[4] where he is going to live now, he will surprise quite a few artists who were too quick to dismiss him.

To painter Antoine Guillemet, Paris, September 3, 1872 (letter 18)

- · -

Aren't you afraid you're mistaken about Monet's[5] talent? In my view, it is very serious and very pure, though of course driven by a different sensibility than the one motivating you; but it is a deeply studied art, based on observation, and with an entirely new sensibility—it is poetry through the harmony of true colors. Monet is a worshipper of true nature.

To his friend, art critic Théodore Duret, Pontoise, May 2, 1873 (letter 21)

- · -

Durand-Ruel, one of the great Parisian dealers, came to see me and took a large number of my oil paintings and watercolors, and offered to take everything I produce from now on.[6] This gives me peace of mind for a while and the means to create important works.

To his niece Esther Isaacson, Paris, January 4, 1881 (letter 84)

- · -

You are not alone in your enthusiasm for Degas, who is certainly the greatest artist of our time.

To his son Lucien, Osny, May 9, 1883 (letter 145)

- · -

I received a visit from Gauguin yesterday; he plans to settle in Rouen for good . . . It's a big decision—he's leaving Paris to devote himself entirely to painting, intent on conquering a place in the art world through relentless work. [. . .] A bold decision, isn't it? He will succeed.

To his friend, collector Eugène Murer, Rouen, November 2, 1883 (letter 186)

- · -

I've just finished my series of paintings, and I look at them a great deal; even I who made them sometimes find them horrible. I understand them only for brief moments, long after completing them, when I've lost sight of them for a while, on days when I'm feeling well-disposed and indulgent toward their poor maker. I sometimes have horrible fears of turning a canvas around, always dreading I'll find a monster instead of the precious jewel I thought I'd made! [. . .] Yet there are moments when I truly find relief in seeing certain things very solid and very much in keeping with my character. But enough of that. Painting, art in general, enchants me; it's my life. What does the rest matter? When you do something with all your soul and all that is noble in you, you will always find a kindred spirit who understands you—it doesn't take legions. Isn't that all an artist should desire? Whew, what a tirade.

To his son Lucien, Rouen, November 20, 1883 (letter 190)

- · -

Manet's exhibition opens on January 5 at the École des Beaux-Arts [. . .]; it is an opportunity to fully appreciate the work of this great artist, who has been so unfairly overlooked.[7]

To his son Lucien, Osny, December 25, 1883 (letter 202)

- · -

My dear niece, I understand perfectly that you may not be familiar with political matters; this is neither surprising nor unusual. However, you should know that universal suffrage, the instrument of domination for the capitalist bourgeoisie, has been definitively condemned by progressive parties—its time has passed. Proud'hon, S. Mill, Spencer[8] *have all declared it fundamentally flawed and harmful to the working classes—it serves only the interests of the rich and powerful! . . . So, with our socialist education, we must seek a new form of political organization, based on a completely different principle than that of representation—it's only logical. If you want a more thorough understanding of what I'm telling you, read Kropotkin's book.*[9]

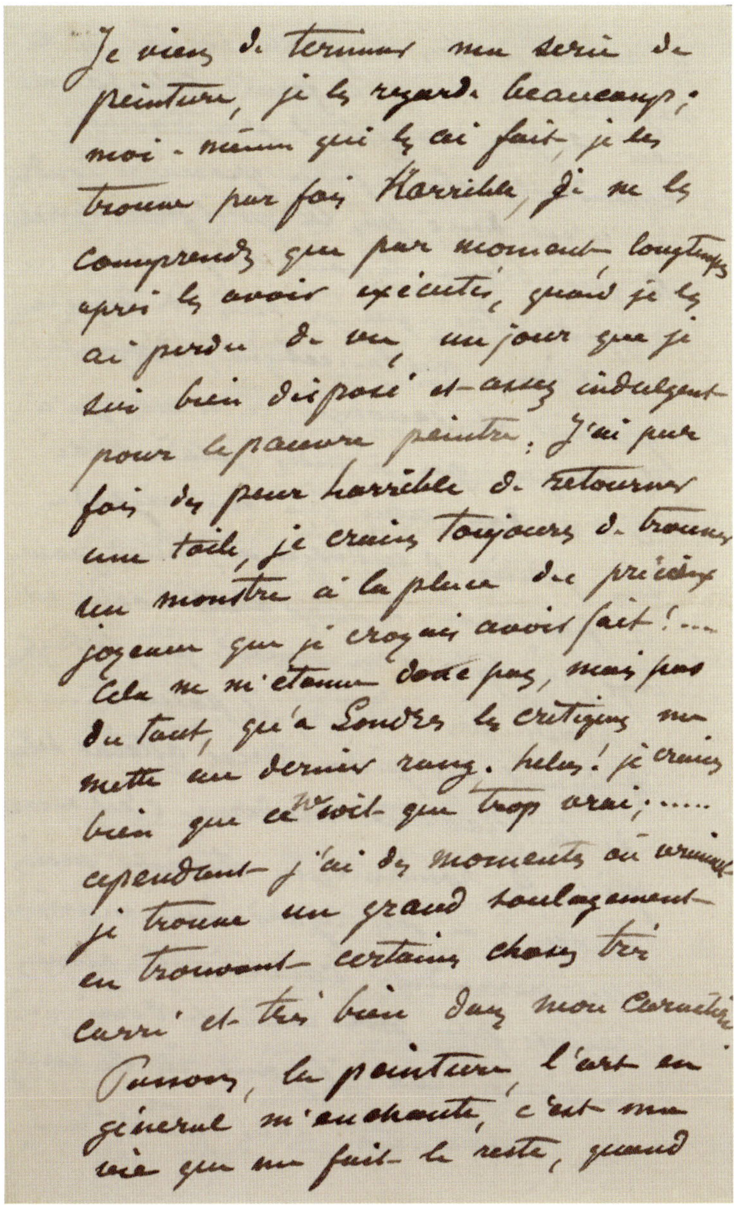

Two pages of a letter from Camille Pissarro to his son Lucien, Rouen, November 20, 1883 (letter 190), The Ashmolean Museum, University of Oxford

You'll easily grasp the absurdity of having one gentleman represent everyone's interests, no matter how brilliant. Suppose that I, as an artist, select the very honorable Beesly,[10] *please tell me how he could possibly serve me; would he, as a professor, ever understand the necessity of tearing down those bastions of art, the École des Beaux-Arts, the academies, the coalitions of big capitalist dealers who make reputations? No, of course not. [...] As for the necessity you mention of having an honest representative, that's a utopia; a man, however honest he might be, cannot represent the thousand interests of an entire class—he would have to be universal, and thus superficial, which makes it absurd. [...] So—no government, no state, no capitalists, and consequently no universal suffrage. For explanations of each of these principles, I refer you to Kropotkin's truly remarkable book, written in a very simple style, easy to read, and as clear as crystal!*

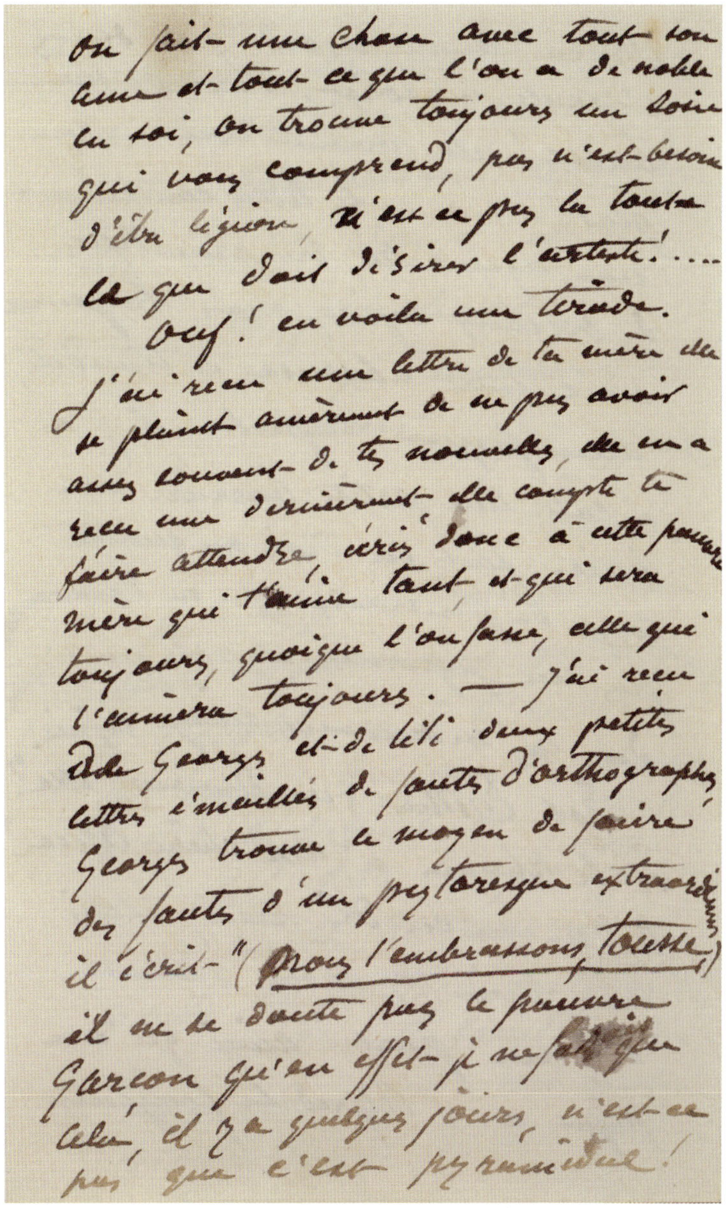

To his niece Esther Isaacson, Éragny-sur-Epte, December 12, 1885 (letter 300)

It's curious, this work with the dot—with time, with patience, little by little, one achieves an astonishing softness.

To his son Lucien, Éragny-sur-Epte, December 30, 1886 (letter 371)

- · -

I'm thinking a great deal here about how to paint without dots [...]. I hope I manage, but I still haven't been able to solve the problem of pure divided color without harshness [...]. What can one do to have both the qualities of purity and simplicity of the dot, and the richness, suppleness, freedom, spontaneity, and freshness of sensation of our Impressionist art? That's the question, and I keep returning to it, because the dot is thin, insubstantial, diaphanous, more monotonous than simple, even in Seurat's works, especially in Seurat's works ... This question is constantly on my mind.

To his son Lucien, Paris, September 6, 1888 (letter 505)

- · -

I'm still penniless—can you send me the remainder of the sum you owe me? You would be doing me a favor. With thanks in advance.

To his dealer Paul Durand-Ruel, Éragny-sur-Epte, October 26, 1888 (letter 509)

- · -

How right I was to have you draw plants—you can see how useful it is to really know them. You should have drawn many more, but you didn't grasp the full importance of it all, it bored you. But later one is glad to have put in a bit of effort when one sees the good results. Be careful, though, you'll still face difficulties because you're only at the beginning. You mustn't get discouraged and give up your work. One has to keep going, one has to want it; it's only through long work that one manages to tame the material.

To his son Georges, Éragny-sur-Epte, July 7, 1889 (letter 530)

- · -

I've examined the drawings you sent, very carefully, and I'm pleased to see that you're making great progress—the overall result is more than satisfactory. Everything I saw is exactly what I thought it should be: a lot of instinct, imagination, spirit. The key is not to lose the natural feeling, the sensation, while gradually acquiring the science—that's the real challenge. Often that precious sensation gets lost through contact with the masters—one abandons one's own personality to pursue that of the master. One must always keep one's feelings present and yet also study the strong ones. [...] I think it would benefit you to compare nature with the work of the Gothics, who as artists drew their elements from nature, and did so with incomparable boldness.

To his son Georges, Éragny-sur-Epte, October 21, 1889 (letter 549)

- · -

Art is indeed the expression of thought, but also of sensation, especially sensation [...]. In all schools you learn to make art—what a huge mistake. They teach you technique, but making art? Never! . . . I began to understand my sensations, to know what I wanted, around the age of forty, but only vaguely; at fifty—that was in 1880—I formulated the idea of unity, without being able to achieve it; at sixty, I am beginning to see how it might be rendered. Well then, do you think this is something that you can learn?

To his niece Esther Isaacson, Éragny-sur-Epte, May 5, 1890 (letter 587)

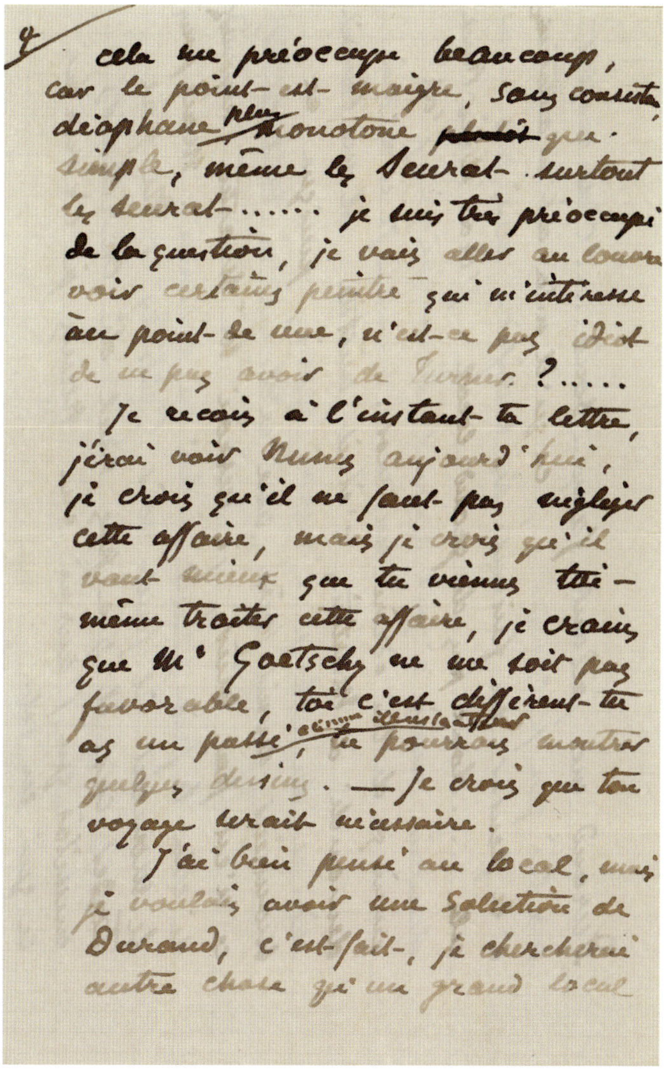

- - -

Two pages of a letter from Camille Pissarro to his son Lucien, Paris, September 6, 1888 (letter 505), The Ashmolean Museum, University of Oxford

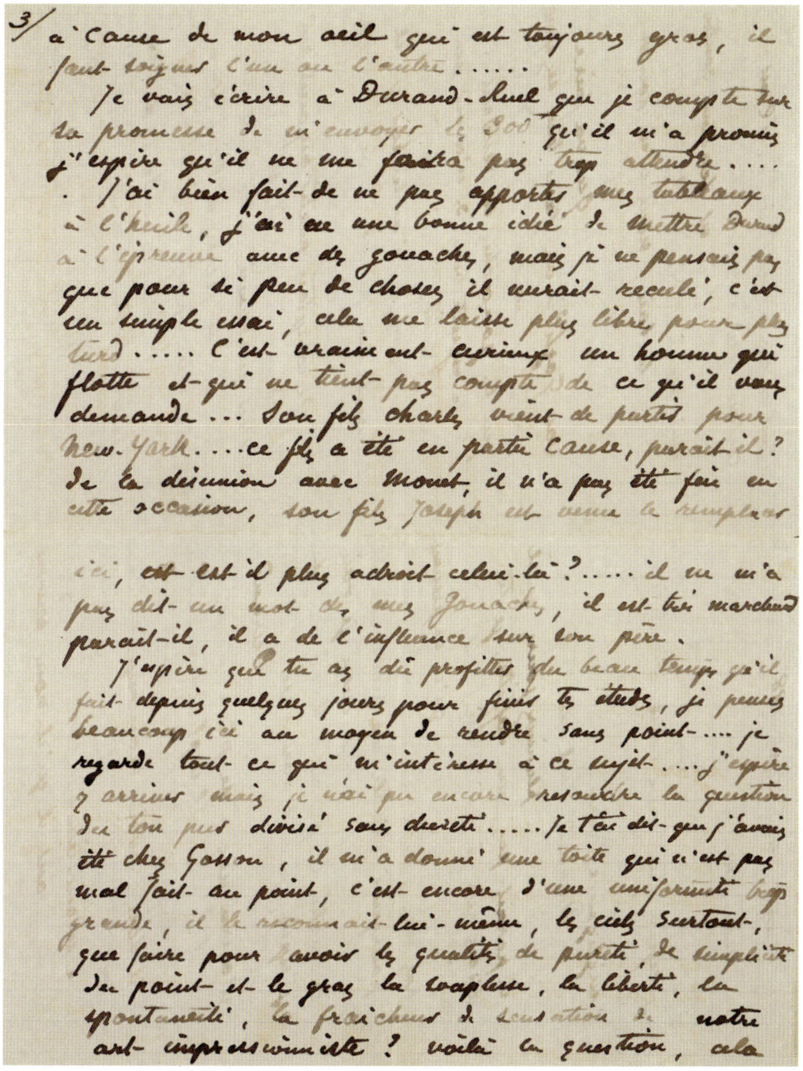

I went to Seurat's funeral yesterday; I saw Signac, who is deeply shaken by this great tragedy. I believe you're right, Pointillism[11] *is finished, but I think other consequences will emerge that will be of great significance for art later on. Seurat clearly brought something new.*

To his son Lucien, Paris, April 1, 1891 (letter 649)

- · -

There are moments when I really wonder if I have any talent at all. Truly, I often doubt it... What is missing then?... or what is there too much of?

To his son Lucien, Paris, April 13, 1891 (letter 653)

- · -

Here I am once again in Paris with my cursed abscess. I underwent the small operation a few days ago; I hope I'll have some peace now for a while, although my eye doctor does not guarantee a complete cure unless nature makes it easier for my tears to flow, but at my age things don't happen so easily. I was happily painting, en plein air, *when it came back; I had to abandon four or five canvases I'd started. I hope to get back to them next month, even though the weather conditions will have changed. It felt so good to work outside—it had been two years since I'd dared to attempt such an adventure.*

To Claude Monet, Paris, July 21, 1891 (letter 677)

- · -

We have again lost a true and devoted friend—Caillebotte has died of a sudden stroke. Here is someone we can truly mourn—he was kind and generous, and what's more, a talented painter.

To his son Lucien, Paris, March 1, 1894 (letter 991)

- · -

Still in Paris, and this time to attend the funeral of our old friend Berthe Morisot, who died following a bout of influenza. You can't imagine how shocked and affected we all are by the loss of this distinguished woman, with her beautiful feminine talent, who brought such honor to our Impressionist group, which is disappearing... Like all things! Poor Madame Morisot—the public barely knows her.

To his son Lucien, Paris, March 6, 1895 (letter 1117)

- · -

I'm constantly worried that something will go wrong with Durand, and there's no way out, no glimmer of hope anywhere. [...] I wonder if Durand is going to reject my next series of paintings; I'm feeling discouraged because there isn't a single other dealer willing to do business! [...] People think I'm rich, but it's always a struggle to make ends meet.

To his son Lucien, Paris, January 17, 1897 (letter 1360)

- · -

Sisley, I hear, is seriously ill; he is truly a fine and great artist—among the greatest, in my opinion; I've seen again works of his of rare breadth and beauty, among others a Flood that is a masterpiece.

To his son Lucien, Paris, January 22, 1899 (letter 1621)

You ask me why, if I don't know where to go, I don't come to stay with you. Well, my dear boy, it's simply because I prefer Normandy, which is just a stone's throw from Paris and Éragny, and one must think about satisfying the art lovers. You know that the motifs are entirely secondary for me: what I'm after is the atmosphere and the effects. Any place at all would suit my purpose. If I followed my own inclination, I would stay in a single town or village for years, unlike many other painters; I always end up finding effects in a given place that I haven't encountered before, and that I've never tried or managed to capture.

To his son Ludovic-Rodolphe, Le Havre, July 6, 1903 (letter 2033)

- · -

Translated from French by Helge R. Dascher

Notes

Introduction

Ortrud Westheider and *Christoph Heinrich*
Pages 7–9

1. Letter from Camille Pissarro to Octave Mirbeau (Éragny-sur-Epte, April 21, 1892), in Bailly-Herzberg 1988, 217, letter 774. English translation in Shikes/Harper 1980, 241.
2. Letter from Camille Pissarro to Lucien Pissarro (Paris, May 13, 1891), in Bailly-Herzberg 1998, 82, letter 661.
3. Timothy J. Clark, "Pissarro's Humility," in Basel 2021, 62–73, here 64.

Essays

"Absolutely Free":
Camille Pissarro's Dedication as an Artist
Claire Durand-Ruel Snollaerts
Pages 12–21

1. Letter from Camille Pissarro to Lucien Pissarro (Rouen, August 12, 1898), in Bailly-Herzberg 1989, 502–03, letter 1573. Unless otherwise noted, all translations are by Helge R. Dascher.
2. Pissarro was Danish by birth and retained his Danish nationality throughout his life. He spoke French, English, and Spanish.
3. Camille's parents, Frédéric Pissarro and Rachel Manzana-Pomié, chose not to send their children to a Jewish school because of tensions in the local Jewish community over their unconventional union. After the death of Rachel's first husband in 1824, his nephew Frédéric was sent to Saint Thomas to help run the family hardware store. Frédéric soon began a relationship with his widowed aunt, and when their first child, Félix Joseph Gabriel, was born in 1826, they asked the synagogue to recognize their union. However, their request was denied, as Jewish law prohibits marriage between a nephew and an aunt, even if not related by blood. It was not until 1833 that their marriage was officially recognized by the rabbinical authorities.
4. The boarding school in question was called Savary, at 46, Boulevard de Passy in Passy (now Rue La Pérouse, Paris).
5. Henry Morel, "Camille Pissarro," in *Le Réveil* (June 24, 1883), 1.
6. Richard R. Brettell (1949–2020), the great American specialist on Pissarro, estimated that more than six hundred graphic works survive from Pissarro's youth, a quantity unmatched by any other Impressionist artist. They are in public and private collections around the world, with significant holdings in three institutions: the Banco Central de Venezuela, the Ashmolean Museum in Oxford, and Olana, the historic home of painter Frederic Edwin Church in Hudson, New York. The catalogue raisonné of Pissarro's work, published in 2005 under the direction of Joachim Pissarro and Claire Durand-Ruel Snollaerts, lists twenty-four oil paintings from this period.
7. Joachim Gasquet, *Cézanne,* Paris 1926, 148.
8. Letter from Camille Pissarro to Eugène Murer (Surrey, June 5, 1871), in Bailly-Herzberg 1980, 123, letter 66.
9. Anton Melbye (1818–1875), Fritz Melbye's eldest brother and also an artist, settled in France in 1847. When Pissarro returned to Paris, Fritz referred him to Anton, who put him to work in his studio and introduced him to the circle of Danish artists living in Paris. The 1859 Salon catalog refers to Pissarro as follows: "Born in Saint Thomas (Danish colonies), pupil of Anton Melbye." At the Salon des Refusés of 1863 and the Salon of 1864, Pissarro presented himself as a pupil of Anton Melbye and Camille Corot, but by 1866, he listed only Anton Melbye as his master. In subsequent Salon entries, he no longer mentioned any teachers.
10. Jean Rousseau, "Le Salon de 1866—IV," in *L'Univers illustré* (July 14, 1866), 447–48, here 447, translated in Pissarro/Durand-Ruel Snollaerts 2005, vol. 2, 96.
11. Émile Zola, "Adieux d'un critique d'art," in *L'Événement* (May 20, 1866), 4, translated in Pissarro/Durand-Ruel Snollaerts 2005, vol. 2, 96.
12. Although Pissarro often worried that his paintings might not sell, the tastes of dealers and collectors were never his primary concern. His sensations always took precedence over aesthetic and commercial considerations.

13 In 1871, much to his parents' displeasure, Camille Pissarro married their former maid Julie Vellay. Together they had eight children—five boys and three girls—born between 1863 and 1884, of whom only five survived their parents.

14 Émile Zola, "Mon Salon: Les Naturalistes," in *L'Événement illustré* (May 19, 1868).

15 Monsieur Musy's house appears in the following works: Pissarro/Durand-Ruel Snollaerts 2005, vol. 2, nos. 133, 147, 161, 206, 216, 225.

16 Louis Leroy, "L'Exposition des impressionnistes," in *Le Charivari* (April 25, 1874), 79–80, here 79, translated in *Art in Theory 1815–1900: An Anthology of Changing Ideas,* ed. Charles Harrison, Paul Wood, and Jason Gaiger, Oxford 1998, 573–75, here 574.

17 Letter from Camille Pissarro to Théodore Duret (Pontoise, May 5, 1874), in Bailly-Herzberg 1980, 94, letter 36.

18 Jules Borély, "Cézanne à Aix" [1902], in *L'Art vivant* (July 1926), 491–93, here 492, translated in Doran/Cochran 2010, 19–26, here 22.

19 For more about their collaboration, see the exhibition catalog New York 2005.

20 Letter from Camille Pissarro to Lucien Pissarro (Paris, November 22, 1895), in Bailly-Herzberg 1989, 121, letter 1175.

21 Paul Gauguin, *Racontars de rapin,* Taravao, Tahiti, 1994, 9.

22 Letter from Camille Pissarro to Lucien Pissarro (Paris, May 8, 1886), in Bailly-Herzberg 1986, 45, letter 334.

23 Pissarro exhibited twenty works in a variety of techniques—nine paintings, four gouaches (including a fan), two pastels, and five etchings—showcasing his versatility and ongoing efforts to renew his practice in response to the diverse tastes of his clients. His subjects included landscapes, figures, animals, and a few views of the town of Rouen, the latter rendered as etchings. Not all of the works were in the Neo-Impressionist style.

24 Jean Ajalbert, "Le Salon des impressionnistes," in *La Revue moderne* (June 20, 1886), reprinted in Berson 1996, vol. 1, 430–36, here 432.

25 Ibid.

26 Letter from Camille Pissarro to Henry van de Velde (Rouen, March 27, 1896), in Bailly-Herzberg 1989, 180, letter 1224.

27 Letter from Camille Pissarro to Théodore Duret (Pontoise, March 12, 1882), in Bailly-Herzberg 1980, 157, letter 100.

28 This is the first exhibition catalog that includes excerpts from Pissarro's extensive correspondence (see Appendix, 226–33).

29 Gasquet 1926 (see note 7).

In Pissarro's Studio:
A Window into Impressionist Experimentation
Clarisse Fava-Piz
Pages 22–31

1 Letter from Camille Pissarro to Lucien, Georges, and Félix Pissarro (Éragny-sur-Epte, September 28, 1893), in Bailly-Herzberg 1988, 374, letter 935, translated in Pissarro/Durand-Ruel Snollaerts 2005, vol. 3, 662.

2 See Brettell/Lloyd 1980; and Richard R. Brettell, "Camille Pissarro: A Revision," in London 1980, 20.

3 In his letters, Pissarro often expressed his frustrations regarding the weather changes and his inability to capture the sought-after artistic effects in the open. See letter from Camille Pissarro to Paul Durand-Ruel (Osny, September 2, 1883), in Bailly-Herzberg 1980, 237–38, letter 179; letter from Camille Pissarro to Lucien Pissarro (Rouen, October 19, 1883), in ibid., 240, letter 181. Unless otherwise noted, all quotations from French are translated by the author.

4 Georges Lecomte, "M. Camille Pissarro," in *Art et critique* 4,88 (February 1892), 50. The same quote appears in the preface by Lecomte in Paris 1892, 8.

5 Kunstler 1930, 190 (italics in original).

6 Scholar Patricia Mainardi has also analyzed the concept of seriality in the context of the history of nineteenth-century collecting. See Patricia Mainardi, "The 19th-Century Art Trade: Copies, Variations, Replicas," in *Van Gogh Museum Journal* (2000), 62–73; Patricia Mainardi, "Impressionist Repetition and the Market," in *Artwork Through the Market: The Past and the Present,* ed. Ján Bakoš, Bratislava 2004, 155–71; and Christian Huemer's talk, "'Voilà des effets terribles du succès': Monet's Serial Production and the International Art Market Around 1900," at the conference *L'Impressionisme à travers les champs,* Musée d'Orsay, Paris, May 2024.

7 Monet also worked serially in his *Stacks of Wheat,* which were painted partially outdoors and partially in the studio. Additionally, technical analysis of the paintings in the collection of the Art Institute of Chicago unveiled both minor and major adjustments and compositional reworks by the painter as part of his artistic process. See Gloria Groom and Kimberley Muir, "Impression, Improvisation, and Premeditation: New Insights into the Working Methods and Creative Process of Claude Monet," in Dombrowski 2021, 129–45, here 132–33.

8 Pissarro/Durand-Ruel Snollaerts 2005, vol. 2, 304, no. 413.

9 Ibid., vol. 3, 593, no. 905.

10 See ibid., vol. 2, 291, no. 388 (1974, High Museum of Art, Atlanta); ibid., vol. 2, 448, no. 669 (1882, Christie's New York, May 12, 1999); and ibid., vol. 3, 594, no. 906 (1891, private collection).

[11] See ibid, vol. 3, 581–82, no. 884 (1890, National Gallery of Art, Washington, DC); ibid., vol. 3, 594–95, no. 907 (1891, private collection, Switzerland).

[12] Ibid., vol. 3, 581. See also Bailly-Herzberg 1986, 353–54, letter 591, and 356, letter 594.

[13] Joachim Pissarro, "Camille Pissarro's Vision of History and Art," in Pissarro/Durand-Ruel Snollaerts 2005, vol. 1, 85–87.

[14] Letter from Camille Pissarro to Lucien Pissarro (Paris, March 1, 1884), in Bailly-Herzberg 1980, 291, letter 222.

[15] Correspondence between Camille Pissarro and Alfred Besnard, see in particular letters from Alfred Besnard to Camille Pissarro (Paris, March 20, 1894, see fig. p. 221; Paris, May 29, 1896; and Paris, June 17, 1896), Pissarro Family Archives.

[16] Letter from Camille Pissarro to Lucien Pissarro (Éragny-sur-Epte, August 27, 1893), in Bailly-Herzberg 1988, 359, letter 921, as translated in Pissarro/Durand-Ruel Snollaerts 2005, vol. 3, 661 (translation modified). The renovation work on Pissarro's studio began in June 1893 and was completed in late October of that year.

[17] Letter from Camille Pissarro to Lucien Pissarro (Éragny-sur-Epte, October 17, 1893), in Bailly-Herzberg 1988, 388, letter 950.

[18] On the sequence of drawings and prints from the 1880s, see Brettell/Lloyd 1980, 48–50.

[19] See Christophe Duvivier, "Camille Pissarro et l'estampe impressionniste," in Pontoise 2017, 21–32, here 31.

[20] Sarah Lees, "Innovative Impressions: Cassatt, Degas, and Pissarro as Painter-Printmakers," in Tulsa 2018, 11–103, here 12.

[21] Letter from Camille Pissarro to Lucien Pissarro (Éragny-sur-Epte, January 3, 1894), in Bailly-Herzberg 1988, 416, letter 975. "Delatre" refers to printer Auguste Delâtre.

[22] See Duvivier 2017 (see note 19), 21.

[23] Lees 2018 (see note 20), 31–32.

[24] Pissarro participated twice in the exhibitions of the Société des Peintres-Graveurs, but in 1891, when the Société became an institution, he was excluded from its membership—because of his nationality—and asked to exhibit as a guest. Michel Melot, "A Rebel's Role: Concerning the Prints of Camille Pissarro," in Lloyd 1986, 117–22, here 119.

[25] See Duvivier 2017 (see note 19), 27.

[26] Lees 2018 (see note 20), 102.

[27] Kisiel 2021, 134. See also *Le Décor impressionniste: Aux sources des Nymphéas,* exh. cat., Musée de l'Orangerie, Paris 2022. While it is documented that Pissarro painted around fifty ceramic tiles, there are only a small number of these ceramic objects known today.

[28] Shikes/Harper 1980, 138.

[29] Brettell/Lloyd 1980, 235.

[30] Sefrioui 2012, 7. Forain showed four and Degas five fans, respectively, at the 1879 Impressionist exhibition.

[31] See Paris 1891.

[32] Sefrioui 2012, 8. See also *Japonisme: Japanese Influence on French Art, 1854–1910,* exh. cat., Cleveland Museum of Art, 1975.

[33] Letter from Camille Pissarro to Lucien Pissarro (Éragny-sur-Epte, November 17, 1890), in Bailly-Herzberg 1986, 366, letter 602 (italics in the original). What Pissarro describes as "l'envers d'une peau, papier pelure d'oignon" in the French original text most probably means the use of a fine leather and very thin transparent paper. "Durand" refers to art dealer Paul Durand-Ruel.

[34] Kisiel 2021, 174.

[35] Armand Guillaumin was the son of a Parisian tailor. During the 1860s, he tried to make his name as a decorative artist by painting signs.

[36] All of Pissarro's late urban views were painted from a window whose jambs were always hidden. See Claire Durand-Ruel Snollaerts's texts on urban views in this catalog, 172–87 and 188–205.

[37] Letter from Camille Pissarro to Georges Pissarro (Paris, March 13,1890), in Bailly-Herzberg 1980, 339–40, letter 579.

Realism or Utopia?
Pissarro's Depictions of Rural Labor
Daniel Zamani
Pages 32–43

1 On the motif of the peasant in French nineteenth-century painting, see *Ceux de la terre: La Figure du paysan de Courbet à Van Gogh,* exh. cat., Musée Gustave Courbet, Ornans 2022. On Pissarro's take on the subject, see notably Brettell 2011, especially chapter 12 ("After the Revolution"), 257–67; and Thomson 1990, especially the sections "Representing the Peasant," 46–58, "Composing an Anarchist Ideal: *The Gleaners,* 1889," 59–80, and "The Late Rural Idylls: Constructing 'the True Poem of the Countryside,'" 81–101.

2 However, Pissarro himself disliked comparison of his paintings with those of Millet, and the quintessential difference between them was already noted by some of his contemporaries, including Octave Mirbeau and Henry van de Velde. See Octave Mirbeau, "Camille Pissarro," in Paris 1904, 1–9; and Henry van de Velde, "Du paysan en peinture," in *L'Art moderne* 8 (February 22, 1891), 60–62. Pissarro's "ambiguous" stance on Millet's paintings is discussed in Thomson 1990, 51–54.

3 George Sand, *The Devil's Pool* (1846), Brétigny-sur-Orge 2024, v.

4 Hans Holbein the Younger's print *The Peasant (or Plowman)* was created around 1526 and first published in 1538 as part of his series of woodcuts related to the theme of "The Dance of Death." There is a copy in the collection of the Metropolitan Museum of Art, New York (inv. 19.57.37).

5 Sand 2024 (see note 3), iii.

6 Ibid., 1.

7 Ibid.

8 Ibid., 3.

9 Ibid.

10 Ibid., 2.

11 Ibid., 3.

12 Boime 2008, 622.

13 On the sociohistorical context of this important series, see Paul Tucker, *Monet in the '90s: The Series Paintings,* exh. cat., Museum of Fine Arts, Boston 1989, chapter 5 ("Of Hay and Oats and Stacks of Grain: Monet's Paintings of Agrarian France in 1890–91"), 69–113.

14 Gustave Geffroy, "Claude Monet Exhibition" (1891), in Charles F. Stuckey, *Monet: A Retrospective,* New York 1985, 162–65, here 163.

15 Roger Marx, "Les Meules de M. Claude Monet" (1891), translated in Paul H. Tucker, *Claude Monet: Life and Art,* New Haven and London 1995, 145.

16 Paul de Saint-Victor in *La Presse,* August 4, 1857, translated in Boime 2008, 122 (italics in the original).

17 On the dramatically changing reception of Millet's paintings, see Bradley Fratello, "France Embraces Millet: The Intertwined Fates of 'The Gleaners' and 'The Angelus,'" in *Art Bulletin* 85,4 (December 2003), 685–701.

18 On this broader context of peasant imagery, see Monica Juneja, "The Peasant in French Painting: Millet to Van Gogh," in *Museum* 36 (1984), 168–72.

19 On Pissarro's scenes of local markets, see Thomson 1990, especially the section titled "The Image of the Market: Exchange between Country and Town," 66–67; and Brettell 2011, chapter 10 ("The Market Economy"), 219–39.

20 See Katherine M. Kuenzli, *Henry van de Velde: Designing Modernism,* New Haven 2019, 16. Excerpts of the lecture were later published as "Du paysan en peinture," in *L'Art moderne* 8 (February 22, 1891), 60–62.

21 Albert Aurier, "Camille Pissarro," in *La Revue indépendante* 3,14 (March 1890), 503–15, here 512, translated in Thomson 1990, 63. Thomson highlights the immense amount of time and energy that Pissarro dedicated to this particular composition and also foregrounds its idealizing nature, writing that "Pissarro's image is as much a construction of rural life as any other gleaning image. His harmonious, light-filled painting, which seems to celebrate woman's 'natural' place in the landscape, proffers an ideal of a classless community which accorded with his anarchist ideology." (Ibid., 65.) On correlations between peasant imagery at the official Salon and Pissarro's Impressionist genre scenes, see Gabriel Weisberg, "Jules Breton, Jules Bastien-Lepage and Camille Pissarro in the Context of 19th-Century Painting and the Salon," in *Arts Magazine* 56 (1982), 115–19.

22 Brettell 2011, 257.

23 On Neo-Impressionism and anarchism, see Roslak 2007.

24 *Stevedores Loading Coal on the Dock at Rouen* (1892, Collection Mount Holyoke College Art Museum, South Hadley, Massachusetts).

[25] A copy of the print is to be found, for instance, in the collection of the Clark Art Institute in Williamstown, Massachusetts (inv. 1962.96). The two other illustrations submitted to *Les Temps nouveaux* in 1896 and 1898 were titled, respectively, *Women Carrying Wood* and *The Homeless.*

[26] Robert L. Herbert, "City vs. Country: The Rural Image in French Painting from Millet to Gauguin," in Herbert 2002, 23–48, here 42. On the same page, Herbert further elaborates on the anarchist ethos of the lithograph: "We see not just a plowman, but one using the old-fashioned wheel plow for, like Millet, Pissarro preferred the unchanging ways of the country. The incarnation of 'modern times' in an archaic plowman did not strike him as an anachronism, because it incorporated his ideas of health, honest labor, and dignity which he set against the pollution and degraded labor of the city. [. . .] The essential Romanticism of Pissarro's view, and its actual disparity with an increasingly urbanized society, shows in the nature of his peasants."

[27] Letter from Camille Pissarro to Lucien Pissarro (April 13, 1891), in Bailly-Herzberg 1988, 63, letter 650, translated in Robert L. Herbert, "Artists and Anarchism: Unpublished Letters of Pissarro, Signac, and Others," in Herbert 2002, 99–114, here 107.

[28] Pyotr Kropotkin, *The Conquest of Bread,* London 1906. Kropotkin's influence on the late work of Pissarro is also highlighted by Thomson: "Pissarro's fiction of a rural idyll was maintained throughout the 1890s, against the odds. First anarchist actions and their suppression and then the Dreyfus Affair preoccupied him; his ideological position engaged him in a struggle against what he saw as oppression and injustice. In his art it seems that his answer was to proffer an almost visionary ideal of *la vie agreste,* ignoring the modernization of rural France and celebrating Kropotkin's utopian concept of rural life." Thomson 1990, 101.

[29] Letter from Camille Pissarro to Octave Mirbeau (Éragny-sur-Epte, April 21, 1892), in Bailly-Herzberg 1988, 217, letter 774, translated in Herbert 2002 (see note 27), 110. Punctuation slightly modified.

[30] Letter from Paul Signac to Henri-Edmond Cross (April 1893), translated in Daniel Zamani, "'To Paint Happiness'? Henri-Edmond Cross's Landscapes," in *Color and Light: The Neo-Impressionist Henri-Edmond Cross,* exh. cat., Museum Barberini, Potsdam 2018, 22–31, here 24.

[31] For a discussion of the Éragny paintings as reflections of an Impressionist utopia, see Allan Antliff, "Utopie vivante," in Paris 2017a, 38–47; and Thomson 1990, especially the section "The Late Rural Idylls: Constructing 'the True Poem of the Countryside,'" 81–101.

[32] This reading through the lens of anarchism is also set out by Richard R. Brettell in his magisterial study *Pissarro's People,* notably chapter 12 ("After the Revolution"); see Brettell 2011, 257–67. Here, Brettell writes, "There is little doubt that Pissarro expected a European revolution to occur in the relatively near future, and that he made works of art in an attempt, like Peter Kropotkin, to 'model' the new anarchist world as it would be after the revolution." (Ibid., 257.)

[33] Mirbeau 1904 (see note 2), 2 and 8, translated in Richard Shiff, "Pissarro: Dirty Painter," in New York 2007, 15–29, here 15–16.

[34] Unpublished and undated manuscript, Archives Signac, Paris, translated in Herbert 2002 (see note 26), 109. The text was in all likelihood the transcript of a lecture and probably penned around 1902.

[35] On Pissarro's and Lucien's work on the series, see notably Brettell 2011, especially chapter 14 ("Les Travaux des Champs"), 285–91.

Catalog of Exhibited Works

Under Palm Trees and at the Port: Artistic Beginnings in the Caribbean
Clarisse Fava-Piz
Pages 44–57

1 The family of his father, Frédéric Pissarro, was originally from Portugal. Frédéric immigrated from Bordeaux to Saint Thomas around 1825. Pissarro's mother, Rachel Manzana-Pomié, was from a prominent Jewish family of merchants from Santo Domingo.
2 McKee 2023, 63. On the history of the island of Saint Thomas and its Jewish community, see also Judah M. Cohen, *Through the Sands of Time: A History of the Jewish Community of St. Thomas, U.S. Virgin Islands,* Waltham, MA, 2004.
3 Brettell 2011, 69.
4 Edward J. Sullivan, *From San Juan to Paris and Back: Francisco Oller and Caribbean Art in the Era of Impressionism,* New Haven 2014, 33.
5 See Richard R. Brettell, "Camille Pissarro and Fritz Melbye: Two Painters 'sans maître,'" in Pissarro/Durand-Ruel Snollaerts 2005, vol. 1, 3–11.
6 On Pissarro's time in Venezuela, see Rewald 1964, Boulton 1966, New York 1968, Paris 1978, Caracas 1992, and New York 1997.
7 Sarah Connors, "Camille Pissarro," in New York 2015, 74.
8 See Copenhagen 2017. See also Natalia Vieyra, *Fragmentary Impressions: Camille Pissarro and Francisco Oller in the Americas, 1848–1898,* PhD diss., Temple University, Philadelphia 2021.

The Path to Impressionism: Modern Landscapes
Clarisse Fava-Piz
Pages 58–79

1 See Pissarro/Durand-Ruel Snollaerts 2005, vol. 2, 96.
2 See the literature with ecocritical perspectives on the Impressionists in general and on Pissarro's work specifically: Rubin 2008, Rome 2010, and Toronto 2019.
3 See Westerby 2022.
4 See Brettell 1990.
5 See Guillermo Solana, "The Road in Pissarro," in Madrid 2013, 14–35. See also André Dombrowski, "Pissarro's Roads," in Basel 2021, 48–61.
6 London 1980, 83.

Family Pictures: Portraits and Still Lifes
Clarisse Fava-Piz
Pages 80–91

1 Brettell 2011, 103. Scholar Richard R. Brettell studied Pissarro's family, friends, and artistic circle in great depth. He dedicated a focused exhibition to the subject, *Pissarro's People,* whose insightful catalog serves as a guide for this contribution.
2 See the selection of excerpts from his letters in this catalog, 226–33.
3 Brettell 2011, 89.
4 Alexia de Buffévent, "A Painter and His Age: Biography and Critical Reception," in Pissarro/Durand-Ruel Snollaerts/2005, vol. 1, 236–37. In June 1892, Julie visited Giverny without telling Pissarro and persuaded Monet to lend them some money to buy the house in Éragny-sur-Epte.
5 Letter from Theo van Gogh to Vincent van Gogh (October 4, 1889), translated in Pissarro/Durand-Ruel Snollaerts 2005, vol. 1, 216. See original in Theo van Gogh, *Lettres à son frère Vincent,* Amsterdam 1932, 69: "Je crois que lui n'a pas grand-chose à dire à la maison où sa femme porte la culotte."
6 For a revealing comparison of *Julie Pissarro Sewing Beside a Window* (cat. 27) and *Portrait of Jeanne Pissarro* (cat. 28), see Callen 2000, 37–38.
7 Ibid., 38.
8 Pissarro submitted a gouache titled *Enfants à table* (Children at the Table) to the sixth Impressionist exhibition in 1881. See Pissarro/Venturi 1939, vol. 1, 266, and Berson 1996, vol. 2, 184.
9 George T. M. Shackelford, "Impressionism and the Still-Life Tradition," in *Impressionist Still Life,* exh. cat., Phillips Collection, Washington, DC, 2001, 20–27.
10 See *Apples and Pears in a Round Basket* (1872, Princeton University Art Museum); and *Still Life with Apples and Pitcher* (1872, Metropolitan Museum of Art, New York).

Painting Outdoors: Pissarro's Impressionism
Clarisse Fava-Piz
Pages 92–105

1 The eight Impressionist exhibitions took place in 1874, 1876, 1877, 1879, 1880, 1881, 1882, and 1886.
2 See the titles of past exhibition catalogs dedicated to Pissarro, including Oxford 2022, Paris 2017b, Wuppertal 2014, and New York 2005.
3 Letter from Camille Pissarro to Paul Durand-Ruel (Éragny-sur-Epte, November 6,1886), in Bailly-Herzberg 1986, 75, letter 358. Pissarro gives a short biography and ends with: "Quant au reste de mon histoire de peintre elle se rattache au groupe impressionniste." Unless otherwise noted, all translations from French are by the author.

4 Brettell 1990, 41–42. Pissarro painted this garden several times during the 1870s. Except for the garden landscapes painted around 1900 at the country home of his friend Octave Mirbeau, this is the only scene of a bourgeois garden in Pissarro's landscape paintings.

5 Joachim Pissarro, "Camille Pissarro's Vision of History and Art," in Pissarro/Durand-Ruel Snollaerts 2005, vol. 1, 61–93, here 61; André Dombrowski, "Camille Pissarro, The Garden of Les Mathurins at Pontoise, 1876," in *French Paintings and Pastels, 1600–1945: The Collections of the Nelson-Atkins Museum of Art*, exh. cat., The Nelson Atkins Museum of Art, Kansas City 2024, https://doi.org/10.37764/78973.5.642.5407.

6 Brettell 2011, 195.

7 Ibid., 183.

8 Theodore Reff, ed., *Modern Art in Paris (1855–1900): Two Hundred Catalogues of the Major Exhibitions, Reproduced in Facsimile in Forty-Seven Volumes*, vol. 23,7: *Impressionist Group Exhibitions: Catalogue de la 7e exposition des artistes indépendants,* New York 1981, no. 107: "Pissarro: Laveuse, étude."

9 Joris-Karl Huysmans, *L'Art moderne,* Paris 1883, 285–301, here 291 (appendix on the 1882 Exposition des artistes indépendants).

10 See Daniel Zamani's essay in this catalog, 32–43.

Rural Community:
Harvest and Market Scenes
Clarisse Fava-Piz
Pages 106–31

1 Richard R. Brettell dedicates two chapters of his catalog *Pissarro's People* (Brettell 2011) to "Rural Workers" (chapter 7, 165–93) and "Rural Subjects" (chapter 9, 207–17). On the comparison with Degas, see ibid., 211.

2 See Timothy J. Clark, "We Field Women," in *Farewell to an Idea: Episodes from a History of Modernism,* New Haven 1999, 94–121. The author situates Pissarro in the world of Élisée Reclus and Pyotr Kropotkin and their publications *La Révolte* and *Le Père peinard,* focusing his analysis on the societal complexity and violence of the 1890s.

3 Brettell 2011, 171.

4 On Pissarro's use of different media and his studio practice, see my essay in this catalog, 22–31.

5 See chapter 10 ("The Market Economy") in Brettell 2011, 219–39.

6 Ibid., 219.

7 On Degas's depiction of laundresses see *Degas and the Laundress: Women, Work and Impressionism,* exh. cat., The Cleveland Museum of Art, 2023. In his essay "Putting People in Their Place: Class and Gender in Degas's Paris," Charles Sowerwine argues that although Degas's laundresses remain nameless and inferior, he pushes the normative boundaries of painting by neither eroticizing nor mythologizing them (45–58, here 54).

8 Ibid., 201.

Garden Views:
The Studio in Éragny-sur-Epte
Nerina Santorius
Pages 132–51

1 [Jules-Antoine] Castagnary, "Exposition du boulevard des Capucines: Les Impressionnistes," in *Le Siècle* (April 29, 1874), 3. Unless otherwise noted, all translations are by Melissa M. Thorson.

2 See Ritter 1963, 18.

3 See Antonia Dinnebier, "Der Blick auf die schöne Landschaft—Naturaneignung or Schöpfungsakt?," in *Projektionsfläche Natur: Zum Zusammenhang von Naturbildern and gesellschaftlichen Verhältnissen,* ed. Ludwig Fischer, Hamburg 2004, 61–76, here 63; and Norbert Fischer, "Landschaft als kulturwissenschaftliche Kategorie," in *Zeitschrift für Volkskunde* 104 (2008), 19–39, here 23–24. This exemplary function of painting is documented, for example, for English landscape parks of the eighteenth century.

4 Mirbeau 1891, 83–84.

5 On this subject, see also Clarisse Fava-Piz's essay in this catalog, 22–31. For Pissarro, the artist's originality lay not in the execution of his paintings but in his specific way of seeing. See Camille Pissarro, letter to Paul Durand-Ruel (Éragny-sur-Epte, November 6, 1886), in Bailly-Herzberg 1986, 75, letter 358.

6 On this newer understanding of landscape, developed in the field of cultural landscape studies based on the work of J. B. Jackson, see *Landschaftstheorie: Texte der Cultural Landscape Studies,* ed. Brigitte Franzen and Stefanie Krebs, Cologne 2005.

A Harmony of Opposites:
Neo-Impressionist Paintings
Nerina Santorius
Pages 152–71

1 Anonymous, "Les On-dit," in *Le Rappel* (March 10, 1890), 2. Unless otherwise noted, all translations are by Melissa M. Thorson.

2 On Neo-Impressionism in Pissarro's work, see also the essay by Claire Durand-Ruel Snollaerts in this volume, 12–21, here 18–20.

3 Letter from Camille Pissarro to Paul Durand-Ruel (Éragny-sur-Epte, November 6, 1886), in Bailly-Herzberg 1986, 75, letter 358. The reference is to French chemist Eugène Chevreul, Scottish physicist James Clerk Maxwell, and American physicist Odgen Nicholas Rood.

4 Fénéon 1887, 139.

5 Ward 1995, 286, n. 11.

6 Fénéon 1889.

7 Cf. Roslak 2007, 28. On Pissarro's relationship to anarchism, see also the essay by Daniel Zamani in this volume, 32–43.

8 Letter from Camille Pissarro to Octave Mirbeau (Éragny-sur-Epte, September 30, 1892), in Bailly-Herzberg 1988, 261, letter 818.

Motors of Progress:
Normandy Port Series
Claire Durand-Ruel Snollaerts
Pages 172–87

1 Gustave Geffroy, "Camille Pissarro," in *Le Journal* (June 25, 1898), 2.
2 Letter from Camille Pissarro to Lucien Pissarro (Rouen, February, 18, 1896), in Bailly-Herzberg 1989, 165, letter 1210.
3 Letter from Camille Pissarro to Lucien Pissarro (Rouen, February 26, 1896), in Bailly-Herzberg 1989, 167, letter 1213.
4 Letter from Camille Pissarro to Lucien Pissarro (Dieppe, August 11, 1902), in Bailly-Herzberg 1991, 255, letter 1926.
5 Letter from Camille Pissarro to Ludovic-Rodolphe Pissarro (Le Havre, July 18, 1903), in ibid., 364, letter 2046.
6 Letter from Camille Pissarro to Pieter van der Velde (Le Havre, July 29, 1903), in ibid., 366, no. 2048. Pieter van der Velde was a Dutch collector who had lived in Le Havre since 1877 and purchased works from Pissarro on a regular basis.

City People:
Paris Series
Claire Durand-Ruel Snollaerts
Pages 188–205

1 Letter from Camille Pissarro to Lucien Pissarro (Paris, May 26, 1895), in Bailly-Herzberg 1989, 75, letter 1138. Unless otherwise noted, all translations are by Helge R. Dascher.
2 Letter from Camille Pissarro to Lucien Pissarro (Paris, February 3, 1897), in ibid., 321, letter 1365.
3 Letter from Camille Pissarro to Georges Pissarro (Éragny-sur-Epte, February 8, 1897), in ibid., 323, letter 1366.
4 Letter from Lucien Pissarro to Camille Pissarro (Epping, February 19, 1897), in Thorold 1993, 529.
5 Letter from Camille Pissarro to Georges Pissarro (Paris, December 15, 1897), in Bailly-Herzberg 1989, 418, letter 1489.
6 Letter from Camille Pissarro to Lucien Pissarro (Paris, March 16, 1900), in Bailly-Herzberg 1991, 77, letter 1699.
7 C. d'H., "Petits salons: Exposition Camille Pissarro," in *Le Moniteur des arts* (June 3, 1898), 559.
8 Ed. S., "Petites expositions: Exposition Pissarro," in *Le Journal des débats* (January 26, 1901), 2.

Excerpts from Camille Pissarro's Letters
Claire Durand-Ruel Snollaerts
Pages 226–33

1 Bailly-Herzberg 1980, 1986, 1988, 1989, and 1991. All excerpts reproduced here are from this edition.
2 This collection is far from exhaustive. Additional letters regularly appear on the market; the unpublished letters currently number in the hundreds.
3 Particularly in terms of punctuation, general comprehensibility was given preference over an exact formal correspondence.
4 For about ten years, until 1882, they worked side by side in the Auvers-sur-Oise region, northwest of Paris.
5 Claude Monet was appreciated by Pissarro not only as an artist but also as a close friend.
6 Due to financial difficulties, Paul Durand-Ruel had been forced to suspend his purchases for several years starting in 1871 but now began to purchase works by Pissarro on a regular basis once again.
7 Manet died on April 30, 1883. He and Pissarro knew each other but were never close.
8 He is referring to French socialist Pierre-Joseph Proudhon and British philosophers John Stuart Mill and Herbert Spencer.
9 Pyotr Kropotkin, with anarchist Élisée Reclus, in 1879 founded the journal *Le Révolté* (The Rebel), which soon after became *La Révolte* (The Revolution). Pissarro was a regular reader of the publication. In around 1885, the articles were compiled into a book titled *Les Paroles d'un révolté* (Words of a Rebel).
10 Edward Spencer Beesly was a professor of history at University College of London, a democrat, and a trade union advocate.
11 The term *Pointillism* is often used by Pissarro in a pejorative way to refer to the technique of applying paint in small dots. Other artists preferred the term *Divisionism,* taking into account color theory and the use of complementary colors. Art critic Félix Fénéon qualified the style as an evolved form of Impressionism when he coined the term *Neo-Impressionism* in 1886. On the range of terms reflecting the different degrees of acceptance of the movement, see Christophe Duvivier, "Neo-Impressionism: Crisis and Continuity in the Work of Camille Pissarro, 1885–1891," in Basel 2021, 98–109, here 98–99.

List of Exhibited Works

* in Denver only
** in Potsdam only

D = Delteil 1999
PDRS = Pissarro/Durand-Ruel Snollaerts 2005
PV = Pissarro/Venturi 1939

1
La Guaira, 1852
Pencil and ink on paper, 10 ⅜ × 13 ¾ in. (26.5 × 35 cm)
Colección Patricia Phelps de Cisneros

2
Landscape with Donkeys, Venezuela, ca. 1854
Graphite on cream wove paper, 10 ⅝ × 14 in. (26.9 × 35.5 cm)
Clark Art Institute, Williamstown, Massachusetts, Gift of Gayllis R. Ward in memory of Chester D. Ward, Jr., Inv. 2009.5

3
Rio de Maiquetía, 1852
Pencil on paper, 13 ½ × 11 in. (34.3 × 27.9 cm)
Colección Patricia Phelps de Cisneros

4
Pariata, 1853
Watercolor and graphite on paper, 8 ⅝ × 10 ⅝ in. (22 × 27 cm)
Colección Patricia Phelps de Cisneros

5
Bridge at Caracas, 1854
Transparent watercolor and graphite on wove paper, 9 ½ × 12 in. (24 × 30.5 cm)
National Gallery of Art, Washington, Collection of Mr. and Mrs. Paul Mellon, 1985, Inv. 1985.64.108

6
A Plaza in Caracas, ca. 1854
Oil on canvas, 10 ½ × 18 ⅛ in. (26.7 × 46 cm)
Colección Patricia Phelps de Cisneros
PDRS 2

7
A Creek in Saint Thomas (Virgin Islands), 1856
Oil on Academy Board, 9 ⅝ × 12 ⅝ in. (24.5 × 32.2 cm)
National Gallery of Art, Washington, Collection of Mr. and Mrs. Paul Mellon, Inv. 1985.64.29
PDRS 16

8
Two Women Chatting by the Sea, Saint Thomas, 1856
Oil on canvas, 10 ⅞ × 16 ⅛ in. (27.7 × 41 cm)
National Gallery of Art, Washington, Collection of Mr. and Mrs. Paul Mellon, Inv. 1985.64.30
PDRS 23

9
Cove with Sailboat, 1856
Oil on canvas, 13 ¾ × 20 ⅞ in. (35 × 53 cm)
Colección Patricia Phelps de Cisneros
PDRS 24

10
Landscape, Saint Thomas, 1856
Oil on canvas, 8 ¾ × 15 in. (47.6 × 38.1 cm)
Virginia Museum of Fine Arts, Richmond, Collection of Mr. and Mrs. Paul Mellon, Inv. 83.46
PDRS 17

11
Farmyard, ca. 1863
Oil on canvas, 15 × 18 ½ in. (38.1 × 47.1 cm)
Private collection, Colorado
PDRS 69

12**
La Varenne-Saint-Hilaire, ca. 1863
Oil on canvas, 19 ½ × 19 ⅛ in. (49.6 × 74 cm)
Szépművészeti Múzeum / Museum of Fine Arts, Budapest, Inv. 377.B
PDRS 74

13
The Banks of the Marne in Winter, 1866
Oil on canvas, 36 ⅛ × 59 ⅛ in. (91.8 × 150.2 cm)
The Art Institute of Chicago, Mr. and Mrs. Lewis Larned Coburn Memorial Collection, Inv. 1957.306
PDRS 107

14
Landscape at Louveciennes (Autumn), 1870
Oil on canvas, 35 × 45 ¾ in. (88.9 × 116.2 cm)
The J. Paul Getty Museum, Los Angeles, Inv. 82.PA.73
PDRS 157

15**
Pontoise, ca. 1867
Oil on canvas, 32 ⅛ × 39 ⅜ in. (81.5 × 100 cm)
National Gallery Prague, Inv. O 3197
PDRS 115

16
Banks of the Oise at Pontoise or *Banks of the Oise at Saint-Ouen-l'Aumône,* 1867
Oil on canvas, 18 × 28 ⅛ in. (45.7 × 71.4 cm)
Denver Art Museum, Gift of the Barnett and Annalee Newman Foundation in honor of Annalee G. Newman, Inv. 2001.310
PDRS 117

17
Quai du Pothuis, Pontoise, 1868
Oil on canvas, 20 ½ × 31 ⅞ in. (52 × 81 cm)
Kunsthalle Mannheim, Inv. M402
PDRS 123

18**
The Seine at Bougival, 1871
Oil on canvas, 17 ⅛ × 23 ½ in. (43.5 × 59.7 cm)
Private collection
PDRS 200

19
The Seine near Port Marly, 1872
Oil on canvas, 18 ⅛ × 22 in. (46 × 55.8 cm)
Staatsgalerie Stuttgart, Purchased with lottery funds in 1965, Inv. 2727
PDRS 234

20
The Lock at Pontoise, 1872
Oil on fabric, 20 ⅞ × 32 ⅝ in. (53 × 83 cm)
The Cleveland Museum of Art, Leonard C. Hanna Jr. Fund, Inv. 1990.7
PDRS 243

21
Route de Versailles, Louveciennes, Rain Effect, 1870
Oil on canvas, 15 ¾ × 22 ⅛ in. (40 × 56.2 cm)
Clark Art Institute, Williamstown, Massachusetts, Inv. 1955.825
PDRS 155

22
The Thaw or *The House of Monsieur Musy, Louveciennes,* 1872
Oil on canvas, 12 ⅝ × 18 in. (32.1 × 45.7 cm)
Denver Art Museum, Frederic C. Hamilton Collection, Inv. 2016.363
PDRS 216

23
Lordship Lane Station, Dulwich, 1871
Oil on canvas, 17 ½ × 28 ½ in. (44.5 × 72.5 cm)
The Courtauld, London (Samuel Courtauld Trust), Inv. P.1948.SC.317
PDRS 189

24*
The House in the Woods, 1872
Oil on canvas, 19 ⅝ × 25 ⅝ in. (50 × 65 cm)
Drs. Tobia and Morton Mower
PDRS 255

25*
The Crossroads, Pontoise or *Square at the Old Cemetery, Pontoise,* 1872
Oil on canvas, 22 × 36 in. (55.9 × 91.4 cm)
Carnegie Museum of Art, Pittsburgh,
Acquired through the generosity of
the Sarah Mellon Scaife Family, Inv. 71.7
PDRS 259

26
Portrait of the Artist, 1873
Oil on canvas, 21 ⅞ × 18 ⅛ in. (55.5 × 46 cm)
Musée d'Orsay, Paris, Paul-Émile Pissarro
Donation, 1930, Inv. RF 2837
PDRS 283

27
Julie Pissarro Sewing Beside a Window, ca. 1877
Oil on canvas, 21 ¼ × 17 ¾ in. (54 × 45 cm)
The Ashmolean Museum, University of Oxford,
Presented by Esther Pissarro, 1951,
Inv. WA1951.225.3
PDRS 534

28
Portrait of Jeanne Pissarro, 1872
Oil on canvas, 28 ⅝ × 23 ⅜ in. (72.7 × 59.5 cm)
Yale University Art Gallery, New Haven,
John Hay Whitney, B.A. 1926, M.A. (Hon.) 1956,
Collection, Inv. 1982.111.4
PDRS 281

29
Jeanne Pissarro (Minette) Holding a Fan, ca. 1874
Oil on canvas, 22 × 18 ⅛ in. (56 × 46 cm)
The Ashmolean Museum, University of Oxford,
Bequeathed by Esther Pissarro, 1952,
Inv. WA1952.6.2
PDRS 325

30
Portrait of Paul-Émile Pissarro, ca. 1890
Oil on canvas, 16 ⅛ × 13 ¼ in. (41 × 33.6 cm)
Private collection
PDRS 878

31
Chrysanthemums in a Chinese Vase, 1873
Oil on canvas, 23 ⅝ × 19 ⅞ in. (60 × 50.5 cm)
National Gallery of Ireland, Dublin, Purchased, 1983
(Shaw Fund), Inv. NGI.4459
PDRS 179

32
Vase of Peonies and Mock Orange, 1872–77
Oil on canvas, 31 ⅞ × 25 ¼ in. (81 × 64 cm)
Van Gogh Museum, Amsterdam
(gift from Sara Lee Corporation),
Inv. s0502S2000
PDRS 556

33
Hoarfrost, 1873
Oil on canvas, 25 ¾ × 36 ¾ in. (65.5 × 93.2 cm)
Musée d'Orsay, Paris, Bequest of Enriqueta Alsop
in the name of Dr. Eduardo Mollard, 1972,
Inv. RF 1972 27
PDRS 285

34
The Pont-Marie Viewed from the Quai d'Anjou, Paris, ca. 1875
Oil on canvas, 19 ½ × 25 in. (49.5 × 63.5 cm)
Colección Pérez Simón
PDRS 406

35
The Boulevards Extérieurs, Effect of Snow, 1879
Oil on canvas, 21 ¼ × 25 ⅝ in. (54 × 65 cm)
Musée Marmottan Monet, Paris,
Gift of Eugène and Victorine Donop de Monchy, 1940,
Inv. 4021
PDRS 618

36
Orchard at Pontoise, Sunset, 1878
Oil on canvas, 18 ⅜ × 21 ¾ in. (46.7 × 55.2 cm)
Wallraf-Richartz-Museum & Fondation Corboud,
Cologne, Inv. Dep. FC 712
PDRS 541

37
The Hills at Le Chou, Pontoise, 1882
Oil on canvas, 23 ¾ × 29 in. (60.3 × 73.6 cm)
Hasso Plattner Collection, Museum Barberini, Potsdam,
Inv. MB-Pis-01
PDRS 673

38
The Highway (La Côte du Valhermeil, Auvers-sur-Oise), 1880
Oil on canvas, 25 ¼ × 31 ½ in. (64.1 × 80 cm)
The Baltimore Museum of Art, The Cone Collection, formed by Dr. Claribel Cone and Miss Etta Cone of Baltimore, Maryland, Inv. 1950.280
PDRS 623

39
The Garden of Les Mathurins at Pontoise, 1876
Oil on canvas, 44 ⅝ × 65 ⅛ in. (113.4 × 165.4 cm)
The Nelson-Atkins Museum of Art, Kansas City, Missouri, Purchase: William Rockhill Nelson Trust, Inv. 60-38
PDRS 448

40
Washerwoman, Study, 1880
Oil on canvas, 28 ¾ × 23 ¼ in. (73 × 59.1 cm)
The Metropolitan Museum of Art, New York, Gift of Mr. and Mrs. Nate B. Spingold, 1956, Inv. 56.184.1
PDRS 640

41
Peasant Girl with a Straw Hat, 1881
Oil on canvas, 28 ⅞ × 23 7⁄16 in. (73.3 × 59.5 cm)
National Gallery of Art, Washington, Ailsa Mellon Bruce Collection, Inv. 1970.17.52
PDRS 661

42
The Shepherdess, 1881
Oil on canvas, 31 ⅞ × 25 ½ in. (81 × 64.8 cm)
Musée d'Orsay, Paris, Bequest of Isaac de Camondo, 1911, Inv. RF 2013
PDRS 653

43
Haymaking at Éragny, 1901
Oil on canvas, 21 ¼ × 25 ½ in. (53.9 × 64.7 cm)
National Gallery of Canada, Ottawa, Purchased 1946, Inv. 4635
PDRS 1393

44
Haymakers, Evening, Éragny, 1893
Oil on canvas, 21 ⅜ × 25 ¾ in. (54.3 × 65.4 cm)
Joslyn Art Museum, Omaha, Nebraska, Museum Purchase, Inv. 1946.28
PDRS 1005

45
The Haymaker, 1884
Oil on canvas, 28 ⅞ × 23 ⅝ in. (73.5 × 60 cm)
Colección Pérez Simón
PDRS 766

46**
Gardener Standing by a Haystack, Overcast Sky, Éragny, 1899
Oil on canvas, 23 ⅝ × 28 ¾ in. (60 × 73 cm)
Isabelle and Scott Black Collection
PDRS 1278

47
Pea Harvesters [recto], ca. 1880
Charcoal and watercolor on heavy wove paper, 9 ⅜ × 12 ½ in. (23.9 × 31.7 cm)
National Gallery of Art, Washington, The Armand Hammer Collection, 1991, Inv. 1991.217.21.a

48
The Plow, 1901
Lithograph, 8 ⅞ × 6 in. (22.5 × 15.2 cm)
Denver Art Museum, Gift of Noëlle and George Beatty, Inv. 2024.705
D 194

49
Peasants Harvesting Hay, 1884
Gouache, watercolor, and pastel on paper, 25 ⅛ × 31 ⅜ in. (63.8 × 79.7 cm)
Denver Art Museum, Anonymous bequest, Inv. 1986.740
PV 1394

50
Landscape with Two Peasant Women on the Left (fan), 1883
Gouache on silk, 10 ½ × 22 in. (26.7 × 55.9 cm)
Colección Pérez Simón
PV 1623

51
Harvest: Peasants Working in the Field (fan), ca. 1880
Gouache on vellum, 11 × 22 ¼ in. (28 × 56.5 cm)
Private collection

52
Herd of Sheep, Setting Sun (fan), 1889
Gouache on silk, 7 ⅞ × 24 ⅜ in. (20 × 62 cm)
Colección Pérez Simón
PV 1641

53
Shepherd and Sheep (fan), 1890
Gouache and pencil on silk, 10 ⅝ × 21 ¾ in. (27 × 55.2 cm)
Colección Pérez Simón
PV 1643

54
The Pork Butcher, 1883
Oil on canvas, 25 ⅝ × 21 ⅜ in. (65.1 × 54.3 cm)
Tate, Bequeathed by Lucien Pissarro, the artist's son 1944, Inv. No5576
PDRS 706

55
The Poultry Market at Pontoise, 1882
Oil on canvas, 31 ⅞ × 25 ⅝ in. (81 × 65.1 cm)
Norton Simon Art Foundation, Pasadena, California, Inv. M.1984.2.P
PDRS 682

56
Saint-Martin Fair, Pontoise (fan), 1881
Gouache on silk, 11 × 21 ¾ in. (27.8 × 55.1 cm)
Private collection
PV 1618

57*
The Marketplace, Gisors, 1891
Opaque watercolor with black conté crayon over traces of charcoal on fabric mounted to cardboard, 14 × 10 ¼ in. (35.6 × 26 cm)
Philadelphia Museum of Art, The Louis E. Stern Collection, 1963, Inv. 1963-181-55
PV 1465

58**
Winter, Return from the Fair (fan), ca. 1878
Gouache on silk, 9 ⅞ × 21 ⅝ in. (25 × 55 cm)
Musée Marmottan Monet, Paris,
Bequest of Hauser Roger, 1990, Inv. 5233
PV 1626

59
Plum Trees in Blossom, Éragny, 1894
Oil on canvas, 23 ⅝ × 28 ¾ in. (60 × 73 cm)
Ordrupgaard, Copenhagen, Inv. 267 WH
PDRS 1030

60
A Corner of the Meadow at Éragny, 1902
Oil on canvas, 23 ⅝ × 32 in. (60 × 81.3 cm)
Tate, Presented by Mrs. Esther Pissarro, the artist's daughter-in-law 1951, Inv. No6003
PDRS 1462

61
Vegetable Garden, Overcast Morning, Éragny, 1901
Oil on canvas, 25 ½ × 32 in. (64.8 × 81.3 cm)
Philadelphia Museum of Art, Bequest of Charlotte Dorrance Wright, 1978, Inv. 1978-1-26
PDRS 1373

62
The Large Walnut Tree, Éragny, Afternoon, 1900
Oil on canvas, 26 × 32 ⅛ in. (66 × 81.8 cm)
Private collection, UK
PDRS 1325

63
Autumn, Poplar Trees, Éragny, 1894
Oil on canvas, 31 ⅝ × 23 ¼ in. (80.3 × 59.1 cm)
Denver Art Museum,
Funds from Helen Dill bequest, Inv. 1935.16
PDRS 1051

64
Peasant House, 1892
Oil on canvas, 23 ⅜ × 28 ¾ in. (59.5 × 73 cm)
Collection of Prof. Mark Kaufman, Monaco
PDRS 957

65
Spring, Gray Weather, Éragny, 1895
Oil on canvas, 23 ¾ × 28 ⅞ in. (60.2 × 73.2 cm)
Collection Art Gallery of Ontario, Toronto,
Purchase, 1933, Inv. 2111
PDRS 1075

66
Spring at Éragny, 1900
Oil on canvas, 25 ¾ × 32 ⅛ in. (65.4 × 81.6 cm)
Denver Art Museum, Frederic C. Hamilton Collection, bequeathed to the Denver Art Museum, Inv. 30.2017
PDRS 1320

67
Saint Anne's Church in Kew, London, 1892
Oil on canvas, 21 ⅝ × 18 ⅛ in. (55 × 46 cm)
Collection of Prof. Mark Kaufman, Monaco
PDRS 940

68
The Tall Beech Trees, Varengeville, ca. 1899
Oil on canvas, 25 ½ × 21 ¼ in. (64.8 × 54 cm)
Colección Pérez Simón
PDRS 1292

69
View of Bazincourt, Clear Sky, 1884
Oil on canvas, 21 ⅜ × 25 ½ in. (54.3 × 64.8 cm)
Colección Pérez Simón
PDRS 756

70
View of Bazincourt, Sunset, 1892
Oil on canvas, 15 × 21 ⅝ in. (38 × 55 cm)
Hasso Plattner Collection, Museum Barberini, Potsdam, Inv. MB-Pis-04
PDRS 960

71
Snow Scene at Éragny (View of Bazincourt), 1884
Oil on canvas, 18 ⅜ × 21 ⅞ in. (46.7 × 55.6 cm)
Fine Arts Museums of San Francisco, Gift of Mrs. Renée M. Bransten, Inv. 1962.20
PDRS 782

72
View of Bazincourt, Snow Effect, Sunset, 1892
Oil on canvas, 12 ⅝ × 16 ⅛ in. (32 × 41 cm)
Hasso Plattner Collection, Museum Barberini, Potsdam, Inv. MB-Pis-05
PDRS 969

73
Woman Breaking Wood, ca. 1890
Gouache on paper, 23 ¼ × 18 ¼ in. (59 × 46.5 cm)
Private collection, courtesy of Pissarro & Associates Fine Art
PV 1455

74
Hoarfrost, Peasant Girl Making a Fire, 1888
Oil on canvas, 36 ½ × 36 ⅜ in. (92.8 × 92.5 cm)
Hasso Plattner Collection, Museum Barberini, Potsdam, Inv. MB-Pis-02
PDRS 857

75**
The Flock of Sheep, Éragny, 1888
Oil on canvas, 18 ⅛ × 21 ¾ in. (46 × 55.2 cm)
Private collection
PDRS 860

76
The Delafolie Brickyard, Éragny, 1885
Oil on canvas, 15 × 18 ½ in. (38 × 46 cm)
The Ashmolean Museum, University of Oxford, Bequeathed by Frank Hindley Smith, 1939, Inv. WA1940.1.12
PDRS 791

77**
The Delafolie Brickyard at Éragny, 1886
Oil on canvas, 22 ⅞ × 28 ⅜ in. (58 × 72 cm)
Private collection
PDRS 826

78
View from My Window in Cloudy Weather, 1886–88
Oil on canvas, 25 ⅝ × 31 ⅞ in. (65 × 81 cm)
The Ashmolean Museum, University of Oxford, Presented by Mrs. Lucien Pissarro, 1950, Inv. WA1950.185
PDRS 825

79
The Garden and Henhouse at Octave Mirbeau's, Les Damps, 1892
Oil on canvas, 28 ⅞ × 36 ¼ in. (73.3 × 92 cm)
Hasso Plattner Collection, Museum Barberini, Potsdam, Inv. MB-Pis-03
PDRS 955

80
The House of the Deaf Woman and the Belfry at Éragny, 1886
Oil on canvas, 25 ⅝ × 32 in. (65.2 × 81.3 cm)
Indianapolis Museum of Art at Newfields, Anonymous gift, Inv. 2002.76
PDRS 827

81
Meadow at Éragny with Cows, Fog, Sunset, 1891
Oil on canvas, 21 ¼ × 25 ⅝ in. (54 × 65.1 cm)
Private collection, Switzerland
PDRS 909

82
Landscape at Saint-Charles, Near Gisors, Sunset, 1891
Oil on canvas, 31 ⅞ × 25 ⅝ in. (81 × 65 cm)
Clark Art Institute, Williamstown, Massachusetts, Inv. 1955.524
PDRS 910

83
Turpitudes sociales, 1889–90 (frontispiece)
Facsimile, Geneva 1972
Reproductions of 30 pen over brown ink over graphite drawings on paper in an album, 12 ⅜ × 9 ⅞ × ⅝ in. (31.5 × 25 × 1.7 cm)
Copy no. 483
Private collection, courtesy of Pissarro & Associates Fine Art

84
The New Idolators (for *Turpitudes sociales,* omitted), 1889
Ink on paper, 12 ⅞ × 9 ⅞ in. (32.7 × 25.1 cm)
Denver Art Museum, The T. Edward and Tullah Hanley memorial gift to the people of Denver and the area, Inv. 1974.395

85
Study for "The Temple of the Golden Calf"
(for *Turpitudes sociales*), 1889
Pen and dark ink over pencil on glazed paper,
8 ⅞ × 7 ⅛ in. (22.5 × 18 cm)
The Ashmolean Museum, University of Oxford,
Presented by the Pissarro Family, 1952,
Inv. WA1952.6.296

86
Study for "The Asphysia" (for *Turpitudes sociales*), 1890
Pen and dark ink over pencil on glazed paper, 9 ⅛ × 7 in.
(23.1 × 17.7 cm)
The Ashmolean Museum, University of Oxford,
Presented by the Pissarro Family, 1952,
Inv. WA1952.6.297

87
The Roofs of Old Rouen, Sunshine, 1896
Oil on canvas, 25 ⅝ × 21 ½ in. (65 × 54.5 cm)
Private collection
PDRS 1115

88
The Roofs of Old Rouen, Gray Weather, 1896
Oil on canvas, 28 ½ × 36 in. (72.3 × 91.4 cm)
Toledo Museum of Art, Purchased with
funds from the Libbey Endowment, Gift of
Edward Drummond Libbey, Inv. 1951.361
PDRS 1114

89
The Great Bridge in Rouen, Rainy Weather, 1896
Oil on canvas, 28 ¾ × 36 ¼ in. (73 × 92 cm)
Staatliche Kunsthalle Karlsruhe, Inv. 2488
PDRS 1139

90
Pont Boieldieu, Rouen, Rainy Weather, 1896
Oil on canvas, 29 × 36 in. (73.6 × 91.4 cm)
Collection Art Gallery of Ontario, Toronto,
Gift of Reuben Wells Leonard Estate, 1937, Inv. 2415
PDRS 1116

91
Pont Boieldieu, Rouen, Effect of Fog, 1898
Oil on canvas, 25 ¾ × 32 in. (65.4 × 81.3 cm)
Colección Pérez Simón
PDRS 1225

92
View of the Quai Cavelier-de-La-Salle, Rouen, 1896
Oil on canvas, 19 ⅝ × 24 in. (50 × 61 cm)
Private collection
PDRS 1147

93
Sunset, Port of Rouen (Steamboats), 1898
Oil on canvas, 25 ⅝ × 31 ⅞ in. (65 × 81.1 cm)
Amgueddfa Cymru—Museum Wales, Bequeathed by
Margaret Davies, 1963, Inv. NMW A 2492
PDRS 1236

94
Harbor at Dieppe, 1902
Oil on canvas, 18 ⅜ × 21 ¾ in. (46.7 × 55.2 cm)
Fine Arts Museums of San Francisco,
Mildred Anna Williams Collection, Inv. 1940.52
PDRS 1444

95
The Anse des Pilotes and the East Breakwater, Le Havre, Afternoon, Sunny Weather, 1903
Oil on canvas, 21 ½ × 25 ¾ in. (54.5 × 65.3 cm)
Musée d'art moderne André Malraux, Le Havre,
Inv. A 494
PDRS 1513

96
The Anse des Pilotes, Le Havre, Morning, Sunshine, Tide Rising, 1903
Oil on canvas, 21 ½ × 25 ¾ in. (54.6 × 65 cm)
Musée d'art moderne André Malraux, Le Havre,
Inv. A 495
PDRS 1509

97
Boulevard Montmartre, Twilight, 1897
Oil on canvas, 21 ¼ × 25 ⅝ in. (54 × 65 cm)
Hasso Plattner Collection, Museum Barberini, Potsdam,
Inv. MB-Pis-06
PDRS 1170

98**
Boulevard Montmartre, Mardi Gras, Sunset, 1897
Oil on canvas, 21 ¼ × 25 ⅝ in. (54 × 65 cm)
Kunst Museum Winterthur, Purchase, 1947, Inv. KV 756
PDRS 1164

99
Morning Sun in the Rue Saint-Honoré. Place du Théâtre Français, 1898
Oil on canvas, 25 ⅞ × 21 ¼ in. (65.6 × 54 cm)
Ordrupgaard, Copenhagen, Inv. 261 WH
PDRS 1200

100**
Avenue de l'Opéra, 1898
Oil on canvas, 28 ⅞ × 36 ⅜ in. (73.3 × 92.3 cm)
Musée des Beaux-Arts de la Ville de Reims,
Bequest of Henry Vasnier, 11/1907, Inv. 907.19.209
PDRS 1202

101
Afternoon Sunshine, Pont Neuf (first series), 1901
Oil on canvas, 28 ¾ × 36 ¼ in. (73 × 92.1 cm)
Philadelphia Museum of Art, Bequest of Charlotte Dorrance Wright, 1978, Inv. 1978-1-24
PDRS 1351

102**
The Pont Neuf (second series), 1902
Oil on canvas, 21 ¾ × 18 ¼ in. (55.3 × 46.5 cm)
Szépművészeti Múzeum / Museum of Fine Arts, Budapest, Inv. 205. B
PDRS 1415

103
The Pont Neuf (second series), 1902
Oil on canvas, 21 ⅜ × 26 in. (54.2 × 66 cm)
Musée des Beaux-Arts de Lyon, Inv. 2000-3
PDRS 1416

104**
The Louvre, Winter Sunlight (second series), 1901
Oil on canvas, 28 ¾ × 36 ¼ in. (73 × 92 cm)
Isabelle and Scott Black Collection
PDRS 1404

105*
The Louvre, Morning, Sunlight (second series), 1901
Oil on canvas, 29 × 36 ½ in. (73.7 × 92.7 cm)
Saint Louis Art Museum, Museum Purchase, Inv. 225:1916
PDRS 1405

106
The Louvre Under Snow (second series), 1902
Oil on canvas, 26 ⅛ × 32 in. (66.3 × 81.3 cm)
The National Gallery, London, Bought 1932, Inv. NG4671
PDRS 1408

107**
The Louvre, Morning, Spring (second series), 1902
Oil on canvas, 25 ½ × 21 ¼ in. (64.8 × 54 cm)
Hasso Plattner Collection, Museum Barberini, Potsdam, Inv. MB-Pis-07
PDRS 1425

108
Statue of Henri IV, Morning, Sunlight (second series), 1902
Oil on canvas, 29 × 36 ⅜ in. (73.6 × 92.3 cm)
Private collection
PDRS 1409
Not exhibited

109
The Tuileries Gardens, Rainy Weather, 1899
Oil on canvas, 25 ⅝ × 36 ¼ in. (65 × 92 cm)
The Ashmolean Museum, University of Oxford, Bequeathed by Mrs. W. F. R. Weldon, 1936, Inv. WA1937.73
PDRS 1258

Documents

Camille Pissarro in front of a window in his studio in Éragny-sur-Epte, no date (unknown photographer)
Gelatin silver print, 3 ⅛ × 3 ⅝ in. (7.9 × 9.3 cm)
Pissarro Family Archives
Not illustrated

Camille Pissarro on the stairs to his studio in Éragny-sur-Epte, no date (unknown photographer)
Gelatin silver print, 4 ⅝ × 5 ⅜ in. (11.7 × 13.5 cm)
Pissarro Family Archives
Fig. p. 26

Camille Pissarro in his studio, no date (unknown photographer)
Gelatin silver print, 7 × 8 in. (17.8 × 20.4 cm)
Pissarro Family Archives
Fig. p. 223

The studio in Éragny-sur-Epte seen from the outside, no date (unknown photographer)
Postcard, 3 ½ × 5 ½ in. (8.9 × 14 cm)
Pissarro Family Archives
Not illustrated

Selected Bibliography

Adler 1978
Kathleen Adler, *Camille Pissarro: A Biography,* New York 1978.

Bailly-Herzberg 1980
Janine Bailly-Herzberg, ed., *Correspondance de Camille Pissarro,* vol. 1: *1865–1885,* Paris 1980.

Bailly-Herzberg 1986
Janine Bailly-Herzberg, ed., *Correspondance de Camille Pissarro,* vol. 2: *1886–1890,* Paris 1986.

Bailly-Herzberg 1988
Janine Bailly-Herzberg, ed., *Correspondance de Camille Pissarro,* vol. 3: *1891–1894,* Paris 1988.

Bailly-Herzberg 1989
Janine Bailly-Herzberg, ed., *Correspondance de Camille Pissarro,* vol. 4: *1895–1898,* Paris 1989.

Bailly-Herzberg 1991
Janine Bailly-Herzberg, ed., *Correspondance de Camille Pissarro,* vol. 5: *1899–1903,* Paris 1991.

Baltimore 2007
Pissarro: Creating the Impressionist Landscape, exh. cat., Baltimore Museum of Art, 2007.

Basel 2021
Camille Pissarro: The Studio of Modernism, exh. cat., Kunstmuseum Basel, 2021.

Berson 1996
Ruth Berson, ed., *The New Painting: Impressionism, 1874–1886; Documentation,* 2 vols., San Francisco 1996.

Boime 2008
Albert Boime, *Art in an Age of Civil Struggle, 1848–1871,* Chicago and London 2008.

Boulton 1966
Alfredo Boulton, *Camille Pissarro en Venezuela,* Caracas 1966.

Brettell 1990
Richard R. Brettell, *Pissarro and Pontoise: The Painter in a Landscape,* New Haven and London 1990.

Brettell 2011
Richard R. Brettell, *Pissarro's People,* exh. cat., Sterling and Francine Clark Art Institute, Williamstown 2011.

Brettell/Lloyd 1980
Richard Brettell and Christopher Lloyd, eds., *A Catalogue of the Drawings by Camille Pissarro in the Ashmolean Museum, Oxford,* Oxford and New York 1980.

Callen 2000
Anthea Callen, *The Art of Impressionism: Painting Technique & the Making of Modernity,* New Haven and London 2000.

Caracas 1992
C. Pissarro: Raíces y vegetacíon; dibujos y acuarelas, Venezuela 1852–1854, exh. cat., Museo de Bellas Artes, Caracas 1992.

Copenhagen 2017
Pissarro: Et møde på Skt. Thomas, exh. cat., Ordrupgaard, Copenhagen 2017.

Dallas 1992
The Impressionists and the City: Pissarro's Series Paintings, exh. cat., Dallas Museum of Art, 1992.

Delteil 1999
Loys Delteil, *Camille Pissarro: L'Œuvre gravé et lithographié / The Etchings and Lithographs; Catalogue Raisonné,* San Francisco 1999.

Dombrowski 2021
André Dombrowski, *A Companion to Impressionism,* Hoboken 2021.

Doran/Cochran 2010
Michael Doran and Julie Lawrence Cochran, eds., *Conversations with Cézanne,* Berkeley 2010.

Fénéon 1887
Félix Fénéon, "Le Néo-impressionnisme," in *L'Art moderne* (May 1, 1887), 138–41.

Fénéon 1889
Félix Fénéon, "Exposition Pissarro," in *L'Art moderne* (January 20, 1889), 21.

Herbert 2002
Robert L. Herbert, *From Millet to Léger: Essays in the Social History of Art,* New Haven and London 2002.

Jerusalem 1994
Camille Pissarro: Impressionist Innovator, exh. cat., Israel Museum, Jerusalem 1994.

Kisiel 2021
Marine Kisiel, *La Peinture impressionniste et la décoration,* Paris 2021.

Kunstler 1930
Charles Kunstler, "Le Centenaire de Camille Pissarro," in *L'Art Vivant* 6,125 (March 1930), 185–90.

Le Havre 2013
Pissarro dans les ports: Rouen, Dieppe, Le Havre, exh. cat., Musée d'art moderne Malraux, Le Havre 2013.

Lloyd 1986
Christopher Lloyd, ed., *Studies on Camille Pissarro,* London and New York 1986

London 1980
Pissarro: Camille Pissarro 1830–1903, exh. cat., Hayward Gallery, London 1980.

Madrid 2013
Camille Pissarro, exh. cat., Museo Nacional Thyssen-Bornemisza, Madrid 2013.

McKee 2023
C. C. McKee, "Bare Feet, Or, The Ambivalence of Emancipation: Camille Pissarro and the Caribbean," in *Black Modernism in the Transatlantic World,* ed. Steven Nelson and Huey Copeland, Washington, DC, and New Haven 2023, 57–78.

Mirbeau 1891
Octave Mirbeau, "Camille Pissarro," in *L'Art dans les deux mondes* (January 10, 1891), 83–84.

Münster 2013
Camille Pissarro: Mit den Augen eines Impressionisten, exh. cat., Kunstmuseum Pablo Picasso Münster, 2013.

New York 1968
Pissarro in Venezuela, exh. cat., Center for Inter-American Relations, New York 1968.
New York 1997
Camille Pissarro: The Venezuelan Period, 1852–1854, exh. cat., Venezuelan Center, New York 1997.
New York 2005
Pioneering Modern Painting: Cézanne and Pissarro 1865–1885, exh. cat., Museum of Modern Art, New York 2005.
New York 2007
Camille Pissarro: Impressions of City & Country, exh. cat., Jewish Museum, New York 2007.
New York 2015
Traveler Artists: Landscapes of Latin America from the Patricia Phelps de Cisneros Collection, exh. cat., Fundación Cisneros, New York 2015.
Oxford 2022
Pissarro: Father of Impressionism, exh. cat., Ashmolean Museum, Oxford 2022.
Paris 1891
Exposition de Pastels, Aquarelles et Eaux-Fortes par Camille Pissarro, exh. cat., Galeries Durand-Ruel, Paris, April 1891.
Paris 1892
Exposition Camille Pissarro, exh. cat., Galeries Durand-Ruel, Paris, February 1892.
Paris 1904
Catalogue de l'exposition de l'œuvre de Camille Pissarro, exh. cat., Galeries Durand-Ruel, Paris 1904.
Paris 1978
Camille Pissarro au Venezuela, exh. cat., Ambassadc du Venezuela en France, Paris 1978.
Paris 2017a
Pissarro à Éragny: La Nature retrouvée, exh. cat., Musée du Luxembourg, Paris 2017.
Paris 2017b
Pissarro: Le Premier des impressionists / The First Among the Impressionists, exh. cat., Musée Marmottan Monet, Paris 2017.
Pissarro 1993
Joachim Pissarro, *Camille Pissarro,* New York 1993.
Pissarro/Durand-Ruel Snollaerts 2005
Joachim Pissarro and Claire Durand-Ruel Snollaerts, eds., *Pissarro: Critical Catalogue of Paintings,* 3 vols., Paris and Milan 2005.
Pissarro/Venturi 1939
Ludovic-Rodo Pissarro and Lionello Venturi, eds., *Camille Pissarro: son art—son oeuvre,* 2 vols., Paris 1939.
Pontoise 2015
Les Pissarro: Une famille d'artistes au tournant des XIXe et XXe siècles, exh. cat., Musée d'Art et d'Histoire Pissarro, Pontoise 2015.
Pontoise 2017
Camille Pissarro: Impressions gravées, exh. cat., Musée Tavet-Delacour, Pontoise 2017.
Rewald 1943
John Rewald, ed., *Camille Pissarro: Letters to His Son Lucien,* New York 1943.
Rewald 1964
John Rewald, *Camille Pissarro in Venezuela* (exh. cat., Hammer Galleries), New York 1964.
Ritter 1963
Joachim Ritter, *Landschaft: Zur Funktion des Ästhetischen in der modernen Gesellschaft,* Münster 1963.
Rome 2010
From Corot to Monet: The Ecology of Impressionism, exh. cat., Complesso monumentale del Vittoriano, Rome 2010.
Roslak 2007
Robyn Roslak, *Neo-Impressionism and Anarchism in Fin-de-Siècle France: Painting, Politics and Landscape,* Aldershot 2007.
Rubin 2008
James Rubin, *Impressionism and the Modern Landscape: Productivity, Technology, and Urbanization from Manet to Van Gogh,* Berkeley 2008.
Saint Thomas 1996
Camille Pissarro in the Caribbean, 1850–1855: Drawings from the Collections at Olana, exh. cat., Lilienfeld House, Saint Thomas 1996.
San Francisco 1986
The New Painting: Impressionism 1874–1886, exh. cat., Fine Arts Museums of San Francisco 1986.
Sefrioui 2012
Anne Sefrioui, *Éventails impressionnistes,* Paris 2012.
Shikes/Harper 1980
Ralph E. Shikes and Paula Harper, *Pissarro: His Life and Work,* New York 1980.
Stuttgart 1999
Camille Pissarro, exh. cat., Staatsgalerie Stuttgart, 1999.
Sydney 2005
Camille Pissarro: The First Impressionist, exh. cat., Art Gallery of New South Wales, Sydney 2005.
Thomson 1990
Richard Thomson, *Camille Pissarro: Impressionism, Landscape, and Rural Labour* (exh. cat., South Bank Centre), London 1990.
Thorold 1993
Anne Thorold, ed., *The Letters of Lucien to Camille Pissarro, 1883–1903,* Cambridge and New York 1993.
Toronto 2019
Impressionism in the Age of Industry, exh. cat., Art Gallery of Ontario, Toronto 2019.
Tulsa 2018
Innovative Impressions: Prints by Cassatt, Degas, and Pissarro, exh. cat., Philbrook Museum of Art, Tulsa 2018.
Ward 1995
Martha Ward, *Pissarro, Neo-Impressionism, and the Spaces of the Avant-Garde,* Chicago and London 1995.
Washington 2001
Impressionist Still Life, exh. cat., Phillips Collection, Washington, DC, 2001.
Westerby 2022
Genevieve Westerby, "Pissarro at Pontoise: Picturing Infrastructure and the Changing Riverine Environment," in *Athanor* 39 (2022), 155–70.
Wuppertal 2014
Camille Pissarro: Der Vater des Impressionismus, exh. cat., Von der Heydt-Museum, Wuppertal 2014.

Authors

Claire Durand-Ruel Snollaerts, a descendant of art dealer Paul Durand-Ruel, received her PhD from Paris 1 Panthéon-Sorbonne University, writing on the relationship between artist Albert André and Durand-Ruel. She has devoted herself to researching and assessing the work of Camille Pissarro. Together with Joachim Pissarro, the artist's great-grandson, she coauthored the catalogue raisonné *Pissarro: Critical Catalogue of Paintings* (2005). She is the author of publications such as *Camille Pissarro: Patriarche des impressionnistes* (2012), *Pissarro: Peindre la ville, Rouen* (2013), *Paul Durand-Ruel: Discovering the Impressionists* (2015), *Les Impressionnistes: Loisirs et mondanités* (2016), and *Camille Pissarro: Fenêtre sur la ville* (2017). She has contributed to numerous exhibitions, mainly focusing on the Impressionist period. Her most recent projects were *Camille Pissarro: Le Premier des impressionnistes* (Musée Marmottan Monet, Paris 2017), *Collections privées: Un voyage des impressionnistes aux fauves* (Musée Marmottan Monet, Paris 2018), *Impressionisti segreti* (Palazzo Bonaparte, Rome 2019), *Paul Durand-Ruel et le post-impressionnisme* (Propriété Caillebotte, Yerres 2021), and *Paul Durand-Ruel y los últimos destellos del impresionismo* (Fundación MAPFRE, Madrid 2024).

Clarisse Fava-Piz is Associate Curator of European and American Art Before 1900 at the Denver Art Museum. She holds a PhD from the University of Pittsburgh and is a specialist of nineteenth- and early twentieth-century sculpture in Europe and the Americas. She previously worked at the Musée du Louvre in Paris, the National Gallery of Art in Washington, DC, and the Getty Research Institute in Los Angeles, among other major cultural institutions. In 2021–23 she was Mellon Curatorial Fellow at the Meadows Museum at Southern Methodist University in Dallas, where she curated the exhibition *In the Shadow of Dictatorship: Creating the Museum of Spanish Abstract Art* (2023) and edited its accompanying catalog. Most recently, she contributed essays to the exhibition catalog *Camille Claudel* (The J. Paul Getty Museum, Los Angeles 2023). Fava-Piz's research has been supported by the Casa de Velázquez, the Smithsonian American Art Museum, and the Terra Foundation for American Art.

Nerina Santorius is Curator and Head of Impressionism at the Museum Barberini in Potsdam. After completing her PhD at the Freie Universität Berlin, writing on ugliness in nineteenth-century French sculpture, she worked at the Städel Museum in Frankfurt am Main from 2009 to 2015, where she was responsible for exhibitions such as the anniversary show *Monet and the Birth of Impressionism* (2015). From 2015 to 2024, Santorius was a curator at the Kunsthalle Munich. There, she developed exhibitions such as *Good—True—Beautiful: Masterpieces of the Paris Salon from the Musée d'Orsay* (2017), *You Are Faust: Goethe's Drama in the Arts* (2018), *Fantastically Real: Belgian Modern Art from Ensor to Magritte* (2021), *Silent Rebels: Polish Symbolism Around 1900* (2022), and *The Myth of Spain: Ignacio Zuloaga 1870–1945* (2023).

Emily Willkom is Senior Curatorial Assistant for the Department of European and American Art Before 1900 at the Denver Art Museum. She received her Master of Arts in museum studies from the University of Leicester, UK, in 2009 and has previously worked at the Philbrook Museum of Art and the Gilcrease Museum in Tulsa, Oklahoma. Since joining the Denver Art Museum curatorial team in 2015, Willkom has worked on several major exhibitions including *Wyeth: Andrew and Jamie in the Studio* (2015), *Glory of Venice: Masterworks of the Renaissance* (2016), *Rembrandt: Painter as Printmaker* (2018), *Degas: A Passion for Perfection* (2018), *Claude Monet: The Truth of Nature* (2019), and *Saints, Sinners, Lovers, and Fools: 300 Years of Flemish Masterworks* (2022).

Daniel Zamani, Artistic Director at the Museum Frieder Burda in Baden-Baden since July 2024, received his PhD from the University of Cambridge, writing on occult and medieval themes in the work of André Breton (2017). He was Curatorial Assistant and then Assistant Curator at the Städel Museum in Frankfurt am Main from 2015 to 2017 and subsequently Curator and Head of Impressionism at the Museum Barberini in Potsdam from 2018 to 2024. He coedited the books *Surrealism, Occultism, and Politics: In Search of the Marvellous* (2018) and *Visions of Enchantment: Occultism, Magic and Visual Culture* (2019). Zamani has curated or cocurated the exhibitions *Matisse—Bonnard: "Long Live Painting!"* (2017), *Color and Light: The Neo-Impressionist Henri-Edmond Cross* (2018), *Monet: Places* (2020), *The Shape of Freedom: International Abstraction after 1945* (2022), *Surrealism and Magic: Enchanted Modernity* (2022), *Maurice de Vlaminck: Modern Art Rebel* (2024), *Yoshitomo Nara* (2024), and *Poetry of Light: Richard Pousette-Dart* (2025).

Colophon

This catalog is published in conjunction with the exhibition

The Honest Eye: Camille Pissarro's Impressionism

Museum Barberini, Potsdam
June 14–September 28, 2025

Denver Art Museum
October 26, 2025–February 8, 2026

Editors:
Angelica Daneo, Clarisse Fava-Piz, Christoph Heinrich, Michael Philipp, Nerina Santorius, and Ortrud Westheider

Exhibition: Claire Durand-Ruel Snollaerts, Clarisse Fava-Piz, Nerina Santorius
Catalog: Clarisse Fava-Piz, Nerina Santorius
Curatorial Assistants: Valentina Plotnikova, Emily Willkom
Catalog Editing: Olga Osadtschy, Nerina Santorius
Image Editing: Valentina Plotnikova, Leonie Schmidt

Museum Barberini, Potsdam

Director: Ortrud Westheider
Assistant to the Director: Dorothee Entrup
Managing Director: Janine Meyer
Chief Curator: Michael Philipp
Curator and Head of Impressionism: Nerina Santorius
Provenance Research Associate: Linda Hacka
Research Associate: Sterre Barentsen
Curatorial Assistants: Valentina Plotnikova, Julia Keinath
Registrars: Anna Seidel, Annelies Legein
Student Assistants: Anna Heling, Céline Véronique Marten, Leonie Schmidt
Communications and Marketing: Achim Klapp, Esther Franken, Marte Kräher, Valerie Maul, Carolin Stranz
Digitization and Information Security: Stefan Scholze
IT Administrators: Sebastian Semmler, Sandra Frank-Kaspuhl
Education and Inspiration: Dorothee Entrup, Isabel Acosta, Andrea Schmidt
Events: Katharina Mench, Kaspar Winkler
Guest Management: Catrin Berendsen, Roswitha Waldheim
Financial Management: Nadine Müller, Irina Palant
Accounting: Heike Kraeft
Ticketing: Yvonne Benesch, Daniela Schaube
HR Administration: Julia Pauline Nowak
Security: Nikolaos Dokalis, Verena Daub
Building Services: Carsten Loeper, Frank Altmann, Dennis Kokert

In collaboration with:

Conservation: Felicitas Klein, Berlin
Friederike Beseler, Berlin
Exhibition Design: Philipp Ricklefs, Berlin
BrücknerAping, Büro für Gestaltung, Bremen
Museum Shop: Museum Barberini. Der Shop, Jörg Klambt
Transport: Hasenkamp, Berlin

Denver Art Museum

Project Team:

Renée Albiston
Eric Berkemeyer
Ruby Dorchester
Erwin Erkfitz
Clarisse Fava-Piz
David Griesheimer
Haley Hartmann
Jeff Keene
Felicia Martinez
Caitlin R. Rumery
Pam Skiles
Lauren Thompson
Emily Willkom

Exhibition Design: Stephen Saitas
Exhibition Graphics: Evan Cotgageorge

Administration:

Director: Christoph Heinrich
Deputy Director, Chief Financial Officer: Curtis Woitte
Deputy Director, Chief Learning and Engagement Officer: Heather Nielsen
Chief of Curatorial Affairs, Collections, and Exhibitions: Angelica Daneo
Chief Marketing Officer: Katie Ross
Chief Development Officer: Arpie Chucovich
Chief Operating Officer: Bryon Thornburgh
Director of Institutional Giving: Chiara Robinson
Director of Registration, Collections, and Exhibitions: Sarah Cucinella-McDaniel
Director of Accounting: Marcy Johnson
Director of Conservation: Sarah Melching
Director of Facilities: Mark Baker
Director of Protective Services: Milagros Torres
Director of Technology: Kevin Beach
Director of Visitor Services: Anna Millholland
Director of Retail: Christine Horvath
Managing Editor: Valerie Hellstein
Associate Director, Development and Events: Elizabeth Dolan
Associate Director, Brand and Design: Tasso Stathopulos

Catalog

1st edition 2025
produktsicherheit@penguinrandomhouse.de
(The above information is mandatory information according to GPSR and should be used for all queries relating to the safety of our books)

Editorial Direction, Prestel: Markus Eisen
Graphic Design and Typesetting: BrücknerAping, Büro für Gestaltung, Bremen
Copyediting: Tas Skorupa, New York
Project Management: Annette Krüger, Hamburg
Translations from French: Helge R. Dascher
Translations from German: Melissa M. Thorson
Production Management: Cilly Klotz
Color Separations: REPROLINE Genceller 2.0, Munich
Printing and Binding: Printer Trento, Trento
Typeface: Neue Haas Grotesk, Lexicon No2A
Paper: 150 g/m² Garda Matt Ultra

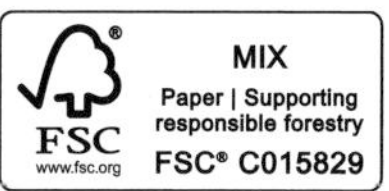

Penguin Random House Verlagsgruppe
FSC® N001967

Printed in Italy

A CIP catalog record for this book is available from the British Library.
Library of Congress Control Number: 2025937548

ISBN 978-3-7913-7788-9
(German trade edition)
ISBN 978-3-7913-7789-6
(English trade edition)
ISBN 978-3-7913-9143-4
(German museum edition, Museum Barberini, Potsdam)
ISBN 978-3-7913-9144-1
(English museum edition, Museum Barberini, Potsdam)
ISBN 978-3-7913-9145-8
(English museum edition, Denver Art Museum)

www.prestel.de
www.prestel.com

Image Credits

Catalog

Alamy, Abingdon: cat. 64 (Vicimages / Alamy Stock Photo); cat. 104 (Artefact / Alamy Stock Photo)
Van Gogh Museum, Amsterdam (Vincent van Gogh Foundation): cat. 32
Courtesy of the Baltimore Museum of Art: cat. 38
akg-images, Berlin: cat. 26 (Laurent Lecat); cat. 33 (De Agostini Picture Lib. / G. Dagli Orti); cats. 46, 59 (Heritage Images / Fine Art Images); cats. 88, 99
bpk, Berlin: cat. 13 (The Art Institute of Chicago / Art Resource, NY); cat. 42 (GrandPalaisRmn, Hervé Lewandowski)
Bridgeman Images, Berlin: cat. 35 (© Photo Josse); cat. 58; cat. 90 (Art Gallery of Ontario / Gift of Reuben Wells Leonard Estate, 1937); cat. 93 (National Museums & Galleries of Wales)
Recom Art, Berlin: cats. 37, 70, 72, 74, 79, 97, 107
Szépművészeti Múzeum, Budapest: cats. 12, 102
© Christopher Burke Studio: cat. 9
© 2015 Christie's Images Limited: cat. 67
© 2017 Christie's Images Limited: cat. 108
© 2023 Christie's Images Limited: cat. 62
The Cleveland Museum of Art: cat. 20
Wallraf-Richartz-Museum & Fondation Corboud, Cologne: cat. 36 (© Rheinisches Bildarchiv Köln, Cologne)
Denver Art Museum: cat. 11 (Christina Jackson); cat. 16 (Jeff Wells); cat. 22 (William O'Connor); cat. 24 (Eric Stephenson); cat. 48 (Christina Jackson); cats. 49, 63 (Jeff Wells); cat. 66 (William O'Connor); cat. 84 (Jeff Wells)
Indianapolis Museum of Art at Newfields: cat. 80
The Nelson-Atkins Museum of Art, Kansas City, Image courtesy of Nelson-Atkins Digital Production & Preservation: cat. 39 (Joshua Ferdinand)
Kunsthalle Karlsruhe: cat. 89
Musée d'art moderne André Malraux—MuMa, Le Havre: cat. 95 (© MuMa Le Havre / Charles Maslard); cat. 96 (© MuMa Le Havre / Florian Kleinefenn)
© The Courtauld (Samuel Courtauld Trust), London: cat. 23
© The National Gallery, London: cat. 106
Private collection, courtesy of Pissarro & Associates Fine Art, London: cats. 30, 73, 83
The J. Paul Getty Museum, Los Angeles, Digital image courtesy of Getty's Open Content Program: cat. 14
© Musée des Beaux-Arts de Lyon: cat. 103 (Alain Basset)
Kunsthalle Mannheim: cat. 17
Colección Pérez Simón, Mexico City: cats. 34, 45, 50, 52, 53, 68, 69, 91 (Arturo Piera)
Yale University Art Gallery, New Haven: cat. 28
The Metropolitan Museum of Art, New York: cat. 40
© Wolfgang Günzel, Offenbach: cat. 18
Joslyn Art Museum, Omaha: cat. 44 (© Bruce M. White, 2019)
© Art Gallery of Ontario: cat. 65
National Gallery of Canada, Ottawa: cat. 43
© Ashmolean Museum, University of Oxford: cats. 27, 29, 76, 78, 85, 86, 109
© Norton Simon Art Foundation, Pasadena: cat. 54
Philadelphia Museum of Art: cats. 57, 61, 101
Carnegie Museum of Art, Pittsburgh: cat. 25 (Art Resource, New York)
© National Gallery Prague 2025: cat. 15
Musée des Beaux-Arts de Reims: cat. 100 (© Christian Devleeschauwer)
© Photo: Francis Rhodes: cat. 87, 92
Virginia Museum of Fine Arts, Richmond: cat. 10 (Sydney Collins)
© Carlos Germán Rojas: cats. 3, 6
Saint Louis Art Museum: cat. 105
Courtesy of the Fine Arts Museums of San Francisco: cat. 71 (Randy Dodson); cat. 94 (Joseph McDonald)
Photograph Courtesy of Sotheby's, Inc. © 2025: cat. 81
© Gregg Stanger: cats. 1, 4
© Staatsgalerie Stuttgart: cat. 19
Tate: cats. 55, 60
Courtesy National Gallery of Art, Washington: cats. 5, 7, 8, 41, 47
Courtesy Clark Art Institute. clarkart.edu, Williamstown, Massachusetts: cats. 2, 21, 82
Kunst Museum Winterthur: cat. 98 (SIK-ISEA, Zurich, Martin Stollenwerk)
© Fotoatelier Peter Schälchli, Zurich: cats. 51, 56, 77

Exhibited Documents

Pissarro Family Archives: p. 26, fig. 6; pp. 221, 223

Comparative Images

Kunstmuseum Basel, Collection Online: p. 39, fig. 8
akg-images, Berlin: p. 12, fig. 1; p. 15, fig. 2; p. 16, fig. 3; p. 17, fig. 4 (André Held); p. 18, fig. 6; p. 19, fig. 7; p. 20, fig. 8; p. 21, fig. 10; p. 27, fig. 8; p. 29, fig. 12 (Cameraphoto); p. 31, fig. 15; p. 206 (Erich Lessing); pp. 208, 209; p. 213 (Heritage Images / Ashmolean Museum of Art and Archaeology); p. 214 (Heritage Images / akg-images / Heritage Art); p. 225 (De Agostini Picture Lib)
bpk, Berlin / RMN-Grand Palais: p. 28, fig. 10 (Patrice Schmidt); p. 30, fig. 14 (Tony Querrec); p. 32, fig. 1 (Patrice Schmidt); p. 34, fig. 2 (Gérard Blot); p. 35, fig. 3 (Patrice Schmidt)
Bridgeman Images, Berlin: p. 18, fig. 5; p. 28, fig. 11 (© Christie's Images); p. 37, fig. 5 (© Photo Josse); p. 222
The Art Institute of Chicago: p. 38, fig. 6
Image courtesy Dallas Museum of Art: p. 39, fig. 7
Photo Archives Durand-Ruel, Paris © Durand-Ruel & Cie: p. 226
Digital image courtesy of Getty's Open Content Program: p. 21, fig. 9
© J. Hyde: p. 41, fig. 10
Courtesy of Pissarro & Associates Fine Art, London: p. 218
Courtesy of The Wildenstein Plattner Institute, Inc., New York City: p. 24, figs. 2 and 3; p. 25, fig. 4; p. 29, fig. 13; p. 40, fig. 9
© Ashmolean Museum, University of Oxford: p. 26, fig. 7; pp. 229, 231
Bibliothèque Nationale de France, Paris: p. 220
© Michel Petit: p. 36, fig. 4
Archives Municipales de Pontoise: p. 210
Musée d'Art et d'Histoire Pissarro—Pontoise: p. 217
Réunion des Musées Métropolitains Rouen Normandie: p. 27, fig. 9 (Photo: © C. Lancien, C. Loisel)
Toledo Museum of Art: p. 42, fig. 11; p. 43, fig. 12
Courtesy National Gallery of Art, Washington: p. 25, fig. 5
Wikimedia Commons: pp. 212, 215, 216

Images have been reproduced from the following publications:
Camille Pissarro: The Studio of Modernism, exh. cat., Kunstmuseum Basel, 2021, p. 290: p. 224
Camille Pissarro: Mit den Augen eines Impressionisten, exh. cat. Kunstmuseum Pablo Picasso Münster, 2013, p. 153: p. 211
Camille Pissarro: Der Vater des Impressionismus, exh. cat., Von der Heydt-Museum, Wuppertal 2014, p. 162: p. 22, fig. 1

Image details have been used on the following pages: pp. 44–45 (cat. 7), pp. 58–59 (cat. 25), pp. 80–81 (cat. 28), pp. 92–93 (cat. 38), pp. 106–07 (cat. 43), pp. 132–33 (cat. 70), pp. 152–53 (cat. 77), pp. 172–73 (cat. 93), pp. 188–89 (cat. 105)

Every effort has been made to locate and contact all copyright holders. Justified claim will of course be settled within the framework of the usual arrangements.